THE ROYAL NAVY AND NAZI GERMANY, 1933–39

STUDIES IN MILITARY AND STRATEGIC HISTORY
General Editor: Michael Dockrill, Reader in War Studies, King's
College London

Published titles include:

Nigel John Ashton
EISENHOWER, MACMILLAN AND THE PROBLEM OF NASSER:
Anglo-American Relations and Arab Nationalism, 1955–59

G. H. Bennett
BRITISH FOREIGN POLICY DURING THE CURZON PERIOD,
1919–24

David A. Charters
THE BRITISH ARMY AND JEWISH INSURGENCY IN PALESTINE,
1945–47

Paul Cornish
BRITISH MILITARY PLANNING FOR THE DEFENCE OF
GERMANY, 1945–50

Robert Frazier
ANGLO-AMERICAN RELATIONS WITH GREECE: The Coming of
the Cold War, 1942–47

Brian Holden Reid
J. F. C. FULLER: Military Thinker

Stewart Lone
JAPAN'S FIRST MODERN WAR: Army and Society in the Conflict
with China, 1894–95

Thomas R. Mockaitis
BRITISH COUNTERINSURGENCY, 1919–60

Roger Woodhouse
BRITISH FOREIGN POLICY TOWARDS FRANCE, 1945–51

Studies in Military and Strategic History
Series Standing Order ISBN 0–333–71046–0
(*outside North America only*)

You can receive future titles in this series as they are published by placing a standing order.
Please contact your bookseller or, in case of difficulty, write to us at the address below with
your name and address, the title of the series and the ISBN quoted above.

Customer Services Department, Macmillan Distribution Ltd
Houndmills, Basingstoke, Hampshire RG21 6XS, England

The Royal Navy and Nazi Germany, 1933–39

A Study in Appeasement and the Origins of the Second World War

Joseph A. Maiolo
Lecturer in Modern History
University of Leicester

 in association with
KING'S COLLEGE LONDON

First published in Great Britain 1998 by
MACMILLAN PRESS LTD
Houndmills, Basingstoke, Hampshire RG21 6XS and London
Companies and representatives throughout the world

A catalogue record for this book is available from the British Library.

ISBN 0–333–72007–5

First published in the United States of America 1998 by
ST. MARTIN'S PRESS, INC.,
Scholarly and Reference Division,
175 Fifth Avenue, New York, N.Y. 10010

ISBN 0–312–21456–1

Library of Congress Cataloging-in-Publication Data
Maiolo, Joseph A.
The Royal Navy and Nazi Germany, 1933–39 : a study in appeasement
and the origins of the Second World War / Joseph A. Maiolo.
p.   cm. — (Studies in military and strategic history)
Includes bibliographical references (p.   ) and index.
ISBN 0–312–21456–1 (cloth)
1. Great Britain—Foreign relations—Germany.   2. Great Britain–
–Foreign relations—1936–1945.   3. Great Britain—Foreign
relations—1910–1936.   4. Great Britain—History, Naval—20th
century.   5. Germany—Foreign relations—Great Britain.   6. Great
Britain. Royal Navy—History.   7. World War, 1939–1945—Causes.
I. Title.   II. Series
DA47.2.M19   1998
327.41043—DC21
                                                          98–12708
                                                          CIP

Contents

List of Tables

List of Figures

Preface and Acknowledgements

For ease of presentation, I have adopted the following conventions. Instead of distinguishing between various grades of senior rank, all Flag Officers are referred to as 'Admiral'. For German naval ranks, the appropriate British equivalent has been adopted. Similarly, throughout the text, to avoid confusion, I have used the terms German Naval Command, German navy and C-in-C [German] Navy, rather than the original German terminology. Employing the original titles would have meant regularly differentiating between those in use before and after 1 June 1935: namely, *Marineleitung* and *Oberkommando der Kriegsmarine, Reichsmarine* and *Kriegsmarine*, and *Chef der Marineleitung* and *Oberbefehlshaber der Kriegsmarine*.

There are a number of institutions and people I would like to pay tribute to for their assistance during my doctoral studies and in the preparation of this book. The following organisations helped to fund my education and research: the Committee of Vice Chancellors and Principals of the United Kingdom, the London School of Economics and Political Science and the Royal Historical Society.

I wish to thank Rear Admiral J. R. Hill, RN, the current editor of *The Naval Review*, for his assistance in identifying the authors of essays in that invaluable publication. Mr T. R. V. Phillips kindly supplied me with relevant documents from the papers of his grandfather, Admiral Sir Tom Phillips. I also wish to thank Professor Thomas Troubridge for permission to consult and cite the privately held diaries of his father, Admiral Sir Thomas Troubridge.

For permission to consult and cite the Neville Chamberlain and Lord Avon Papers I thank the Rare Book Librarian, the University of Birmingham, and Lady Avon. I acknowledge the Trustees of Churchill College Archives, Cambridge, for permission to consult their holdings. Crown copyright material in the Public Record Office appears by permission of the Controller of HM Stationery Office.

I am indebted to the archivists and support staff of the Public Record Office, Churchill College Archives, the Cambridge University Library, the

Admiralty Library, the British Library, the National Maritime Museum, the Imperial War Museum, the Birmingham University Library, the National Library of Scotland, and the British Library of Political and Economic Science. For assistance in locating official documents and private papers, I am indebted to Mr R. W. A. Suddaby, Keeper of the Department of Documents, Imperial War Museum, and to Mr I. D. Goode, Deputy Departmental Records Officer, Ministry of Defence.

I owe a great deal to friends and colleagues too numerous to list individually. I especially wish to thank my tutors at the University of Toronto, Professor Sidney Aster and Professor Wesley Wark. Thanks are also due to Dr Michael Doran, Dr Anthony Best and Professor John Ferris for comments and advice on draft chapters. Professor Richard Overy and Professor George Peden, my PhD Examiners, were likewise very generous with their observations, encouragement and assistance. I wish to thank Ms Annabelle Buckley, the Senior Commissioning Editor at Macmillan, Dr Michael Dockrill, the Series Editor, and Ms Anne Rafique for editorial assistance.

My profoundest gratitude and admiration go to my thesis supervisors, Professor Donald Cameron Watt and Dr David Stevenson.

Finally, I owe an incalculable debt to the support and patience of my family, and to Sally Merriman. I dedicate this book to her and to my grandparents.

List of Abbreviations

ACNS	Assistant Chief of the Naval Staff
ADM	Admiralty
AIR	Royal Air Force Documents
ASW	Anti-Submarine Warfare
ATB	Advisory Committee on Trade Questions in Time of War
CAB	Cabinet
CB	Confidential Book (Admiralty)
CCC	Churchill College Cambridge
C-in-C	Commander-in-Chief
CID	Committee of Imperial Defence
CNS	Chief of the Naval Staff
COS	Chiefs of Staff
CP	Cabinet Papers
DBFP	*Documents on British Foreign Policy*
DCM	Disarmament Committee Ministerial
DCNS	Deputy Chief of the Naval Staff
DCOS	Deputy Chiefs of Staff
DGFP	*Documents on German Foreign Policy*
DNC	Director of Naval Construction
DNI	Director of Naval Intelligence
DPP	Defence Plans (Policy) Sub-Committee
DRC	Defence Requirements Committee
FO	Foreign Office
FPC, FP	Foreign Policy Committee (Cabinet)
IFC	Industrial Intelligence in Foreign Countries Sub-Committee
IIC	Industrial Intelligence Centre
Inkavos	*Ingenieurskantoor voor Scheepbouw*
JIC	Joint Intelligence Committee
JPC, JP	Joint Planning Committee
MIR	Monthly [Naval] Intelligence Report
mtg	meeting
NCM	Naval Conference (Ministerial) Committee
NID	Naval Intelligence Division
NMM	National Maritime Museum, Greenwich
OIC	Operational Intelligence Centre (Admiralty)
OPC	Offensive Planning Cell

PD	Plans Division
PM	Prime Minister
PREM	Prime Minister's Office, Records
PRO	Public Record Office, London
RAF	Royal Air Force
SAC	Strategic Appreciation Committee
SIS	Secret Intelligence Service (MI6)
T	Treasury
TINA	*Transactions of the Institution of Naval Architects*

Introduction

On 4 June 1935, at the Foreign Office in London, Herr Joachim von Ribbentrop, Adolf Hitler's Ambassador Extraordinary and Plenipotentiary, opened discussions on naval disarmament by confronting his hosts with a blunt proposition. Breaking with conventional diplomatic practice, the German emissary insisted that the British accept forthwith, as a precondition to further negotiations, the German Chancellor's claim to a fleet equal in strength to 35 per cent of the Royal Navy. Two days later, the British agreed. Once the wording had been settled, the Anglo-German Naval Agreement was formally concluded on 18 June with an exchange of notes between Ribbentrop and Sir Samuel Hoare, the British Secretary of State for Foreign Affairs.

News of the Naval Agreement caused surprise and rancour in Europe, especially in Paris. After all, it had looked like the powers were combining to check resurgent German militarism. In April, Britain joined France and Italy at Stresa to censure Hitler's flagrant violations of the military restrictions imposed on Germany by the 1919 Treaty of Versailles. The League of Nations added its disapproval. To many onlookers, the British decision to accept Hitler's 35 per cent offer thus appeared to be short-sighted and self-serving. Historians have likewise interpreted the Agreement as a low point in interwar British diplomatic and naval history. Not only did it break-up the so-called 'Stresa Front', but the Agreement also permitted the German navy to equip itself unfettered for war. Even those scholars who sympathise with the British decision regard it as a diplomatic blunder, albeit an understandable one.

What follows offers a different interpretation of Anglo-German naval relations in the 1930s. It focuses on the prime mover in Whitehall behind naval armaments diplomacy with Nazi Germany, the Admiralty. It addresses three interrelated questions: How did the Admiralty view German naval armaments expansion under Hitler as a problem for British maritime security? Based on that perception, how did the Admiralty seek to influence defence and foreign policy-making in Whitehall as a whole? And what does this political and strategic analysis reveal about the broader relationship between London and Berlin in the period preceding the outbreak of war in 1939?

One of the main weaknesses of previous accounts of these issues is that they usually begin and end their analysis with the exchange of notes on

18 June 1935. Interpretations of the 1935 Naval Agreement by diplomatic historians reflect the general trends in scholarship on British appeasement.[1] Initially, the 1935 accord was dubbed by some as the first act of 'appeasement', that is in the pejorative sense. British statesmen, the so-called 'guilty men', failed to grasp Hitler's ruthless aims, and so pursued a pusillanimous policy of concessions. Deluded into the belief that they could trust Hitler, and cowed by the fear of another Tirpitzian naval contest, the British fell for the Führer's offer to limit his fleet to a 35 per cent ratio. Consequently, in one bold stroke, Nazi diplomacy ruined the burgeoning anti-German bloc of April 1935 and, more importantly, spoiled any chance of potent Anglo-French cooperation.[2] Subsequently, with access to British government records, revisionist historians explained appeasement as a rational response to Britain's precarious international and domestic circumstances. Though still a mistake in execution, the naval accord appeared to be a reasonable attempt by London to lessen its global defence burden. Saddled with a pacific public, troubled finances and the advance of Japan against Britain's East Asian possessions, revisionists argue that British decision-makers had little option but to leap at the chance to cap the German naval arms build-up.[3]

Interpretations of the Anglo-German Naval Agreement in the naval literature also differ. The Royal Navy's official historian underscored the chimera of disarmament and the evils of the Treasury's tight grip on defence expenditure as the main reasons why the Admiralty so readily fell prey to Hitler's 35 per cent ruse. Desperate for some control over German sea armaments, the British were hustled by Nazi diplomatic tactics into the arrangement with an 'unseemly haste' and in 'too trustworthy a spirit'.[4] The standard account of modern British naval history regards the 1935 accord as symptomatic of Britain's great power decline. Faced with an expiring industrial base, shrinking revenue and the development of air power, the Royal Navy desperately sought to retain enough strength to fight in Europe and the Far East at once. Hence the 1935 accord was a rearguard action by a decaying sea power seeking to retreat safely from escalating liabilities.[5]

Diplomatic and naval accounts share the view that the Admiralty's eagerness for naval talks with Hitler typified its dogged blindness to the Nazi menace. Obsessed with the Japanese threat, so the argument goes, the Royal Navy was lulled into a false sense of security by the 35 per cent bargain. As senior British naval officers retreated into complacency and dreamed of a future battleship contest in the South China Sea, the German navy grew rapidly, cheated on warship tonnage limits and perfected its U-boat arm for another drawn-out campaign against oceanic trade. A recent study of British intelligence has backed up these claims. In fact, 'the poor state of intelligence on German naval construction played a significant role in bringing the British to the negotiating table in June 1935'. Once the Naval Agreement was signed, the Admiralty endorsed it as 'proof' of Berlin's desire to be on friendly terms with London, and of its willingness to confine its maritime ambitions to the Baltic Sea. Evidence that contradicted the Royal Navy's Japan first policy preconceptions were either interpreted to fit them or ignored.[6]

In reality, the Admiralty's enthusiasm for naval armaments diplomacy with Nazi Germany was more rational, more ambitious and more complex than earlier studies would suggest. Nor was the Royal Navy's strategic calculus ever static. The only way to interpret Anglo-German naval diplomacy is to reconstruct it as an intricate process of interaction beginning well before and ending long after the June 1935 deal. In doing so, it is possible to expose, at each point in the relationship, the often overlooked patterns of power – that is power as influence and ideas.

Consequently, this study is not the orthodox tale of a reactive and bungling policy born of great power decline, but a positive and ingenious project born of strategic confidence. It argues that British naval armaments diplomacy helped to co-opt Berlin into pursuing from London's viewpoint the *least* dangerous type of warship building programme. This book demonstrates that Admiralty war planning and intelligence *vis-à-vis* the German navy were far better than previous works suppose. It evaluates the significance of a little-known proposal from within the navy in late 1937 to change the emphasis in naval war plans against Nazi Germany from the defensive to the offensive. Above all, a focus on the much overlooked programmatic (or temporal) dimension to Admiralty thinking distinguishes this monograph.[7] Briefly stated, the Admiralty wanted to pursue a long-term programme intended to remodel the international naval balance, with resolute armaments diplomacy and naval building, to bolster Britain's prospects as the leading global sea power.

Another unconventional feature of this book is that it endeavours to combine diplomatic and naval history. Diplomatic historians generally overlook the technical, financial, industrial and strategic aspects of maritime power. They treat the Anglo-German Naval Agreement as an error because of their fixation with the negative impact it had on European co-operation against Hitler. What they fail to appreciate is that the June 1935 accord, from the standpoint of the Admiralty and some FO officials, represented the use of naval armaments diplomacy to fashion the technological, financial and international conditions crucial to Britain remaining a global power. On the other hand, naval historians understand the arcane technical issues – such as the influence of ship design on naval war planning – but they have failed to see how crucial armaments diplomacy had become to the ascendancy of the Royal Navy. The fundamental problem with treating the naval and the diplomatic sides of these issues in isolation is that Admiralty policy-makers never considered them in watertight mental compartments, but perceived them as inextricably linked in their strategic calculus.

Why a fresh look at Anglo-German naval relations? Apart from revising the existing literature, this study offers several significant benefits. First, by examining the subject as a whole, it sheds light on an important aspect of Anglo-German relations before the Second World War that up to now has only been investigated in a fragmentary fashion. Second, in agreement with current studies of the Royal Navy, which dispute the theory that economic factors predestined the demise of British naval supremacy between the wars,[8] this book also underscores the contingent nature of that downfall. Third, what follows has implications for the ongoing debate about British appeasement. Several recent studies have argued that the revisionist case has gone too far. Historians have forsaken their interpretative duties for the allure of the archives; they have forgotten that the search for a détente with Hitler was an option *chosen* by the Prime Minister, not one *determined* by external factors. The abundant, orderly documents prepared for the Chamberlain Cabinet were drafted to justify a pre-selected policy, not to probe alternative ones. To explain appeasement, the counter-revisionists contend, analysis must focus once again on how Chamberlain's temper skewed British foreign and defence policy.[9] However, the evidence from the Admiralty records suggests that, *independent* of Chamberlain, the leadership of the Royal Navy had realistic strategic incentives to *select* his German policy.

This argument is founded on a thorough and comprehensive study of British Cabinet, Admiralty and Foreign Office (FO) records. Admiralty records alone are insufficient, and their apparent abundance is deceptive. No single set of files exist that constitute a coherent record of the navy's internal decision-making. At the same time, it is impossible to decipher the meaning of single documents without reconstructing the overall strategic, financial, industrial or technical framework of naval policy. Obtaining such an outlook requires an interdepartmental approach to research. In a period when armaments diplomacy was crucial in shaping Admiralty thinking, the files of the FO are as significant as those of the navy itself. Although the analysis benefits from the recent release of some Whitehall intelligence material, this study represents a novel interpretation of documents that have been open to scholars for some time, and the exploitation of hitherto neglected sources – such as the archives of the Department of Naval Construction. The incomplete paper trail for Admiralty intelligence and war planning remains problematic, but the private papers, diaries, and correspondence of key personalities are invaluable for filling in the gaps. Finally, since some of the shrewdest commentators on British sea power resided in the German Naval Command, this study also makes extensive use of the published primary sources and the rich secondary literature on German naval policy in the Nazi era.

To relate the story of Anglo-German naval relations in the 1930s, it was essential to explore several levels of analysis: international relations, Whitehall politics, and decision-making and intelligence appraisal inside the Admiralty. The chapters are therefore organised to combine a narrative of diplomatic events and Whitehall policy-making with a thematic examination of Admiralty thinking about Germany. The middle three chapters are thematic, the outer four are chronological. Chapter 1 looks at the making of the Anglo-German Naval Agreement within the framework of the Admiralty's long-term strategic aims. Chapter 2 recounts Anglo-German naval relations from July 1935 to July 1937. Chapters 3 to 5 deal with the Royal Navy's image of German naval policy, technical intelligence and the fleet's role in British strategy. Chapter 6 is devoted to how the Admiralty sought to triumph in inter-service politics and to sway foreign policy. It also describes how the navy's grand design miscarried during the approach to Munich. The final chapter investigates two largely separate issues. First, the role of naval diplomacy during the unravelling of appeasement in 1938–9. Second, it examines how the new Admiralty leadership tried to transform naval policy to match post-Munich realities. Before commencing, however, it is necessary to set out the structure of the British foreign and defence policy-making machinery as well as that of the Admiralty.

THE DECISION-MAKING PROCESS

The Cabinet was collectively responsible for Britain's external relations, but it relied on the Committee of Imperial Defence (CID) to co-ordinate the formation of strategic policy and for its implementation by the government overall. Chaired by the PM, and serviced by a combined military and civilian secretariat, the CID normally comprised the Chancellor of the Exchequer, the Foreign Secretary, the three service ministers, the three service Chiefs of Staff (COS) and the permanent heads of the Treasury and the Foreign Office. During the interwar period, the CID was supported in many of its specialised tasks by a regularly expanding network of expert subcommittees. To manage defence preparations across departmental boundaries, the CID received professional advice on strategy, supply, industrial intelligence and (after July 1936) joint military intelligence, from a hierarchy of inter-service subcommittees.[10]

The most important of these was the COS Sub-Committee. Formed in 1923, the COS was charged with supplying the CID with military guidance on strategic matters as a whole. Its members were the three professional heads of the armed forces – the Chief of the Naval Staff (CNS), the Chief of the Air Staff, and the Chief of the Imperial General Staff – who rotated in the chairmanship. After 1927, under the direction of the COS, the task of drafting regular imperial defence reviews, war plans and strategic appreciations was delegated to a Joint Planning Sub-Committee (JPC). The JPC comprised the heads of the planning and operations cells of the three service staffs.[11]

Although the CID system was intended to establish a high degree of consensus on national strategy, differences between departments often persisted. At times, the CID proved incapable of adjudicating disputes. The three service ministries, the Treasury and the FO guarded their turf and autonomy jealously, but strove to advance their own vision of what strategic policy ought to be. Certainly, inter-service disputes could become unruly, especially the persistent battle for aviation resources between the two older arms and the Royal Air Force (RAF). Nonetheless, defence, finance and foreign policy were interconnected, and so interdepartmental collaboration was required to get policies sanctioned by Cabinet; moreover, power relationships in Whitehall were dynamic. Generally, the Treasury and the FO had the edge over the Admiralty, Air Ministry and the War Office, yet no one department completely dominated at all times.[12]

The Admiralty benefited from its glorious past and the importance of oceanic trade to Britain,[13] but this was not enough to secure its policies. The view in the press and Parliament that the bomber had made the battleship obsolete vexed senior sailors. In the early 1930s, the Treasury exploited this and the theories of naval heretics to question battlefleet replacement and to assert its own scheme for an air-based deterrent. Second, the legacy of COS squabbles in the 1920s and of the Admiralty's factious attitude had damaged its credibility: sailors 'are splendid people', one Whitehall insider wrote, 'but their notion of an argument closely resembles an order from the quarter-deck'.[14] On both counts, in the 1930s, the navy profited from the leadership of Admiral Ernle M. Chatfield. In 1935, for instance, during an inquest on the 'Vulnerability of Capital

Ships', he skilfully framed his pro-battleship case to create sufficient doubt in political minds: if 'the airman is wrong and our [bombers] cannot destroy the enemy's capital ships, and they are left to range with impunity on the world's oceans and destroy our convoys, then we shall lose the British Empire'. Equally, as chairman of the COS, Chatfield displayed a remarkable capacity to unite the COS and, as a result, to further the navy's interests.[15]

From the 1830s onwards, the Royal Navy had been operated and administered through the Board of Admiralty, which collectively advised its political master, the First Lord, on *matériel*, financial and personnel matters. The First Sea Lord, as the top professional naval officer, retained the prerogative in technical questions, policy and war plans.[16] Despite the Prussian example of what could be achieved by the application of methodical staff work to warfare, First Sea Lords before 1914 showed a marked reluctance to decentralise authority. The drawback of relying on one personality for strategy and operations was exposed at the celebrated CID meeting of 23 August 1911, when Admiral A. K. Wilson, the First Sea Lord, failed to offer a cogent naval war plan against Germany. As a result, Winston Churchill was made First Lord to institute reform. But all the new First Lord achieved was the creation of a new post, an independent Chief of the Naval Staff (CNS). It was not until 1917, partly as a result of agitation by reform-minded junior officers, but mostly as an urgent countermeasure to the U-boats, that a proper naval staff was set up. The offices of CNS and First Sea Lord were combined. And finally, in 1921, the government issued instructions for a Naval Staff.[17]

Naturally resistance on the part of many senior officers to staff work and decentralisation did not vanish overnight. Some fleet commanders were notorious for leaving their staffs to expire from boredom. But the Naval Staff was given an immense boost from Admiral David Beatty, the First Sea Lord from 1919 to 1927. Beatty understood his main task to be fighting the navy's corner in Whitehall. To free himself from routine work, he installed in key posts men he could trust to execute his ideas.[18] Consequently, the Naval Staff evolved into the navy's policy-making, war planning, operations and intelligence elite. Formal authority for administration, construction, personnel and finance still belonged to the Board, but in practice policy-making power resided with the Naval Staff.

The First Lords did not usually assume a large role in detailed policy-making. During the 1930s, four ministers held the post: Bolton M. Eyres-Monsell (1931–6), Samuel Hoare (1936–7), Alfred Duff Cooper (1937–8) and Earl Stanhope (1938–9). This high turnover rate made it very difficult for the later First Lords to master nuances of naval issues. And while

Monsell, a one-time naval officer and Conservative Chief Whip, and Hoare, a former Secretary for India and (very briefly) Foreign Secretary, were significant personalities in Cabinet and Parliament; Chamberlain's appointees, Duff Cooper and Stanhope, were regarded by their colleagues as feeble.[19]

The First Sea Lord (and the Chief of the Naval Staff) was the Admiralty's foremost personality. He represented the navy at the COS and other CID subcommittees. The CNS had the final word on policy, strategy and technical matters, but the C-in-Cs of the Home and Mediterranean fleets were important sounding-boards for his thinking. The CNS also relied on his subordinates to scrutinise policy and to refine his broad instructions. The Naval Staff was divided under the Deputy and the Assistant Chief of the Naval Staff (DCNS and ACNS). The ACNS was responsible for the Training and Staff Duties, Tactical, and Naval Air Divisions – in other words, upholding fighting efficiency. Setting the fleet's aims was the remit of the DCNS, who directed the Naval Intelligence, Operations and Plans Divisions. Although the Admiralty's work was conducted across departmental and divisional boundaries to ensure that policy was compatible with *matériel*, the formation of policy and plans remained within the purview of the DCNS.[20] To reconstruct Naval Staff thinking, therefore, it is essential to concentrate on the dialogue between the CNS, the DCNS and Plans and Intelligence Divisions.

Plans Division could only trace its lineage to 1917, but between the wars it became the CNS's top advisor on all questions of naval policy and maritime warfare. The planners greatly influenced ship design and construction, personnel policies and detailed financial planning. During the 1930s, its average strength was 14 officers, who were divided into three sections: plans, trade defence and local defence. The Director of Plans Division was second only to the CNS in the role of chief advocate of the Admiralty's strategic vision within the CID mechanism. As a member of the JPC, in co-operation with his War Office and Air Ministry counterparts, he was responsible for drafting regular strategic appreciations and defence reviews, and overseeing production of war plans and operations orders. During the protracted bargaining leading to the second London Naval Treaty of 1936, he and the DCNS acted as Admiralty liaison officers and technical advisors to the American Department of the FO, which guided naval armaments diplomacy. Finally, the Director of Plans was one of the Admiralty's chief consumers and assessors of intelligence.[21]

In the co-ordination of intelligence, the Naval Staff was unique among the three services. The Air Ministry and the War Office subordinated their intelligence to their operations cell, but the Admiralty assigned a senior officer and a division solely to it.[22] Its mandate was to collect, classify and distribute naval intelligence. Inter-service intelligence co-operation became the responsibility of the Deputy Director in July 1936, who attended the newly formed Joint Intelligence Committee (JIC).[23] The Director of Naval Intelligence (DNI) was routinely consulted before major policy decisions were made and could propose new policies based on incoming data. Naval Intelligence Division's capacity to influence the decision-making process, though, was largely determined by its director's personality and the way in which he perceived his role, rather than by any formal bureaucratic procedure.

Naval intelligence officers outnumbered the planners by a third and were subdivided into many more sections. The geographic sections compiled data about potential enemies and their navies; the technical sections monitored foreign developments in weapons technology and gunnery effectiveness. Special sections included the liaison officers to the government organisation responsible for codes and wireless intelligence, the editors of secret publications, and an officer assigned to plot the location of foreign warships and merchant vessels.[24]

The diversity of its work and its dependence on other agencies for information prevented Naval Intelligence Division (NID) from monopolising intelligence. While reports about the training, organisation, tactics, and doctrine of potential foes were the domain of naval officers, technical and scientific intelligence called for the input of experts. To estimate the capabilities and qualities of foreign warships, for instance, the skills of the Admiralty's civilian design professionals, the Department of Naval Construction, were required. NID also shared the job of forecasting the output and evaluating the production methods of foreign ship industries with a research cell of the Department of Overseas Trade, known as the Industrial Intelligence Centre (IIC).[25] Besides published sources and the exchange of warship characteristics between the naval powers, the only sources of intelligence controlled by the DNI were the naval attachés assigned to British Embassies, who were also subordinated to the FO, British Naval Missions abroad and ships on overseas stations. Despite the navy's pioneering work in the interception and analysis of wireless messages, these activities had been largely assigned in 1919 to the Government Code and Cypher School,[26] which was controlled by the Secret Intelligence Service (SIS). The SIS, which was nominally under the FO, exclusively supplied NID with reports obtained from espionage.[27]

In setting out the decision-making structure of the Naval Staff and its position within the CID organisation, it is hazardous for the historian to let the mechanical metaphors suggested by orderly organisation charts go too far. The components of the machine were men. The Royal Navy's leaders in the 1930s were conditioned by their experiences and their strategic imaginations were circumscribed by the inescapable limits of human cognition. In assessing the Naval Staff's response to the rise of German naval power in the 1930s, therefore, one must reconstruct and compare several degrees of understanding.

The first is the image of the German navy and German policy cultivated by the Naval Staff. The second, which is frequently neglected, is the image entertained in the minds of senior naval officers about the Royal Navy's strengths and capabilities in relation to its potential foes. This is important because when naval officers imagined the outcome of a potential war with Nazi Germany or framed competitive policies designed to adjust the future maritime balance, overestimating their own capabilities proved as dangerous as underestimating those of their potential opponents. Finally, evaluating this knowledge requires comparing it to the reality with which it was presumed to correspond – the parallel processes of policy-formulation, war planning and warship construction taking place in the Nazi state – and with the more objective view of the Royal Navy's relative strategic position made plain by hindsight.

1 The Naval Staff and the Anglo-German Naval Agreement of June 1935

In the early 1930s, the rise in global tensions contrasted with the relative strategic vulnerability of the British Empire compelled London to reassess Britain's foreign and defence policies. To the Royal Navy's leadership, the onset of this process was viewed as an occasion to achieve long-term policy goals. A coherent set of financial, industrial, technical, diplomatic and strategic imperatives shaped the Admiralty's blueprint for naval revival. It is essential to analyse the Naval Staff's response to the rise of German naval power under Hitler and the navy's influence on the formulation of British foreign policy towards Nazi Germany in this context. This approach reveals how the Anglo-German Naval Agreement of June 1935 was consistent with an elaborate programme that aimed to adjust the international naval order to advance Britain's long-term prospects as the world's leading sea power. The first part of this chapter will set out the Admiralty's programme; the second will investigate the calculations behind the Naval Agreement from the viewpoints of the key personalities in both London and Berlin.

THE ADMIRALTY'S PROGRAMME

In the 1930s, the Admiralty deemed naval armaments diplomacy to be a fundamental instrument of strategic policy. To understand why, one must begin with the legacy of the 1922 Washington and 1930 London Naval Treaties.

By formally agreeing at Washington to set a 5:5:3:1.67:1.67 battleship tonnage ratio between Britain, the United States, Japan, France and Italy, London abandoned the two-power standard in favour of parity with the US Navy. The Admiralty accepted this quantitative relationship because it granted the British fleet a virtual two-power standard against Japan, Britain's Far Eastern rival, and France, the largest European naval power. But in 1930, Franco-Italian antagonism proved irresolvable and both powers refused to limit their fleets. A naval competition between them threatened to erode the Royal Navy's capability to secure European waters while defending Britain's interests in the Far East.[1]

The London Naval Treaty's clauses about cruisers and battleships were even more vexing for the Naval Staff than was the abstention of the two middle-ranking powers. Washington had left cruiser limitation largely in abeyance by defining only an upper qualitative limit per vessel of 10 000 tons and 8-inch guns. At Geneva, five years later, an attempt was made to extend the capital ship ratios to all the auxiliary classes; however, an Anglo-American row over cruisers scuttled the talks. The real issue was British fears about blockade enforcement and trade defence, versus American fears about neutral trading rights; this translated into opposite views about cruiser numbers and types. The United States claimed parity and preferred for doctrinal reasons to build large vessels with 8-inch guns. The British, however, sought to limit this type according to the 1922 ratios, and to build light 6000-ton/6-inch gun ships in numbers greater than required by the genuine trade defence needs of the United States or Japan. In 1930, to prevent another transatlantic squabble, PM Ramsay MacDonald agreed to hold temporarily Britain's cruiser strength at 50 ships.[2] This over-rode the advice of naval planners: they believed that 70 (15 heavy and 55 light) cruisers in service were the minimum required to safeguard oceanic commerce and to wage trade warfare.

Further, under the 1930 London Treaty the United States, Japan and Britain once again reduced capital ship forces. Britain agreed to cut to 15 by scrapping four pre-1914 ships and demilitarising another. It also accepted an extension to the end of 1936 of the ten-year capital shipbuilding holiday agreed to at Washington. This had dire effects on the Navy's industrial strategy. During the 1920s, with subsidies and a trickle of orders, the Admiralty hoped to sustain capacity to replace the battlefleet in 1931–41, with enough reserve plant to lay down a crash programme to trump aggressive building by rival naval powers. As senior officers warned, the extended holiday might doom the specialised ship industries to atrophy below this essential strategic standard. MacDonald was willing to gamble on a peaceful future and looked to the forthcoming World Disarmament Conference to eliminate the peril by establishing a tranquil security environment.[3]

The Cabinet did authorise some limited cruiser, destroyer and submarine building. But it was not enough. The onset of the global financial crisis in 1929 combined with the effects of the 1930 London Treaty to hit both the warship and mercantile private sectors: from 1929 to 1935, British maritime building capacity, including large slipways, specialist labour and armour plate firms, shrank by one half.[4] This industrial calamity marked the structural low-point of the service's fortunes. In September 1931, cuts in public wages forced upon MacDonald by the sterling crisis compounded the Royal Navy's miseries by sparking elements of the Home Fleet to mutiny at Invergordon. And in 1932 the lowest interwar naval estimates were presented to Parliament.[5]

Nonetheless, an omen eminently suited to inducing British politicians to reflect upon the needs of sea power coincided with Invergordon. In the same month, a conspiracy of Japanese army officers staged an 'incident' in Southern Manchuria to instigate the annexation of the province. While the League of Nations struggled with war in Asia and the World Disarmament Conference assembled at Geneva, the British COS reacted to Japan's aggression by urging the Cabinet in February 1932 to begin rearmament. In March, the Cabinet abandoned the Ten Year Rule, under which since 1919 the services had framed their estimates on the precept that there would be no major war for a decade. Plans Division began to draft rearmament proposals.[6] But the mutiny had discredited the Admiralty Board. Senior officers quarrelled about the credibility of the CNS, Admiral Sir Frederick Field.[7] Hence, as a first step to reversing the Royal Navy's fortunes, the priority of Sir Bolton Eyres-Monsell, the newly appointed First Lord, was to change its leadership.[8]

Admiral Sir Ernle Chatfield, Monsell's substitute for Field, took command in January 1933. No adequate account of Admiralty policy in this period can be given without considering his personal stamp upon it; yet it is equally essential to underscore the powerful continuities in strategic thought and shared experience that his tenure personified. Chatfield's schooling in the pitfalls and possibilities of armaments policy and diplomacy was unrivalled. As a junior officer, he had excelled in gunnery and had impressed the colourful prewar naval reformer, Admiral 'Jackie' Fisher. At Jutland, he served as Flag-Captain in the Battlecruiser Squadron. After 1918, Chatfield was appointed ACNS, attended the Washington Conference, and went on to command both the Home and Mediterranean fleets. From 1925 to 1928, as the Third Sea Lord responsible for warship building and supply, he skilfully defended the Navy's separate procurement system from centralisation; and, more importantly, this key appointment placed Chatfield in a position to appreciate the industrial predicament overtaking British sea power.[9]

Two premises underpinned Chatfield's thinking on foreign and defence policy. First, without its overseas Empire, Britain would 'carry as much weight in the councils of the world as Italy or Spain'. Second, without the prestige and security afforded by a powerful fleet, Britain would lose its Empire.[10] His aim was to restore the Navy to a position equal to this task. Internally, this required raising morale, rebuilding the battle fleet, increasing cruiser strength and bringing to an end the arrangement by which the Admiralty shared control of naval aviation with the Air Ministry.[11] In terms of industrial output, when Chatfield arrived at his post, the downward spiral ensuing from MacDonald's gamble was by no means irreversible. Despite the great damage, Britain still possessed the world's largest warship industry. In the medium run, however, the trouble was that there was only enough capacity for modernisation and replacement. Significant expansion at sea and building up shipyard potential would have to wait until after 1939–40. More perilous still, there would be during this period little spare plant to match aggressive building by rivals bent on toppling the maritime order.[12] Externally, therefore, Chatfield's goal required forestalling any radical changes in the global naval balance. To achieve success on all fronts, the Naval Staff had to influence several financial, technical and international variables. .

Of course the British had never had boundless funds for defence, but postwar indebtedness, the rise of expenditure on social services and government parsimony had impressed senior admirals. In December 1926, Chatfield and other leading officers openly voiced their anxiety about the soaring cost of warships.[13] By the early 1930s, the economic depression had made it abundantly clear that Edwardian levels of spending on naval armaments were a thing of the past.[14] To make it acceptable to the Cabinet, any future standard of naval strength would have to be fine-tuned to the state's diminished fiscal capacity. Technically, the Admiralty could curb the price of sea power by keeping the overall size of the fleet to a minimum; by decreasing the dimensions of warships (Table 1.1), which in turn made them serviceable in existing dockyards; and by extending operational lifespans to put off expensive replacement building. Since 1927, for instance, the Naval Staff had proposed to reduce the treaty displacement and main armament of capital ships from 35 000 tons with 16-inch guns to 25 000 tons with 12-inch guns, and to stretch their treaty life spans from 20 to 26 years.[15] The Admiralty, however, did not control these crucial factors. The building plans of potential foes and the types of ships

Table 1.1   Comparison of capital ship size and unit cost

Displacement (tons)	Gun size (inches)	£ (millions)
28 000	12	5.5
35 000	14	8.0
45 000	16	10.5

Sources: FO, 28 Mar. 1934, A2417/1938/45, FO371/17596; Sea Lords Meeting, 4 May 1938, PD06786/38, ADM116/3735.

they built determined, especially in the minds of admirals, the relative quantity and quality of the British fleet.

The primary means by which Admiral Chatfield and his staff attempted to adjust the international naval balance was to replace the expiring 1922 Washington and 1930 London Treaties with one better suited to British maritime interests. The use of diplomacy to safeguard British sea power, of course, was not unprecedented. By formally accepting parity with the US Navy at Washington in 1921, the British negotiators had cleverly defused a potential American bid for naval supremacy without jeopardising any vital interests.[16] Since naval power had to be cultivated over long periods by methodical and costly industrial organisation, and because the cycle of production, employment and replacement of warships was calculated in decades, the status quo possessed its own momentum.[17] Adroit naval armaments diplomacy could stand in to uphold the pre-eminence of the Royal Navy while British industrial and financial capacity could not. Admiral Chatfield and his colleagues grasped this lesson.[18] If the other powers could be persuaded by tenacious bargaining in 1935 to play sea power according to fundamentally British rules, then the period of structural vulnerability created by the 1930 London Naval Treaty might be traversed with British sea power intact.

The cardinal rules of the game that the Naval Staff planned to refine in the new treaty were the measures for the international exchange of warship construction data and qualitative limitation.[19] To reduce mistrust, the two earlier treaties required the signatories to declare to the others the principal dimensions and features of their new ships once the keels were laid. This traffic proved invaluable to the Navy's technical intelligence apparatus for evaluating foreign designs. Hence the Naval Staff proposed that the new treaty should provide for an even greater trade in data, including engine power, designed speed, type of fuel, the number and calibre of all guns, and whether ships would carry mines and torpedoes.

Qualitative limitation required the placing of warships into categories and defining the maximum size and gun calibre of each category. The first two treaties had set important precedents, but the Naval Staff desired to close three perilous loopholes in the third. First, the Washington Treaty had fixed the upper limit for cruisers at 10 000 tons and 8-inch turrets. The Naval Staff regarded this type, which the powers began to build in numbers after 1922, as useful solely for the pre-eminently anti-British activities of breaking blockades and attacking convoys. Although the London Treaty prohibited 8-inch guns on cruisers, after 1930, the Americans and the Japanese began to lay down ships up to 10 000 tons bristling with 6-inch guns.[20] In the new treaty, the Naval Staff hoped to ban production of all vessels above their preferred size of 7000 tons with guns up to 6 inches, so that the existing larger types would become extinct in 1945 by the cycle of obsolescence and replacement. Second, the Admiralty hoped to extend limitation by categories[21] – that is maintaining the relative strength of the powers in each class – to check immoderate cruiser and submarine building, such as the French had undertaken in the 1920s. Third, it wanted consensus on non-construction zones between categories to outlaw commerce destroying hybrids like Germany's 10 000 ton/11-inch gun *Panzerschiffe* (colloquially 'pocket' battleships), which were designed to be faster than more heavily armed battleships and more heavily armed than faster cruisers.[22]

The supreme object of this elaborate exercise in warship taxonomy was to prevent revolutionary escalations in design. As the master of technological one-upmanship Admiral 'Jackie' Fisher put it: 'There is no progress in uniformity.' Chatfield craved for uniformity to kill 'the principle of going one better'.[23] During the formative years of their careers, he and his contemporaries had witnessed the expensive evolution of battleships, from 17 000 ton/12-inch gun dreadnoughts to 30 000 ton/15-inch gun super-dreadnoughts. The Italians reinforced the lesson in June 1934, when they announced the construction of two 35 000 ton/15-inch gun ships in reply to France's new 26 500 ton/13-inch gun *Dunkerque* class battlecruisers. Not only were the larger ships and guns more expensive, but qualitative escalation threatened to topple the treaty edifice and with it British sea security. Fisher defended British maritime security through technological innovation; Chatfield attempted to safeguard it with qualitative standstill legislated by treaty. But this was not an entirely retrograde policy. As Chapter 4 will demonstrate, the Admiralty believed that they acquired a singular advantage from qualitative limitation because they could design and construct superior fighting vessels within any given set of balanced dimensions, so long as the other naval powers built their ships reasonably close to treaty standards.

Naturally, the major hurdle to the Admiralty shaping the new treaty to suit its purposes was gaining international consent. Although the events of the second London Naval Conference are recounted elsewhere, it is necessary to sketch out here the overall situation to locate the Anglo-German Naval Agreement within the wider framework of the Royal Navy's strategic programme. After the Admiralty and the FO had drafted position papers in the first four months of 1934, a Ministerial Committee (NCM) was formed in April to oversee the preliminaries.[24] In May, delegations from the other five Washington powers were invited to London for pre-conference discussions. Negotiations with the Americans began formally in June. It quickly became evident that they would reject 70 cruisers for the Royal Navy, the proposal to reduce the size of the battleship and any tampering with the ratios. The Japanese, who arrived in October, proposed a 'common upper' limit of tonnage, within which every power could build the ship types it deemed necessary for its security. The British effort to steer a middle course between the two positions, plus accurate press reports about elements in Whitehall advocating an accord with Japan, antagonised Washington. But an open clash between the two Western powers was prevented by the mutual desire to oppose Japan with a united front.

In retrospect, the negotiations were doomed owing to the underlying political struggle between the Pacific powers. At the time, however, the Naval Staff supposed that the fuel of Japan's discontent was the ratio system itself, which wounded the *amour propre* of the states saddled with inferiority.[25] Evidence supporting this peculiar idea existed. Despite the American claim in 1922 for a navy 'second to none', for example, the Congress refused to vote the annual funds necessary to build even up to treaty strength until 1934.[26] Franco-Italian enmity appeared to stem from the objection of each to recognising equality with the other, rather than from any detached reckoning of maritime potential. Also, the FO's negotiator planned to tame Tokyo's aversion to inferiority by admitting its 'theoretical' equality in the same way that Germany's equality of status had been accepted by the powers in December 1932 to entice it back to the Geneva disarmament talks.[27] Similarly, the Admiralty hoped to moderate the naval ambitions of the other powers by granting them the 'theoretical' right to do as they pleased.[28] By replacing the ratios with a scheme by which each signatory would negotiate a five-year building plan and observe qualitative limits, the Naval Staff anticipated that the maritime balance would stabilise at roughly the Washington Treaty levels. In the new ratio-free world, where fleet strength would become proportional to needs and national resources, Chatfield hoped to persuade the Cabinet to increase the size of the battle fleet incrementally. This expansion had to be gradual so as not to incite rivals into systematic opposition and to cloak the period of relative industrial vulnerability. The Royal Navy's true ambition was to reach by the mid-1940s an unchallengeable two-power standard over Japan and the largest European fleet.[29]

By the close of 1934, however, the CNS was pessimistic about the probability of realigning the global naval order. Unless the ratio system was abandoned, Tokyo would not negotiate qualitative limits; Washington refused to uncouple qualitative from quantitative limitation.[30] The Naval Staff correctly anticipated that Japan would issue notice in December of its departure from the Washington Treaty. Opposition within the CID to the Admiralty's aims had also proved formidable. And the connection between internal and external goals was critical: even if the Cabinet granted the Navy all it desired, the other powers could check Britain's maritime revival by pursuing policies inimical to it; if naval diplomacy fostered a favourable situation abroad, the opportunity could still be squandered by a vacillating Cabinet. Indeed, months earlier, from both the FO and the Treasury, came proposals to scale down British defence policy from a global perspective to a narrow European one, principally by a concentration on airpower and the conclusion of a *rapprochement* with Japan.

Chatfield first encountered these 'disturbing' ideas in the Defence Requirements Committee (DRC). The DRC was set up in November 1933 by the Cabinet to 'prepare a programme for meeting the worst [defence] deficiencies'.[31] It consisted of the COS, the permanent heads of the Treasury and the FO, Sir Warren Fisher and Sir Robert Vansittart, and was chaired by the Cabinet Secretary, Colonel Sir Maurice Hankey. The COS, under Chatfield's chairmanship, came to the DRC to haggle over the money. The CNS, who probably expected that events in China would bear out his priorities, intended his share to pay for the modernisation of the existing battle fleet, more cruisers and naval aircraft, reserve fuel, ammunition and ASDIC sets, and the completion of the advance fleet base at Singapore. Moreover, he anticipated the DRC would underwrite a long-term building plan. But when the DRC convened, Vansittart and Fisher, who both wished to frame a single strategy, tenaciously argued that Germany was the 'ultimate potential enemy'. Even the CNS conceded that Japan was unlikely to move against British interests in Asia unless they were first entangled in a European conflict. Influenced by the near universal fixation with the supposed apocalyptic capabilities of bombing planes,[32] the two civilians further proposed concentrating on defence measures against the nascent German air force. Hankey, however, Chatfield's powerful CID ally, successfully negotiated a compromise: in the DRC's report of February 1934, Germany was labelled the principal threat, but the Navy's deficiency scheme was largely endorsed.[33]

This first DRC report might have been an Admiralty victory had its price tag not exceeded the original budget by a third. Warren Fisher and the Chancellor of the Exchequer, Neville Chamberlain, who generally overpowered his weaker Cabinet colleagues, exploited this overshoot to press for economy and deterrence in Europe through airpower. In April 1934, Fisher proposed to the NCM the negotiation, even at the cost of offending Washington, of a 'thorough and lasting' settlement with Japan which would obviate the need for the Navy's expensive two-power standard and 'make available for immediate concentration our maximum force' against Germany. Fisher's bold thesis failed to persuade MacDonald, Monsell or Sir John Simon, the Foreign Secretary, all of whom preferred alignment with Washington to Tokyo in the naval talks.[34] In June 1934, though, while the DRC report was being examined by the Ministerial Committee on Disarmament (DCM),[35] the Chancellor made clear the fiscal benefits of Fisher's plan. He reduced the total cost of the DRC package by slashing the naval and military measures in favour of relatively inexpensive air defences, and proposed abandoning battleship building altogether. In his view, enhancing security in Europe was pressing: air armaments would supply a deterrent (the image of German bombers releasing a torrent of poison gas and high explosive bombs over London was foremost in the public mind) and British safety from Japanese opportunism entirely rested upon peace in Europe. Although the Singapore base should be finished, he added, its defence should be left to submarines and light craft.[36]

Chatfield angrily accused Chamberlain of inventing an entirely new formula for British defence policy: 'What is the cheapest way in which we can "keep face" with the world?' Ironically, the Admiralty's blueprint for naval security was largely premised on this question. For the Naval Staff, who were vexed by claims that the bomber had made the battleship obsolete, the truly irksome point of the Treasury proposal was the substitution of air for naval forces.[37] At the DCM, Monsell defeated Chamberlain's proposed cuts to the Navy's deficiency plan, but did not obtain a decision about long-term building, which was postponed until after the naval conference.[38] Chatfield, though discouraged, had sound reason to believe that latent Cabinet support for the Navy existed, if only the Whitehall deadlock could be broken by what one later Director of Plans called the right 'psychological moment'.[39] Getting there hinged on the naval negotiations. After Tokyo played its hand in December, progress on that front required unanimity in Europe, and that meant bringing Germany on board.

THE GERMAN PROBLEM

Despite defeat in 1918 and the encumbrance of the Treaty of Versailles, which outlawed the possession of substantial armed forces and required the payment of reparations, Germany remained potentially Europe's pre-eminent military and economic power. Since Germany no longer presented a serious naval or colonial challenge, the problem of British policy in Europe was reconciling the craving of successive Weimar Chancellors for treaty revision with the French wish for security from German attack.

Without a formal Anglo-French alliance, however, French statesmen were reluctant to contemplate altering Versailles.

British political elites viewed French policy as short-sighted. French delay in accepting the suspension of reparation payments in June 1931, which was followed by the collapse of the Reichsmark, and French opposition to limited German rearmament, which confounded the Geneva disarmament talks, reinforced this opinion. The advent of Hitler's bellicose regime in January 1933 and its withdrawal from the Geneva talks later that year were regarded by the British as attributable to these events. In April 1934, the new hard-line government in Paris rejected a British proposal to permit limited German rearmament and ruled out future talks. Undaunted, Whitehall persisted in trying to mediate a Franco-German settlement and to put a lid on covert German rearmament.

Before March 1935, the future of the German navy was only a subcomponent of this larger foreign policy predicament. In June 1935, seemingly from nowhere to onlookers, the issue leaped to the forefront of British policy. The Cabinet agreed to a bilateral naval agreement with Berlin. The accord represented a break in the ostensible anti-German front and a Nazi diplomatic victory. While historians have admitted the crucial role played by the Admiralty and strategic motives in this decision, they have failed to appreciate the utter audacity of the Admiralty's grand objective. To reiterate the point, Admiral Chatfield and his staff planned to remodel the international naval balance to buttress Britain's status as a great power. How this ambitious strategic programme was permitted to impinge on the formulation of Whitehall's European policy, and how the Admiralty regarded the bilateral Naval Agreement with Nazi Germany as the harbinger of the right 'psychological moment' it sought, requires a look at policy-making on both sides.

One reason why historians have overlooked the consistency and continuity of strategic purpose underlying the Royal Navy's enthusiasm for the June 1935 Naval Agreement is that they have focused exclusively on the years 1933–5. In fact, the Admiralty's efforts to ensure that German naval expansion conformed to its framework predated Hitler's Chancellorship. Although the Treaty of Versailles banned German possession of U-boats and naval aviation, and limited the German surface fleet to six armoured ships of 10 000 tons, six light cruisers of 6000 tons, 12 800 ton destroyers, and 12 torpedo boats, German naval planners cleverly exploited the capital ship limits to lay down in February 1929 a powerful 10 000-ton *Panzerschiff*. This conspicuous departure from orthodox warship design was perceived by the Admiralty not only as a danger to British maritime communications but also to qualitative uniformity. In November 1930, a six-year building plan was tabled in the Reichstag that included eight such *Panzerschiffe*: six for service and two for reserve. Paris protested. Berlin explained that the two extra ships had been sanctioned by a decision of the Versailles powers in March 1920, which allowed Germany to lay up two vessels against accidental loss or extended repairs.[40]

What is striking and characteristic about the Royal Navy's approach to this Franco-German dispute is the desire to use armaments diplomacy to serve broad strategic goals. The Admiralty hoped to avoid joining the French in a formal objection that might jeopardise Berlin's assent to the Draft Disarmament Convention, which was designed, among other things, to forestall European naval competition before the 1935 conference.[41] More specifically, Berlin's adherence to qualitative limitation would kill the destabilising *Panzerschiffe*, and switch German ship production to conventional types. Conversations with German naval officers at the Geneva disarmament talks that indicated that they also wished to conclude a deal to 'bridge' the period between Versailles and full equality at the forthcoming conference encouraged this policy.[42] Hence the Admiralty's chief planner equated what was strategically useful with what was internationally just when he declared in March 1932 that Germany had 'a moral right to some relaxation of the treaty'.[43]

The recognition in December 1932 of Germany's equality of status signalled a renascent German fleet on the strategic horizon, without settling the issue of its size and shape. On 7 February 1933, perhaps in an effort to test the new Chancellor's desire for good relations with London as espoused in *Mein Kampf*, Admiral Bellairs, the British naval delegate at Geneva, renewed his efforts to convert his German counterparts to the British view of naval disarmament.[44] He made no headway. In April, acting on increasingly hardline instructions, the German delegates rejected the British Draft Convention (the MacDonald plan) because it denied them U-boats and full-size battleships before 1937.[45] Six months later, Hitler pulled out of the Geneva talks and the League of Nations. He told European statesmen that they should either disarm to Germany's level or accept German rearmament. But he also sent word to London that he would eschew a Tirpitzian style challenge.[46] Indeed, as the year closed, there were no visible signs of an increase in the German building plan.

The Admiralty's only concern was whether a fourth *Panzerschiff* would be laid down in 1934 to join the three being built. Admiral G. Durand-Viel, the French CNS, had told Chatfield that he required two 26 500 ton *Dunkerque* class battlecruisers to combat three German *Panzerschiffe*.[47] The Naval Staff hoped that if France only laid down one battlecruiser, the naval situation in Europe might remain stable. But if Berlin began a fourth

10 000 ton ship and Paris followed with a second battlecruiser, an Italian reply was inevitable. In December, Captain Edward L. King, the Director of Plans, reported that the C-in-C of the German Navy, Admiral Erich Raeder, had told the British naval attaché that work on the fourth ship would begin as planned, but Hitler had told the British Ambassador that it would be delayed.[48] Reluctant to enquire lest they provoke the unwanted response, and calculating that Berlin would postpone long-term plans until after the naval conference, the Naval Staff and the FO decided to 'let sleeping dogs lie'.[49]

Yet the reality of the new Chancellor's ambitions meant that European waters would not remain tranquil for long. Examining the dynamic propelling German naval diplomacy on this course is indispensable to a full account of the origins of the Anglo-German Naval Agreement, and to a balanced appraisal of the Royal Navy's role. But the key point to bear in mind is that German diplomacy did not force the Admiralty to improvise nor substantially to adjust its policy. As we shall see, German naval proposals as presented in June 1935 were endorsed by the Admiralty and recommended to ministers because they were compatible with the Navy's scheme to use armaments diplomacy to promote strategic conditions favourable to British sea power.

Of course Hitler's naval diplomacy was guided by his own purposes. Days after coming to power, at a private gathering of military and foreign-policy officials, and again at a cabinet meeting on 8 February 1933, Hitler affirmed that his priority was to expedite rearmament. When German military power was restored, he spoke of 'throwing off the shackles of Versailles' and vaguely about establishing hegemony in Europe by the conquest of living-space (*Lebensraum*) in the East.[50] While Hitler consolidated his grip on the state, however, he proved reluctant to tempt diplomatic isolation or provoke intervention. Rather than exit from Geneva early in 1933, he drew out the bargaining, and assuaged London and Paris by talking publicly of disarmament. Hitlerian diplomacy, however, was not directed at peace: it was camouflage for subversive intentions and the stockpiling of arms, a tool to disrupt the formation of an anti-German coalition and the penultimate step before aggression.[51]

In the execution of his policy, Hitler was solely consistent with *Mein Kampf* in his attempts to procure alliances with Britain and Italy as a precondition for a *Drang nach Osten*. He acknowledged London as the greatest potential obstacle to his success and criticised the Kaiser's government for antagonising Britain by a naval challenge. He asserted that in future Germany should forgo maritime ambitions in exchange for London's indifference to German dominance on the continent. The new Chancellor even imagined that a German guarantee of the British Empire coupled with an offer of the use of its small fleet would make Germany appear to London an attractive ally.[52]

Admiral Raeder, who harboured armaments ambitions of Tirpitzian proportions, was uncomfortably aware of the new Chancellor's opinion of sea power.[53] Since he took command in 1928, Raeder had concentrated his unbounded tenacity on rebuilding the navy and raising its reputation among German political elites. He rejected attempts by several Weimar defence ministers to limit the navy's operational horizon to the Baltic and instructed his planners to look to the Atlantic as the proper theatre for the fleet.[54] During the Geneva talks, the C-in-C Navy was anxious that the navy's interests might be sacrificed in exchange for concessions on land weapons. His staff looked to the forthcoming naval talks for a 'new start'. In their view, joining the sea power conference in 1935 would annul the Versailles naval limits and would leave Germany free to rebuild its fleet.[55] In February 1933, Hitler's stress on a continental policy and the appointment of the influential Nazi-party official, Hermann Göring, as Air Minister confirmed Raeder's fears that the navy would be relegated to third place in rearmament. Admiral Raeder, however, showed himself to be an adroit Tirpitzian. At their first private interview in April, he played to Hitler's foreign policy preconceptions by stressing how a small fleet would enhance Germany's eligibility for an alliance. By persistent lobbying, he established a favourable relationship with Hitler and could boast in September 1933 that the new Chancellor had come to grasp the political and strategic significance of sea power.[56]

Six months after obtaining Hitler's permission to increase the tonnage of the next two planned *Panzerschiffe*, designated ships D and E, to 18 000 tons in October 1933 (converted again in 1935 to the 31 800 ton battlecruisers *Scharnhorst* and *Gneisenau*), Raeder considered a new building timetable drafted by his staff. It was a project for eight *Panzerschiffe*, three aircraft carriers, 18 cruisers, 48 destroyers, and 72 U-boats to be completed by 1949.[57] Although this timetable ignored Versailles Treaty limitations, Raeder's planners had an even more lofty medium-term scheme in mind. As early as March 1932, Admiral Otto Groos, the Head of the German Naval Command Office, told the British naval attaché that the German navy desired equality with France in any future naval treaty.[58] On 6 February 1934, Raeder's subordinates reasserted what they considered to be their minimum objective for the immediate future to the Foreign Ministry in anticipation of joining the naval talks. Groos wrote that the Naval Command planned for qualitative equality and quantitative parity with France and Italy, and only a brief transitional period before obtaining these goals.

Hitler's idea of a special agreement with London based on a 33.3 per cent naval ratio first appears in a document prepared for the C-in-C Navy in April. In June, Admiral Raeder instructed his staff to 'use the figure of one-third of the British tonnage as the standard for settling the strength of the German fleet'. Although it was later revised to a 35 per cent ratio with the Royal Navy to equal France's Washington Treaty battleship and aircraft carrier quota, his staff pointed out that this figure was insufficient for parity in cruisers, destroyers and U-boats (Table 1.2). Since war plans envisaged defending the Baltic against a Franco-Soviet combination while conducting offensive sea operations against the French in the Atlantic and the Mediterranean, the 35 per cent ratio was deemed strategically unacceptable.[59]

During discussion in the summer of 1934 about whether Germany should join the naval negotiations, however, Raeder failed to make Hitler grasp the distinction between the Naval Command's 'parity with France' and the Chancellor's arbitrary figure of one-third the British fleet.[60] For the master of carefully crafted oratory, the formula of 'one-third of the British fleet except in cruisers, destroyers, and submarines, in which we demand parity with France' was too much of a mouthful. It also failed to convey the ostensible generosity of his political ploy. Hitler and Konstantin von Neurath, the Foreign Minister, disappointed Raeder and his staff by rejecting their proposal to seek direct participation in the multilateral naval conference as a means to nullify the naval clauses of Versailles and to win prestige by joining the global maritime order.[61] In early November, the Chancellor renewed his bid for a bilateral accord by issuing instructions that London should be informed of the 35 per cent offer.[62] On 27 November, Admiral

Table 1.2   German Naval Command, tonnage calculated from 50 and 33.3 per cent ratios compared with British and French naval strength, 16 June 1934

| | *Britain* | *Germany* | | France |
		50%	*33.3%*	
Capital ships	525 000	262 500	175 000	175 000
Aircraft carriers	135 000	67 500	45 000	60 000
Heavy cruisers	146 800	73 400	48 933	70 000
Light cruisers and destroyers	342 200	171 100	114 066	197 431
U-boats	52 700	*	*	81 989

* U-boat tonnage would vary according to what would be decided at the 1935 naval conference.
Source: Dülffer, *Marine*, 567.

Raeder, adjusting his policy, told Captain Muirhead-Gould, the British naval attaché, that 'Germany would welcome direct negotiations with England as to the strength of Germany's fleet on the basis of an agreed percentage of England's strength in various categories.' Perhaps still hoping to refine the Chancellor's 35 per cent ratio during bargaining, the C-in-C Navy added that 'these percentages [to be decided by naval experts] would be surprisingly low'. At a meeting the next day, though, Sir Eric Phipps, the British Ambassador in Berlin, heard Hitler utter in a 'torrent of words' his idea of setting a 35 per cent naval ratio.[63]

Only a year before, both the FO and the Admiralty had greeted Raeder's clumsy offer of a naval treaty and an anti-American alliance with the contempt his staff had predicted,[64] while Hitler's envoy, the champagne salesman turned diplomatic interloper, Joachim von Ribbentrop, was treated politely but sceptically by MacDonald and his Lord President, Stanley Baldwin. Despite official reports to the contrary, the Naval Staff and the FO still anticipated that Berlin might delay its fourth *Panzerschiff* until 1935.[65] In April, just before Paris refused another settlement mediated by MacDonald, Phipps was again told by Hitler and his Defence Minister, General Werner von Blomberg, that they had no wish for another naval antagonism. The message was repeated in October, but to no avail.[66] Throughout 1934, the naval issue was of secondary importance. In December, however, British priorities began to shift. A Cabinet subcommittee recommended that the European crisis could not be left to 'drift', and that they would have to act with Paris to gain some 'control' of the German military build-up. And in reply to the German overtures in November, the Central Department of the FO, which was responsible for relations with Germany, proposed to the NCM an Anglo-German exchange of views on naval questions.[67] As 1935 opened, therefore, the course of the international naval negotiations described in the previous section, plus the Cabinet's outlook on European security, combined to enhance London's responsiveness to Hitler's persistent wooing.

Externally, however, events in early 1935 did not convey this image of British policy. A new and seemingly more reasonable government in Paris offered some hope of treaty revision. The Franco-Italian *rapprochement* in January, spurred on as a result of a bungled coup by Austrian Nazis in the previous summer, and the advance of Franco-Soviet talks appeared to give Hitler reason to pause. In early February, French and British ministers met in London to draft a new settlement. They issued a communiqué opposed to unilateral treaty modification and offered a Western air pact and an Eastern treaty of mutual guarantee. London thus gained the pledge of collective action against air aggression in the West, without accepting entanglements in France's alliance system in Eastern Europe. The next step was for Sir John Simon and his deputy, Anthony Eden, to visit Berlin to get Hitler on board. The Admiralty took the opportunity to bring naval armaments diplomacy into play. To succeed, the broad strategic programme described in the section above had to be supported by a sturdy set of international agreements. Chatfield's deputy, Admiral Charles Little expressed the Navy's principal concern at this moment: 'The longer we put off coming to grips with Germany on the naval question, the more difficult it will be to get an agreement with her at a level which is likely to find acceptance in Europe generally.'[68] On 27 February, therefore, Monsell, the First Lord, asked Simon to sound the Germans out on the naval question.[69] But Hitler postponed the meeting in reaction to the British rearmament plan announced in a White Paper on 4 March. Calculating that London would concern itself mainly with restraining French and Italian reaction rather than opposing his unilateral denunciation of Versailles, Hitler reinstated conscription in Germany and bluffed that he now controlled an air force as large as Britain's.

The alarm generated by Hitler's bluff also confirmed to the Cabinet the merit of Monsell's request for naval talks. But Chatfield and his staff were not being stampeded. By this stage, they had a well developed view of how big a German navy was compatible with British security and how fast Berlin would expand its fleet. They had also acquired a reasonably accurate picture of German warship construction. On these points, though, historians have been critical of the Admiralty. Roskill sees the Navy as victims of lightning bargaining tactics: Ribbentrop rushed the Admiralty into accepting the 35 per cent deal with an 'unseemly haste'. Equally, Wark depicts the Naval Staff, which failed to make any 'systematic' enquiry into how fast Germany could expand its fleet, as accommodating itself to Hitler's ratio due to an overwhelming desire to reach agreement. 'The poor state of [Admiralty] intelligence on German naval construction', he adds, 'was a significant factor in bringing the British to the negotiating table.'[70] These assertions are incorrect. Tackling them will mean departing from the chronological narrative, but it is worth taking the detour because it will provide further insight into the long-range calculations behind the Admiralty's search for a naval accord with Nazi Germany.

The Naval Staff consistently viewed the ratio of naval armaments assigned to France by the Washington Treaty (a 35 per cent ratio with Britain in capital ships and aircraft carriers) as 'the highest that we could accept for any European power'.[71] The problem was that the expansion of the German and Italian fleets would compel the French to add to their tonnage. In anticipation of Anglo-French naval talks, Captain King concluded in late June

1934, just as Raeder's planners had found, that a comparison between French and German seaborne trade and geostrategic factors would render a claim for Franco-German parity 'difficult to resist by logic'. But the Director of Plans assumed that French hostility combined with Berlin's desire to please London would deter Germany from making this strategically reasonable bid. He advised informing the French that Germany should be held at 188 000 tons (roughly a 16 per cent ratio with Britain), which would grant Berlin at least Baltic supremacy.[72] Thus, the Naval Staff's belief that German naval planners would accept less than treaty parity with the French was not premised on a detached strategic analysis of reasonable German sea security needs but on diplomatic factors that might influence Hitler.

In December, Plans and Intelligence Divisions considered the potential rate and magnitude of German fleet expansion up to the years 1939 and 1942. Captain King started with three assumptions: one, that Germany would join the next naval treaty; two, Hitler's priorities would be the army and air force; and three, that Admiral Raeder's 'immediate' aim would be to secure the Baltic from Russia and to protect German merchant shipping from French interdiction. He therefore projected a growth rate that would bring the German navy near one-third the size of the Royal Navy by 1942.[73] Admiral Gerald C. Dickens, the DNI, questioned this notion. Dickens, who delighted in playing devil's advocate, asserted that with experience German constructors would increase the building tempo and mobilise idle yard capacity. If Germany desired, he added, it could finance an ambitious schedule of parity with France by 1939 and a naval challenge to Britain by 1942.[74]

In reply, Captain King revised his 1939 forecast to account for an acceleration in the rate of assembly, but he was not prepared to extrapolate at this pace beyond 1939. Cost-effective policy had to be premised on what foreign armaments planners would probably do, and periodically adjusted to match what they actually did. Any prognosis beyond 1939, King had argued, was 'highly speculative'. In any case, the Director of Plans credited German naval strategists with sufficient imagination to envisage an alternative to Tirpitz's defunct programme of a symmetrical armaments competition. If they planned for war with Britain, then German admirals would reject qualitative limitation and build an asymmetrical offensive fleet. This fleet, composed of 'improved' *Panzerschiffe*, fast-light craft and submarines, would be capable of evading the Royal Navy's superior heavy surface forces to strike a deadly blow to Britain's oceanic commerce.[75] Here lies a crucial point: King recognised that if Berlin was bent on a direct challenge to Britain, then German naval planners would not commit themselves to a *pattern of naval development* that was the *least* dangerous from the Royal Navy's viewpoint, as well as being the one that would concretely reinforce the existing order of sea power and with it British interests generally.

On 15 January 1935, during an informal meeting in the FO, King summarised the implications of his earlier study for Vansittart. He said that Admiralty policy was to propose to Berlin that it adhere to the British compromise plan: namely the combination of qualitative limits and announced five-year building plans. Statements about the ultimate size of the German fleet should be avoided; instead, they should endeavour to discover what ships Germany intended to lay down by 1942. He added that the Naval Staff could accept German parity with France, but this was unacceptable to Paris.[76]

Captain King, however, was well aware that Raeder intended to build a conventional fleet to match at least that of the French. The drive for 'equality of status' implied an aspiration to possess standard warships. As early as 1932, the German navy planned to construct its fourth and fifth capital ships, D and E, as improved *Panzerschiffe* of 15 000 to 18 000 tons. The Admiralty evidently had some knowledge of this intention. Chatfield told the DRC in November 1933 that the fourth German capital ship would 'probably' be some 15 000 to 17 000 tons, only about ten weeks before the keels of D and E were laid to accommodate 18 000 tons.[77] By late January 1934, Captain Gerald Muirhead-Gould had noted that the diesel engines with which the *Panzerschiffe* were powered had not been ordered for D, which suggested an alteration in design. He was told in April by Raeder's chief of staff, Captain Hermann Densch, that if the naval talks failed, they would build 25 000-ton ships with 12-inch guns.[78] A month later, though, intelligence obtained by the SIS from the naval yards at Kiel presumably confirmed that ship E was still being built to displace only 18 000 tons.[79]

Anyway, it appears that the Naval Staff assumed throughout the summer of 1934 that both ships would be only 17 000-ton improved *Panzerschiffe*. Admiral Raeder, however, ordered work on the ships to halt in July. He thrashed out a new design with his constructors that month with difficulty because of a lack of technical intelligence about the *Dunkerque*, but they eventually settled on three 11-inch gun triple turrets and 31 800 tons.[80] Muirhead-Gould reported the work slowdown on D and E and speculated that they were being reassembled as replies to the *Dunkerque*. In January 1935, the DNI ordered him to confront the Germans with a questionnaire about the features of their new warships. Muirhead-Gould presented it to Densch, and boldly exploited the latter's anxiety over relations with Britain by insinuating that the questionnaire was evidence that the DNI no longer believed that Muirhead-Gould had Raeder's confidence: 'My remarks apparently caused [Densch] acute embarrassment.'[81] Two weeks later, Raeder and Densch reassured him that their reticence was politically inspired, but they added unofficially that D and E would conform to the new qualitative limitations. Although the German C-in-C Navy later refused to release design details, NID informed the FO that D and E would probably 'attain very large proportions – and constitute an effective answer to the Dunkerque'.[82]

To monitor submarine development, the British had the advantage of a well placed spy. In 1919, a former naval engineering officer, Otto Krueger, had been recruited by the SIS to keep track of covert rearmament. A talented engineer, who was later awarded an honorary doctorate in engineering, Krueger evidently became associated with the Dutch company *Ingenieurskantoor voor Scheepbouw* (Inkavos), which had been set up in 1922 by the German navy to continue U-boat work outside Germany to evade detection by the Allied Control Commission. From 1927 to 1932, through a secret office in a private Berlin engineering firm (Igewit), German U-boat constructors directed experiments with three prototypes of 250, 500 and 700 tons, laid down in Finland, Holland and Spain.[83]

Within days of Hitler's advent to power, Blomberg authorised the establishment of a U-boat School at Kiel to train crews for the first submarines to be built in Germany. Contracts were later awarded to Inkavos to lay down 250-ton boats at Kiel, while experiments continued with the prototype in Finland. Political conditions did not permit rapid development in 1933, but by the end of the year components for the first six 250-ton types were being shipped and stored at Deutsche Werke for final assembly. Hitler had cautioned Admiral Raeder in June 1934, in view of the Saar plebiscite, to maintain absolute secrecy about U-boat preparations. To camouflage the assembly of the first six, work was started in December 1933 on large huts to cover the exposed Deutsche Werke slipways. In November 1934, at Germania Yard, where a second batch of six 250-ton boats were to be built, the identification numbers of six new minesweepers, which were supposed to be under construction in the shipyard, were painted on the iron fencing which surrounded the existing slipway building. By the end of the year, Raeder had the required parts for the first six U-boats ready for assembly, preparations for an additional batch of six in motion, and had advanced plans for the first two 700-ton boats at Bremen.[84]

Thanks to Dr Krueger and other sources, NID had a good picture of Inkavos's activities.[85] Even so, espionage was not always necessary. In January 1930, the Communists raised the issue of the U-boat being built in

Spain in the Reichstag; in April 1932, word from friendly but not clandestine sources reached the FO about the U-boat under construction in Finland.[86] The DNI recounted for the Naval Staff in the summer of 1933 how Inkavos was constructing U-boats to German specifications in Spain and Finland.[87] It is very likely that some of the secret arrangements for the six 250-ton boats from Inkavos were known to NID. Significantly, the Naval Staff framed policy to match this technical intelligence. As Chatfield told his DRC colleagues at the end of 1933, he was prepared to see Germany build 'submarines of up to 250 tons'.[88]

On 31 October 1934, the head of French military intelligence, the *Deuxième Bureau*, informed the British naval attaché in Paris that U-boat construction had begun at Kiel. As proof, he produced for the DNI a blurred photograph and a sketch diagram of the disguised slipways. The Admiralty was aware that German submarine constructors were making progress. The technical specifications of engines for ocean-going U-boats being manufactured by Krupp had arrived at NID in May 1934. But Phipps thought the report was an example of how the *Deuxième Bureau*'s eagerness to authenticate German treaty violations engendered a propensity for exaggeration. On 28 November 1934, Captain Muirhead-Gould reported that, although he believed that plans for submarines existed, none had yet been laid. He added that minesweeper building at Germania Yard appeared to have prompted the French accusation.[89] The naval attaché was correct about the keels not having been laid even if plans were ready – the assembly sheds contained the required components – but he was misled by the minesweeper deception.

Admiral Raeder gave the order to begin assembly of the first six 250-ton U-boats on 8 February 1935.[90] Six weeks later, in the wake of Hitler's denunciation of the military clauses of Versailles, Admiral Dickens summed up for the CNS and the FO what NID expected to hear about the German navy. In the case of U-boats, the NID memo stated that they would not 'be entirely surprised to hear that submarines are, in fact, being constructed at Kiel'. It cited two reports about the storage of 'submarines in parts, ready for assembly, at short notice'. Since early March, sources indicated that perhaps ten boats were being built at Germania Yard in Kiel, where minesweepers were supposed to be being assembled, but it was impossible to be certain because observers could not penetrate beyond the slipway screens. Concerning the size of ships D and E (the future *Scharnhorst* and *Gneisenau*), weeks before German constructors actually began to re-lay the new 31 800 ton keels the memo reiterated the Naval Staff's perfectly sound conviction that they would be effective replies to the *Dunkerque* and would 'have a displacement of about 30 000 tons'.[91]

At a moment when Hitler's claim to have achieved air parity caused havoc with the assessments of their Air Ministry colleagues,[92] NID's knowledge of the German naval construction, when compared with the reality, was reliable. The Naval Staff were not driven by a paucity of intelligence or even faulty analysis. Dependable data about the increasing scale of German sea expansion backed, but did not determine, the policy of coming 'to grips with Germany on the naval question'. Although the DNI's conclusion about U-boats was couched in probabilistic language, it is unreasonable to expect that it could have been otherwise. Inferences made from disparate reports of varying reliability were not conducive to certainty – one SIS informant, for instance, saw U-boats on the river Elbe months before the first one was launched.[93] As in the King–Dickens debate about the rate of naval growth, intelligence judgements inevitably boiled down to calculating the probability of competing hypotheses. Even Krueger could not supply a definitive date when U-boat assembly would start because of the marginalisation of Inkavos after 1933, during which time the Naval Command assumed greater formal control for managing U-boat production, and great secrecy was attached to the assembly stage.

To sum up, the foregoing analysis reveals three important findings: first, the 35 per cent ratio equalled in the Admiralty's view the maximum tonnage level for any European fleet; second, the Admiralty rightly concluded that Germany would likely aim to expand its naval forces to that level by about 1942; and third, the Admiralty's knowledge of the details of German warship construction before June 1935 was quite accurate. Far from being the outcome of an Admiralty hustled into an ill-considered position by Nazi diplomacy or compromised by poor intelligence, therefore, the decision to endorse Hitler's offer must be interpreted as an attempt by the Naval Staff to use armaments diplomacy to advance its long-range strategic programme. What remains is to examine the last round of diplomacy before the German delegation arrived in London, the first meeting, and how the Cabinet arrived at its decision.

As noted earlier, Hitler's use of the Luftwaffe as a tool to foment friction between the Western powers also added impetus to the cause of an Anglo-German naval accord. London reacted to open German rearmament by dispatching Simon and Eden to Berlin at the end of March to discuss the Western air pact and a European settlement, while the French suggested immediate consultation with Britain and Italy to co-ordinate opposition and advanced negotiations with Moscow about a mutual assistance treaty. During the Berlin talks, Hitler skilfully played on the Soviet bogey to sidestep a new security structure, but encouraged the belief that he might sign an air pact. He also welcomed Simon's invitation to send a naval delegation to London for an exchange of views.[94] The discouraging outcome of the Berlin talks notwithstanding, the British Cabinet continued to seek a negotiated settlement. Although the mid-April meeting at Stresa between British, French and Italian ministers, followed closely by the conclusion of the Franco-Soviet alliance and a resolution of the League of Nations condemning Hitler's unilateral action, appeared to be foundations for an anti-German front, London continued to play intermediary.

Despite Stresa, Sir Robert Craigie, the head of the FO's American Department, which was responsible for naval armaments diplomacy, pressed for the Anglo-German naval talks to begin without delay. As King had recommended to Vansittart in January, Craigie planned to avoid all mention of ratios and to extract from the Germans a five-year building plan that could be smoothly inserted into the general package that he was trying to sell to the naval powers. He agreed with King's December 1934 judgement that the German navy was unlikely to expand beyond 35 per cent before 1942.[95] Craigie and the Naval Staff planned to ensure that the Germans arrived in early May with the brief that they desired. On 17 April, while Muirhead-Gould was in London, he was ordered by Chatfield to deliver a personal message to Raeder that he expected his negotiators to present detailed qualitative proposals and a concrete building timetable.[96]

Hitler, however, had told Raeder that he had rejected the British compromise proposal during his talks with Simon. He would continue to push for a bilateral accord. The Chancellor added that he did not want any dramatic public statements about naval armaments which would complicate matters for the British.[97] On 12 April, therefore, when Muirhead-Gould was briefed by Captain Leopold Bürkner, Admiral Raeder's liaison officer, about the 1935 building schedule, he was informed about the two capital ships (D and E), two new cruisers and 16 destroyers to be completed, but not a word about U-boats. Muirhead-Gould nonchalantly enquired 'why [are there] no figures for submarines?' Bürkner replied 'we hadn't got that far'. 'I had the impression', the liaison officer later reported to his C-in-C, 'that we could have given the British Naval Attaché simultaneous information about submarine construction without arousing unfavourable reactions; he is certainly thoroughly prepared to hear such news, and so, I suppose, is the Admiralty.'[98] Bürkner was right. Only three days before, a report reached NID which confirmed that 12 U-boats had been ordered.[99] Captain Muirhead-Gould had himself discovered a month earlier that gear boxes, which had to be incorporated into the hulls in the early stages of U-boat assembly, were being manufactured for 12 boats.[100]

Clearly, the Naval Staff was not perturbed by learning about U-boat assembly without it being officially broached. Perhaps influenced by Bürkner's report or by a desire to strengthen his bargaining position, Admiral Raeder decided to inform the Admiralty about the U-boats. On 25 April, when Muirhead-Gould delivered Chatfield's message to the German C-in-C, Bürkner told him about the twelve 250-ton U-boats. The British naval attaché protested that his briefing of 12 April was supposed to have been definitive. Bürkner later explained that the decision to move from the preparation of components to assembly was authorised by Hitler only on the day of his original briefing.[101] This vain attempt at damage control was undermined by partially erroneous intelligence obtained by NID that ocean-going U-boats of 1015 to 1550 tons displacement were also being built from prefabricated parts and that powerful diesels for large submarines were being produced by the MAN works at Augsburg-Nürnberg.[102] Press rumours about the 250-ton U-boats were confirmed by Simon in Parliament on the 29th. Admiral Raeder reacted angrily to the public notification of what he had intended to be a strictly confidential communication. He bitterly accused Muirhead-Gould of breaking his confidence and permitting the FO to leak the U-boat story to scupper the negotiations.[103]

Ironically, this incident helped convert FO sceptics about the wisdom of Anglo-German naval discussions.[104] Although on 2 May PM MacDonald reaffirmed the policy of a negotiated European settlement to the House of Commons, and said that he still intended to hold naval talks with Berlin on the same terms as his government had conducted with the other naval powers, Hitler now intended to delay the meeting until after he made a statement to the Reichstag in rebuttal of the League of Nations condemnation on 21 May.[105]

Meanwhile, reports that the Japanese would not return to the conference table without European maritime unanimity focused Craigie's attention.[106] He and Admiral Little still hoped to obtain from the discussions German qualitative preferences and naval programme intentions. Then they would promptly reopen talks to get French and Italian acquiescence. Equipped with that 'valuable weapon', the DCNS surmised, 'a world-wide treaty embodying qualitative limitation [was] a practical proposition'.[107] Since Craigie and the Navy regarded ratios as obsolete, they hoped to discourage Hitler's talk of a 35 per cent deal. Eric Phipps was instructed to drop hints about this in the right quarter.[108] Admiral Dickens made contact with Ribbentrop's unofficial intermediary in London, T. Philip Conwell-Evans, probably with similar intentions.[109] And a now very frustrated Muirhead-Gould endeavoured to educate a prevaricating Bürkner in the drafting of a building programme.[110]

But Hitler could not be diverted from his bilateral stratagem. On 21 May in the Reichstag, he declared, among other seemingly concilia-tory gestures, that his concession of a 35 per cent ratio was 'final and abiding'.[111] The next day, the Cabinet decided to initiate the naval talks.[112] Phipps telegraphed the FO that Hitler's pledge should be accepted forthwith, now that he had publicly committed himself; no opportunity should be lost, he added, 'owing to French shortsighted-ness'.[113] Craigie was also relieved that Germany was now committed to a fleet inferior to the French by 15 per cent, but he suggested that the con-cession should be neither accepted nor rejected.[114] Eager 'to get the European situation cleared up' by the summer, Chatfield considered it impossible to 'oppose [Hitler's offer] but what the reactions of the French will be to it are more uncertain, and its reaction on our own battleship replacement still more so'.[115] Captain King had the answer to the CNS's second concern prepared. In an elaborate piece of analysis designed to project the naval balance for a decade (see Figure 1.1), the Director of Plans demonstrated that a German navy limited to 35 per cent was compatible with plans for a two-power standard.[116]

Figure 1.1   Plans Division, comparative forecast of available capital ships, May 1935 (assuming: (a) completion of the British capital ship modernisation and replacement plan; (b) the three German *Panzerschiffe* counted as one capital ship; (c) Japanese fleet holds at nine capital ships).

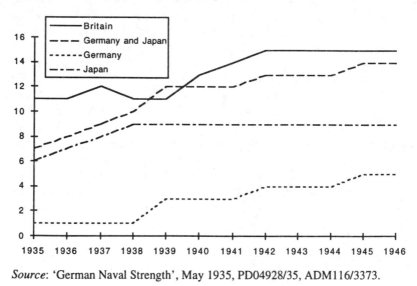

Source: 'German Naval Strength', May 1935, PD04928/35, ADM116/3373.

The first Anglo-German naval meeting took place in the Admiralty on 4 June.[117] Ribbentrop, who headed the German delegation with the grudging consent of Neurath, calculating that failure would discredit him, followed his instructions dogmatically. Hitler had told him to insist on recognition of the 35 per cent ratio. To this end, Ribbentrop took steps to ensure that Simon was present at the opening talks.[118] He greeted the Foreign Secretary with the unpalatable news that acceptance of Hitler's ratio was a precondition of further bargaining. The next morning, MacDonald's Cabinet, with the distraction of an imminent reshuffle on their minds, declined to make an immediate decision about the German ultimatum. Although the unfavourable diplomatic ramifications of condoning a departure from the disarmament clauses of Versailles were admitted, the ministers considered that this 'was a matter in which we were entitled to lead'. As a result, they delegated decision-making authority to the NCM committee and instructed the negotiating team to discover what in practice the 35 per cent meant.[119]

Craigie and Admiral Little had already extracted from Ribbentrop and Admiral Karlgeorg Schuster, Raeder's intermediary, agreement that neither French nor Russian building would alter the ratio. During discussions on 5 June, the German team also agreed to calculate their tonnage by categories instead of global tonnage.[120] For the Naval Staff, these concessions, and the expectation that Germany would join future treaty rules for qualitative limitation and the exchange of information, settled the issue.[121] A blueprint of German naval expansion compatible with the Admiralty's scheme for defending British maritime security was on the market. Even Schuster's claim to the right to parity in U-boat tonnage could not blemish the value of the bargain. The crucial issue here for the Naval Staff and Craigie was not whether it was indeed feasible for Germany to construct a fleet of 35 or 50 per cent by 1942, the precise details of the existing German programme, or even the true motive behind the German gesture: more decisive than any of these concerns was their acute awareness that if Hitler uttered even a hollow threat to strive for a higher percentage, it would utterly demolish their diplomatic strategy for shaping the global naval order to conform to British interests.

The NCM agreed with the advice of its negotiators and accepted Hitler's 35 per cent ratio on 6 June.[122] Simon told them that the remaining issues were how to inform the other powers and whether to link the deal with one on air parity with France. Baldwin, who believed that the naval agreement might serve as a yardstick of Hitler's future intentions, and Monsell, the First Lord, both objected to a coupling of air and naval questions, and convinced the committee that Paris, instead of being consulted, should only be informed of the intention to agree to the ratio. Simon reported that MacDonald had said that 'we could not put our future in French hands', and that he wanted the assurance of the Admiralty's satisfaction with the proposal. The First Lord left no doubt. Admiral Chatfield added that the accord should be well defined and permanent because Hitler had overruled his own naval planners in proposing the 35 per cent ratio. Finally, Chamberlain objected that he had not had time to consider the implications of the Admiralty's claim that German naval expansion would require 'a more rapid replacement' of the battle fleet. Baldwin, one day before he became PM in the reconstructed National Government, told the Chancellor that it was not the occasion to discuss it.[123] This was the CNS's first taste of how German sea expansion would boost his case in Cabinet for a two-power standard.

ARMAMENTS DIPLOMACY AND MARITIME POWER

In retrospect, historians have viewed the conclusion of the 1935 Anglo-German Naval Agreement as a low point in interwar British diplomacy; consequently, they also see the Naval Staff's decisive support for it to be based on defective decision-making and springing from a sense of strategic decline. Retrospective scrutiny, however, has diluted the flavour of contemporary analysis. From the Naval Staff's viewpoint, the Naval Agreement was but one signpost on the road to a bold objective. It represented the use of diplomacy to shape the global maritime balance to bolster Britain's great power status. Specifically, diplomacy was the tool to fashion the technological, financial and international conditions that the Naval Staff perceived as fundamental to remaining the pre-eminent maritime power. Unfortunately, as we shall see, unlike Admiral 'Jackie' Fisher's programme of maritime hegemony by technical supremacy, Admiral Chatfield's programme of qualitative standstill legislated by treaty lacked flexibility or margin for error, and it did not furnish a solution to the European crisis.

Chatfield perceived the Naval Agreement not only as an important tool against warship design revolutionaries abroad, but also as a weapon with which to defeat Treasury and air power heretics at home. He regarded the bilateral naval accord as the precursor of the 'psychological moment' he sought to convince the Cabinet to restore the two-power standard and to restore maritime power to its former place in national policy. Moreover, reassured by accurate intelligence that Hitler had sprung his 35 per cent political solution on Admiral Raeder and his disgruntled staff in the hope of buying British goodwill, the CNS apparently believed he had bamboo-zled his German counterpart by obtaining a permanent treaty. And as Chatfield later explained, he believed that Hitler received nothing in return for his trouble.[124]

Yet Hitler reckoned that he had achieved a great deal with his bilateral ploy. The solidarity of the Stresa front should not be exaggerated, but the accord did rescue Berlin from diplomatic isolation, strain Franco-British relations and legitimise Hitler's violations of the disarmament clauses of Versailles. In what was perhaps the Naval Agreement's most disastrous legacy, it also substantiated Ribbentrop's spurious credentials as a diplomat and launched his vainglorious search for the Anglo-German alliance dreamed of by his Führer.[125] Admiral Raeder took consolation in the self-assurance that it was nothing more than diplomatic camouflage to be discarded once naval construction within the 35 per cent ratio was unworkable.[126]

At the highest level, both parties entertained incompatible expectations of what the Anglo-German Naval Agreement would do for their European policies. Hitler imagined that he had freed himself from British interference with his aggressive designs on Central and Eastern Europe. The Cabinet was receptive to the Admiralty's influence because the deal offered a much needed relief from policy drift. Annoyance at Paris for frustrating successive efforts to redraft the Versailles settlement, and the conviction that in serving their own interests the British were also serving those of the French, were also important.[127] Even sceptical FO officials concurred because, as Craigie repeatedly told Ribbentrop, the Anglo-German Naval Agreement 'was designed to facilitate further agreements within a wider framework and there was no further thought behind' it.[128] Ultimately, however, it failed to satisfy the grand strategic or foreign-policy aspirations coveted by any of its authors.

2 Anglo-German Naval Relations, June 1935 to July 1937

Most accounts of Anglo-German naval relations end with the exchange of notes on 18 June 1935.[1] The Naval Agreement's formal recognition of Nazi Germany's freedom from the naval clauses of the Treaty of Versailles and the resulting damage to Anglo-French relations naturally attracts the eye of diplomatic historians. In this period, the Admiralty is normally interpreted as retreating into complacency about Nazi ambitions as a consequence of the accord. But the story does not end in June 1935. In the two years that followed the 1935 Naval Agreement, the Naval Staff and the FO jointly negotiated a second bilateral accord to regulate both the calculation of the 35 per cent ratio and the exchange of warship construction schedules. Concurrently, NID and the IIC monitored German naval expansion.

One reason why historians overlook the naval relationship in 1935–7 is that it was removed from the mainstream of Anglo-German affairs. The exchange was delegated in both states to diplomatic and naval officials on the second rung of policy-making. In Britain, the Cabinet rarely discussed the rationale for the ongoing relationship, and only then in a cursory fashion. The Foreign Secretary, the FO's permanent head and the Central Department regarded these talks as either an irrelevance or a nuisance, and so the technical haggling was left to Craigie and the Admiralty. In Germany the making of the second Naval Agreement was mostly the handiwork of Ribbentrop and the navy.

Of course the impediment to these talks maturing into anything politically concrete was the underlying conflict of expectations buried within the 1935 Naval Agreement. With its signature, Hitler had hoped that the British would disassociate themselves from the continent; the Cabinet hoped that Hitler would co-operate in Europe. But neither signatory grasped nor satisfied the hopes of the other. The German armaments build-up, the Italian aggression in East Africa and attempts to remodel the 1925 western security pact (Locarno) were foremost on the minds of European statesmen. Even so, the continuance of naval diplomacy in 1936–7 was tolerated by principal policy-makers in both London and Berlin because the negative consequences of ending it outweighed any positive incentive for excavating its original premises.

Even if progress on the substantive aims behind the 1935 accord were shunted or pursued along other diplomatic tracks, the course of these naval negotiations and the parallel analysis of the German warship industry are significant for two insights they provide us about the formation of Admiralty policy. First, the Admiralty possessed a quite accurate picture of the bottlenecks that impaired the advance of Admiral Raeder's warship programme. Second, the 1936–7 experience taught the Naval Staff that naval diplomacy could not be isolated from the upheavals in Anglo-German relations overall. If the search for a détente miscarried, then any beneficial naval association was doomed.

Like the first round of Anglo-German naval talks, it is necessary to place round two in its international context before detailed analysis.[2] Once again the main imperative for British negotiators was to obtain a global treaty on qualitative limitation. Japan's declaration in December 1934 of its intention to allow the existing naval treaties to lapse and its insistence on a 'common upper limit' were hardly encouraging. But London remained committed to two top diplomatic objectives: securing qualitative limitation and setting up a general system for the exchange of naval programmes. Although the British did not persuade Washington to reduce the maximum size of the capital ship to 25 000 tons, Craigie and Admiral Chatfield convinced their American counterparts to accept the British compromise plan and to co-operate in opposing Japan.

In December 1935, when the naval conference convened in London, it quickly became apparent to the Japanese that a positive reception for their ideas was unlikely and so they withdrew from the talks. In late February, Mussolini also refused to sign any naval treaty while League of Nations sanctions over his October 1935 Abyssinian aggression were in force. On 25 March 1936, the three remaining Washington powers, Britain, France and the United States, signed the second London Naval Treaty, with ample provision of 'safeguarding' clauses against third-party building. The ratification and longevity of the three-power treaty rested on London's ability to coax the non-signatory powers to adhere to it. Craigie and the Naval Staff anticipated that an Anglo-American harmony coupled with agreement in Europe might induce Tokyo to reverse its policy.[3] And once again agreement in Europe meant agreement with Nazi Germany.

JUNE 1935 TO FEBRUARY 1936

During the technical discussions from 15 to 22 June 1935, the Germans indicated that they would support Britain in the bid to negotiate an international naval treaty. They agreed to divide their 35 per cent ratio by warship categories and to the qualitative limits proposed by the British, including the 25 000-ton capital ship. They also assured their hosts that Germany would participate in any future international régime for the reciprocal trade of naval building plans. Ribbentrop and Admiral Schuster especially impressed Craigie and Admiral Little with emphatic assurances that third-party naval expansion would not upset the 'permanent and definitive character' of the 35 per cent ratio.[4] Ribbentrop further insisted that there should be no denunciation clause within the Naval Agreement as a safeguard against temporary political difficulties between the two governments.[5]

The initial phase of bargaining dealt with how to accomplish the naval ratio in practice. On 4 July, Craigie handed Captain Wassner, the German naval attaché, a document which set out the points for future discussion. It stated that the size of the German fleet would be calculated from the aggregate tonnage of the Royal Navy since no new quantitative relationship would be fixed among the Washington powers.[6] This presented several technical difficulties. First, the 35 per cent ratio was not exactly divisible in every category. The 1935 Naval Agreement stipulated that such anomalies would be hammered out by the transfer of surplus tonnage from one category to adjust a shortage in another within limits. In the capital ship category, Craigie and Little proposed that the shortfall for Germany's eighth ship – 10 000 to 15 000 tons depending on the new maximum treaty displacement – should come from the heavy cruiser category.

The second problem concerned the British plan to retain ten overage cruisers and 50 000 tons of overage destroyers for trade defence. Since the existing underage lifespans for cruisers and destroyers were 20 and 16 years, it would take Germany decades to build up sufficient vessels to match Britain in overage tonnage. To compensate Germany, the British memo suggested reducing the normal lifespan of existing cruisers and destroyers to 15 and 12 years. In the case of the three *Panzerschiffe*, the British left it to the Germans to suggest what reduction in the standard 20-year operational life might be reasonable.

Admiral Raeder, upon receiving a copy of the document from London, vented his scepticism about the British position by decorating it with curt marginalia. He suspected that Craigie intended to squeeze German sea expansion tightly within the bounds of the 35 per cent framework, perhaps by deliberately underestimating forecasts of British strength. The C-in-C Navy as well feared that participation in a general naval conference might entail further concessions or grant the French an opportunity to breathe new life into the Versailles Treaty.[7] Sensitive to criticisms from within the navy over the 35 per cent deal, he briefly toyed with the idea of proposing to London that the three *Panzerschiffe* should be categorised as heavy cruisers to release 30 000 tons for an additional battleship. The idea – and it is difficult to conceive of one more eminently suited to torpedoing the talks – was dropped. The knowledge, as Hitler had intended, that 'the success of the [naval] agreement [lay] principally in the political sphere', tempered Raeder's scepticism.[8]

To confound further interference from treaty restrictions without arousing British antagonism, however, Raeder planned to delay any firm commitments to London until after the Naval Conference had been convened. He expected the conference to fail and to leave naval limitation in perpetual abeyance. Ribbentrop, who had Hitler's authority to conduct the negotiations, provided the best means to achieve this end. In Raeder's eyes, the universally despised plenipotentiary had demonstrated two redeeming characteristics during the London talks: first, he was unlikely to make concessions because he had no authentic diplomatic skills; and, second, he was content to leave complex technical matters to the admirals. In contrast, the Foreign Ministry under Konstantin von Neurath, the Foreign Minister appointed by President von Hindenburg, might reach a swift settlement with London. Raeder thus collaborated with Ribbentrop, who coveted Neurath's position, in excluding the professional diplomats from naval talks, and employed the German naval attaché in London as his personal agent to cultivate the favour of the Admiralty.[9]

At the end of July, Ribbentrop and Admiral Günther Guse, the Head of the Naval Command Office, drafted a reply to the British. On 31 August, the Foreign Ministry was again bypassed when Wassner handed the document directly to Craigie.[10] The German note disputed the proposal that the tonnage for their eighth capital ship should be transferred from the heavy cruiser category. It argued that the required 15 000 tons, a three per cent excess of the naval ratio, did not represent a 'substantial' deviation and should be regarded as temporary. It accepted the offer to reduce the operational life of Versailles type cruisers and destroyers. But presaging future trouble, the note stressed that any compromise on this issue was subject to revocation if other powers eventually possessed stronger naval armaments. In answer to the question about the three *Panzerschiffe*, it proposed a 15-year operational existence.[11]

Ironically, Craigie expected the German document to be far more objectionable than it turned out to be.[12] His outlook stemmed from the knowledge that 'naval circles in Germany were by no means pleased at Herr Hitler's offer',[13] combined with an awareness of the Raeder-Ribbentrop effort to exclude Neurath from the talks.[14] The memo reaffirmed the impression that Berlin was co-operating with the attempt to obtain an international treaty, although it was obviously drafted to 'drive a hard bargain'. Berlin's assent to his insistence that only German overage cruisers would be used to balance British overage cruisers was agreeable. But Craigie rejected the temporary three per cent deviation as an attempt to obtain 38 per cent in capital ships tonnage 'by the back door'.[15] He suggested to the Naval Staff exhausting the possibilities of transfer and adjustment before contemplating such a concession. Captain Danckwerts, the Plans Division officer responsible for the navy's preparations for the naval conference, readily agreed.[16]

By mid-October, Prince Bismarck, deputy to Leopold von Hoesch, the German Ambassador in London, had received the British rejoinder. Alluding to Hitler's May 1935 proclamation that the naval relationship was eternal, it questioned the validity of a temporary three per cent deviation. To reinforce the message, Craigie told Bismarck to inform Ribbentrop that the political harm of an attempt to obtain 38 per cent in capital ship tonnage would certainly outweigh the extra 15 000 tons of battleship they might build.[17] The memo added that transfer into the capital ship category would be acceptable so long as it did not exceed half the tonnage of a standard size vessel. The German proposal that the three *Panzerschiffe* should be scrapped and replaced with a single ship after 15 years of service was accepted.

When Raeder discovered that Bismarck had largely endorsed Craigie's reply, he took steps to ensure that Hoesch was not sabotaging Ribbentrop's work.[18] Meanwhile, Craigie anxiously pondered whether the rejection of the adjustment claim and his verbal warning to Ribbentrop might have provoked intransigence. But despite Raeder's grumbling, the German note of 27 November turned out to be reasonable. The only point of contention remained the tonnage shortfall for Germany's third 35 000-ton ship. The memo argued that 'transfer' and 'adjustment', described by the Naval Agreement in separate paragraphs, were thus separate concepts; the decision of which concept to employ had to satisfy both parties. In that vein, it conceded the British formula for the maximum size of an adjustment to be half the size of a standard capital ship and linked it to a ten-year limit for adjustments.[19] Craigie regarded the German counter-proposals as meeting him halfway. Again his low expectation shaped his perception of German tactics: 'The fact that the Germans have been reasonable should ... be counted unto them for righteousness.'[20]

Nevertheless, Craigie was alive to the danger of Ribbentrop using the talks as a channel to promote wider political objectives. Back in June, Simon and Craigie resisted a bid by Ribbentrop to keep the naval talks secret.[21] Secrecy would have destroyed any chance of a global treaty and it would have suggested to other capitals that more than just maritime matters had been settled. Craigie also thwarted Admiral Raeder's attempts to deal with the Admiralty directly. In the weeks that followed the 1935 accord, the FO accepted the practice whereby the German naval attaché delivered the building timetable and later amendments directly to the Admiralty, but only until the formal exchange between the foreign ministries through the embassies had been established. In mid-August, however, Wassner requested that this practice should continue.[22] 'There is so much political dynamite in this naval question,' Craigie balked, 'that there is a distinct risk in the Admiralty handling these questions direct with the Naval Attachés.' He instructed the German attaché to make all communications to him and to keep Hoesch informed.[23]

While Craigie checked this manoeuvre, he also countered a ploy to isolate Captain Muirhead-Gould. Before April 1935, the German Naval Command had made every effort to woo Muirhead-Gould with special treatment. But in the aftermath of the submarine episode that month, which Raeder unjustly attributed to the naval attaché being in cahoots with the FO,[24] he was ostracised and became the target for petty insults. The German liaison officer even refused to give him routine construction data before it was sent to London.[25] In November, Muirhead-Gould complained bitterly to the DNI and Sir Eric Phipps, suggesting that the German Naval Command was deliberately delaying sending the details of their 1935 programme to London.[26] Craigie and the DNI solved the problem by establishing with Wassner how the system of exchange should work: in future, Muirhead-Gould would receive the German timetable when the Admiralty did from Wassner and then the British naval attaché would submit supplementary technical questions.[27]

Yet Muirhead-Gould, as he confided to the diplomatic correspondent of *The Times* in April 1936,[28] also remained personally aggrieved by the April 1935 U-boat fiasco. It had converted him from an advocate of friendly Anglo-German relations to a student of the misdeeds of 'teutonic truthfulness'. The FO and NID viewed the U-boat affair as precisely the type of secret building the Naval Agreement was designed to prevent. When they instructed the naval attaché to enquire about the speed of U-boat assembly, he replied:

I should have thought by now that the Foreign Office would have realised that the German official never tells the truth except when it suits his purpose, and that he considers that his duty to his country entitles him to tell any story which he thinks will be believed. It is humiliating to me to know that the German [Naval Command] have so low an opinion of my intelligence and professional ability that they believe they can stuff me up with fairy stories as the building of a submarine in 2 months ... I no longer believe anything I am told by the [Naval Command] unless I can obtain corroboration.[29]

Outbursts like this discredited his message: Craigie told his colleagues that they had to be 'cautious'; but he considered that the naval attaché, who had a propensity to make 'a mountain out of a mole-hill', had made 'unnecessarily heavy weather over [the] whole business of exchange of information – and was certainly not very helpful in preparing the way for the naval agreement'.[30]

The beleaguered naval attaché had the same effect on the new DNI, Admiral James A. G. Troup, who had replaced Dickens in July. He saw the whole 'misunderstanding' as arising from Admiral Raeder's efforts to 'short-circuit' the German Foreign Ministry. Troup's immediate priority was to get the 'official' trade of information flowing to test its accuracy against alternative sources.[31] Significantly, although Raeder had fed Muirhead-Gould 'evasive answers' and even 'direct fabrications', the DNI was not distressed. He had no intention of relying on German 'truthfulness'. Troup reassured Vansittart that sources aside from the attaché 'would not fail to inform' the Admiralty if Germany violated the Naval Agreement.[32] This confidence was fortified in early 1936, when an allegation by the Italian naval attaché in Berlin that two aircraft carriers had been laid at Kiel instead of the one officially reported, was easily discredited by Muirhead-Gould alone.[33]

In the six months of naval negotiations after June 1935, information from official and unofficial channels sustained the positive image made by the German negotiators in London. Both the FO and the Admiralty looked to the Naval Conference with the knowledge that at least they carried Berlin with them. Oddly, it was the equilibrium between Craigie's low expectation of the German bargaining position and the actual Raeder-Ribbentrop bargaining position, tempered by Hitler's wish to placate London, which fostered this image. More importantly, though, Craigie was careful to keep the talks strictly within the scope of naval armaments diplomacy.

RHINELAND, 10 000 TON CRUISERS AND CRAIGIE'S THEORY

In naval affairs, the Japanese bid for parity dominated the first two weeks of 1936, which closed with Japan's withdrawal from the conference.

Within a month, London and Berlin exchanged brief notes in which Britain accepted the German time limit on tonnage adjustments, but left the issue of whether there would be a three per cent deviation to future negotiations.[34] No substantive issue[35] prevented Germany from signing the planned naval treaty. Yet the French, still perturbed about the 1935 Naval Agreement, refused to advance naval disarmament while European security remained unresolved. Viewed from Whitehall, however, the naval talks seemed concordant with the policy of drawing Berlin back into the League and buttressing Locarno with a convention on aerial bombing.[36]

On 26 February, Sir Anthony Eden, the new British Foreign Secretary,[37] informed Hoesch that Germany would have to join the multilateral naval treaty by a second bilateral agreement with London because France had blocked their entry into the conference. Hoesch and Wassner urged their superiors to accept Eden's offer to gain the navy's technical objectives.[38] They needed little convincing. Plans existed to send another Ribbentrop-led delegation to London to demand recognition of Germany's freedom from Versailles as a precondition to participation, yet there was little appetite for it. Eden's proposal suited Hitler's abhorrence of multilateral talks and his hope to string the British along with naval appeasement. Neurath accepted Eden's offer.[39] The FO and Admiralty expected Germany to sign onto the treaty shortly after Britain, France and America, but Hitler's brinkmanship in Central Europe intervened.

The targets of Hitler's move were the provisions in the Versailles and the Locarno treaties for the demilitarisation of Germany's western frontier. On 7 March, regular German troops occupied defensive positions in the demilitarised zone on the west side and 50 kilometres from the east bank of the Rhine. Hitler judged rightly that neither Paris nor London were prepared to use force. The coup was timed deliberately to exploit both France's ratification of the Franco-Soviet mutual assistance pact on 27 February and the continuing quarrel over the East African war between the co-guarantors of Locarno, London and Rome. But the Führer's motives were primarily strategic: an exposed frontier in the west precluded a more active foreign policy elsewhere.[40]

Given that Hitler had already overturned the military restrictions imposed under the peace treaty, Paris and London regarded the remilitarisation of the Rhineland as inevitable but not imminent. The French government, which recognised that it could not act unilaterally if Germany moved into the western zone, was perplexed by London's pursuit of economic sanctions against the co-Locarno guarantor, Rome. Though Britain had reaffirmed with Italy its Locarno commitment at the Stresa conference, the Cabinet did not regard the continued existence of the Rhineland régime as a vital interest. British policy aimed to discourage France or Germany from any provocation. Eden and his advisors planned to swap remilitarisation in exchange for Germany's pledge to a western air pact and the inviolability of the Franco-Belgian border. But Hitler dismayed them by not waiting long enough for the offer to be made.[41]

In the Admiralty, the breach of Locarno caused disquiet. Up to now, Hitler had argued that he would not recognise imposed treaties, but would be bound to those signed voluntarily. By implication, the military clauses of Versailles were allocated to the former category, while the pledge of the inviolability of the Franco-German and Belgo-German frontiers in the Locarno Treaty and the 1935 Naval Agreement were assigned to the latter category. The Rhineland crisis, however, challenged this distinction: 'The really serious thing he's done this time', explained one naval planner, 'is to tear up one scrap of paper which he did <u>not</u> sign <u>under compulsion</u>. For that reason only his present offers about non-aggression pacts etc. automatically lose all their value. So does his blaring about the British Government's "realism" about the Anglo-German Naval Treaty.' Admiral Roger Backhouse, the C-in-C Atlantic Fleet, expressed the same concern to Chatfield.[42]

Nonetheless, the Naval Staff, which discouraged action likely to cause war with Germany while war in the Mediterranean against Italy remained possible,[43] perceived the Rhineland crisis as the predictable outcome of a failure to arrive at a general settlement, largely owing to French intransigence. Captain Tom Phillips, who had replaced Captain King as Director of Plans Division in August 1935, believed that the solution to Europe's trouble lay in a European agreement that redressed German grievances as a whole.[44] Admiral Chatfield expressed similar views in late March 1936, and wondered whether Britain might soon be faced with either breaking with France or creating a hostile Germany.[45] For the Naval Staff, however, the immediate problem was to shelter Anglo-German naval diplomacy from the fallout of the crisis.

As the Locarno powers assembled in London to discuss measures against Berlin on 12 March, Craigie informed his colleagues that the Admiralty was willing to sign the three-power naval treaty and trust to the 'escalator' clause against Japan, but not against Japan and Germany.[46] He argued that it was absurd to lose an opportunity for a bilateral accord with Germany, and thereby fortify the naval limitation globally, when it was within grasp. He proposed continuing the talks 'unobtrusively' until relations with Berlin either improved or deteriorated irreversibly. Central Department officials replied with trenchant comments. But the point of contention was not whether there ought to be a naval agreement, but on priorities. 'The naval negotiations must take second place', Vansittart wrote, 'at least for the time being anyway ... [and added] the delay may not need to be long.'[47] But there was little choice between employing delaying tactics or continuing 'unobtrusively'. Against Eden's advice, the Cabinet sanctioned low-level naval talks, but the signature of a second agreement would be postponed until after the crisis.[48]

In the flurry of diplomatic activity resulting from the crisis, London pressed Paris to remain calm, and sought to emerge from the crisis with an enhanced western security pact. Hitler played on the universal desire for peace by offering to rejoin the League, to replace Locarno with fresh arrangements including one on bombing, and a string of non-aggression treaties. Eden asked Hoesch for a conciliatory gesture, such as a withdrawal of some forces. The troops stayed in place. The only punitive action taken was a condemnation by the League Council on 19 March. In early April, the British pledged to assist France and Belgium against unprovoked attack. A plan to initiate negotiations with Berlin was also issued. In mid-month, limited staff talks between the three powers were held. It was left to London to discover whether Hitler's protestations of reasonableness were authentic. On 6 May, a British questionnaire was dispatched to Berlin that pointedly probed Hitler's position on 'genuine treaties'.[49]

In the meantime, real progress with Germany over a second naval agreement was on hold. On 18 March, the First Lord asked the Cabinet for authority to sign (but not to ratify) a three-power naval treaty without waiting for Germany's signature on a parallel bilateral accord.[50] On 25 March, the remaining Washington powers concluded the second London Naval Treaty. In late April, however, the German naval attaché reported to his C-in-C that the mood in the Admiralty towards Berlin was now 'cool and reserved'. Wassner was horrified to discover that Admiral Troup's outlook on European affairs originated from the *Daily Telegraph* and *Morning Post,* two conservative newspapers noted for their antipathy to Nazism.[51] Still, Chatfield and his staff looked to a successful resolution of the diplomatic impasse to pave the way for Berlin's adherence to the new global qualitative treaty, but they soon suffered another disappointment at German hands.

It came to Craigie in the form of a memorandum delivered on 13 May by Captain Wassner. The memo listed the conditions under which the German government would conclude a second bilateral agreement. Among other things, the memo stated that because of French and Russian cruiser construction, Germany intended to construct two 10 000-ton cruisers armed with 8-inch guns (designated A category) besides the three already under construction. In response, the normally imperturbable Craigie unnerved Wassner with his barely controlled anger.[52] For nearly a decade, Craigie had taken part in the British effort to either outlaw or restrict these blockade-busting ships; they were an anathema to Admiralty planners, who saw economic pressure exerted from the sea in war as ultimately decisive. The culmination of that effort was Article VI of the March 1936 London Treaty. Article VI prohibited A-category cruiser building during the seven-year life span of the Treaty. The German decision, which contradicted an unconditional pledge of 26 February 1936 to back the heavy cruiser holiday, now threatened to destroy it.[53]

Craigie's outrage plus his own fears about the chilly climate in the Admiralty convinced Captain Wassner of the wisdom of retaining the memo and questioning his superiors.[54] He made no impression. In mid-March, Admiral Raeder had rejected Craigie's request that he forgo the third A-class ship on the grounds that it was ordered before the building holiday was settled. As to the fourth and fifth heavy cruisers that Germany was nominally entitled to under the 35 per cent ratio, besides Raeder's general precept that warship quality and construction tempo should be unfettered by diplomacy, technical reasons – the lack of a satisfactory light cruiser design[55] – pointed to this heavy cruiser policy. But the technical motives were in themselves insufficient for the C-in-C Navy to settle on a position so likely to raise Britain's ire.

The rest of the explanation lies in Hitler's attitude towards Britain. Before March 1936, he intended to use the naval talks to mollify London and perhaps to hammer out an arrangement; in the wake of the crisis, they had become an instrument (along with demands for the return of Germany's former colonies) by which the Führer could apply pressure on London. The British reaction to Rhineland, pledges of aid to France and Belgium and a questionnaire that probed his position to the existing territorial and political status quo did not correspond with what he expected in reward for his naval ratio. Yet there was no need nor desire at this time for a break. German diplomacy aimed to string the British along. The questionnaire was left unanswered. The German Foreign Ministry used discussions over a new five-power western security pact to obfuscate well into 1937.[56]

Accordingly, Wassner returned to the FO six days later with the German memo unaltered, but he told Craigie that his government was prepared to address the British objection in the manner of previous transactions.[57] The door was ajar. Craigie now believed the German move was a 'try-on' because the justification, the Franco-Soviet Pact, was a 'little thread-bare'. Neither power had laid down a heavy cruiser for some time, nor would they do so under the building holiday. Vansittart was sceptical and feared that the German decision would vindicate the rancour in Europe that had followed the 1935 Naval Agreement if it was not reversed. He recommended to Eden that they should apply diplomatic leverage. At the Admiralty, Captain Phillips concurred with the FO plan but was pessimistic: 'It seems almost certain that the cruiser holiday will go west.'[58]

The British launched their diplomatic offensive on 29 May. Eden skirmished with Bismarck (Hoesch had died in April), expressing the Cabinet's displeasure with the German decision. The First Lord delivered the main assault with Craigie and Phillips in an interview with Ribbentrop, who was in London to further Anglo-German friendship and 'spread influence' with invitations to the Munich Olympics.[59] Monsell told him that the political effect of the German plan was out of proportion with the potential naval advantage and that the Admiralty would certainly be alienated. This was a potent message coming from a Cabinet minister whom Ribbentrop knew to favour détente with Germany.[60] He promised to speak to Hitler. But Craigie remained restless. A few days later he tackled Ribbentrop unofficially. Craigie made 'no perceptible impression' while the German complained about London's objection to the Rhineland occupation.[61]

Nevertheless, the message, augmented by warnings from Wassner and Bismarck, was received. In a memo dated 7 June, the Naval Command contrasted military and political reasons for firmness or compliance on the issue. But at this stage neither Hitler nor Ribbentrop, who was currently attempting to persuade Baldwin to visit Berlin, could contemplate a clash with London of the magnitude entailed in building the two extra heavy cruisers. Only two days later, Ribbentrop instructed Wassner to inform the FO that Germany would lay down two 10 000-ton ships armed with only 6-inch guns (thus making them B-category), unless France or the Soviet Union built additional A-class ships.[62]

The German caveat left residual unease: Phillips wrote to Chatfield that Russian cruiser expansion would probably trigger German A-class construction.[63] Still the news was welcome. Vansittart and Eden congratulated Craigie and the Admiralty on their performance.[64] The sudden turn surprised Craigie. It appeared to confirm the theory that he had been developing since early June. The whole episode arose from 'a problem inherent in the over-centralisation of a dictatorship'. From remarks made by Wassner, Bismarck and Ribbentrop, Craigie surmised (and Phillips agreed) that at the end of April a meeting was held in Berlin to discuss the document that the German naval attaché presented to him on 13 May. At this meeting, in view of the Franco-Soviet pact, Hitler decided that Germany required five

8-inch gun cruisers. No one present had the moral courage to point out that a promise to abide by the cruiser holiday had already been given to London. Now Ribbentrop, who insisted that neither he nor Hitler knew about the 26 February pledge, was in Craigie's view imitating 'the overweening self-confidence of the Führer' in this belated attempt to obtain two more 8-inch gun cruisers.[65]

Craigie's theory was viewed with scepticism. Eden and others had been disillusioned by Hitler's refusal to atone for his treaty breach and to reply to the British questionnaire; they had become convinced that a durable détente was improbable. Ralph Wigram, the head of the Central Department, wondered why Hitler should respect the cruiser pledges when he had scant regard for his own peace proposals. Vansittart could not accept that Raeder had promised to observe the cruiser holiday without first obtaining Hitler's permission. To test German trustworthiness, Vansittart proposed that they send Phipps a narrative of events according to Craigie's theory and leave it to him to discover the facts.[66] The Ambassador replied on 19 June, only three days after receiving it. 'The mistake', he wrote, 'undoubtedly arose through slackness on the part not only of the Chancellor but of Ribbentrop. Neither of them had any office experience and neither realises the importance of reading through documents before giving important decisions or initialing the said documents.' According to his 'informant', who had apparently explained the error to the Chancellor and had obtained the policy reversal, Raeder accepted Hitler's order for the two cruisers on the assumption that the Chancellor was aware of the 26 February pledge. Phipps thus acquitted them of a breach of faith and added that conceit had prevented either Hitler or Ribbentrop from admitting that they were at fault.[67]

It is difficult to know whether Phipps's 'informant' was spinning misinformation. At the end of April, Hitler did chair a meeting to decide the final text of the German reply, but no record of it has survived.[68] If he insisted that Raeder build five 8-inch gun ships, then the C-in-C Navy was unlikely to resist. The 26 February note was under Neurath's signature with only Ribbentrop's initials. And Ribbentrop's private office exemplified administrative chaos.[69] After his meeting with Monsell on 29 May, Ribbentrop had Wassner compile a report of what had been said about heavy cruisers. Perhaps Ribbentrop and Hitler were not wholly aware of the pledge, but it is certain that they underestimated the British reaction to the use of the cruiser issue as leverage. Ribbentrop even found it difficult to grasp that reducing the German demand by one heavy cruiser would not solve the problem.[70] A blend of muddle and mendacity therefore seems likely. Ribbentrop had blundered into a difficult situation, and lied his way out of it.

It was subsequent behaviour, however, that exposed the true attitude in Berlin towards Britain and the Naval Agreement. As the lead time for placing contracts approached, the Naval Command again raised the gun calibre issue. In September 1936, it had issued orders for the assembly of both 6-inch and 8-inch turrets, but this would entail delays. A few weeks before the first keel was to be laid, Raeder offered the Führer three alternatives. First, build two A-category ships, break the building holiday and invite retaliatory building by France and Russia. Second, ostensibly honour the pledge to mount 6-inch guns, but install 8-inch turrets and prepare a bogus excuse for violating the holiday for January 1939. Third, adhere to the promise and construct B-category ships, but at the cost of a two-year delay in further A-category building. Hitler selected option two.[71]

The Rhineland crisis and the cruiser dispute altered the Admiralty's perception of naval talks with Germany. Obtaining Berlin's adherence to the second London Naval Treaty – the next step to framing the global naval order to suit British interests – was no longer going to be an agreeable experience. But the apparent success of the British diplomatic offensive in reversing the German cruiser decision and the test result of Craigie's theory helped to restore the Naval Staff's confidence. Moreover, the change in tenor of the talks also appeared to authenticate the gravity with which Berlin viewed the negotiations. As Captain Phillips wrote in November 1936, it was difficult to believe that Berlin eventually intended to overthrow the Naval Agreement because of the 'meticulous' attention they paid to technical issues like overage tonnage, transfer and adjustment.[72]

THE SOVIET FLEET AND 'ELBOW ROOM'

Craigie's awareness of Ribbentrop's truncated channel for conducting the naval talks was fundamental to his theory: while the dabblers in diplomacy were in charge, it was plausible that the cruiser episode was an administrative blunder rather than deliberate manipulation. Ironically, weeks before the cruiser dispute, Admiral Raeder and Ribbentrop (as a result of Craigie's refusal to negotiate through Wassner) arrived at a compact with the professional diplomats to employ the normal diplomatic apparatus for the negotiations.[73] It was therefore left to Raeder and Neurath (Ribbentrop was appointed Ambassador to London in August 1936) to press the most vexing condition upon the British for a second bilateral agreement: the simultaneous conclusion of an Anglo-Soviet naval agreement.

It had been suggested in March 1935 that Moscow should be invited to the naval conference, but Ribbentrop's insistence in June 1935 that third-party building would not upset the 35 per cent ratio made it unnecessary in the short term. Once it became clear a year later that Berlin would not sign a qualitative agreement without Moscow, Craigie began to make informal enquiries at the Soviet Embassy.[74] By May 1936, these overtures matured into a formal exchange of views. Although the details of this exchange are not wholly relevant, it is instructive to set out the important features of the Russian position and the British perception of Stalin's bid for naval power.[75] First, because of Japan's departure from naval limitation, the Soviet negotiators demanded that their Far Eastern Fleet be exempt from the new treaty. Second, they desired to lay down two capital ships armed with 15- or 16-inch guns, despite the current limitation of 14 inches. And third, they reserved the right to construct ten 7.1-inch gun/8000-ton A-category cruisers.[76]

By October, Craigie was convinced that Moscow's conditions could be accommodated. The other powers could permit the Soviet Far Eastern reservation, which amounted to Article 25 of the London Treaty, the so-called 'escalator clause', because the Soviet negotiators made it clear that it would exceed the qualitative limits only if Tokyo did. If Japan initiated a naval competition, then the entire treaty would be wrecked anyway. Craigie also believed he could persuade the other powers to accept the Russian demand for 15-inch guns, which was reasonable since France, Italy and Germany, in reply to each other, had each laid down two 35 000-ton ships armed with 15-inch guns. Finally, after many hours of tedious bargaining, he managed to reduce the Russian demand for ten A-category cruisers to seven if Germany stood at three.[77]

Still, dealing with the Soviets was a particularly frustrating experience for Craigie and the Naval Staff because they knew that Moscow's pretension to sea power was greatly exaggerated. Up to October 1936, the Admiralty did not even consider it necessary to post a naval attaché to Moscow. Although the Red navy possessed large subsurface forces and a potentially large shipbuilding capacity, intelligence analysis suggested that they were incapable of launching significant surface units during the seven-year life span of the 1936 London Naval Treaty. The principal obstacle was technical expertise, which could only be obtained rapidly from an accomplished maritime power. The USSR lacked the standard 6- and 8-inch naval guns and Phillips rightly believed that they were incapable of manufacturing 15- or 16-inch gun battleship turrets.[78] The maximum programme the British projected for Moscow in June 1936 – two battleships, seven 7.1-inch gun/8000-ton cruisers, a number of destroyers and a very large number of submarines – was verified as correct in February 1937 by the newly appointed British naval attaché.[79]

The Germans, however, resisted the idea that Russia did not possess the capacity for a sudden burst of expansion at sea. In July 1936, they also began to cast doubt on the premise that third-party construction would not upset the naval ratio between Britain and Germany. A now familiar German claim that the Franco-Soviet Pact effectively rendered the two navies a single unit was advanced, along with a new allegation about the international conference at Montreux. It had been convened from 22 June to 20 July to address a Turkish government request to revise the 1923 straits convention and the demilitarisation of the Bosphorus and Dardanelles. Although they criticised the new rules governing the passage of warships through the straits, Raeder's principal strategic concern was the fortification of the Dardanelles. It would permit a concentration of the Red fleet in the Baltic, while the vacated Black Sea was defended by Turkish shore batteries.[80]

Craigie countered German protests without success.[81] On 1 July, in reaction to rumours that the new straits convention might grant Russian warships passage if the Franco-Soviet Pact was invoked, Neurath warned Phipps that Germany would in such circumstances demand an amendment to the naval ratio. The warning worked. The Admiralty sought to ensure that the new convention signed on 20 July provided Berlin with as few grounds for complaint as possible.[82] But the negative signalling continued unabated. On 12 September, Bismarck complained to Craigie that the new convention subjugated Turkey to Soviet interests and created a safe haven for the Red fleet in the Black Sea. Resonating with the anti-communist propaganda emanating from Berlin, especially with Soviet intervention in the civil war in Spain and a Popular Front government in Paris, Hitler authorised a barbed diplomatic memo, which was handed to the FO on 5 October: 'If the Anglo-Soviet Naval Agreement is concluded in the form of the existing draft,' it stated, then 'the German naval situation will deteriorate to a considerable extent.'[83]

Some of Admiral Raeder's anxieties about the strategic balance in the Baltic were genuine and originated from an accurate knowledge (probably supplied by Rome) of Moscow's warship plans. In November, he ordered Wassner to hand to the Admiralty intelligence about Soviet building. It tallied with NID information, including naval attaché reports of a Soviet cruiser being assembled in Italy.[84] Even a limited threat from Soviet light surface and subsurface forces to the vital iron ore trade with Sweden would pose difficulties for the German fleet, especially when war plans called for an Atlantic offensive against the French. And Raeder's inflated remarks about the possibility of cruisers and battleships being built in British yards for Moscow and the 'astonishing speed' of Soviet expansion at sea were not only an external smoke screen, but also calculated to promote the navy's interests within the Third Reich's decision-making machinery.[85]

The signals to London about renegotiating the 35 per cent ratio, however, were tactical rather than strategic. Both Raeder and Neurath agreed to employ the threat as leverage to safeguard German interests, but the C-in-C Navy was too ardent. The Foreign Minister cautioned him that the June 1935 Naval Agreement only sanctioned a revision of the ratio under mutual consent and only then in the case of extraordinary third-party building. Too aggressive a posture at this stage might provoke the British. Raeder knew the navy could not expand much beyond the current programme before 1940 without a substantial increase in its share of skilled labour and raw materials. The time was not yet ripe to jettison the diplomatic camouflage. As Admiral Guse realised in late September, it was sensible to reserve a few plausible arguments to justify future deviations from the accord.[86]

Yet Admiral Raeder still desired to temporise. In October and November 1936, he refused Craigie's offers to come to Berlin to speed up the bargaining.[87] Although Hitler's decision to construct five 8-inch gun cruisers meant that he had escaped the only potential sacrifice he would have had to make, he wrote to the Foreign Ministry that they should continue to obfuscate. In reply, the diplomats reminded him how important the British perceived the naval treaties to be. Germany could not appear to be 'guilty or partly guilty' for the demise of the naval limitation. Further, they assured him, with the number of reservations stacked upon its creaking framework by the naval powers, the new treaty had only 'theoretical significance' and was bound in the end to collapse.[88]

Since they had reliable intelligence on the pace of Soviet expansion, Craigie and the Naval Staff regarded German complaints about it as 'inadmissible'. In early July, Monsell's replacement as First Lord, Sir Samuel Hoare, contacted Craigie to express concern about Berlin exploiting Montreux 'to pile up purely imaginary grievances'. But Craigie remained optimistic. At the end of July, the Cabinet decided to move to the final stage.[89] The remaining obstacles had been cleared. The Soviets agreed to reduce their heavy cruiser programme to seven vessels and the British accepted the German demand for a 17 500-ton 'adjustment' to the 35 per cent ratio.[90]

On 21 October, however, it became apparent to Craigie that German protests amounted to a 'desire to collect ammunition against the day when

Germany may ask for an increase'. Ribbentrop confirmed this to Craigie in December. Bitter about his failure to deliver to Hitler his much promised Anglo-German alliance, he complained about Franco-Soviet naval building upsetting the Anglo-German ratio and the lack of concrete political results arising from the German gesture.[91] Captain Phillips reported these remarks to the Naval Staff. He explained that Hitler had no genuine reason to be discontented with the naval balance. With the plan for a new two-power standard in mind, however, he suggested heading off the German bid for treaty revision by informing them of the planned increase in the Royal Navy's tonnage for 1937 and dropping hints about a potential increase in the number of British battleships.[92] The idea was accepted. On 24 February 1937, after the Cabinet had approved the naval programme, Craigie met with Ribbentrop's deputy, Ernst Woermann, to notify him of the 300 000-ton expansion in aircraft carriers, cruisers and submarines, 'which in turn would, of course, give Germany some more "elbow-room"'. Additionally, he explained, in future the British government might not stand at 15 capital ships if the other powers began to increase the size of their battle fleets. Captain Wassner returned to the FO that afternoon to confirm Craigie's statements. Wassner later reported rumours that Britain might begin a capital ship programme of five keels a year. Although the German Naval Command was sceptical about that report, it had little reason to doubt Craigie.[93]

In early March, with all the German and Soviet demands met, it seemed to Craigie that 'things might move very quickly in the next few days'. He was right. The Soviets now threw a massive spanner into the works. Ivan Maisky, the Russian Ambassador, told Craigie that his government found it impossible to sign a bilateral agreement. He proposed another multilateral conference to discuss the supervision of warship construction. Moscow's *volte-face* caused disgust in Whitehall.[94] Germany would not join qualitative limitation without Russia, and Britain could not ratify the three-power treaty without Germany. Hoare pleaded to Eden. 'Unless we can get Russia to change her mind,' the First Lord wrote, 'it seems to me that the whole fabric of limitation which we have built up may collapse and that we shall be faced with the prospect of unrestricted building by all countries.'[95] Much to Craigie's and the Navy's relief, after representations by Eden to Maisky, on 23 March, Moscow again reversed its policy. The initial turn appears to have been motivated by anxiety about German warship building and the desire to secure British technical aid. As Maisky told the Foreign Secretary, Moscow had 'disquieting information' about the 'design and character' of German ships and was disgruntled by the Admiralty's objections to Soviet naval orders being placed with British firms.[96]

At this stage, the only definite information Maisky disclosed was about Germany's fourth and fifth 10 000-ton cruisers. Soviet intelligence reported that they were being built to convert quickly from 6- to 8-inch gun mountings.[97] This revelation probably did not surprise Phillips, who had been pessimistic about the cruiser holiday since June 1936. In December, his view was supported by the Department of Naval Construction. Given the required lead time for manufacturing the ordnance, the constructors concluded that the decision to mount 8-inch guns had already been made.[98] The Soviet allegation also corroborated data obtained by NID in 1936 about interchangeable turrets on German battlecruisers.[99] Craigie and Phillips, as their interrogation of the German negotiators about the interval of gun conversion reveals, presumably suspected this ruse. In April 1937, when the Germans complained about Russia building seven heavy cruisers and now demanded the right to build more than five A-class vessels by tonnage transfer from light cruisers and destroyers, Phillips's pessimism was vindicated. But Craigie again saved the day by persuading the Soviets to build fewer than seven A-category vessels in exchange for British 6-inch gun technology.[100] The cruiser holiday was resuscitated. If Hitler later choked it, then the speed of conversion to 8-inch guns would be a yardstick for the Naval Staff of German good faith; the opportunity to apply it, however, did not arrive.[101]

On 17 July 1937, Berlin and Moscow exchanged bilateral agreements with London which pledged adherence to the second London Naval Treaty. This ought to have been a triumph for Craigie and Phillips. But the German negotiators had convinced their British counterparts about the frailty of the supposedly 'permanent and definitive' 35 per cent agreement. Indeed, two weeks before the signature of the second Naval Agreement, the British Ambassador in Berlin reported that 'I have an uneasy feeling that Hitler often feels like denouncing the agreement'.[102] To maintain it, the Naval Staff in concert with the FO signalled to Berlin the intention to expand the Royal Navy proportionally with other powers and to possibly increase the size of the battle fleet. Naval Staff hopes for a two-power standard and the future of the Naval Agreements with Germany were thus linked.

ESTIMATING GERMAN FLEET EXPANSION

The Admiralty wished German naval development to take place within the framework of naval limitation because it considered Germany to be a serious rival. From the early 1930s onwards, the Naval Staff expected that

Berlin would reclaim its presence at sea; the real questions were how quickly the German fleet would expand and what form it would take. The second issue is dealt with in the next chapter. As we saw in the last chapter, two hypotheses on the first question emerged at the end of 1934. The Director of Plans Division expected a moderate growth rate for German naval armaments, limited by the likely financial, labour and raw material requirements of the army and air force. The DNI, however, playing devil's advocate, fancifully envisaged a much higher rate of output, especially after 1939, unfettered by competing material or financial needs.

On 20 June 1935, during technical discussions, Admiral Schuster partially resolved the question by presenting the German building programme up to 1942. It called for up to six capital ships, three aircraft carriers, 18 cruisers, 37 500 tons of destroyers and 17 500 tons of submarines. Craigie and Little, concerned about the effect of a rapid German building on France, argued that German building should be 'slow and systematic'. Ribbentrop replied that 'Germany intended to have her fleet as soon as possible'. In his absence, though, Schuster said that slipway capacity might disrupt Raeder's construction timetable. But Ribbentrop's later assertion that 'it would, of course, be possible to build up much faster, but Germany preferred method and system in their reconstruction', probably left the British delegates somewhat puzzled. Indeed, later that day, Captain Danckwerts interrogated Wassner about potential obstacles to expansion.[103]

For the Naval Staff, discovering what proportion of Germany's warship industry would remain idle due to the tonnage ratio and when the 35 per cent fleet would be reached were clearly important. If Germany possessed spare shipyard, armour and ordnance capacity, then the potential for an acceleration in building was a constant hazard. Wark argues that the Naval Staff's faith in the 1935 accord was predicated on the belief that the German navy, exercising political restraint, was capable of far greater growth than permitted by the naval accord.[104] However, this argument, as we shall presently see, is flawed for two reasons. First, it is founded on a document composed almost entirely to silence Whitehall critics about the value of the Naval Agreement. Second, it ignores the routine inflow of industrial intelligence from a variety of sources. A sampling of these documents from 1936–7 illustrates that the Admiralty's understanding of the limits of Nazi Germany's naval industry was far more accurate than hitherto recognised.

In every strategic appraisal issued by the Naval Staff after 1935, Germany was correctly described as striving to reach 35 per cent by 1942. It was in fact Admiral Raeder's minimum objective. At Hitler's instigation, he had already ordered ship construction to be accelerated in early 1934. The start date for Germany's first aircraft carrier was brought forward. By April 1935, the German yards and skilled labour force had reached capacity. The Defence Minister convened a meeting of the three service chiefs on 18 November 1935 to order additional speed. Financial restraint was lifted and the naval budget for 1936 rose to over a billion Reichsmarks, nearly doubling the money available for ship construction. The German Naval Command once again advanced start dates and invested in infrastructure to sustain even greater expansion in the future.[105]

In January 1936, Admiral Troup set out what NID had pieced together about these developments. According to reliable observers, German building was proceeding 'at high pressure' and rumours suggested that Raeder's timetable had been accelerated. Captain Muirhead-Gould reported orders for floating docks and confirmed that 'neither money nor effort is being spared to produce a powerful fleet with the least possible delay'. NID had thus grasped that Germany's naval industry was operating at full capacity just to build up to the 35 per cent limit by 1942. The DNI explained that naval intelligence intended to produce a survey of Germany's shipyards and to carefully monitor their output.[106] Indeed, in contrast to aircraft, tank and U-boat production, which could take place in relative secrecy, the assembly rate of large warships was quite easy to monitor.

The appraisal of Germany's potential building capacity was a collaborative effort between NID and the agency usually responsible for estimating the war potential of foreign economies, the IIC. It took over six months for the two departments to produce a final report. In the meantime, the IIC circulated secret information about German mobilisation plans for the mass production of U-boats, which will be studied in Chapter 4.

The July 1936 report on 'German Naval Construction', proved to be a simple arithmetic exercise. Using wartime and postwar activity as a yardstick, it set out the current and maximum output rates, from laying down to commissioning, for each warship category: for instance, 37 months for a battleship. It then estimated the peak output of each naval yard, plus that of any other firms capable of building warships. Two projections were thus made. The first, which assumed the current output rate of only those yards already building warships, found that the German fleet would be just short of the 35 per cent ratio by 1940 and well beyond it by 1942 (columns (A) in Table 2.1). The second, which postulated the maximum output tempo of the entire national capacity, projected that Nazi Germany's naval strength for both 1940 and 1942 would be far larger than that permitted by the 1935 Naval Agreement (columns (B) in Table 2.1). Contrary to Berlin's stated target of 1942, the report unblushingly declared that the

Table 2.1 Comparison of 35 per cent fleet, NID/IIC forecasts of German
expansion and actual strength by September 1939

	35 per cent by 1942	31 December 1940		31 December 1942		Sept. 1939
		(A) Current rate	(B) Maximum rate	(A) Current rate	(B) Maximum Rate	
Capital ships	8	7	9	11	14	5
Aircraft carriers	3	2	3	3	3	0
Cruisers (all types)	15	12	20	15	30	8
Destroyers	38	84	92	121	135	22
Submarines	44	73	89	98	118	57

Sources: CID 1252-B, 22 July 1936, CAB 4/24; Dülffer, *Marine*, app. B.

35 per cent ratio 'might not only be completed, but considerably exceeded
by the end of 1940'.

However, this remarkable assertion, which Wark interprets as typical of
Naval Staff thinking, did not follow from the report's suppositions. The
colossal effort envisaged by the second forecast was considered 'beyond
the national capacity', owing to financial, raw material and especially
skilled labour shortages. Further, 'the engineering capacity of the country
would hardly support a greater programme [than the 35 per cent one]
while so much of it is still engaged on military and air rearmament.'[107]
The sound forecast was the first one, which estimated that Germany could
achieve the 35 per cent level by about 1940–1. When the report was
handed to the CID on 30 July, Sir Edward Crowe, the IIC's chairman, was
obviously diffident about a forecast premised on the national effort of the
Third Reich being redirected from military and air to naval armaments: the
study, he said, 'contemplated what might, and not what would actually
happen'. The First Lord added that Germany was 'unlikely to reach the
figures given in the report' because 'in practice it was not considered that
the construction to this scale was practical'.[108]

If the Admiralty and the IIC saw it as industrial fantasy, then why was
the thesis asserted? Timing is important. The Naval Staff had it circulated a
week before the Cabinet was to decide whether to sanction a second naval
accord with Berlin. Its embellished message was thus largely intended for
advocacy.[109] Moreover, to have the CID endorse a memorandum that
advanced the hypothesis that Berlin was actively abstaining from a naval

challenge was insurance against questions being raised in Whitehall about the material value of the Naval Agreement. In June 1938, as we shall see later, Plans Division revived the IIC/NID document in a skirmish with the FO expressly for this purpose.

In reality, the obstructions cited by the July 1936 report caused the German Naval Command severe headaches. The shipbuilding industry was saturated in April 1935. The slipways had to be cleared for new ships to be laid. Yet right from the outset the gap between goals and results expanded. Part of the problem was numerous design changes and the application of untried technology. The re-laying of *Gneisenau* and *Scharnhorst* in the summer of 1935 entailed a setback of at least 18 months; teething troubles with their turbine installations compounded the delay. A shortage of skilled workers and inadequate deliveries of steel and non-ferrous metals proved to be the chief bottlenecks. Despite the Reich's hunger for foreign exchange, the navy did not have the slipway space nor the raw materials for foreign orders from Chile, Brazil and other budding naval powers. No new contracts for large warships or even destroyers were issued in 1937. Only 26 months after the signature of the 1935 Naval Agreement, Admiral Raeder's aim of 35 per cent by 1942 had foundered: capital ship, aircraft carrier and cruiser production had fallen from eight to 18 months behind schedule.[110]

A sampling of the routine influx of intelligence shows that the Admiralty was well aware that German shipyard performance was a disappointment to Raeder. Significantly, NID first detected the slackening in the pace of German building six weeks *before* the joint NID/IIC report was promulgated. On 21 May 1936, Captain Muirhead-Gould reported a production slowdown. His successor, Captain Tom Troubridge, reiterated the message in his annual report for 1936 and drew attention to persistent boiler troubles retarding destroyer building. An IIC survey dated May 1937 estimated that the 35 per cent fleet would not be completed before 1943 even with the naval yards working at peak capacity. It underscored a shortage of skilled labour, particularly naval draughtsmen, as the 'serious limiting factor for some time to come'.[111] By June, there was no doubt: 'The laying down of warships and other naval construction', Troubridge wrote, 'has taken rather an unexpectedly long time to complete.' He later reported that the building rate of the battleships *Bismarck* and *Tirpitz* was 'by no means high'. At the end of 1937, another IIC report cited raw material and labour shortages as the chief causes of the conspicuous slowdown in warship building, and added that 'administrative blunders' and 'technical defects' had exacerbated the problem.[112] In November 1937, Admiral Chatfield wrote that the 35 per cent ratio had probably been dictated by German building potential.[113]

NAVAL DIPLOMACY AND INDUSTRIAL INTELLIGENCE

The story of Anglo-German naval diplomacy from 1935 to 1937 reveals that the Admiralty's view of the Naval Agreement was not static but shifting. In the summer of 1935, the Germans adopted a co-operative posture. After Rhineland, as attempts to resolve European tensions foundered, things changed for the worse. The Germans made progress more difficult. The aspiration of Craigie and the Naval Staff to shelter naval diplomacy from broader political developments had proved to be impossible.

Admiral Chatfield believed that he had exploited Hitler's desire to settle with Britain in 1935 without incurring serious costs. Despite Ribbentrop's pledges about the eternity of the naval ratio, reports in the summer of 1937 that the Führer was unhappy because he believed the British had betrayed his naval magnanimity caused the Naval Staff alarm. The British responded by signalling to Berlin that likely increases to the size of the British battle fleet would provide them with ample scope for expanded warship building. More significantly, the experience of 1936–7 convinced Chatfield that they had to press the Cabinet to intensify the effort to seek a workable détente with Berlin. The repercussions of this belief on British foreign and defence policy will be examined in Chapter 6.

In this vein, though, it must be recognised that Admiralty anxiety was not inspired by a fear of the potential output of the Third Reich's warship industry. The Naval Staff was well informed about the industrial bottlenecks that were frustrating Admiral Raeder's objective to reach 35 per cent by 1942. Its fears were long term, or more precisely, programmatic. The Admiralty wished to prevent Hitler from destroying the framework of qualitative limitation by ending the Naval Agreements before its plan to restore Britain's naval pre-eminence had matured; furthermore, the Naval Staff wished Germany, when it reached 35 per cent some time in the mid-1940s, to stop. The sinister image of German shipyards poised ready to outbuild the Royal Navy was concocted by the Navy to hush sceptics. Given the readiness of Eden, Vansittart and the Central Department to sidetrack the naval negotiations in March 1936, this is hardly surprising.

Ironically, the policies pursued by top naval officials in both Berlin and London were to some degree at variance with the policies of their political masters. In this period, Admiral Raeder chafed against the naval talks and made claims that would have torpedoed them; but Hitler was not ready yet for a total break with London. Equally, the Cabinet had no real incentive to cut off the naval dialogue while the prospects for a settlement existed. The conflicting policy expectations buried within the 1935 accord remained so in 1936–7. Notes on qualitative limitation were exchanged and the way was clear for Britain to ratify the 1936 London Naval Treaty. The Admiralty saw this as another measure to remodel the naval balance to uphold British maritime security; the German Naval Command regarded it as an ephemeral gesture to a moribund order, whose collapse would signal the onset of another Tirpitzian challenge to British supremacy at sea.

3 Naval Staff Perceptions of German Naval Strategy, 1934–39

The geostrategic asymmetry between Britain and Germany shaped their opposing approaches to naval strategy in war. Germany, at the centre of the European continent, judged its viability as a great power by the extent to which it dominated the states that surrounded it. As an island state, Britain relied on the unimpeded access of its unrivalled merchant fleet to its Empire and to world markets. The Royal Navy's task was the security of maritime commerce. Short of a 'bolt from the blue' invasion, the nightmare of Whitehall planners and the inspiration to thriller writers in the late nineteenth century,[1] Britain could only be conquered or starved into capitulation by the cutting of its oceanic lines of communication. In 1917 U-boats had come close to achieving this grim object. Likewise, the Royal Navy's hold on the North Sea and the Allied blockade contributed to the final collapse a year later of Imperial Germany's bid for continental hegemony.

In the 1930s, these geostrategic imperatives supplied the framework within which planners in both capitals studied the prospect of a second contest at sea. This chapter seeks to reconstruct the Naval Staff's perception of how Germany might employ its navy against Britain. (The next two chapters will examine how the Royal Navy assessed its likely performance in war.) The best way to comprehend how the Admiralty developed its thesis about Admiral Raeder's strategy is to examine the planning process, including intelligence analysis. To do so, it is first necessary to describe British naval strategy in general and Whitehall's expectations about a European war, the existing literature on this subject, and the process by which strategic appreciations and naval war plans were drafted.

British national greatness was founded on the doctrine of battle fleet supremacy. From the late 1880s, as the other European powers rejected alternative patterns of naval power and began to assemble capital ship fleets, Britain tenaciously defended its top ranking. This tenacity climaxed in a healthy superiority in dreadnoughts over the Royal Navy's most dangerous rival, the German High Seas Fleet. Similarly, between the wars, by the concentration of an efficient and properly 'balanced' fleet (one composed of battleships, supported by aircraft carriers, cruisers, destroyers and submarines) for battle against any opponent, the Admiralty was certain that it could safe-guard the sea for commercial and belligerent purposes. London hedged its capacity for victory by maintaining a standard of naval strength which was a proportional measure of fleet size *vis-à-vis* potential foes.[2] Formal parity with the US Navy (the one-power standard) in the 1920s was acceptable to the Admiralty because it granted a virtual two-power standard over France and Japan. This would permit the Royal Navy in any likely war to concentrate concurrently sufficient strength in Europe and in the Far East to deter rivals from exploiting the situation and to engage the enemy offensively. By the early 1930s, however, this margin of strength had been eroded by French and Italian expansion, and by the lack of steady modernisation to uphold fleet efficiency.[3] Moreover, work on the planned fleet base at Singapore, the Naval Staff's logistical precondition to a successful Japanese war, was curtailed and twice stopped by successive cash-conscious Cabinets.[4]

Consequently, Admiral Chatfield stressed at the DRC the necessity for the Cabinet to complete the Singapore base and to reconsider the naval standard. The Naval Staff desired a new standard to match Germany in the North Sea and the Imperial Japanese Navy in the South China Sea. Of course the Admiralty's appetite for a return to a two-power standard was as much about CID politics as it was about a reply to objective external threats. Yet the Navy's computation of this new standard was premised on what British planners regarded as a precept well tested 'alike in the wars of the Eighteenth Century and the War of 1914'. 'Our naval strategy', as Admiralty papers consistently explained, 'is based on the principle that a fleet of adequate strength, suitably disposed geographically and concen-trated against the enemy's fleet, provides the "cover" under which security is given to widely dispersed territories and or mercantile marine and trade routes.' Since the 'cover' of the battle fleet could not be absolute, it would be necessary to operate cruiser patrols to hunt down enemy raiders on the trade routes and, if necessary, to organise shipping into convoys.[5]

What Admiralty strategists called 'cover' was a readiness on the part of the battle fleet, when in position, to achieve victory in a decisive battle of annihilation over the enemy's main concentration, or at least to keep an inferior surface force from venturing from its fortified anchorage. In the 1930s, with the reach provided by a global network of bases, strategic geography favoured the Royal Navy. From Singapore, the Royal Navy could 'cover' trade in the Indian Ocean and deter attacks on Australia and New Zealand. During the Abyssinian crisis, control of Gibraltar and Suez counterbalanced the temporary loss of commercial traffic between the Mediterranean exit points.[6] As 1914–18 had shown, the Royal Navy had a commanding geographic position over Germany. The British Isles obstructed German access to the North Atlantic; the North Sea remained devoid of strategic targets for a true offensive. Derisively, the figure formed by Shetlands–German Bight–Dover was labelled by German naval strategists as the 'wet triangle' or 'dead angle'.[7]

Decisive battle was viewed as the most effective means by which to win (and lose) undisputed use of the sea. Yet it was not the ultimate task of the Navy in British strategy. The First World War had instilled in European strategists the creed that national financial and industrial endurance would be decisive in future war.[8] The British fleet would once more serve as a weapon with which to damage the German war economy by denying it seaborne foodstuffs and raw materials. Other vital components of this enterprise, which was the business of many CID subcommittees, included efficient industrial, manpower and agricultural mobilisation, targeting German industry and transport for bombing, and the management of neutrals and their commercial traffic.[9] Two motives inspired these activities. The first was the prevalent view that the land commitment of 1914–18 had been a costly aberration from Britain's historic peripheral strategy that should not be repeated. The second motive was the conviction that Britain's industrial and financial staying power, allied with France, and combined with the sea and air blockade, would prevail in another prolonged macroeconomic slugging match with Germany. The COS admitted that Berlin's drive for autarky under the Four-Year Plan had enhanced its resistance to economic leverage. Even so, the grand strategic calculus was deemed to be unequivocal: Britain and its allies were sure to win a long war; Nazi Germany was sure to lose anything but a short and decisive one.[10]

Turning to the historiography, three overall criticisms have been levelled against the Admiralty: first, that it wrongly assumed that it derived strategic advantage from the 1935 accord; second, that it did not study war with Germany in sufficient depth; and third, that when studies were made, the analysis was defective. Marder and Roskill agreed that the Royal Navy failed to prepare for the Second World War because it was obsessed by a resolve 'to make the next Jutland [against the Japanese navy in the South China Sea] a Trafalgar'. Kennedy has concluded that 'this surface battle obsession made it difficult for the Admiralty to react to a German naval challenge that would be expressed partly by individual raiding cruisers ... and chiefly by a renewal of the U-boat attack on merchant ships, a danger that the Admiralty greatly underestimated.'[11] Wark puts this complacency down to a lack of inquisitiveness: the Naval Staff clung inanely to the fantasy that the German fleet was strictly intended to control the Baltic Sea for safe access to Swedish iron ore against the threat from Nazism's ideological antagonist, Soviet Russia.[12]

Before testing these assertions, it is necessary to describe the process by which British naval plans were drafted. The Cabinet, on COS advice, designated potential enemies and issued instructions to begin war planning. The detailed work was done at two levels. Each service planning cell produced its own forecast of opposing forces and the range of feasible enemy courses of action, as well as the method best suited to thwart a foe's likely strategy. At the JPC, the service estimates were then collated with economic and political studies by the IIC, and after 1936 the FO, to compose a coherent appreciation. Once the COS and the CID had endorsed it, the appreciation formed the framework for detailed plans and operational orders, which were prepared by each service staff. Together with four appreciations of war with Germany drafted between October 1934 and January 1939, the naval and air staffs produced special studies on trade defence.

These documents are excellent barometers of military opinion as war approached and illustrate how military estimates were used to influence policy decisions.[13] But these records do not reveal the entire picture. The most valuable Admiralty sources – the early drafts of plans and appreciations, along with the concomitant marginal notes, revisions, and minutes by senior officers – were either lost or destroyed.[14] It is indeed the absence of a complete paper trail that explains why scholars have habitually concluded that the Royal Navy simply ignored the German threat. Yet, from CID level records, fragments of Naval Staff level planning and intelligence documents and private papers it is nevertheless possible to reconstruct a remarkably different picture of Admiralty thinking about war with Nazi Germany than the one usually advanced.

For ease of presentation, it is useful to divide Admiralty thinking about Germany into two phases: the first, from 1933 to the end of 1934, and the second, from 1935 to 1939. In phase one, the Naval Staff considered Admiral Raeder's *optimal* warship policy against Britain. A comparison of this formula with the reality of German naval thinking in late 1938 illustrates how British naval armaments diplomacy helped to co-opt Berlin into pursuing what was from London's viewpoint the *least* dangerous pattern of naval expansion. In phase two, the Naval Staff became convinced by a steady influx of reliable intelligence that German strategists, having taken to heart the lessons of 1914–18, intended in a future war to launch an aggressive air-sea offensive against British maritime lines of communication.

A 'FREAK' NAVY ?

British naval diplomacy in the 1930s was a key component of an ambitious attempt to induce the naval powers to pursue warship policies compatible with British security. The objective was to prevent revolutionary innovation in warship design. It was even necessary at the Disarmament Conference, along with the Japanese and American delegations, to kill a wildly ambitious proposal from the small powers for the abolition of the battleship. This diplomatic defence, however, did not arise from an irrational attachment to obsolete concepts of sea power, but from the sound conviction that Britain was particularly but not exclusively well served by the doctrine of battle fleet supremacy.[15]

The antithesis of battle fleet doctrine was the *guerre de course*. It was articulated in the 1870s by the French *jeune école* naval theorists: Admiral Aube and his followers maintained that the torpedo and the high-speed torpedo boat furnished France with a weapon to break the Royal Navy's close blockade and to mount a potentially decisive counter-blockade. Orthodox theorists held that a privateering campaign could do no more than impair a dominant battle fleet's sea command. It was regarded as the cheap but ultimately ineffective option for continental states. Yet the 1917 U-boat campaign had come uncomfortably close to vindicating the *jeune école*, even if the opposite lesson was accepted by experts. We shall see in the next chapter how this experience inspired one German engineer to seek a technological innovation to perfect the *guerre de course*. In the Royal Navy, it left lingering doubts about whether in future an enemy might successfully prepare in peacetime sea armaments designed solely to evade the main fleet and to disrupt the mechanism of British imports.[16] One manifestation of this anxiety was the British diplomatic effort to abolish or at least limit the effectiveness of submarines.[17]

In the early 1930s, the only power with a substantial building capacity in a position to pursue a truly heretical naval policy incompatible with battle fleet supremacy and the naval treaty system was Germany. In 1934 it became steadily clear that German naval expansion would be subordinated to Hitler's desire to procure British goodwill, but the Naval Staff still took the possibility of a revisionist German naval policy seriously. The Weimar Republic's warship programme had already exhibited these tendencies. The 10 000-ton/11-inch gun *Panzerschiffe*, which were faster than more heavily armed ships and more heavily armed than faster ships, with a large cruising radius generated by diesel plants, were regarded by the Naval Staff as ideal for disrupting British sea communication. In fact the Admiralty informed the FO in 1932 that it was prepared to permit the German navy to possess U-boats as a *quid pro quo* for a halt to *Panzerschiff* construction.[18]

Admiralty anxiety about the *Panzerschiff* menace to its operational concept of battle fleet 'cover' stemmed from war and postwar experience. The exploits of the raiders *Emden* and *Karlsruhe*, in attacking evasively routed merchant ships and dodging British pursuers,[19] exemplified what might have been possible had Germany possessed more numerous, self-sufficient and purpose-designed vessels. Similarly, in late 1917, the destruction of two British Scandinavian convoys by pairs of German cruisers and destroyers underscored one important lesson: convoys intended to protect ships against U-boats were very exposed to destruction by strong surface units, unless a powerful escort was present.[20] And in the 1930s, fleet exercises confirmed the tactical effectiveness of cruisers, 'hunting in couples', in both the attack on and the defence of trade.[21]

Consequently, in late 1933, when it was unclear in which direction the Nazi regime might take its warship policy, Chatfield told the DRC that he thought it might be wise to allow Raeder to lay down 'standard' ships, instead of 'hybrids' like the *Panzerschiffe*, which were 'extremely inconvenient'. The CNS explained correctly that German constructors were working on designs for an improvement on the *Panzerschiff* class of 15–17 000 tons displacement. In November 1933, therefore, the DRC warned against a proliferation of 'hybrid' sea weapons: 'A force of such vessels might possess great destructive potentialities on the trade routes of the Empire.'[22]

The hypothesis that Berlin might attempt to reify the antithesis to British sea doctrine by building a fleet of hybrids was broached again when the COS initiated planning in October 1934.[23] As a first step, the JPC tasked each service to estimate the forces which Britain and Germany would possess by 1939 and 1942.[24] For the Admiralty, however, war in 1939 – a date selected according to the period required to prepare British industry for mobilisation[25] – was improbable on its time-line. Neither navy would be ready.[26] Indeed, the essence of naval policy was the competitive management of warship programmes over time.[27] The Naval Staff thus intended to restore British sea power through incremental fleet expansion after 1938 to achieve by the mid-1940s an unchallengeable two-power standard. As long as the other powers adhered to qualitative limits, the Naval Staff expected to cultivate successfully the crushing *matériel* and industrial preponderance essential to battle fleet supremacy. Admiral Chatfield and his staff knew that potential rivals were guided by the same strategic logic: 'The world knows we can do it,' they affirmed, 'and seeing us make a determined start may realise the futility of challenging us.'[28]

Of course the historical precedent underpinning this confidence was the arms race with Admiral Tirpitz. To wrestle supremacy away from Britain, a rival would have to win a symmetrical naval competition – an impossible task for Germany alone unless British building stood still. Hence, when Captain King formulated his forecasts of German strength in December, he knew that Admiral Raeder had two broad choices. The option least harmful to British security was the creation of a balanced fleet aimed against a Franco-Soviet combination, with the task of securing the Baltic and defending North Sea trade. According to diplomatic channels, and King's reasonable assumption that Hitler would give priority to land and air armaments, he concluded that this was to be Berlin's 'immediate' naval policy. Alternatively, 'if Germany's policy was to be determined by the possibility of war against us,' King reckoned, 'she would probably aim at the development of forces which could inflict the greatest damage on our trade by evading our principal naval forces.' This purpose-built *guerre-de-course* fleet would consist of 'improved' *Panzerschiffe*, high-speed light craft and submarines.[29]

Admiral Dickens, however, was not convinced. In line with orthodox thinking, which held that only 'balanced' fleets could be decisive at sea, he pointed out that 'in war "freak" navies have always been defeated'.[30] Dickens, by mustering details about a potential acceleration of the output rate of German shipyards, asserted that Raeder could effectively launch, from a position of parity with France, another Tirpitzian style bid for naval supremacy over Britain after 1942.[31] Subsequent intelligence proved that the DNI's forecasts had massively overrated the German capacity for concurrent rearmament of its air, land and sea forces, as King and other staff officers recognised.

Nevertheless, the Director of Plans appreciated the compelling incentives for Germany to adopt a radical sea strategy. By engaging in an asymmetrical arms competition, Raeder could effectively circumvent the obstacles that foredoomed Tirpitz: time and the British quantitative lead. Moreover, a *guerre-de-course* fleet applied against oceanic commerce could generate strategic leverage disproportionately greater than its relative size.[32] The Royal Navy would be compelled to disperse its main assets: convoys would require powerful escorts; a strong deterrent fleet would have to be based at Singapore to check Japan; and several 'composite squadrons', consisting each of a battlecruiser, two heavy cruisers and an aircraft carrier, would have to be formed to hunt down the German surface raiders.[33] In short, in contrast with the 1917 U-boat campaign, not only would potentially ruinous damage be inflicted upon British seaborne trade, but concentration, the essence of battle fleet supremacy, would be unravelled.

By reconstructing King's image of Raeder's *optimal* sea strategy against Britain, it is possible to comprehend the reason why the Naval Staff was convinced that it would derive substantial strategic benefits from German conformity to qualitative limitation. Conventional doctrine and historical precedent dictated that a numerically inferior and 'balanced' fleet could not decisively threaten Britain. But the heretical *guerre-de-course* force was a novel peril. Conceivably, it might generate sufficient strategic leverage to undermine British security. Keeping Captain King's hypothesis in mind, it is rewarding to compare it with the final results of German prewar planning to appreciate the similarity of ideas conceived by the leading planners in both navies.

Broadly, German naval planning between the wars can be divided into two phases. Before May 1938, British neutrality was postulated as the prerequisite to a successful outcome; after that date, war with the Royal Navy was embraced formally as the problem. Outwardly, however, this pattern is deceptive. From Tirpitz onward, within the German naval officer corps, the craving to revise the prevailing maritime constellation was the burning ambition. This continuity of intent was expressed in a memo prepared for Raeder in 1934: 'The scale of a nation's world status is identical with the scale of its sea power.' Throughout the 1920s and the early 1930s, despite *matériel* inferiority against the fleets of France and its potential allies, Poland and Russia, German strategists steadily expanded the navy's operational horizon out from the Baltic Sea to the North Sea and the Atlantic. Of course these blue-water aspirations invariably foundered on the problem of German sea power's ultimate geographic and naval obstacle, Britain.[34]

The German Naval Command's desire for parity with France in 1934 must therefore be interpreted as a 'provisional' goal. Before November 1937, while Hitler remained content with a limited navy to defend the supply of Swedish ore during the continental stage of his programme, Admiral Raeder was focused on a long-term bid to revise Germany's world-power position.[35] To this end, and in keeping with battle fleet doctrine, the German Naval Command endeavoured to construct a balanced or 'normal' navy, within the 35 per cent ratio, capable of securing the Baltic and mounting operations against the French in the North Atlantic and the Western Mediterranean. To offset quantitative inferiority against the combined Franco-Soviet fleets, Raeder intended to employ an aggressive-diversionary strategy with ships of superior speed and endurance and large U-boats to disperse French forces, which might then be favourably engaged piecemeal.[36]

Although Raeder entertained intentions in the long run to close the *matériel* gap with Britain, the C-in-C Navy and his staff agreed with King's estimate that the projected balance of sea armaments in the mediumterm effectively ruled out war with Britain. War games conducted in the 1930s arrived at this conclusion. The navy's draft battle instructions of May 1936 specified that no operational order for a victorious war against Britain and its allies could be issued. In October 1936, Commander Hellmuth Heye, the first operations officer, reiterated the prevailing view: 'The prerequisite to a successful German sea war against enemies in the

West and East is English neutrality.' In February 1937, the only alternative that he could devise to overcome British ascendancy was an utterly improbable alliance with either France or Soviet Russia.[37]

If these conclusions confirmed the Royal Navy's conviction that an inferior battle fleet across the North Sea did not pose a potentially lethal menace, then German naval plans after the first Czech crisis of May 1938 are even more revealing. As Hitler's policy moved against Britain, the German navy shed the wishful pretence that London would permit Germany to execute an offensive in the Atlantic against France without joining in. To meet Hitler's demands for armaments acceleration, Raeder ordered in June work to begin on a study of the possibilities of 'conducting a naval war against Britain and the resulting requirements for strategic objectives and the build-up of the navy'.[38] The way in which they responded confirms that King's estimate of Germany's *optimal* sea strategy was in its essential features shared by leading German planners.

It fell to Commander Heye to draft the key document in reply to Raeder's instruction.[39] Heye grasped that it was pointless to challenge the British battle fleet under unfavourable geographic and *matériel* conditions. Like Captain King four years before, he perceptively identified Germany's true offensive objective if command of the sea could not be won in 'one big battle'. As an extension of aggressive plans against France, and to exert the maximum strategic leverage, the operations officer wanted to disrupt the British economy by attacking its sea communications. This would compel the Royal Navy to disperse its heavy units and so loosen its blockade of the North Sea, thus permitting Germany to reinforce its raiders. The exchange of strategic aims had implications for future ship construction. 'Indeed, the standard ship types defined by international treaty and the cultivation generally of opinion about the composition of a "normal fleet",' Heye correctly reasoned, was 'an important method for the preservation of British supremacy at sea.' Warship programmes had to match national geostrategic imperatives. Heye thus advocated, with the blessings of Admiral Günther Guse, Raeder's chief of staff, the rapid build-up of a *Kreuzerkrieg* fleet, designed for an assault on British commerce, consisting of improved *Panzerschiffe*, light cruisers and U-boats. By inference, the battleship had lost its top status. Yet, in deference to Tirpitzian tradition, Commander Heye assigned to the navy's heaviest vessels the task of covering the raiders en route and engaging detached surface units of the British fleet in the North Sea.[40]

In late August, a senior committee approved of the *Kreuzerkrieg* strategy and endorsed specific ship types: 19 000-ton *Panzerschiffe*, 7800-ton Type-M cruisers and large destroyers. But as Heye had probably anticipated, the role of the battleship became a point of contention. The main issue for the committee was how to correlate effectively the future ship programme with that of the British. Heye stressed the need for forces that could be produced relatively quickly. Along with Guse, he had openly voiced concerns that Hitler's policies might provoke a general war before Germany was ready.[41] In contrast, the fleet chief, Admiral Rolf Carls, was less concerned about the question of a general war in the shortrun, than with the foundations of a future German world empire with a supreme battle fleet. He called for the building of four blue-water battle groups – each with a battleship (H-Type, 56 000 tons/16-inch guns), a *Panzerschiff*, an aircraft carrier and auxiliaries. The battle groups would be deployed to disrupt British shipping, while the *Bismarck* and *Scharnhorst* types tied down a proportion of the Royal Navy in its bases. This tension between unrealistic long-term and perhaps achievable short-term armaments policies muddled later decision-making. Although ten battleships, 15 *Panzerschiffe*, five heavy, 24 Type-M and 36 light cruisers, eight aircraft carriers and 249 U-boats were provisionally projected for 1945, various building schedules emphasising either a combination of the heavy and light units, or a rapid assembly of four *Panzerschiffe* by the end of 1942 were tendered.[42]

As we shall see later, the main impetus behind the increase in the German warship programme was Hitler's growing antagonism towards London. Although the C-in-C Navy was anxious about the weak state of his fleet, he engaged his remarkable aptitude for blinkered thinking and accepted Hitler's assurances in 1938–9 that war with Britain would not come before 1946. However, in late October and early November 1938, he endorsed plans for the swift production of four *Panzerschiffe* and the postponement of battleships. The output delays imposed by industrial bottlenecks and the prospect of the *Luftwaffe* being assigned war tasks against the British at the navy's expense probably influenced Admiral Raeder's tally of priorities. A staff paper of 17 November concluded that with extra resources the navy could complete eight *Panzerschiffe*, 18 Type-M cruisers and the entire U-boat plan by 1943. Nevertheless, as Jost Dülffer convincingly argues, Hitler was now expressly aiming at a future world conflict with the Anglo-American sea powers after achieving the mastery of Europe. The Führer thus angrily demanded the laying down immediately of six H-class battleships at the expense of small vessels and rejected several attempts by Raeder to gain priority for the *Kreuzerkrieg* navy.[43]

A comparison of King's December 1934 and Heye's summer of 1938 ideas of what was Germany's *optimal* naval armaments policy uncovers a significant finding: it shows that the Admiralty's conviction that it derived strategic benefits from the Naval Agreements was not without foundation. As Heye recognised, orthodox doctrine about what constituted a 'normal' fleet, which had been codified by international treaty, helped to sustain British sea security. Britain could not stop Hitler from building a navy, but what type of navy he built would make a difference. In war, an inferior German battle fleet would generate disproportionately less strategic leverage than was justified by its size and the resources invested to create it.[44] If Germany later attempted to contest British battle fleet superiority, Chatfield calculated that by the time such a bid could be launched, Britain's *matériel* preponderance and renewed warship building capacity would thwart it. The German navy could not win by playing according to British sea power rules.

For example, some scholars have argued, as Karl Dönitz did at the time, that Germany should have invested entirely in that quintessentially anti-British weapon, the U-boat. With 300 boats in the early phases of the war, Raeder's successor was convinced that he might have had a good chance at a rapid decision.[45] To illustrate, instead of building the *Bismarck*, Germany could have procured about 50 Type VII U-boats.[46] The problem with this counterfactual thesis, however, is that it was the least likely German naval policy. The lesson of 1917–18, as accepted in naval circles, was that the failed U-boat offensive had shown the limitation of over-reliance on a single weapons system.[47] In the summer of 1938, Heye correctly asserted in his study that attacks from surface, subsurface and air weapons in combination would achieve greater results than any one type alone.[48] Furthermore, with the collective ambitions of the naval officer corps set on a bigger project, the belief that 'a U-boat power is not a [global] sea-power' was unyielding.[49]

Moreover, as Geoffrey Till has suggested, perhaps Raeder was right and Dönitz was wrong.[50] U-boats alone did not achieve decisive results. U-boats, a sizeable surface fleet and a concerted air offensive might have been more potent. The devastation inflicted by combined attacks on convoys (exemplified in 1942 by the ill-fated PQ17) might have disrupted the whole apparatus of British overseas supply. Was the colossal Z Plan (Table 3.1) the right sort of navy for Germany? It was closer to the battle groups advocated by Carls than Heye's modest *Kreuzerkrieg* fleet and thus entirely utopian in conception. Like the Tirpitz plan, the Z Plan was unlikely to unfold without an energetic British reply. Although Hitler insisted that the six H-class battle-ships be laid down in 1939 and matched that order with giving the navy priority in resource allocation, that frame of priorities was unlikely to last due to continental exigencies. The slow pace of officer and crew training, astronomical oil needs and lacklustre shipyard output, all should have forewarned the C-in-C Navy that his Z Plan was unrealisable.[51] So the answer to the question posed above is the one proffered by King and Heye: Germany would have been better served by *Kreuzerkrieg* and should have built more 'hybrid' type raiders earlier.[52] Indeed, during the war, the German navy's historical branch criticised Raeder for failing to endorse this policy.[53]

Table 3.1   German Naval Command, Z Plan, provisional timetable, January 1939
(units operational)

Warship category	1939	1940	1941	1942	1943	1944	1945	1946	1947	Target
Type-H battleship						4	4	6	6	6
Bismarck type			1	2	2	2	2	2	2	2
Scharnhorst type	2	2	2	2	2	2	2	2	2	2
Old *Panzerschiffe*	3	3	3	3	3	3	3	3	3	3
New *Panzerschiffe*					4	4	8	8	10	12
Aircraft carriers		1	2	2	2	2	2	3	4	8
Heavy cruisers	2	5	5	5	5	5	5	5	5	5
Type-M cruisers				3	3	4	5	8	12	24
Light cruisers				2	6	9	12	15	20	36
U-boats*	66	84	111	130	161	194	229	240	249	249

* All types, including coastal defence, minelayers and U-cruisers.
Source: Adapted from Dülffer, *Marine*, 569–87.

Of course this is conjecture. Still it must be emphasised that the counterfactual corresponds with the *optimal* German sea strategy against
Britain envisioned by senior war planners in *both* navies. It is significant
that King considered the idea months before it became evident that
Germany would join the treaty system. Dülffer admits that Raeder's
desire for the prestige of 'equality of rights' and his wish to follow the
Tirpitz tradition helps to explain his disinclination to develop special
commerce raiders. Yet he rejects the argument that the Naval
Agreements blocked alternative sea strategies because the officer corps
desired a 'normal' fleet anyway.[54] But this misses the point. Heye was
right: concepts of sea power mattered. Britain benefited from the
abstract influence exerted by the prevailing norms and historically conditioned responses about what constituted authentic sea power encoded
into the international order by treaty. It was not coercive, but cogent.
In the German case, revisionist aspirations at sea were twice confounded by the craving of its leadership to emulate the British battle
fleet standard.[55]

THE KNOCKOUT BLOW AGAINST SHIPPING

The 1935 Naval Agreement ended further Naval Staff speculation about
the possibility of Hitler following a heretical naval policy. Instead, the

planners turned to the question of how Germany would employ its small balanced fleet in a potential anti-British strategy.

As noted, strategists in London were convinced that Britain and its allies would inevitably win a long war of endurance and that Germany was bound to lose anything but a short and decisive one. It was assumed that military staffs in Berlin, by similar reasoning, would plan for a rapid victory. One offshoot of this thinking, well known to historians, was the Air Ministry's thesis that the *Luftwaffe* was being built to deliver a 'knock-out blow'. It presumed that if Germany inflicted massive casualties in London with a torrent of high-explosive and poison gas bombs, the ensuing collapse in public resolve would compel politicians to seek an immediate peace. It reflected widespread beliefs cultivated by futuristic novels and the popular press, about the apocalyptic capacity of air power. It also mirrored the RAF's conviction that bombing would be the next war winner.

Less well understood by historians, however, is the Admiralty's own version of the knockout-blow thesis. Instead of civilians, the Naval Staff considered that the *Luftwaffe* might pummel the 'import system',[56] in conjunction with an all-out surface and subsurface campaign, to realise what U-boats alone could not achieve in 1917. The scenario originated in March 1935, shortly after Hitler's dramatic unveiling of the *Luftwaffe*, and steadily developed thereafter to include indiscriminate mine warfare. Although it was conceived of as a worst-case hypothesis, the strictly naval component of this knockout-blow scenario – that in contrast to 1914–18, the German fleet would be used *offensively* – became the accepted premise of British planning in 1937. The exposition of this theme below will establish that the Royal Navy's perception of the German threat was not blinded by the preconception that Hitler's fleet was being built for the Baltic, nor by an irrational obsession to re-enact Trafalgar with the Japanese in the role of the vanquished.

It will be recalled that in December 1934, as the first step in the joint planning process, the Naval Staff projected that Germany would procure a small balanced fleet aimed at a Franco-Soviet combination. The next step was for each service to envisage how Berlin might employ its forces in 1939. In March 1935, King and his staff prepared two studies. The first looked at the global implications of a war with Germany, and the second described Germany's probable courses of action at sea.[57] In the first, the planners assumed, as they would consistently during the 1930s, that Japan would exploit a European war to further its imperial ambitions in Asia at British expense, and hence put pressure on the Royal Navy to set aside a credible deterrent force.

In the second memo, it was accepted that the German battle fleet was not going to sail into the North Sea and offer itself up for annihilation. Instead, Captain King argued, as a later document put it, that 'the task of the German navy in wartime would be to engage sea forces weaker than her own, but principally to damage enemy trade and to protect her own merchant shipping.'[58] King did not anticipate that Raeder would 'achieve any vital results' by dispersing his small balanced fleet into the Atlantic. The security of the Baltic would be the most likely task of surface units, including the *Panzerschiffe*. Some heavy ships might be employed on 'tip and run' raids against sea links with British forces on the continent, but only disguised armed merchant cruisers would be used to dislocate British commerce. Alternatively, since U-boat numbers would be too few to mount an effective *guerre de course* alone, King imagined that Germany might gamble on the 'unknown' potentiality of an unrestricted air attack, combined with an aggressive surface/subsurface assault, on east coast shipping and the Port of London.[59]

Admiral Dickens generally agreed. But he believed that King had under-rated Germany's offensive potential. The DNI argued that a U-boat menace could develop in war as Germany mobilised its productive capacity. Also, he did not accept that Raeder would be inhibited by defensive tasks. The Russians could be bottled up in the Gulf of Finland and the Royal Navy fenced out of the Baltic with a generous distribution of the 12 000 mines Germany was believed to possess. This would release the surface units for blue-water commerce hunting. Accordingly, Dickens concluded that:

> If Germany used all her surface ships, including the [*Panzerschiffe*], to attack shipping she might, along with air attacks on London and shipping there and ruthless submarine operations against shipping between Portland and the Tees, hope to defeat us mainly by economic pressure. She will remember the narrow margin between failure and success which she was able to reach in the last war.

King accepted the DNI's critique.[60] In October, his revised memo was printed as the naval subsection of the JPC's 'provisional' report of war with Germany. The image it painted represented a compromise between the tolerable level of sea denial exerted by Germany that he anticipated and the lethal air-sea strike envisaged by Dickens.[61]

Further study of the navy's knockout-blow thesis in 1936 tended to play it down. The Naval Staff reckoned that the very large number of long-range bombers required and the effect of indiscriminate sinking of merchantmen on neutrals would deter Berlin from resorting to it in all but the most desperate circumstances. In March, Plans Division asserted that an air attack upon shipping could only be economically and profitably executed in the coastal approaches to east coast ports, especially the Port of London, where one-third of the food supply was delivered. Still, the planners maintained that by organising the shipping which could not be diverted to ports outside of bombing range into convoys, particularly at night, and by providing merchantmen with anti-aircraft guns and escorts, losses would be reduced to an acceptable amount. A potential enemy was more likely to risk its valuable air forces on more 'attractive' targets: 'On balance,' the planners concluded, 'the air threat to shipping is not considered to be as serious as attack by surface raider.'[62]

In July 1936, however, a joint Air Ministry/Admiralty study argued that in future the increasing range (greater than 300 miles from Germany) and numbers of aircraft in the aerodromes of Europe would enlarge the danger to shipping. Surface and subsurface attacks would be manageable, but when added to the unknown factor of air attack with bombs and torpedoes, the resulting 'shipping losses, combined with the dislocation at the docks and other vital points in the distribution system ... might affect the maintenance of our supplies to an extent we have never hitherto experienced'. Even if cargoes could be diverted to and smoothly unloaded at safe western ports, the existing rail and road network serving the west coast did not have the capacity for the prolonged distribution of goods. Dismissing the navy's faith in the lethality of anti-aircraft gun fire, the Air Ministry regarded convoys approaching east coast ports as plum targets for bombers.[63]

Finally, in December 1936, in a study intended to explore the 'worst case' from the standpoint of British survival in a war with Germany,[64] the knockout blow against the British import system was thoroughly described. It envisaged the use of warships and armed merchant cruisers both in sporadic raids on British coastal routes and in distant waters. Attacks might even originate from ostensibly neutral states. The 42 large U-boats available to Berlin in 1939 would only permit ten to be stationed on a continuous patrol in home waters, but the study also suggested that the entire force might be deployed at the onset of a conflict to obtain a shock effect. As to the *Luftwaffe*, the paper predicted that the initial effort would be directed against ports and the inland distribution system which served them; and subsequently, as local air defences improved, the main effort would be shifted to merchant vessels approaching harbours on the east coast.[65]

Aside from the instruction to adopt a 'worst case' approach, one reason for this progressively grim tone was the increasingly gloomy diplomatic situation, and not any direct evidence that Germany was actually planning a knockout blow.[66] In the interval between the first JPC appreciation in

October 1935 and the second in late 1936, Italy had invaded Abyssinia, civil war had broken out in Spain and Nazi Germany had occupied the Rhineland. Captain Tom Phillips, who had replaced King in August 1935, was no more convinced than his predecessor that Germany would unleash a knockout blow,[67] but together with his JPC colleagues, he sent a decidedly pessimistic message to the Cabinet to criticise the slow pace of British rearmament.[68]

In their October 1936 appreciation, the joint planners pictured the currents of power shifting away from Britain and her potential allies and coalescing in Germany's favour. Totalitarian methods of peacetime mobilisation, they argued, granted the Nazi state an increasing capacity to resist economic pressure as well as incentives to launch a first strike. The JPC believed that the German high command, cognisant of the decisive long-term advantage in economic and industrial resources that Britain and France possessed, would exploit its initial lead in armaments, particularly in bombing aircraft, to achieve a quick victory over one of its enemies: either a mechanised push into France supported by the balance of the *Luftwaffe*, or the knockout blow against Britain. Both the Air and Naval Staffs' versions of the knockout blow sustained the joint planners' dark message. If the hammer was to fall on Britain, then Berlin would either attempt to demoralise civilians with high-explosive, incendiary and gas bombs, or seek to disrupt the raw material and food supply with an all-out attack against the import system.[69]

The Cabinet Secretary and the Deputy Chiefs of Staff edited out the especially gloomy predictions advanced in the JPC's draft appreciation in November 1936. Hankey, Chatfield and the other COS were no less critical of the rate of British rearmament, but the JPC report undermined their claim that the FO could and should construct a durable détente with Germany.[70] Moreover, Phillips, who was perhaps motivated by a desire to reach a JPC consensus, evidently did not appreciate that too great an emphasis on the 1939 deadline and the Navy's own 'worst case' thesis would vitiate the Admiralty's long-term aims. Nonetheless, two points about Naval Staff thinking in 1935–6 should be emphasised. First, the Admiralty believed that the only way in which German surface and subsurface forces could be made deadly was to combine them into a rapid all-out air strike on the British import system. Second, again to be decisive, German air and U-boat attacks had to be concentrated in the Atlantic approaches and British coastal waters.

The true turning point in Naval Staff thinking occurred in early 1937. Thereafter, the Admiralty correctly believed that Raeder would not permit his heavy forces to remain idle in any future conflict. On 12 January, Chatfield first articulated this point as the COS considered revisions to the JPC's 1936 appreciation. He told his colleagues about the change in German outlook. He said he was convinced that the Germans would not repeat the mistake they made at the beginning of the last war. He felt that we must anticipate that German battlecruisers would be sent out into the Atlantic to attack our trade at the outset of a war and we should have a big problem on hand to deal with them.[71]

Subsequently, all COS, JPC and Admiralty papers accepted this judgement. Both a revised Plans Division study drafted in the spring of 1937 and the JPC appreciation of July 1938 assumed that German surface units would be employed in a 'vigorous' attack on British oceanic trade. With only a small force and mines employed in the Baltic, the anti-British attack would be conducted by the bulk of the fleet available in 1939, including the *Scharnhorst* class battlecruisers, the *Panzerschiffe*, 8-inch gun cruisers, merchant cruisers and U-boats.[72] This expectation percolated down to detailed 'Operation Instructions' issued to British fleets and naval stations. In September 1938, the 'Enemy Naval Information' paragraph of the instructions warned local commanders that the Admiralty 'anticipated that [Germany's] navy will be employed to the fullest extent in delivering a series of heavy blows, designed to force an early decision'.[73]

Although it is difficult to be certain, it appears that this trend was reinforced by accumulating intelligence. In the next chapter, we shall see how technical data about the high-performance propulsion systems installed in Admiral Raeder's capital ships provided a vital clue about their future deployment. Other less secret sources, however, were as influential. A significant one was the observations made of German warships in Spanish waters. The section on 'Strategy and Tactics' in NID's handbook on the German navy was considerably rewritten in light of information from Spain and other sources in mid-1937.[74] Unfortunately, the only surviving copy is the interim summer of 1936 edition.[75]

It is very likely, however, that most of the fresh information concerned the German navy's application of 'group' tactics, and how effective those tactics would be if employed to dislocate British seaborne commerce. The 1936 NID handbook referred to this doctrine. It pointed out that the German officer corps was divided between two schools of thought: conventional thinkers who advocated the rigid 'Line of Battle' system, and supporters of flexible 'groups'. For an offensive against trade, the latter proposed to deploy the *Panzerschiffe* (and future battleships) as the core attack vessels, while supporting cruisers, destroyers and U-boats intercepted merchant vessels. If enemy cruisers attempted to engage the group, the core ship would provide cover; if an opponent concentrated superior strength against the group, then it would withdraw behind a U-boat screen. Once the German navy had sufficient heavy units, the battle fleet would also be organised into groups ('divisions' in British parlance) for tactical flexibility.[76] During 1937–8, in Spanish waters, on average at least one *Panzerschiff*, one cruiser, a division of four destroyers, and a number of U-boats were stationed on patrol.[77] Consequently, observation of the operational behaviour of these vessels and perhaps the analysis of their wireless traffic probably confirmed that the German navy intended to follow the 'group' system.[78]

In any case, the possession by Germany of a small fleet of fast capital ships challenged the Naval Staff to think differently about sea warfare. The German menace hastened the British movement to flexible 'divisional' battle fleet tactics.[79] In late 1937, Admiral James, the DCNS, predicted that in future

> the western Powers will not deploy a great number of capital ships in a slow moving line, and though in a Far Eastern war it is probable that the issue would be decided by a main action between battle fleets, these battle fleets will be not only relatively small in numbers but will possess very high speed and high powers of manoeuvrability.[80]

From early 1937 onwards, therefore, one of the chief concerns of the Royal Navy was how to deal with fast German capital ships operating singly or in groups in the Atlantic. A list of 'Strategical and Tactical Problems' suggested by various commands provides some indication of this anxiety.[81] The Director of the Staff College submitted a proposal for a war game in which the German Naval Command adopted group tactics in the offensive. The 1st Cruiser Squadron conducted its own exercise and found that Admiral Raeder could do greater harm by employing his ships singularly. The C-in-C Home Fleet was concerned with pre-emptive operations and thwarting a German breakout. A scenario inspired by a NID report envisaged Germany deploying its merchant navy as commerce raiders.[82]

As early as December 1934, Captain King had proposed to establish hunting groups to cope with the surface threat.[83] The task for these groups was to defeat the German offensive quickly enough to resume a reasonable level of imports. If the Germans dispatched the majority of their heavy units into the Atlantic, there would be insufficient battleships available to provide convoy escorts. Until the trade routes were safe, the entire shipping system would have to be suspended. Vital supplies could be transported by very large convoys escorted by battleships, but the disruption of the system would still be considerable.[84] As fleet exercises had shown on several occasions, the use of aircraft carriers and a pair of cruisers was ideal for quickly locating and attacking raiding forces.[85] The lesson was applied on a larger scale. As Captain Phillips wrote in March 1938, the ideal hunting force would consist of battlecruisers working in conjunction with aircraft carriers.[86] Indeed, France was expected to provide one hunting group consisting of the two *Dunkerque* battlecruisers, heavy cruisers and an aircraft carrier.[87]

British and German naval planners recognised that the greatest obstacles to the German navy sustaining an effective surface attack on Britain's oceanic trade links were geography and logistics. The Naval Staff assumed that the offensive would diminish in the long run because Germany lacked bases outside the North Sea. The long distances (1200 miles) to Atlantic stations also severely curbed U-boat patrol periods. In late 1938, Commander Heye estimated that even his *Kreuzerkrieg* fleet could only remain at sea for three months without resupply.[88] German naval planners hoped that the dispersion forced upon the Royal Navy by their offensive and the threat from Japan and Italy, and resupply at sea, would permit them to replenish their raiders. More boldly, one German theorist and several admirals advocated occupying Denmark, Norway, Holland or even the French coast to solve the geographic predicament.[89]

The Admiralty, however, as events in 1940 proved, wrongly assumed that Berlin would be less ambitious. In response to an FO inquiry about a potential German attack on Norway to seize the air base at Stavanger, the Admiralty replied that, although it would be of 'great strategic importance' to Berlin, in its opinion, Germany still had more to gain by Norway's neutrality than its partnership in an 'unwilling' alliance.[90] The Naval Staff took it for granted that the German navy would use clandestine bases in friendly/neutral states, namely Franco's Spain,[91] to overcome replenishment problems. This expectation was encouraged by some scant intelligence. In late 1936, the French naval attaché reported that the German Naval Command was planning to make use of the Bissagos Islands (off the African Gold Coast), but corroborating evidence eluded NID.[92] Reports of German, Italian and even Japanese covert activities in Central and South America induced the C-in-C of the American and West Indies Station to compile details in the hope of identifying in advance possible refuelling and storage bases for enemy submarines and surface raiders.[93]

The support given to the Naval Staff's thesis that Admiral Raeder would adopt a 'vigorous' offensive by the influx of evidence about German strategy, tactics and covert overseas bases was matched by intelligence of German literature on naval warfare. Historians usually fault the Admiralty for failing to scrutinise German theoretical works, particularly for neglecting Admiral Wolfgang Wegener's 1929 monograph *Die Seestrategie des Weltkrieges*.[94] Wegener castigated Tirpitz for premising his strategy on the belief that the British would mount a reckless offensive in search of a second Trafalgar. He realised that the Royal Navy had achieved its aim – defending sea communications – with a defensive blockade, while the German navy, moored to its worthless position by technical and geographic handicaps, had achieved very little of strategic value. Rejecting the one-big-battle as an end in itself, Wegener advocated that Germany should aim to outflank Britain by securing bases in Scandinavia, from which it could launch a deadly strike at British trade in the Atlantic.[95] In sum, Wegener argued that German naval war plans and warship construction had to be premised on an offensive sea strategy.

According to previous studies, Wegener's book languished unread and untranslated in the NID library until word reached Vansittart in April 1939 that Hitler had expressed 'unbounded admiration' for it. The Naval Staff then belatedly ordered its attaché in Berlin to write a précis of Wegener's thesis.[96] This interpretation, however, is wrong for two reasons. First, it assumes that this episode was typical of the British approach to the published German sources. Second, it presupposes that the Admiralty ignored or misunderstood the chief message of post-1919 German scholarship on sea warfare.

Actually, the Royal Navy had two means for the dissemination of information about foreign thinking on naval warfare: the semi-official and restricted publication, *The Naval Review*, and the official and *confidential* 'Monthly Intelligence Report' (MIR). The purpose of the former was to encourage discussion about current affairs, strategy, tactics and any other related topics. It published articles and reviews written by naval officers.[97] The MIR was produced by NID for circulation to all officers. It usually contained a wide-ranging section on the international situation, current naval intelligence, miscellaneous articles submitted by naval officers and extracts from the international press.

The Naval Review printed studies of the official German naval histories of 1914–18, as well as articles on cruiser warfare and intelligence translated from the French *Revue Maritime* and the German *Marine Rundschau*.[98] Admiral Alfred Dewar, a proponent of naval education, penned a perceptive critique of Wegener's book in 1929, in which he detected its Spenglerian and anti-British overtones.[99] In the early 1930s, articles tended to focus on international affairs, but major theoretical and historical monographs were regularly appraised. In 1937, the naval attaché in Berlin, who also lectured at the various staff colleges on the German navy, invited subscribers to comment on a list of 'themes for discussion' extracted from *Marine Rundschau*.[100] It is impossible to chart precisely the journal's influence, but it is notable that all senior staff officers were members.[101]

At any rate, as the MIRs bear out, the interpretation of German naval historiography that was fed into the Admiralty for war planning purposes penetrated the well-documented process of suppression of scholarship critical of Tirpitz and, hence, appreciated the key lesson propounded by Wegener and like-minded theorists: the need for an offensive sea strategy. Too literal a reading of the official histories and Admiral Raeder's 'celebrated' feud with Wegener, ironically, would have been utterly misleading.[102] Although Raeder labelled Wegener's work 'sacrilegious', he expropriated the latter's thesis in a lecture in February 1937. He told Hitler and top officials that, in contrast to 1914–18, the fleet would adopt an 'energetic' Atlantic offensive against an enemy's sea links.[103]

This 'change in outlook', as Admiral Chatfield had described it, was reported in the MIRs. The November 1937 edition cited an article by Admiral Otto Groos, one of the navy's official historians and often Admiral Raeder's mouthpiece. 'Germany could also have made it impossible for England', he wrote, 'to have retained indefinitely an overpowering fleet in the North Sea by taking full advantage of the strategical possibilities of cruiser warfare and submarine warfare against commerce.' In the next edition, an account of the German fleet exercises in September 1937 emphasised that the 'study of the last war, to say nothing of wars before that, has taught the German Navy the value of the offensive in war'. The author added that commanders were being inculcated to 'ensure that offensive strategy is a good deal more in evidence in any future maritime operations undertaken by the German Navy, than it was in the past'.[104] And finally, Captain Troubridge, the naval attaché in Berlin, encapsulated in his 1937 annual report the cardinal message of post-1919 German scholarship on naval strategy:

> Much emphasis is now laid on the necessity for offensive action, and criticism of wartime operations is generally levelled at the smallness of the scale on which they were conducted rather than on the nature of the operations themselves, and in this connexion the progressive school of naval writers continually emphasise that naval operations cannot be undertaken without risk.[105]

All of this overthrows the argument that the Naval Staff were ill-informed about German sea strategy. The Admiralty had a better appreciation of the chief premise of post-1919 German scholarship than has been previously acknowledged.

Moreover, the Admiralty was also convinced that Raeder had solved the other main defect of German First World War naval operations: a divided and thus indecisive chain of command. Appraisal of the German navy's order of battle and command structure by officers at the Naval Staff College in 1938 arrived at this conclusion.[106] In 1937, the swift and brutal attack upon Almeria in reply to the attack on the *Deutschland* by Spanish government bombers was interpreted by Troubridge as indicative of this potent organisation.[107] According to the available sources, the Naval Staff also rated the man at the top highly. NID described Admiral Raeder as 'an outstanding personality whose influence in the direction of Naval policy is incalculable'.[108] As to Hitler, Admiral Chatfield and his subordinates were well aware that the German chancellor's naval policy was his British policy. It was also correctly reported that Hitler was a 'naval expert' of the nuts-and-bolts, *Jane's Fighting Ships* variety, for whom Wegenerian or Mahanian abstractions about sea power were a mystery.[109] As Dülffer has shown, it was the land-minded Führer who insisted that the German navy give priority to battleship construction in the Z-Plan, which the Naval Command regarded with some scepticism.[110]

Additional evidence about a German sea offensive came in the form of intelligence about mine warfare. The Naval Staff knew about Admiral Raeder's illicit mine arsenal in 1930, shortly after he first procured them. By February 1934, the total reached 12 000. Thereafter, the IIC attempted to monitor output.[111] In 1937, it estimated that stocks had surpassed 100 000 units and manufacturing capacity exceeded that 'warranted by peace requirements'.[112] This steady flow of industrial data was matched by reliable technical intelligence on mine-laying capacity. Although NID did not know about plans for a large mine-laying U-boat, it did know that Rome had given Berlin its system for deploying mines by submarine.[113] In March 1938, the Director of Tactical Division noted that Germany could operate seven cruisers, 15 destroyers, 12 torpedo boats and 26 minesweepers, all equipped to lay mines. Finally, the conversion of 40 fishing vessels to mine-layers and sweepers in September 1938 confirmed the assumption that Germany was prepared to embark on 'a vigorous mine-laying policy'.[114]

The prospect that Germany would scatter mines indiscriminately on British overseas and coastal trade routes as part of its knockout-blow scenario was disturbing enough, but in April 1939, the IIC issued a frantic warning.[115] It reported that the German stock of mines had reached at least 200 000 and was steadily growing. According to the IIC, Germany had procured in peacetime more mines than the total number laid by Britain and its allies (including the USA) in 1914–18. This grossly inflated estimate, however, was based on an ingenious yet entirely misleading source. In late 1936, the IIC became aware that the German navy was purchasing a 'special mine paint'. Experts in NID calculated how much paint was required to coat the average mine. Since the IIC wrongly believed that the paint was exclusively used for the mines, it kept track of the German inventory by the deliveries made of the 'special mine paint' suppliers. It was not until March 1940 that the JIC determined that the IIC's mine-paint-based estimates were 'fallacious' and correctly estimated that the German stock was probably much less than 15 000.[116]

This episode not only bolstered the Royal Navy's belief in the German offensive, but it also influenced NID's estimate of the types of mines Germany manufactured. An unconfirmed report about novel designs reached NID in 1939,[117] but it seems that the naval planners were spellbound by the colossal numbers being charted by the IIC. They probably assumed that German planners were counting on mass attack with conventional mines to overwhelm British minesweeping forces: not the exploitation of a novel design to circumvent existing countermeasures. Consequently, the Royal Navy was befuddled by Germany's development of detonators for mines triggered by a passing vessel's magnetic field. Ironically, the German design was based on models deployed by the British off the coast of Flanders in 1918. The German navy procured its first batch in 1929, but production was limited. In October 1939, Raeder hoped that mass use of the weapon, against which the British had yet to develop proper defences,[118] might prove decisive. The mines caused great disruption to shipping and nearly closed London to imports. But insufficient stocks (1500 in September 1939), especially of the air-dropped model, and their premature use permitted the Admiralty to save the day with 'de-gaussing' – a method of rendering ships magnetically neutral and so immune to this form of attack.[119]

Unfortunately, while the Admiralty took great interest in discovering the realities of German capabilities at sea, it did not devote as much attention to the air component of its own knockout-blow thesis before 1939. One reason for this was the long-running battle with the Air Ministry about the effects of bombing and the control of naval aviation.[120] Consequently, although the two services shared common ground on the knockout blow, the fierce debate and the scramble for funds tended to polarise views and propel technical thinking into the theoretical realm.[121] An attempt by the JIC to resolve the problem by studying air warfare in Spain from May 1937 produced few results.[122] The final report concluded that 'the effort to cut off sea communications by air [in Spain had] been so diffuse, ill-coordinated and inaccurate as to be inconclusive on the issue.'[123]

The slow development of a German fleet air arm contributed to the lack of interest. The Naval Staff could readily empathise with Raeder's frustration at failing to obtain control of his naval air assets or even to co-ordinate preparations for an air-sea campaign.[124] In May 1938, in a brief prepared for a war game, NID noted that Germany lagged behind the other powers in the development of the torpedo as an air weapon for purposes other than coastal defence.[125] In the frenzied atmosphere of early 1939, when war scares and speculation about Hitler's next diplomatic move swept through Whitehall, the DNI, Admiral Troup, attempted for the first time to co-ordinate with the Air Ministry a study of the probable role in war of elements of the *Luftwaffe* devoted to the navy.[126]

Sarcastically, the air attaché in Berlin wrote to his superiors that much of the data requested on the composition of the *Luftkommando See* was in the possession of the Air Ministry and that 'closer touch' between the two services was 'desirable'. He outlined a force scarcely capable of delivering a decisive blow. The *Luftkommando See* consisted mostly of older models, organised into fleet based and embryonic carrier squadrons, some fighters, flying boats, and a large number of long-range reconnaissance planes.[127] Troubridge added that there was very little evidence to suggest the way in which German naval aircraft would be employed in war; however, he appended an extract from an article written by the head of the *Luftwaffe* staff college that appeared to indicate that escort and reconnaissance were the prime duties of German naval aviation.[128]

Still, nothing could overturn the well entrenched belief that Germany might risk an attempt to knock Britain out of the next European war with air power.[129] Anxiety about a 'bolt from the blue' vexed Naval Staff attempts to relieve the sense of tension in the fleet in the summer of 1939.[130] Despite the fact that Germany had clearly failed to develop the air dropped torpedo, which both services regarded as possessing great potential against shipping, and the geographic disadvantages for Germany in mounting such an attack, a joint Admiralty/Air Ministry report in June on the protection of trade did not rule out a rapid all-out air strike against the import system.[131] In anticipation of this, the diversion of shipping to west coast ports was introduced as a precaution two days before the outbreak of war.[132] On 19 September, as his armies raced across Poland, Hitler threatened to unleash a 'secret weapon' that would undermine the unassailable defence the Royal Navy had previously afforded the British Isles. Asked by the COS what the Führer meant by his threat, the JIC pondered a number of utterly fantastic notions, including a 'death ray' and a 'super cannon'. In the end, the JIC response resonated unmistakably with five years of sensible Naval Staff thinking when it concluded that 'the form which the weapon or method of warfare referred to [by Hitler] might take may be an intensive attack on sea-borne trade by air, submarine and surface craft, and the indiscriminate use of mines'.[133]

4 Admiralty Technical Intelligence and the German Navy, 1936–39

Historians have criticised the Admiralty for placing too much faith in the Nazi regime's willingness to abide by the 1935 Naval Agreement and for failing to grasp the threat of German expansion at sea. The oppressive atmosphere of complacency cultivated by the Naval Agreement, so the argument runs, stifled efforts on the part of naval intelligence to discover the realities of German naval expansion.[1] This version of events is largely based on the cogent memoirs of Admiral John H. Godfrey, the Director of Naval Intelligence from January 1939 to 1943. The former DNI blamed the Royal Navy's technical intelligence assessors for overlooking compelling evidence that the bilateral Naval Agreements were employed by Berlin to 'steal a march' on battleship building and to conceal its true intentions. He also attributed to Admiralty technicians an aversion to crediting Germany with progress in U-boat technology.[2]

This chapter tests Admiral Godfrey's contentions by reconstructing Admiralty technical intelligence analysis about German capital ships, cruisers, destroyers and U-boats from 1936 to 1939. It argues that historians, by accepting Admiral Godfrey's critique, have not appreciated the complexities involved in this process. Evidence from the Department of Naval Construction demonstrates that technical assessors performed better than has been previously acknowledged. Where errors in judgement occurred, they can be attributed to faults other than misconceptions generated by German deceit or by a dearth of reliable data.

Apart from correcting earlier accounts, a fresh look at these issues has two benefits. First, a reconstruction of capital ship intelligence illuminates the intricate balance of calculated risks underlying the Admiralty's battleship policy. It reveals how naval planners, confronted with the dangerous predicament of maritime challenges from Germany, Japan and Italy, wagered on a combination of armaments diplomacy and the presumed qualitative supremacy of their own forces to formulate a victorious strategic scenario. Appreciating the features of this venture helps to render the Admiralty's attachment to the Naval Agreement with Germany after 1935 comprehensible. Second, the technical analysis of U-boats explains why the Royal Navy underrated the subsurface menace. Before proceeding, though, it is necessary to set out how the Admiralty's technical intelligence apparatus worked and what obstacles it encountered.

THE APPARATUS

In an era when mutual inspection to verify compliance with arms limitation treaties was universally regarded as an intolerable violation of sovereignty, the burden of vigilance within the Admiralty was shouldered by the DNI, the Director of Plans Division and the Director of Naval Construction (DNC). The technical and geographic sections of NID, which initially collated and provisionally analysed incoming information, circulated reports for assessment through the DNI, via Plans Division, to the DNC and then on to other relevant technical departments. If a report contained data about the ballistics of a potential opponent's guns, then the distribution list would include the Director of Naval Ordnance. Contingent on the scope of the report, therefore, the process could expand to encompass several technical and scientific departments. Nevertheless, surviving records indicate that technical intelligence analysis was coherent and well co-ordinated. Routinely, the DNI and Director of Plans deferred to the counsel of the DNC and other experts on complex technical questions.

The technical intelligence apparatus relied on both covert and overt sources. Although the records of the former will remain closed to historians until the archives of the SIS become available, it is still possible to identify some of Britain's technical espionage successes. As noted, Dr Otto Krueger, a consulting marine engineer at Kiel, was a precious source on U-boats. Two similarly well placed agents in Washington and Tokyo delivered intelligence about the US Navy's advances in anti-aircraft target acquisition systems, the results of American bomb and torpedo aircraft attack experiments[3] and details about Japanese torpedoes.[4]

The Admiralty's primary sources of technical intelligence, however, were less sensational than espionage. The international system of reciprocal visits to warships and naval installations by naval attachés, and courtesy visits by warships to foreign ports, presented opportunities for visual inspection. Not only could the length, beam and number of guns and their calibre be checked on sight; a trained observer could even formulate judgements about a warship's stability and sea-keeping qualities.[5] The Royal Navy itself was part of the overt intelligence-gathering network. Although they were cautioned to avoid exposing the service to accusations of systematic spying, officers at sea exploited every occasion to acquire information requested by periodic NID questionnaires.[6]

In February 1937, for example, the intelligence officer of the cruiser *Guardian* produced a composite photograph, taken unnoticed through the ship's scuttles, of the 10 000-ton *Panzerschiff Deutschland* while it was berthed nearby at Gibraltar. Studies of the composite photo led the Director of Naval Ordnance to alter estimates of the maximum and minimum elevations of the ship's secondary batteries and to revise the accepted figure for its normal deep water draught.[7] Two months later, analysis of the damage inflicted on the *Deutschland* by Spanish government bombers added considerably to the Admiralty's knowledge about its protective scheme.[8] Modest data like this, progressively accumulated, eventually congealed into warship profiles, valuable for tactical decision-making: such as approximating the navigational limitations of a potential combatant or determining what depth to set torpedoes for greatest effect.[9]

Although most naval technical intelligence work was gradual, laborious and mundane, one intelligence bonanza occurred in the summer of 1936 when the Italian cruiser *Gorizia*, damaged off the coast of Spain during a storm, had to dock at Gibraltar for repairs. The 1922 Washington Naval Treaty set a size and gun-power limit for cruisers of 10 000 tons and 8 inches. Since Italy was a party to the Treaty, the *Gorizia* should have conformed to this standard. In 1927, when Mussolini's heavy cruiser programme began, an Italian engineer told the British naval attaché in Rome that they were all 1000 tons over the limit, but proof was elusive. During the repairs in August 1936, however, the British dockyard engineers secured limited access to the cruiser's drawings, accurately measured its draughts and estimated the thickness of its armour and the weight of its unloaded stores.[10] By December, calculations made by the DNC, based on these measurements, established that *Gorizia* was 1000 tons overweight.[11]

The *Gorizia* episode, however, was an exceptional opportunity to put a theory about a naval deception to a swift empirical test. In the mid-1930s, the fundamental predicament for the Admiralty, particularly concerning the renascent German surface fleet, was how to discover the characteristics and fighting qualities of warships not yet built. Empiricism was impossible. To arrive at judgements (where espionage failed) about vessels that existed only as ideas in the minds of those who had ordered and designed them, or as partially assembled hulks on shielded slipways, the British relied on official treaty data. To reduce mistrust, the 1922 Washington and 1930 London Naval Treaties bound the signatories to declare the principal specifications of every new warship laid down: namely, standard displacement, length, beam, draught and the calibre of the main batteries. Evaluation of these data, however, was not a purely abstract exercise. Since all warship designers had to balance the distribution of weight between several desirable attributes – mainly hitting power, speed and protection – within particular dimensions, the DNC applied the weights of British ordnance, fire control apparatus and machinery, as well as known foreign design practices, as guides to probe foreign warship configurations.

The problem of obtaining empirical evidence was not the only obstacle to accurate appraisal. In the minds of the assessors, the terminology used to describe warship characteristics, with the exception of standard displacement,[12] was sufficiently ambiguous to prevent warship comparison from becoming a science. As a November 1937 Plans Division memorandum explained, how foreign navies estimated 'speed' and 'gun power' was problematic. It described the Italian practice of running their warships at maximum power under unusually favourable trial conditions, for instance, to obtain impressive speeds for transmission to the other powers. In contrast, the British custom of calculating speed from designed horsepower underrated potential top machinery performance under operational conditions. Determining the relative gun power of comparable ships was also a source of ambiguity. A cruiser like USS *Wichita*, with three triple 8-inch turrets, appeared to outgun the HMS *Norfolk* which mounted only eight guns in four turrets; yet, the planner confided, the large 'spreads', characteristic of the unwieldy and tightly packed American triple mountings, nullified any advantage gained by the extra gun.[13]

Both the lack of a swift empirical test to verify the claims of foreign powers and the ambiguity of the terminology used to describe warship performance, created considerable scope for conjecture. Consequently, when the Admiralty began to evaluate German capital ships and to consider the characteristics of their own vessels from 1936 onwards, self-images entertained in the minds of senior policy-makers – that is, how they viewed the Royal Navy's strengths and capabilities *vis-à-vis* its potential opponents – significantly influenced decision-making.

CAPITAL SHIPS

As we have seen in earlier chapters, despite the June 1935 Naval Agreement, Admiral Raeder harboured blue-water ambitions of Tirpitzian proportions. He regarded the 1935 accord as a temporary measure to be abandoned once the 35 per cent tonnage ratio became unworkable.

Moreover, Hitler had made it clear that German warships should be qualitatively superior to their foreign counterparts.[14] It is hardly surprising, therefore, that the German C-in-C Navy did not permit treaty obligations to impair the fighting power of his ships. To maintain the fiction of treaty compliance, however, spurious technical data were sent to London. Admiral Godfrey argued that this ruse 'hoodwinked' the technical assessors, who accepted the enticingly concrete German data, and misled senior officers, who took refuge from the unpalatable possibility that Nazi Germany might be cheating in technical equivocations. The deception stifled NID suspicion, adversely influenced the design of British battleships, which conformed to treaty standards, and supported the comfortable delusion that the German fleet was directed solely against Soviet Russia in the Baltic Sea.[15]

The record, however, does not support Godfrey. From 1936 to 1939, the technical assessors acknowledged a gap between the image that the declared German data was intended to project and the reality they imagined. This is particularly true about their estimate of the *Scharnhorst* and *Gneisenau*. In November 1935, the first official report appeared to confirm the NID conviction that they were replies to the two French 26 500-ton *Dunkerque* class battlecruisers.[16] But the declared 26 000-ton displacement for *Scharnhorst* and *Gneisenau* fell short of the 30 000 tons NID had predicted in March 1935,[17] and their 11-inch guns were outweighed and outranged by the 13-inch gun batteries of the two French ships. Admiral Raeder's apparent failure to achieve his goal of equality in armaments, particularly *vis-à-vis* the French, left the Admiralty suspicious about their ultimate characteristics.

In late 1936, reliable intelligence indicated that the two German ships were built to permit the ready interchange of their inferior main battery for 13.8-inch gun turrets.[18] Stanley V. Goodall, the DNC from July 1936 to 1944, ordered the calculation of a ship's legend – a list of a vessel's specifications, including the weights of the armour protection, ordnance, and machinery – and drafting of alternative drawings of the German battlecruisers to evaluate their design and to investigate the feasibility of swapping turrets.[19] His subordinates found that 700 tons of the additional 1200 tons displacement required for the installation of three triple 13.8-inch gun turrets must already be built into their frame.[20] Although the calculations made by Goodall's constructors were incorrect (they assumed 26 000 tons, not the true 31 800 tons), the intelligence about the intended 13.8-inch gun turrets was reliable. Raeder was planning to upgrade the guns once the second generation of German battleships had cleared the slipways.[21]

The accurate intelligence about the guns of *Scharnhorst* and *Gneisenau*, however, had a negative influence on a different puzzle. In February 1936, Goodall noticed that the beams and draughts of the second and third *Panzerschiffe*, *Admiral Scheer* and *Admiral Graf Spee*, had increased and decreased, respectively.[22] It struck him as a mystery. Small variations in the dimensions of ships of the same class were not unusual but, in this case, there appeared to be no obvious explanation. A combination of technical and tactical analysis, however, appears to have solved the problem. The building of the *Dunkerque* class battlecruisers effectively checked the deployment of the *Panzerschiffe* against French convoys transporting reinforcements from North Africa to the Western Front in any future Franco-German war. Considering the reliable knowledge about the interchangeable guns of *Scharnhorst* and *Gneisenau*, the assessors presumed that *Admiral Scheer* and *Admiral Graf Spee* would also eventually mount 13.8-inch guns.[23]

In reality, the different dimensions of the second and third *Panzerschiffe* stemmed from the installation of larger machinery and additional armour for increased speed and protection.[24] The declaration of bogus figures for the draughts cloaked the 20 per cent violation of the 10 000 ton limit. Yet the inherent plausibility of the interchangeable-turret explanation, based on reliable intelligence, and the issue's minor strategic significance arrested further enquiry. Indeed, the hypothesis persisted into the war.[25] Still, the detection of *Scharnhorst* and *Gneisenau*'s interchangeable turrets and the application of that discovery to the *Panzerschiffe* demonstrates that, even in the early phase of the process, the technical assessors approached the information furnished by Berlin critically.

The evidence also challenges Godfrey's argument that technical appraisal misled Admiralty planners about German strategy. At the end of 1936, a technical study of the likely speed of the *Scharnhorst* and *Gneisenau* reinforced accumulating strategic intelligence about the German navy's 'offensive' doctrine. In January 1937, Admiral Chatfield correctly concluded that German strategists would not repeat the error of the 1914–18 war of remaining on the defensive; instead, they would immediately send their battlecruisers into the Atlantic against British trade.[26] The technical study determined the two ships to be eminently suited to that role. Working without official German data about speed and engine power, the DNC's staff estimated the probable engine capacity to be about 100 000 horse power, generating a maximum speed of at least 30 knots (1.5 knots short of the correct figure).[27] Unlike the relatively slow 28 knot *Panzerschiffe*, even the Royal Navy's three fast battlecruisers would have difficulty in overtaking and compelling *Scharnhorst* and

Gneisenau into combat. Moreover, intelligence that German capital ships were propelled by advanced high-temperature, high-pressure steam machinery, which approached the efficiency of the unique diesel plants installed in the *Panzerschiffe*, indicated that they would have high fuel economy and thus the wide cruising radius necessary for offensive operations. Consequently, studies made in Plans Division of German naval strategy correctly credited German capital ships with ample endurance for aggressive Atlantic sorties against British commerce.[28]

Even the initial appraisal of the 35 000 ton *Bismarck* revealed the German navy's desire to employ its capital ships offensively. When the official German note about its characteristics arrived in the Admiralty on 1 July 1936,[29] Goodall was struck by its great length, broad beam and shallow draught.[30] The waterline length, he noted, would permit efficient power to speed ratios at full power, but penalise the vessel at cruising speeds. He correctly estimated a top speed of 28–30 knots, which would be useful for evading the Royal Navy on commerce-destroying raids into the Atlantic. As to the other two dimensions, Goodall, a member of the team that dissected the High Seas Fleet's most advanced design after the war, knew how Imperial Germany had exploited its advantage in large docks to build broad battleships.[31] A wide beam was a great advantage for stability, important for effective gunnery; a slight draught was practical in the Baltic's shallow approaches. Captain Tom Phillips, the Director of Plans Division, perceived the *Bismarck*'s wide beam as a sensible continuation of the prewar practice. The draught also suggested to him that the German navy was 'looking towards the Baltic [that is, Russia] more than in the past'.[32] Historians have mistakenly followed Godfrey in citing this assertion in isolation as evidence that the Admiralty inferred from *Bismarck*'s reported draft that German maritime aspirations were confined to the Baltic. But Phillips's inference must be viewed within the entire technical analysis. Collectively, Goodall's estimate of *Bismarck*'s speed, the known efficiency of German machinery and the reported draft informed Admiralty planners that German strategists desired a 35 000-ton ship suitable for checking Russia in the Baltic and capable of striking Britain's Atlantic traffic. Even with these offensive and defensive design features in mind, the reported dimensions appeared to Goodall as an extraordinary stretch on a 35 000-ton displacement.[33] Without knowledge of the number and type of gun turrets, the designed horsepower and speed, and the other details exchanged under the 1936 London Naval Treaty, however, his technical appreciation could go no further.[34]

Of course the peculiarity of *Bismarck*'s dimensions perceived by Goodall was the result of a falsehood. The German navy's Construction

Office, true believers in heavy protection and high stability, informed Raeder in December 1934 that they could not build a well-balanced battleship armed with the anticipated 14-inch gun treaty maximum on a standard displacement of less than 37 200 tons. In January 1935, it was decided to achieve optimal fighting capacity by disregarding treaty displacement. As the design was thrashed out, the weight steadily grew. By the spring, Raeder had approved sketch drawings for a 42 000-ton battleship capable of 28–30 knots and mounting eight 15-inch guns. Since the length and beam could not be hidden from foreign observers, the official dimensions, to conceal the excess displacement, listed a phoney draught, well below the true figure.[35]

Goodall followed up his curiosity about *Bismarck* by requesting from Admiral James Troup, the DNI from 1935 to 1939, intelligence that might explain its curious proportions. There were no immediate results. Not only was secret intelligence unavailable, but, as we saw in Chapter 2, the second round of Anglo-German naval negotiations, which were intended to bring Germany into the 1936 London Naval Treaty rules for information exchange, were bogged down in tedious bargaining until July 1937. Nonetheless, during the interval, and despite the paucity of data, suspicion within the Admiralty about German shipbuilding persisted.

In late 1936, after he had personally calculated the displacement of the Italian heavy cruiser *Gorizia*, Goodall's general misgivings increased due to the implications of the Italian deception. On his instructions, Goodall's constructors worked out what they could do if the Royal Navy cheated on cruiser displacements.[36] They found that 1000 extra tons would double weight available for armour protection.[37] While policy-makers grappled with what to do about this discovery, the Russians made accusations about Raeder's capital ships. In March 1937, Ivan Maisky, the Russian Ambassador, informed Eden, the Foreign Secretary, that Soviet Intelligence had 'disquieting information as to what Germany was doing in regards to the design and character of the ships which had either already been built or were at present under construction'.[38] Captain Phillips reacted by urging the FO to press Maisky for details. 'Any suspicions or definite information that we may acquire from the Russians', he wrote, 'may be of use to us in checking other sources of information.'[39]

The information the Soviets provided in the summer of 1937 intensified the ongoing technical debate.[40] It is evident from Goodall's diaries, though, that Moscow supplied concrete intelligence only about the true size of *Scharnhorst* and *Gneisenau*, not about *Bismarck*. Hence Goodall focused his scepticism on the battlecruisers, but suspended his judgement about the German battleships. The question was raised at an NID meeting.

The head of the German section, Commander C. Swinley, probably with the Soviet allegations in mind, distrusted the official German data. But the head of technical section, Commander J. Charley, like the DNC, required empirical proof before accepting that any German ship ordered after *Deutschland* 'substantially' exceeded treaty standards. Admiral Troup agreed with his technicians.[41]

In July, Captain Phillips devised a method of measuring the displacement of foreign battleships by a weight coefficient. He took the products of the lengths, beams and draughts of the British and foreign battleships as denominators under the known and unknown displacement and then solved the equation for the unknown displacement. According to the results, the Italians, the Germans and the French were all cheating on their 35 000-ton designs by about 3000 tons.[42] Unlike the evidence about *Gorizia*, however, Phillips's coefficient was too crude to warrant official protests, nor was it necessarily a sign of duplicity. As Goodall explained on 5 August, a three to five per cent error in design displacement was an acceptable tolerance, particularly since foreign constructors, unlike their British counterparts, were not 'meticulously accurate'. For the 35 000-ton ships under construction in Europe, he thus recommended that they accept a displacement of 36 000 tons.[43]

At first glance, considering the peril, the reaction within the Admiralty to the Soviet allegations, Commander Swinley's misgivings and the results of Phillips's displacement coefficient appears remarkably stoical. To understand this stoicism at the technical level, it is necessary to peruse the self-images entertained in the minds of the senior policy-makers about the qualitative superiority of British naval architecture and construction, combined with the undiminished legacy of Admiral 'Jackie' Fisher's battlecruisers.[44]

An Admiralty paper in October 1937, written to calm FO anxiety about Italy's intention to build four fast 30-knot battleships with 15-inch guns, against Britain's five 28-knot *King George V* class ships with ten 14-inch guns,[45] succinctly sets out the features of this self-image. It promised that 'the immense experience of our Naval constructors will ensure that the ships we build are fully the equal *in fighting power* of those built by other nations'.[46] 'Fighting power', not the base comparisons between speed and gun calibre, the planner explained, was the key. Like Raeder's constructors, the DNC had found it impossible to design a sufficiently protected ship armed with 15-inch guns on only 35 000 tons. The selection of 15-inch guns by the European powers (exempted from the 1936 London Naval Treaty) and the trend to high speed signalled to the British that their potential enemies had sacrificed protection for gun and engine power. The planner cited the battlecruiser engagement at Jutland between *Derfflinger* and *Queen Mary* to illustrate the danger of distorted configuration. Although the former had an inferior speed and gun calibre, the latter's deficient protection made it vulnerable and caused its destruction by the first enemy salvo. The 'well balanced' *King George V* class, however, were adequately protected against 15-inch shells, torpedoes and 'any' form of attack by aircraft 'yet' foreseen, and the high rate of fire from their 14-inch guns would compensate for the lighter projectiles. 'If foreign nations exceed 35,000 tons then [their] new ships *may* be better fighting machines than ours,' the paper concluded: 'if they stick to treaty limits they are *unlikely* to produce a better article than we can [my italics].'[47]

In the 1930s, the Admiralty's conviction that, in a future European conflict, the new generation of British battleships would play the *Derfflinger*s to their potential opponent's *Queen Mary*s, blended with the confidence in the qualitative supremacy of British design and construction, even if other states were violating treaty limits by several thousand tons, was a powerful brew. The mixture originated primarily, but not exclusively, in the shared formative experiences of two of the leading personalities involved in warship design: the DNC and the CNS. Both Goodall and Chatfield participated in the post-mortem examination of the German High Seas Fleet conducted by the Institution of Naval Architects in the spring of 1921. At that conference, Sir Eustance T. D'Eyncourt, the then DNC, and his junior, Goodall, responding to their vociferous wartime critics, presented papers which celebrated the qualitative supremacy (significantly, in all but battlecruiser protection and diesel engines) of British naval *matériel*. The ex-German battleship *Baden*, their most advanced design, was labelled an 'inferior copy' of the *Queen Elizabeth* class. Chatfield summed up the general tenor of the discussion when he said 'we have little to learn from our late foe'.[48] The immodesty of the victorious aside, the legacy of the defeat of Tirpitz's fleet was to vindicate the belief that the nation that had produced Nelson could and would always lead the way in naval armaments. Goodall's enormous capacity for work, his exceptional talent as a naval architect and his meteoric rise to DNC[49] ensured that this ethos animated British warship design. Indeed, even after learning the true details of *Bismarck* in 1942, Goodall staunchly maintained that it was little more than an improved *Baden*, while the *King George V* exemplified advanced design.[50]

For Chatfield, combat in the North Sea was not just the second-hand observation of a naval constructor, but a profound career-defining experience. As Admiral Beatty's Flag Captain in the battlecruiser squadron at

Jutland, his own ship, the *Lion*, in the same class as *Queen Mary*, had narrowly escaped a similar fate.[51] Between the wars, the threat to the decks and undersides of battleships from plunging gun fire and air attack with bombs and torpedoes, and his staunch defence of the survivability of battleships in the face of that threat and against its critics,[52] reified his early impressions. In October 1935, Chatfield, now the chief naval advisor to the Cabinet, assuaged Prime Minister Baldwin's fears about Germany outgunning the Royal Navy with 15-inch turrets to the British 14-inch by declaring that the 'gun was asserting itself over armour and therefore you needed better protection'.[53] During his tenure as CNS, like Fisher before him, he was determined to take his 'share of the responsibility for design'.[54] 'Given a good ship, that will not be destroyed by a lucky blow,' Chatfield affirmed, 'we will always win.' In March 1936, therefore, he induced the other Sea Lords to reject the penultimate design of the *King George V* in favour of a heavier armoured version. 'I came away feeling sad,' Goodall wrote in his diary that day, '... I still think the pendulum has swung too far away from Jackie Fisher's poorly protected ships.'[55]

The intensity of this self-image, or more precisely the value of it, even after 15 years, is understandable. The Admiralty, with the renewal of battleship building in the mid-1930s, perceived themselves to be engaging in a dangerous exercise akin to what game theorists have dubbed the 'prisoner's dilemma'. Just as the imagined crime suspects are confronted with either co-operation or non-cooperation,[56] each naval power had to choose between sticking to the treaty clauses and optimising their designs within the limits, or cheating and obtaining an advantage in battleship quality. Anxiety that some of the powers might cheat coexisted by necessity in the minds of senior naval staff officers with the knowledge that the entire edifice of the treaty system ultimately rested upon the good faith of the signatories. Hence, bearing in mind the five to six years it took to produce a battleship, and the enormous difficulties of altering production once it was set into motion, it was absolutely crucial to make the right decisions about design and fighting characteristics long before the technical intelligence machinery could ever *feasibly* deliver conclusive discoveries about rivals.[57] Certainty about British qualitative supremacy not only reduced the inherent risk of this venture in the minds of the senior decision-makers, but it was also a prerequisite to entering into the game. And clearly, the possibility of cheating by some states within limits was considered better than a costly escalation in battleship fighting power without limits.[58]

Despite all this, the Admiralty remained vigilant. While Plans Division drafted memos in late 1937 about the unmatched excellence of British *matériel*, the DNC collated the Soviet intelligence to ponder whether

Admiral Raeder was deliberately cheating. The focus of his attention was the intelligence accumulated about *Scharnhorst* and *Gneisenau*. The details of how his incisive mind deciphered the conflicting dimensions, attempted to account for them, reflected upon the Soviet data and eventually penetrated beyond the German deception is unclear. Goodall's diary entry for 2 November 1937, however, records the result: 'I believe the Hun is cheating.'[59]

The assembly of *Scharnhorst* and *Gneisenau* had begun before German warship building above 10 000 tons was legal. Consequently, and partly because of the interchangeable turrets thesis, the assessors always viewed the two German battlecruisers with suspicion. This suspicion, and the self-image described above, absorbed the impact of Goodall's discovery. Opinion probably remained divided about whether the evidence revealed systematic cheating or an isolated violation to compensate for an inadequate design. Still, for promulgation in fleet reference books, the horsepower and speed of the German battlecruisers were raised to the quite accurate figures of 150 000 horsepower and 32 knots, suggesting a greater machinery weight and a larger displacement.[60]

The Admiralty's preoccupation with foreign and defence policy considerations – which will be explored closely in the penultimate chapter – adds another layer of explanation to its stoical response to German and Italian treaty transgressions. Attempts to formulate a policy in the *Gorizia* case were derailed by the priority of pulling the Italians out of the German orbit. The Admiralty advised the CID that it served the ends of naval armaments diplomacy better to impress the Italians with the British intelligence discovery only after Mussolini had signed up to the 1936 London Naval Treaty.[61] In contrast, the Naval Staff did not inform the CID of Goodall's discovery about the German tonnage deception on the *Scharnhorst* and *Gneisenau*. Earlier, Craigie had argued that the *Gorizia* episode proved how difficult it was to cheat without detection. He speculated that the excess tonnage probably stemmed from shoddy construction and a cover-up by the Italian naval authorities.[62] In all likelihood, the CNS rationalised Goodall's discovery on similar grounds. Further, Chatfield probably feared that if Goodall's findings were reported to the Cabinet, then it could be exploited at every turn by the FO to destroy his case for the Naval Agreements. In fact, as late as April 1939, he told the CID that despite patent prevarication about the size of the *Luftwaffe*, technical information supplied by Berlin about its navy 'invariably proved to be correct'.[63]

On 4 December 1937, Germany communicated under the 1936 Treaty rules for technical exchange the designed speed and horsepower of its capital ships.[64] For *Bismarck* and its twin *Tirpitz* (42 900 tons), it listed a maximum of only 26 knots and 80 000 horsepower (the true figures were 30 knots and 160 000 horsepower). In a minute to his colleagues, G. G. Fitzmaurice, the legal advisor to the naval negotiations, who had worked closely with the naval planners during the Anglo-German talks, paraded his knowledge of the Admiralty design doctrine. 'It is evident,' he wrote, 'that the Germans, in the matter of 35 000 ton battleships, are refusing to be lured by the will-o'-the-wisp of excessive speed, and the deduction is that they are devoting the weight and space saved to additional armour protection.'[65] But the data about the battlecruisers was puzzling. Fitzmaurice wondered how *Scharnhorst* and *Gneisenau* could possibly perform their role with a speed of only 27 knots. Were they not outclassed by the French 29.5-knot *Dunkerque* battlecruisers, as well as the 28-knot *King George V* battleships? A request was sent to Plans Division for an explanation.[66]

At the Admiralty, the same questions were already being asked. On 18 January 1938, Admiral Troup enumerated for Phillips and the technical departments the important features of the German communication that were at variance with the expectations cultivated by two years of Goodall's technical analysis. For *Scharnhorst* and *Gneisenau*, the reported horsepower was 80 000, 47 per cent less than anticipated, generating 5 knots below the 32 knots the DNC predicted in November 1937. As for *Bismarck*, the official German report challenged Goodall's July 1937 supposition that the reported length revealed a desire for efficient machinery performance at high speeds.[67]

Enquiry into these discrepancies continued in early 1938. Evidence about warship construction delays in Germany and increased British rearmament, however, drew Goodall's attention away from the issue. The FO's query went unanswered. In mid-March, to close their file, they prodded Commander L. H. Bell of Plans Division by telephone. He said that they had 'no views to express'.[68] Despite their reticence, however, the planners did not alter strategic appreciations premised on high speeds and large cruising ranges for German capital ships.[69] And Chatfield, as late as July 1939, continued to cite correctly *Bismarck*'s speed to be 28–30 knots.[70]

The crisis over Hitler's diplomatic offensive against Czechoslovakia in September 1938 injected renewed urgency into solving the riddles of German capital ships. Since at least one of the two German battlecruisers might be ready for war, Admiral Troup again interrogated Goodall about their top speed. In reply, the DNC presented the full range of possibilities postulated by his earlier studies. If they accepted the German specifications, then the two ships steamed at about 27.5 knots maximum under operational conditions. Under trial conditions, at standard displacement, they might have attained speeds between 28.5 and 29 knots. To outpace the Royal Navy's three battlecruisers by surpassing the 30-knot hurdle, however, his original estimate of approximately 160 000 horsepower engines in *Scharnhorst* and *Gneisenau* would have to be correct.[71]

During the final phase of the Admiralty's technical analysis of German battleships, from the Czechoslovakian crisis to war, the issues examined since 1936 remained unresolved. Concerning the speed of the *Scharnhorst* and *Gneisenau*, Goodall's subordinates, after further dissection in late 1938, supported his estimate that the reported horsepower was too low, but not as high as he had calculated in November 1937.[72] Mixed evidence about *Bismarck* continued to surface. Shortly after its launch in February 1939, observations of the new ship in the water provided the first empirical clue to its real size. The British Vice-Consul in Hamburg reported that it was 'drawing a good deal more than she should'.[73] The German decision to mount eight 15-inch guns in four turrets, however, instead of concentrating them into three triple turrets, to save weight for armour, was yet another sign of poor protection. Goodall was particularly unimpressed with the four inches of horizontal protection provided by its two armoured decks.[74] Photographs obtained in January 1940, though, confirmed his judgement about *Bismarck*'s high speed.[75] Evaluation of the declared German data of their second generation of battleships, designated H and J, the 56 000-ton behemoths with which Raeder intended to settle 'the British question conclusively', left Stanley Goodall utterly perplexed.[76] Just like his reaction to *Bismarck*'s official proportions, the true length and beam of H and J on the falsely declared displacement of 40 000 tons, appeared 'contrary to all our ideas' about battleship design.[77]

It was during this final stage of the process that Godfrey assumed the post as DNI and formed his views about the accomplishments of his predecessors. It is hardly surprising that his views were critical. In 1939, the intelligence requirements of Britain's defence machinery shifted from a conjectural posture for planning purposes to an appetite for operational intelligence and strategic warning. To operate under these circumstances with the cupboard of tentative analysis the new DNI inherited, particularly under the arduous demands of a new First Lord, Winston Churchill, must have been frustrating.

However, the prewar performance of naval technical intelligence was not as culpable as Godfrey recalled. Except for the *Panzerschiffe*, the Royal Navy had little contact with Raeder's new capital ships before 1939.

Without an empirical test of German veracity, the technical assessors approached official German data sceptically, often arrived at the correct deduction from it, and used conflicting intelligence from covert sources profitably. Senior policy-makers appreciated the gamble of relying on other powers to play the game honestly. The DNC even discovered that likely foes were taking liberties with the rules. Yet design decisions had to be made long before technical intelligence could *feasibly* become a reliable guide. What made the risk worthwhile for Admiral Chatfield and his staff was the conviction that the Royal Navy acquired a singular advantage from qualitative limitation because they could design and construct superior warships within any given set of balanced specifications, so long as the other powers built their ships reasonably close to the treaty standards.

CRUISERS AND DESTROYERS

The appraisal of German cruiser and destroyer designs from 1936 to 1939 is significant because it supported the Admiralty's assumption that Admiral Raeder's desire for rapid 'production' had resulted in inferior workmanship and design.[78] In turn, this conviction upheld the self-images about British design supremacy evident in the technical analysis of Nazi Germany's capital ships.

In many respects, in the study of cruisers and destroyers, the Admiralty assumption was right on the mark. NID, for instance. knew about the persistent boiler troubles that plagued destroyer production.[79] The installation of advanced high-temperature, high-pressure steam turbines in both destroyers and cruisers before obtaining any operational experience resulted in chronic breakdowns and exceptionally long repair times during the war.[80] Goodall's criticisms of German destroyer design, especially the lack of structural strength, would have found sympathisers across the North Sea.[81] Ironically, an oversight by the British may have contributed to their poor design. The drafters of the Naval Agreement failed to stipulate, as they had in the second London Naval Treaty, that vessels of over 1500 tons could only take up 16 per cent of the total destroyer tonnage.[82] The German Naval Command, therefore, did not hesitate to expend all of their allotted tonnage on vessels of the maximum size. And, to elevate these large destroyers to the status of light cruisers, the German navy crammed in every bit of fighting power possible; but this design policy ultimately spoiled their operational performance as either cruisers or destroyers.[83]

Although systematic cheating on cruiser and destroyer displacements by the German navy went undetected, this did not impair the Naval Staff's perception of their intended wartime mission as commerce raiders. But contacts with Germany's pre-1935 light cruisers in Spanish waters exposed their inadequacies for this mission: a fact quite readily admitted by German naval officers.[84] The slow production of the post-1935 cruiser types, and the 1939 construction start dates for the fast 7800-ton Type-M mercantile attack ships called for by the Z-Plan, obviously limited the Admiralty's scope for first-hand technical appraisal.[85]

U-BOATS

The appraisal of U-boats presented an entirely different problem to the technical assessors. Submarines were not built to engage other submarines; they were isolated from the dynamics of competitive building that virtually dictated surface warship characteristics. The 1936 London Naval Treaty stipulated that the maximum size of submarines was to be 2000 tons with 5.1-inch guns, but the danger was not that Germany might cheat on the weight of individual submarines, but on numbers.

Thanks to Dr Otto Krueger, the former German naval officer turned SIS informant, this was not initially a major anxiety.[86] His steady supply of reliable intelligence on Inkavos and later as a consulting engineer at Kiel served to authenticate the claims of the official German U-boat programme. Consequently, the central issue for the technical intelligence apparatus was the quality of the new German submarines. In this respect, Godfrey was correct in arguing that the DNC and his colleagues were averse to crediting German marine engineers with developing a technical innovation before his own constructors had successfully done so.[87]

It is impossible to separate the assessment of U-boat quality from the parallel analysis of their method of production. From the start, knowledge about German industrial mobilisation plans decisively influenced the technical appraisal. The brief period from the initial detection of U-boat assembly on 9 April 1935 to the first commissioning only six weeks later shocked the Admiralty. In the summer of 1935, the DNC and NID became convinced that German constructors, applying the principle of mass production, had built the first U-boats by connecting on the slipways prefabricated sections from inland factories.[88]

In early 1936, Krueger corroborated this judgement. He transmitted through the SIS network in Holland the details of the German navy's submarine mobilisation plan. The IIC, responsible for estimating the war potential of foreign economies, immediately circulated his report to NID with only preliminary observations. It described how select squads of workers, already numbering 4000, but with a target figure of 13 000, were being intensively trained in 'drills' to complete swiftly what were normally complex and time-consuming tasks. The plan was to employ this method at six shipyards, 24 hours a day, to a maximum output of one unit every 100 working hours. At that rate, and recalling U-boat production in 1917, the IIC analyst considered a frequency of seven launchings per month or 87 annually was not at all 'fantastic'.[89]

The staff in the German navy's Office for Construction Mobilisation Planning (*Amt für Rüstung und Wehrwirtschaft*) agreed. The 1936 emergency plan they drafted called for the manufacture of four large and four small U-boats per month, but only after the first 15 months of war. During the initial phase, the German planners anticipated fabricating only 37 boats, mostly the small 250-ton type. Neither Krueger's intelligence, nor the IIC's analysis, however, acknowledged this inevitable gap between instituting a large-scale industrial enterprise and achieving maximum output. The error, which led the Admiralty to overestimate U-boat production after September 1938, resulted partly from the indelible impression created by the quick fabrication of the first submarines (entirely the result of the protracted period of preparation and the delayed decision to go on to final assembly), and partly from the ill-conceived stereotypes about German efficiency.[90] NID later compounded the misjudgement by adding that the German navy could undertake the mass training of U-boat crews by 1938.[91]

The belief in a latent German capacity for the sudden mass production of U-boats became an Admiralty orthodoxy. However beneficial this knowledge may have been to British naval planners, it was accompanied by an even more significant deduction from Krueger's intelligence. The mass production of complex machines, by definition, meant the fabrication in large quantities of standardised models. If the German navy had taken up the principle of mass production to U-boat construction, then German submariners would be forced to commit themselves to a few standard U-boat designs.[92] The questions for the technical assessors were what types would the German navy adopt and what combat quality would they have?

The large dossier of Krueger's intelligence about the activities of Inkavos provided the answer to the first question.[93] Even though they now had the freedom to embark on the manufacture of novel types, the official reports from Berlin between July and November 1935 signalled the decision to continue with the three designs covertly evolved by Inkavos in Spain, Finland

and Holland before 1935: namely, the 250-ton training and coastal defence boats and the larger 500- and 700-ton vessels for overseas and fleet operations.[94]

Once it was established what types Admiral Raeder had decided to rely upon, the technical intelligence apparatus transferred its attention to considering their quality. The first available evidence about the German navy's evaluation of their new U-boats demonstrated a resolve to construct tough but not revolutionary designs. Reports that the German navy had gone as far as depth-charging four 250-ton submarines to test their high pressure hulls fascinated Goodall.[95] Although little was known about the important Baltic trials of the newly launched 500-ton Type VII and 712-ton Type I boats in the summer of 1936,[96] German treaty notifications fortified the theory of reliance on standard types.

In May 1936, the German decision to build additional 250-ton boats (substantiating NID's thesis about mass training) and their determination to press on with four more 500-ton Type VII U-boats before operational experience had been gained with the first six, surprised Admiral Troup.[97] The German Naval Command's U-boat strategy became clear to the Admiralty's technical assessors: the potential quality of the new U-boat arm was being sacrificed to the dictates of mass production. Rather than pioneering revolutionary prototypes by years of experimentation, time, money and resources were being expended to put into place the industrial infrastructure necessary to fabricate large quantities of merely adequate types.[98] Once that fixed infrastructure was in place, it would be extremely difficult to introduce novel designs without jeopardising the output of large numbers. Like the Ford Motor Company, which was rolling millions of identical Model Ts off its Detroit assembly lines, the technical assessors imagined that the German navy planned to mass produce in wartime hundreds of standardised U-boats. These boats would be tough and reliable, but they would not be revolutionary victory-winning machines. Indeed, it surprised Goodall that German naval strategists had decided so readily to invest in the plant required to produce the existing models. In November 1935, a technical analysis of the three current types concluded that 'antisubmarine measures since the war has had little effect on German ideas … th new German submarines show but a slight advance on those of the [1914–18] period'.[99] In the summer of 1936, therefore, Goodall summed up NID's official appraisal of the U-boat menace as 'Don't worry they're rotten' submarines.[100]

While the Admiralty attempted to evaluate the quality of the renascent U-boat fleet, Captain Karl Dönitz, the recently appointed head of U-boats, was wrestling with the same problem. During the summer trials of 1936, he developed a preference for the medium 500-ton Type VII U-boat (the mainstay of his future Atlantic Campaign force). In his mind, it outperformed its larger 712-ton Type I cousin and was well suited to his innovative 'wolf-pack' tactics. The German Naval Command, however, which envisaged sustained operations against French troop transports in the Western Mediterranean, preferred the larger boat and pressed for the design of an improved 740-ton Type IX with a maximum range of about 13 000 miles. From 1936 onwards, during the tug-of-war between these two camps, Admiral Raeder proved indecisive, and sanctioned the construction of both an improved 500-ton Type VII, as Dönitz advocated, and the long-range 740-ton Type IX boats; but ultimately his conception of future maritime warfare compelled him to favour the larger cruiser type submarines and to authorise the production of a 2000-ton boat armed with 6-inch guns.[101]

The Admiralty's technical analysis that matched this struggle reflected an anxiety about the latter eventuality. The possibility of U-cruisers, with an enormous endurance and armed with both large calibre gun and torpedo armaments, suddenly and unexpectedly appearing in distant waters, destroying commerce and then moving on to another zone of operations – like the famous surface raider *Emden* but submersible – vexed the minds of Admiralty planners. In the 1920s, they had been conditioned to expect German constructors to move in this direction by intelligence about plans for a 'submarine cruiser' capable of carrying eight to 16 aircraft or a large mine-layer armed with a 6-inch gun.[102] In 1935–6, Krueger and other sources had reported rumours about plans for large U-boats of 1000 to 1550 tons, but no corroborating evidence ever emerged.[103] The 712-ton Type I design, however, with its reported surface endurance of 12 500 miles at 10 knots,[104] was probably perceived to be a precursor to U-cruisers. Still, although there were features of the new U-boats that were considered 'dangerous', Goodall wrote in October 1936 'that there was nothing outstanding in the design'.[105] In December, the introduction of the 740-ton Type IX aroused curiosity, but Krueger was unable to supply drawings of the boat until the summer of 1937, when Turkey placed an order for a variation of it through Inkavos.[106] In contrast to the concern about the largest U-boats, Dönitz's prize boats, the 500-ton Type VIIs, received passing attention. Unlike the relatively accurate appraisal of the 700-ton Type I and IX boats, the assessors grossly underestimated the endurance of the 500-ton Type VII.[107]

By the beginning of 1937, the thesis about Germany's reliance in wartime on the mass production of standard U-boat designs of second-rate quality was firmly entrenched. Captain Tom Troubridge, the British naval attaché in Berlin, reported Raeder's complete satisfaction with the experimental cruise to the Azores in February of one each of the 500-ton and 700-ton class boats. Moreover, as a result of his conversation with Raeder, he incorrectly dispelled any residual fears of Germany's development of a U-cruiser in the immediate future.[108] The 1937 trend in U-boat production and submariner training seemed to demarcate a period of consolidation. After a burst of rapid construction in 1935–6, only one U-boat launching took place in 1937 (the result of Raeder's procrastination over crucial construction decisions).[109] Limited slipway space was even turned over to foreign U-boat contracts from China, Turkey, Yugoslavia and Romania – all reported by Krueger well before official German notification.[110] It was also no secret that the twenty-four 250-ton U-boats were being used to train more crews than were required to man the existing fleet.[111]

The resilience of the standard-types thesis is demonstrated by the Admiralty's response to intelligence that Germany was actually revolutionising submarine design by developing a single-drive. Conventional submarines in the era of the two world wars – perhaps more appropriately classified as submersible torpedo boats – had divided propulsion systems. John Philip Holland, a radical Irish nationalist, invented the dual-drive system in the 1870s to sink British men-of-war for the Fenian Brotherhood. His 'Holland boat' was powered on the surface by an oxygen consuming combustion engine that also charged batteries for an electric motor to propel the vessels below the surface.[112] Obviously, limited engine space, plus the divided plant, resulted in inferior surface and subsurface speeds, and severely curbed the tactical effectiveness of early submarines. Despite considerable advances in diesel technology between the wars, submarines could neither keep up with fast surface forces nor could they manoeuvre quickly into favourable attack positions from patrol stations. Moreover, battery capacity hindered even their primary tactical advantage, remaining unseen when submerged.

The discovery of a single-drive would eliminate these handicaps. It would propel a vessel at great speeds above and below the surface and allow a submarine to remain submerged for longer periods than dual-drive models. Had this technology arrived on the eve of the Second World War, it might have revolutionised maritime warfare as the combination of large aircraft carriers and high performance torpedo-bombers actually did. Single-drive U-boats infesting the waters around the British Isles and the North Atlantic could have decisively cut the island's vulnerable sea lines of communication. Although a counterfactual from our standpoint, in the early 1930s this proposition was the fantasy of a gifted engineer working for the Germania Yard at Kiel, Professor Hellmuth Walter, who, like Philip Holland before him, aspired to undermine British sea power by technological innovation.[113]

During experiments on high-performance gas turbines, it occurred to Walter that it was feasible to construct a single diesel power plant for a U-boat that when submerged would obtain its oxygen in a closed cycle from the disintegration of hydrogen peroxide. In an October 1933 letter to the German Naval Command, he presented his idea. Despite scepticism about the immediate applicability of his theory, senior officers were impressed. At a time when U-boats ran at 8 knots below the surface, Walter had promised to create a 300-ton submarine with a subsurface speed of 30 knots. At the end of the year, they authorised plans for an experimental single-drive U-boat. However, although Walter's experiments had advanced sufficiently in 1936 to obtain his own research establishment at Kiel, the first contract for a single-drive U-boat was not issued until 1939.

The extent to which Krueger was personally familiar with Walter's work at Kiel is uncertain, but NID records demonstrate that the Admiralty was being kept informed. In July 1935, secret sources reported that four different institutions in the Third Reich were conducting experiments with single-drive motors employing hydrogen and oxygen as propellants, including the Germania Yard. Significantly, in March 1936, one intelligence informer confirmed that research was being carried out 'daily' at Kiel, and described the 'specially constructed' workshop where the trials with a prototype were taking place, and the fundamentals of how it worked.[114]

Secrecy of course was the hallmark of German rearmament, but experiments with closed-cycle diesel engines, although sensitive, were not treaty violations. It was a matter of international record that they had taken place in Germany during the decade before 1914.[115] And one German commercial firm, from November 1930 onwards, persistently sought to convince the Admiralty to purchase its experimental single-drive system – the so-called Erren motor.[116] The Erren motor, named after its German inventor, Rudolf A. Erren, was a closed-cycle internal combustion steam-engine operating on hydrogen. The Admiralty's technical and scientific experts, however, seriously doubted the feasibility of turning the Erren system into an operational method of submarine propulsion.[117] Undeterred in their efforts to persuade the Admiralty otherwise, Erren and his British business partners transferred the entire Erren Engineering Company from Berlin to London in 1933.[118]

To arrive at a considered judgement, the Admiralty set up in late 1936 a Submarine Propulsion Committee to examine the potential application of Erren's ideas, as well as the general question of new engine systems. In August 1938, it rejected the Erren design as unsuitable for technical reasons.[119] The committee's negative conclusion, therefore, appears to substantiate Admiral Godfrey's reproach of the Royal Navy's technical and scientific experts, although, in fairness, whether Erren could have matched, with the Admiralty's backing, the achievements of Walter's research programme remains an open question. Moreover, despite recurrent yet false rumours that the German navy had two 250-ton U-boats propelled by single-drives, intelligence from technically competent German sources invariably played down the immediate applicability of the embryonic technology. In fact, in July 1937, the Admiralty was not at all alarmed to discover from the Security Service (MI5) that Erren Engineering was in close touch with the German Naval Command.[120]

The Admiralty's confidence that the German navy was nowhere near a major technological breakthrough in U-boat propulsion, with or without the assistance of Erren Engineering, is confirmed by the DNC's reaction to press leaks about Nazi Germany's most secret submarine research. In a series of three articles in the *Daily Telegraph*, printed in September 1936, Hector C. Bywater, the former Great War naval intelligence agent turned naval correspondent,[121] who had broken the news about the assembly of the first six U-boats in April 1935, was doing the same with the story of Walter's research. Under the headline 'How Science May Reinforce a Sinister Weapon', he described how German engineers, 'after years of research and experiment', had foiled contemporary anti-submarine defences by developing a single-plant 'which is said to drive a submarine with equal facility on the surface and under water'. After recounting the near defeat U-boats had inflicted upon Britain in 1917, Bywater comforted his readers, and thereby undoubtedly revealed his source, 'that there is every reason to believe that our own naval authorities are fully informed of the new development, and are giving it their attention'.[122] Bywater was right. An incensed Goodall was giving the articles his full attention. The DNC complained bitterly about Bywater's 'rotten' articles to the Deputy DNI, Captain C. P. Hermon-Hodge. In response, Hermon-Hodge, responsible for Admiralty press liaison, contacted the *Daily Telegraph*'s editor to quash any further reporting of the single-drive.[123]

Goodall's reaction to the *Daily Telegraph* articles did not just stem from the obvious falsehoods: for instance, Bywater claimed that the existing

U-boat fleet had single-drive plants. Rather, the DNC, reflecting the prevailing Admiralty judgement founded on sound technical and industrial evidence, remained unshakeably convinced that the German naval strategists endorsed a submarine policy of the mass production of conventional designs and not a strategy of technological surprise.

CONSEQUENCES

The question remains of whether Chatfield's faith in British design supremacy was a sound hedge against German cheating. It is instructive that when Goodall calculated *Bismarck*'s true displacement in 1942, it was 'the size of the official German lie' that surprised him most. After comparing designs, he certainly would have welcomed the freedom German constructors had to improve the speed, endurance and underwater protection of *King George V*. Yet Goodall, and others since, have maintained that *Bismarck* was an old-fashioned ship with an outmoded distributive armour pattern.[124] Wartime performance did not resolve the issue. *Bismarck*'s fatal raid did not end in an engagement with *King George V* class ships alone. *Bismarck* sank the obsolete if ostensibly formidable *Hood*, but British 14- and 16-inch gun ships quickly rendered *Bismarck* defenceless. British ships suffered from technical faults, but for German ships serious structural defects (*Bismarck*'s stern separated while sinking), chronic breakdowns and prolonged repair times, and cruising ranges well below expectation substantiate NID's assumption that Raeder's desire for rapid 'production' had resulted in a 'lack of attention paid to "design and details"'.[125] Regardless, it was the torpedo-bomber that proved fatal to both *Bismarck* in May and *Prince of Wales* in December 1941. Ultimately, though, even if we concede some substance to Chatfield's conviction, its ranking as a prime factor in the Admiralty's strategic calculus is eloquent testimony to the magnitude of the problem posed to British strategists in the 1930s by insufficient resources against the triple threat from Germany, Japan and Italy.

For U-boats, wartime evidence is less ambiguous. Walter's fantasy about deploying single-drive U-boats to devastate British seaborne commerce did not come about. His progress was slow. Despite Admiral Dönitz's enthusiasm for the single-drive project, even he proved reluctant in the end to endanger the steady mass production of conventional 500-ton Type VIIs and 740-ton Type IXs until improvements in Allied anti-submarine warfare techniques forced him to seek a corresponding advantage in the attack: the combination of the schnorkel and high underwater speed.

But the first 24 operational Walter U-boats, ordered in January 1943, like the other Nazi technological advances, did not emerge in time to influence the war.[126] The prewar judgement of NID and the DNC was sound: with the exception of better speed, diving capacity and communications, First World War German submariners would have found few novelties in the second generation U-boats; mass production did mean a reliance on standard designs of adequate quality. Dönitz, the composer of the 'wolf packs', however, dubbed it a reliance upon 'proven' types. Unfortunately for the Royal Navy, the innovation that finally shaped Germany's approach to war at sea in the 1940s was not technical but tactical.

5 The Naval Staff, British Strategy and the German Menace, 1934–38

In his memoirs, Admiral Chatfield differentiated between the qualities of a tactician and a strategist. Tactics call for the keen eye, rapid judgement and the decisiveness of an athlete. Strategy, like the game of chess, demands the grasp of first principles, the capacity to abstract the complexities of projecting power over time and space, and the study of past masters. 'Faulty tactics may lose an opportunity of victory,' he wrote; 'faulty strategy may more certainly lose an empire.' Unquestionably, as First Sea Lord and Chairman of the COS, Chatfield aimed to get British strategy right.[1]

This chapter seeks to explain how Chatfield's desire to save an empire by safeguarding its sea power shaped his strategic counsel in the 1930s. It focuses on how the Naval Staff imagined the role of the Navy in British strategy *vis-à-vis* Germany, and how it predicted the fleet's likely performance in battle. In so doing, it traces the chief reason why the Royal Navy was ill-equipped to thwart the German U-boat threat. As will become apparent, the programmatic dimension to British naval policy was the most critical. The Naval Staff placed its confidence in ultimate victory over Germany on the slow-acting effects of 'economic warfare' and the latent fighting potential of Anglo-French power, and sacrificed short-term improvements to its immediate prospects in a European war – such as fully upgrading trade defence or developing offensive war plans – for long-term measures to reassert British naval supremacy. Also, in striking contrast to the formal process of enquiry into German sea strategy, the Naval Staff's faith in the superior fighting qualities of the Royal Navy, and the efficacy of British sea and economic power in Allied strategy, were accepted without systematic analysis.

SEA POWER AND ECONOMIC WARFARE

The Naval Staff perceived an offensive by the German fleet in a future war within the overarching long-versus-short war framework. Germany's sea and air forces might be wagered in a risky yet calculated attempt to knock Britain out of the conflict. Chatfield considered the Navy's thesis of the air-sea strike against the British import system more likely and more dangerous than the Air Ministry's nightmare scenario of a ruthless German bombing offensive against the inhabitants of London.[2] Still, with sufficient anti-aircraft escorts, rerouting, and other proven measures, the Naval Staff believed that they could keep up the inflow of essential commodities. In their minds, the development of potent anti-aircraft defences, principally on warships, was quickly bringing to an end the 'temporary ascendancy' of the bomber. Rudimentary plans to employ the air force to attack the German fleet at berth and to damage the Kiel Canal were drafted.[3] And with the benefit of air reconnaissance in good weather over the North Sea, and perhaps signals intelligence in inclement conditions, naval war planners were confident that the Home Fleet could frustrate most attempts by the German surface raiders to break out into the North Atlantic.[4]

Primarily, the Admiralty envisaged exercising strategic leverage against the Nazi state by means of a distant supply blockade: destroying or capturing German shipping and persuading/coercing neutral merchantmen away from the temptation of carrying contraband cargoes to enemy ports.[5] Blockade of course was not a new stratagem in the British war-making repertoire. In the 1930s, however, it took on an enhanced status in Whitehall thinking. The legacy of 1914–18 was crucial: specifically, the precedent of the British Ministry of Blockade and the unquestioned assumption that the Allied siege had brought about Germany's unexpected collapse in 1918.[6] Consequently, European general staffs anticipated that any future conflict would be a test of endurance, to be decided by the relative capacity of states to earn foreign exchange and mobilise credit abroad, produce weapons, obtain raw materials, grow food and to muster fighting units and an efficient workforce.[7] After 1936, as the CID elaborated its plans, the use of sea power to cripple German war-making capacity was seen as an essential form of 'economic pressure' in the larger concept of 'economic warfare'.[8]

Economic warfare was regarded as having defensive (mobilisation) and offensive (economic pressure) dimensions. This was reflected in the structure of the mechanism the CID had developed to prepare for it. On the defensive side, there was the Principal Supply Officers Committee. It consisted of the top supply officers of the armed services and a Board of Trade official. Its task was to ready industry for the mass production of arms and munitions.[9] On the offensive side, since 1919 there existed the Advisory Committee on Trade Questions in Time of War (ATB). In the

1920s, it was preoccupied with providing expert counsel for the international negotiations on the legalities of exercising belligerent rights. In the 1930s, it was concerned with the possible imposition of League of Nations sanctions and the drafting of war plans.[10] Naturally, mapping out the vulnerable points of an adversary's economy was a prerequisite to planning. To furnish the vital economic topography, the CID set up in March 1931 a research cell, affiliated with the Department of Overseas Trade, known as the Industrial Intelligence Centre. Since air bombardment provided a promising means with which to strike at German industry and communications, the IIC established a subcommittee in early 1936, in reply to an Air Ministry request, designated as the Air Targets Sub-Committee.[11]

The strategic hypothesis underlying these bureaucratic activities was the prevailing conviction within Whitehall that Britain and its potential allies could mobilise, in a prolonged conflict, a preponderance in war-making resources. Britain and France were sure to win a long conflict; Germany was certain to be defeated in anything but a short and decisive one. The COS and JPC envisaged a future European war moving through two phases, broadly similar to the 1914–18 cycle of events. During the first, Germany would launch a calculated bid for a rapid victory. In the opening battles, the Allies would have to be ready to stave off this initial assault and achieve a stalemate on the continent. This would permit London and Paris to develop their tremendous yet untapped industrial, financial and especially extra-European manpower reserves. In the second stage, the Allies would accumulate a commanding superiority in armaments and supplies for a final offensive. Concurrently, with the combined efforts of a naval blockade, air attack and the diplomatic and commercial management of neutral powers, the Allies would endeavour to apply direct pressure on Germany's national organisation.[12]

This scenario was based on an agreeable and accurate reading of Germany's weak resource base. Here, the message promulgated by the IIC was important. Fixed firmly on a combination of preconceptions about totalitarian/teutonic efficiency and a steady flow of often reliable intelligence about the ultimate objective of German economic plans, the IIC consistently painted a picture for CID planners and politicians of the Nazi state thoroughly preparing itself for total war. Even Hitler's inauguration of the Four-Year Plan in the autumn of 1936, which openly committed Germany to a drive for autarky, was not perceived as a departure from previous policy. From the start of its analysis, however, the IIC cited as the obvious weakness in these preparations Germany's shortage in key materials, including iron ore, petroleum and access to foreign exchange. As a result, British planners hoped by creating 'an extreme scarcity of everything' through the exercise of sea power and diplomacy, and by bombing the industrial Ruhr–Rhineland–Saar area, it would be feasible to bring Hitler's military machine to a grinding halt.[13]

Similarly, the expectation that in a lengthy war the balance was bound to swing in favour of an Anglo-French alliance was founded on a number of well entrenched beliefs. Foremost among these was a widespread conviction that there should never again be a continental commitment on the 1914–18 scale.[14] It was too costly in blood and treasure for the British to defeat land powers by becoming a sizeable land power. Rearmament was to act as a deterrent to aggression, while diplomacy eliminated the causes of war. Deterrence meant procuring adequate strength to rule a knockout blow out of Hitler's calculations. In the wake of the global financial crisis of 1931, and the loss in 1934 of the United States as a source of credit (due to punitive legislation passed by Congress which barred Britain access to American financial markets for having defaulted on previous wartime loans), it also meant husbanding financial resources and cultivating a steady commercial recovery. 'Nothing operates more strongly to deter a potential aggressor from attacking this country', the Cabinet agreed in early 1938, 'than our [economic] strength.'[15] Taken together, therefore, the CID's perception of British financial power, combined with the promise of strategic bombing and blockade, coalesced in a faith in 'economic warfare', which, in the words of the official historian, was elevated to the status of a 'secret weapon'.[16]

Seemingly, most of the Admiralty's institutional interests coincided nicely with the development of economic warfare. Although the RAF's bomber fleet shared centre stage, blockade still afforded the Royal Navy a significant offensive and war-winning assignment in British national policy. Nevertheless, in sharp contrast to the debilitating influence of the fear of German air power on Whitehall crisis management, British strategists repeatedly advised ministers that economic warfare was a very blunt and unwieldy instrument when it came to attempts to coerce Hitler.[17] Moreover, no less convinced of the power of economic warfare than any other CID policy-makers, Chatfield and his planners were faced with an exceptionally vexing dilemma. The untimely application of the British 'secret weapon' against Germany would signal the demise of the Admiralty's aspiring programme to defend British sea power. A brief survey of the points at which economic pressure was considered as a potential instrument of diplomacy will reinforce this interpretation.

In May 1933, the ATB's Economic Pressure subcommittee considered economic sanctions as a means to compel Germany to adhere to the Versailles Treaty. The Naval Staff was instructed to report on the question of a League of Nations blockade in peacetime. In addition to the usual Admiralty antipathy to risking ships for League of Nations purposes, the Director of Plans at the time, Captain H. Moore, regarded enforcement as unworkable.[18] If German escorts were present, or, worse, if a non-League power like Soviet Russia attempted to run the blockade, and the Royal Navy used force, then Britain might technically become the 'aggressor'. Hence, until Moscow joined the League in 1934, the ATB endorsed the Navy's view that potent sanctions were impossible without sea power, and that ships could not blockade effectively without a state of war.[19] Besides an unwanted war with a non-League power, British interests were likely to be 'gravely injured' well before Germany faced a crisis. 'The results of such a blockade would not be felt seriously by Germany for some time,' Moore wrote, 'and in effect such action would amount to "cutting off one's nose to spite one's face".'[20]

Moore's remark pithily sums up the Naval Staff's attitude to blockade as a coercive instrument and to the possibility of war with Germany before the mid-1940s. It was all a question of timing. First, Chatfield was convinced that a dangerous confrontation with Berlin before 1942 was improbable. As we shall see in the next chapter, he argued that avoiding a European conflagration, at least in the medium term, was more a matter of exploiting Hitler's desire to win British goodwill than a question of deterrence or containment. Second, sound naval policy was about the competitive management of warship programmes over time. While protecting the fleet's qualitative fitness and keeping its cost down with armaments diplomacy, the Naval Staff planned to expand the fleet incrementally to a two-power standard by 1946. Expansion had to be gradual (as well as inconspicuous) because Britain no longer had reserve building potential for a sudden burst in output in every warship category.[21] A repeat of the laying down of eight dreadnoughts in 1909 to close the gap with Tirpitz was impossible in 1936 due to the atrophy of the shipbuilding industry.[22] To achieve his ultimate aim, the CNS forced the tempo of battleship assembly to the relative neglect of cruisers and destroyers. Since he believed that time was on the side of British sea power, this was sensible given the five-year lead time for capital ships. As he said in July 1935, if he really expected war in 1939, then he would at once demand far more auxiliaries than allowed under the 1930 London Naval Treaty.[23] A major European conflict before the mid-1940s was seen as dangerous because it would abort the Admiralty's project; it would signal the end of the Naval Treaties and incite warship innovation and expansion globally; and it would prematurely divert Britain's national effort from a systematic one on the oceans to an impromptu one on the continent.

Accordingly, as the Naval Staff looked to a future of peaceful industrial and naval renewal, the CID predicated its plans for economic warfare on an indefinite period of German endurance. A report by the ATB in March 1936, in the aftermath of the Rhineland crisis, once again stressed that it was impossible to foresee how long it would take for a blockade to work.[24] As detailed planning for economic warfare against Germany began in 1936,[25] the key question was how long might the stockpiles of strategic materials possessed by Germany last? The IIC tended to be cautious in its estimates.[26] Thus, when the ATB circulated the final draft of its German war plan, it hedged its bet on this issue. The ATB plan stated that it was impossible to make an accurate forecast, and it dispelled any optimism about obtaining early results by cutting off one key commodity – namely Swedish iron ore or Romanian oil.[27]

Consequently, in 1938, despite confidence in the long-war scenario and the superiority of Anglo-French naval strength over Germany (Table 5.1), the Naval Staff interpreted the impending crisis in Central Europe as a hazard to its programme for global maritime ascendancy and not as a question of the strategic merits of keeping Czechoslovakia intact. Once

Table 5.1   British Naval Staff estimated comparative naval strength at 1 January 1938

Types of ship	Britain	Germany	France	Italy	Russia	Japan
Capital ships:						
Pre-war design:						
not modernised	5				3	
partly modernised	3	3				
modernised	1		3	2		7
War design	1					2
Postwar design	2	3*	1			
Total available	12	3	7	2	3	9
Under modernisation	3			2		1?
Grand total	15	3	7	4	3	10?
Aircraft carriers	5		1			5
A-Class cruisers	10		7	7	1	7
B-Class cruisers	49	6	40	15	7	25
Destroyers	161	28	33	111	63	111
Submarines	53	36	76	80	184	60

* Three 10 000-ton *Panzerschiffe*, with perhaps one 26 000-ton battlecruiser.
Sources: Adapted from JP242, 28 Oct. 1937, CAB55/10.

more, the trinity of sea power, financial 'staying power' and economic pressure did not supply policy-makers with a rapid military solution if diplomacy failed to discourage Hitler from aggression. As the COS gloomily warned the Cabinet in March 1938, in terms which resonate with Chatfield's thinking, 'we can do nothing to prevent the dog getting the bone, and we have no means of making him give it up, except by killing him by a slow process of attrition and starvation.' And, given the predatory policies of Italy and Japan, not only would a German attack on the Czech state be transformed into a European war, but a European conflagration would surely escalate into a global conflict.[28]

Still, some attempts were made to use the Royal Navy to deter Hitler. At the urging of the British Ambassador in Berlin, ministers held back a definite diplomatic threat of British intervention, but on 10 September, in accordance with FO instructions, Admiral Troup attempted to send a warning via the German naval attaché. The DNI told Captain Leopold Siemens, in reply to his enquiry about preparatory naval measures announced in the press, that 'everybody in England knew that if France was involved in war, we should be likewise'. Siemens, 'overwhelmed' by the news, replied that he had not considered war possible 'until the present moment'. Troup was delighted with the result and wished to recall Siemens for a second round of 'rubbing it in'.[29] The naval attaché's reaction also pleased Chamberlain because it 'had just the effect we intended'.[30] Two days later, it was the turn of the Americans. As the Minister for the Co-ordination of Defence, Sir Thomas Inskip, recorded in his diaries, the US Ambassador had arranged for two US Navy heavy cruisers, sent to prepare for the evacuation of American citizens, to berth at Gravesend and Portland. Sources reported that the move had 'impressed' Berlin,[31] and a bewildered Siemens was informed that the two vessels were being retained due to the crisis.[32]

Yet fleet mobilisation, which Vansittart (now the Cabinet's Chief Diplomatic Advisor) endorsed, was rejected in fear that it would provoke Hitler. Alexander Cadogan, the new permanent head of the FO, wondered whether the naval moves taken so far had had any 'irritation' effect at all.[33] Regardless, Chamberlain, acting from an optimistic reading of Hitler's intentions, was determined on mediation. He planned to corner Hitler into a summit meeting by flying to Germany. In Cabinet, on 14 September, even the First Lord, Duff Cooper, who had intended to propose mobilisation, 'preferred' the PM's ploy.[34] But after Chamberlain had twice flown to Germany (15 and 22 September) and had convinced Paris and Prague to cede the Sudetenland, Hitler refused an orderly transfer and threatened force. On 26 September London stated that it would join the French in a war triggered by German aggression. The next day, spurred by a report of Göring's scornful response to the threat of a British blockade, Duff Cooper implored Chamberlain to mobilise the fleet at once. At an 'inner' Cabinet meeting that day, Admiral Backhouse (who had just succeeded Chatfield) stressed the need for a long interval between mobilisation and the start of war. The PM agreed to mobilise the Navy as a precaution, not as a act of deterrence. He even failed to announce it in his radio broadcast that night.[35]

The oversight made little difference. Not long after the broadcast, Hitler's letter offering to join in an international guarantee of Czechoslovakia had reached Whitehall before word of the mobilisation had arrived in Berlin.[36] If the letter was the first sign of Hitler's change of plan, then it is evident from the timing that the naval threat did not influence his decision. Alternatively, if it was an attempt to split the British from the French and the Czechs, then the naval threat may have been more consequential: on the morning of the 28th, after news of the British action had reached him, Hitler accepted Mussolini's plan for a four-power conference to break the deadlock.[37] Even so, the real question was whether Hitler was prepared to see what he had hoped to be the swift conquest of the Czech state escalate into a conflict against Britain and France. Broader considerations are critical here. Chamberlain's shuttle diplomacy had put the Führer on the spot: to go ahead with the attack meant being painted as the enemy of peace, not the champion of German minorities. The effect of this on civilian morale was evident to Hitler in the grim reaction given by onlookers to troop parades in Berlin on the 27th. As his later anger would reveal, Hitler was not ready to take the plunge: after all, since late May, he had been berating his hesitant generals for questioning his assurances that Britain would stand aside.[38] In any case, NID was unable to arrive at any definite conclusion about to what extent the deployment of the Royal Navy contributed to Hitler's last minute climbdown.[39]

In summation, the combination of sea power, financial robustness and blockade, which underpinned British grand strategy, appeared to offer very little clout to British diplomacy on the continent. Of course given Chamberlain's preference to deter German aggression with air power, it was the prevailing belief in the minds of ministers that Britain and France had lost the race in the air and that Hitler might opt for a knockout blow against London that skewed Cabinet decision-making. In compensation, the Naval Staff did not offer an offensive plan for the use of naval strength to alter the gloomy psychological state in Whitehall. On the contrary, it was predominantly Chatfield who had set the foreboding tone to COS counsel that buttressed Chamberlain's policy during the crisis.

As historians have rightly pointed out, it was the COS's 'worst case' analysis of the military balance, correlated with the PM's 'best case' appraisal of Hitler's aims, that propelled appeasement in 1938.[40] They add that the COS were wrong on two counts. First, the military balance was not stacked in Hitler's favour. The Czechs would have been defeated, but the COS ignored the way in which even victory would have exposed material flaws in the Wehrmacht's speedy expansion. The *Luftwaffe*, for technical and logistical reasons, was incapable of devastating London. Most important of all, if a general war ensued, Germany would have to wage it from the inferior foreign exchange and raw material base that the IIC had accurately mapped. It can be argued that appeasement assisted Germany in escaping this predicament: it allowed Hitler to absorb Austrian and Czechoslovakian war-making assets in 1938–9, to expand his continental resource base further with a series of rapid conquests in 1939–40, as well as to conclude a materially profitable non-aggression pact with Stalin.[41] Second, the COS failed to examine more closely Britain's own financial and economic stamina in the event of a long war. The Treasury's dire warnings about excessive defence spending, an unfavourable balance of payments and Britain's shrinking gold and dollar reserves should have injected some realism into long-range prognostications.[42] In the event, despite London's desire to fight on even after the fall of France in 1940, financial ruin in 1941 was narrowly averted by American Lend-Lease.[43]

It is not the purpose here to refute the details upon which these criticisms are based. Yet the two points should be tempered with the knowledge that it was not a faulty strategic insight nor an irrational preoccupation with military unreadiness and imperial overstretch that caused Chatfield to advance the 'worst case' in 1938. Instead, he was motivated by a legitimate and realistic grand strategic proposition.[44] In 1934, he warned against basing plans on a 'worst case' because it would inflate the forces demanded by the other services since they would be scaled to meet what was by definition improbable.[45] What caused him 'uneasiness' was the scope for excessive fiscal and industrial capacity being devoted to weapons for continental warfare. What compelled him in 1938 was the recognition that a general European war beginning that year would occasion Britain's descent from its position as the leading global power. Within his scheme of priorities, a tactical capitulation over the Sudetenland was worthwhile to secure the preservation of Britain's long-range prospects.[46] The next chapter will explore the reasons why Admiral Chatfield backed Chamberlain's policies in 1937–8, and the CNS's estimate of what the outcome would be if Nazi Germany conquered parts of Central and South-Eastern Europe.

Several additional points should be borne in mind when considering the Naval Staff's faith in economic blockade and Britain's financial stamina. Recollections of the last war were more significant in shaping beliefs than comparative economics. The way in which the German officers, sent to negotiate the surrender of the High Seas Fleet in 1918, picked a leg of mutton clean to the bone at dinner imprinted on Chatfield's mind an indelible link between the blockade and German defeat.[47] Also, Chatfield was acutely aware of Britain's financial dilemma. He optimistically hoped to avoid bankrupting the Exchequer with his elaborate defence of Britain's global dominance by diplomacy, reducing the estimates of the other services and cutting social spending.[48] It should also be underscored that the Naval Staff's programme was intended to avert the sort of transition in Britain's world position *vis-à-vis* the United States that was marked in 1941 by the enactment of Lend-Lease.[49] And finally, that in 1938–9 Hitler impetuously deviated from his own stated programme of preparing Germany for total war, and consequently transformed his previously dire geostrategic position as compared with that of the Allies,[50] as well as over-turning the reasonable expectations of many Whitehall strategists, does not vitiate the calculations upon which the Naval Staff based its ambitious project. After all, despite severe setbacks in 1939–40 and near bankruptcy in March 1941, it was sea power (albeit Anglo-American instead of Anglo-French) that enabled London to engineer the strategic context of Hitler's defeat.[51]

ANTI-SUBMARINE WARFARE

For nearly fifty years now, historians have endeavoured to explain why the Royal Navy was unprepared for the Battle of the Atlantic. Early studies criticised the Navy for an abhorrence of convoy operations and a hankering after a fresh Trafalgar. The official and semi-official historians attributed the error to the Admiralty's inability to learn the lessons of the first unrestricted submarine campaign and a lack of operational research to elucidate the key principles of convoy doctrine.[52] Although recent scholarship rightly continues to hold several institutional inadequacies responsible for the Naval Staff's neglect of anti-submarine warfare (ASW) between the wars,[53] naval historians have become more forgiving of some aspects of the Royal Navy's shortcomings.

It is now clear, for example, that the Royal Navy was as ready to defend against a U-boat campaign as the German navy was ready to mount one.[54] Scholars have also begun to discard the teleology-of-failure approach – that is tracing back from wartime technical deficiencies on the presumption that they must be linked to some prewar ineptitude. By doing so, they have found, as with research into the development of naval air and battle fleet doctrine,[55] that it was not a poverty of imaginative thinking, but a paucity of potent *matériel* that adversely influenced fighting performance. Planners accepted that convoys would be needed at the outbreak of war, and that aircraft were an integral part of convoy defence.[56] Naval planners also recognised that Berlin would not abstain from indiscriminate U-boat warfare simply because in November 1936 Germany had become a party to the rules banning it in the second London Naval Treaty.[57] And lastly, until the defeat of France in the summer of 1940 had radically transformed the geographic make-up of the Atlantic campaign, the Naval Staff's prewar anti-U-boat strategy proved largely correct.[58]

Nevertheless, certain conspicuous shortcomings in Admiralty ASW preparations – for instance the failure to perfect a prototype of an oceanic escort for mass production in wartime[59] – require analysis. Yet the whole subject of Royal Navy ASW between the wars, that is the dynamics of interaction between technological progress, doctrinal evolution, finance and the quality of training, is extremely complex, deserving of its own study and beyond the scope of this one. Instead, what will be pursued here, in step with the overall theme of this chapter, is an analysis of how the grand strategic framework entertained in the minds of senior Admiralty decision-makers governed the state of ASW readiness. To reiterate, it is essential to appreciate the programmatic nature of Naval Staff calculations. Prewar decisions were made on the basis of arranging the shipbuilding timetable to win the battle for global maritime dominance by the mid-1940s, not to prepare for the Battle of the Atlantic as it unfolded from August 1940 onwards.

For Chatfield and his staff, as noted above, this set of priorities entailed a calculated risk in the medium term. The superstructure of sea power, the battle fleet and its allied industrial infrastructure, were being reconstructed urgently, at the relative expense of improvements to operational capabilities in trade protection, which were only marginally upgraded.[60] The Admiralty's policy for ASW, anti-aircraft and minesweeping auxiliaries was based on the build-up in peace of a skeletal force capable of rapid expansion in war. Existing units would prevent a fatal blow to shipping, while wartime forces would evolve to meet the enemy's attack as it developed. The nascent organisation included the provision of sufficient ASDIC (sonar) units for installation into old destroyers, light patrol boats and trawlers to be manned by reservists.[61] The Naval Treaties were drafted, for instance, to allow for rapid expansion of these units during the diplomatic crisis that was expected to presage a conflict.[62] The Naval Staff as well thought it conceivable that a future foe might observe the rules banning unrestricted submarine warfare long enough to cover the period between the war's outbreak and full ASW mobilisation.[63]

Obviously, maintaining a minimal auxiliary fleet in peace was a component of the Admiralty's attempt to calibrate the cost of maritime power to Britain's fiscal capacity.[64] Yet it was also a policy scaled to the Admiralty's analysis of the U-boat threat. As we saw in the last chapter, the Admiralty's technical intelligence apparatus had become convinced that the German navy planned to mass produce in war hundreds of standardised U-boat types. The combat quality of these boats was only marginally better than those of the 1914–18 period. Although German negotiators in June 1935 had insisted on a submarine ratio of 45 per cent with Britain, and reserved the right to parity in certain circumstances, the development of the U-boat arm before 1939 indicated that it would only possess the numbers and, more importantly, the endurance to menace British home waters. The Naval Staff concluded that the only way in which U-boats could become lethal was if they were part of an all-out air, surface and mine offensive against shipping.

To decide on the optimal number and types of vessels to counter this threat, as Captain Phillips recognised in July 1936, meant an inevitable compromise between the need to re-equip neglected defences and 'the rapid progress in science and engineering [that was] changing many aspects of naval warfare'.[65] In other words, given that the Naval Staff's policies were predicated on a long cycle of quiet renewal, it was reluctant to invest prematurely in the capacity to mass produce an available model (as Germany had apparently done with U-boats), when the not too distant future might bring a more advanced yet still simple to produce variant. Instead, in late 1937, the Admiralty undertook to accumulate a nucleus of premium escorts by ordering two or three per annum. They would be in place to deter or defeat a German knockout blow. Thus, the resulting 1300-ton *Black Swan* escorts were armed not only with ASW apparatus, but also with elaborate anti-aircraft batteries. Although these 'thoroughbred' escorts later proved effective in combat, they were as expensive to procure per ton as fleet destroyers and contained a complex machinery, which taken together made them unsuitable for mass production.[66]

The major fault of the *Black Swan* class, and later frigates and corvettes improvised for large-scale production in 1938–9,[67] was insufficient endurance to act as proper transatlantic escorts. Clearly, this was a product of the Naval Staff's knockout-blow thesis. As noted earlier, British naval planners anticipated that Germany would concentrate its air and subsurface strike on shipping in British coastal waters, especially along the approaches to eastern ports and the Thames estuary. As a result, anti-aircraft defences, not oceanic endurance, were the prime concern in escort design. Likewise, it appeared that since Admiral Raeder had expended his submarine tonnage to build up a large number of small to medium sized boats, most of them could not possess the cruising capacity to reside in the North Atlantic for very long, except with the development of the capability for refuelling at sea,[68] or the use of overseas bases belonging to alleged neutrals.[69]

Another consequence of NID's conviction that the new U-boats were nothing more than minor refinements on First World War models was its rosy correlation with the Naval Staff estimate that ASW had advanced considerably since 1919 with the evolution of ASDIC.[70] In 1921, as ACNS, Chatfield believed that the progress of ASDIC would cause 'all our present tactical and strategic theories as affected by submarines [to] require alteration'.[71] The navy worked to integrate the new device into a coherent ASW doctrine between the wars.[72] In contrast with the orthodox judgement, it is not entirely true that the Royal Navy exaggerated the degree to which ASDIC sets alone had solved the subsurface threat. The Naval Staff admitted important limitations, and early operational results were mixed.[73] A memo prepared for the CID in March 1937 pointed out that successful ASW would depend on the training and skill of the ASDIC operators, sea conditions and preparedness of the ASW system as a whole, including aircraft. 'There is much to be done', the Admiralty forewarned, 'before [a] desirable state of affairs is achieved.'[74]

Roskill argues that the near successful attack by the Italian submarine *Iride* on HMS *Havock* in August 1937 should have shaken the Admiralty's confidence in ASDIC.[75] Ironically, it had the opposite effect. In early 1938, an inquest by Tactical Division into the incident was critical of *Havock*'s performance. The *Iride*'s torpedo was sighted by a sentry as it passed a few feet astern. He raised the alarm, but sonar sets were unmanned and depth charges were unready. Evasive manoeuvres by *Havock* interposed its wake between the ASDIC oscillator and the submarine several times, thus interfering with the contact. It was concluded that the destroyer's actions had ruined any chance for a potent counter-attack.[76] Luckily for *Havock*'s captain, the Deputy DNI interceded with 'most secret' intelligence that correctly confirmed that *Iride* had been depth charged, although the extent of its damage, if any, was unknown.[77] This tactical intelligence appeared to show that, despite *Havock*'s serious operational errors, the combination of ASDIC and depth charges was effective under combat conditions. Tactical Division softened its critique.[78] More importantly, the CNS interpreted the navy's ASW experience in the Mediterranean positively,[79] and a progress report on ASW issued in June 1938 cited the *Havock* episode as evidence of ASDIC reliability.[80]

The key Admiralty oversight with respect to U-boats was the absence of enquiry into how the German navy might overcome the presumed technical mediocrity of its subsurface weapons with cunning tactics. One problem was that the views advocated by Germany's foremost theorist on submarine warfare, Captain Dönitz, were not accepted by senior German naval staff officers.[81] Consequently, although there is little documentary evidence to reconstruct thoroughly what NID reported about the German Naval Command's accepted U-boat doctrine, it can be safely assumed that when it was accurate it was entirely misleading. In November 1934, for instance, Captain Muirhead-Gould, the British naval attaché, contrary to his own expectations, reported that 'the German navy has very little faith in the future of the submarine, and believes that modern AS methods are so excellent that a submarine will have no chance against a well prepared enemy.' One former submariner confided to him that he considered a U-boat attack on a well protected convoy as gratuitous suicide.[82] It is significant that Captain Troubridge, who succeeded Muirhead-Gould in 1936, was most intimate with senior officers who disputed Dönitz's innovative thinking. According to his diary, which was intended to be a record of German personalities, Troubridge did not encounter Dönitz.[83]

In any case, there was evidence about fresh approaches to submarine war available from the activities of the Royal Navy's own subsurface fleet. British submariners studied ways of pressing home an attack despite the presence of ASDIC-equipped destroyers.[84] The efficacy of submarines in reconnaissance and assault roles when co-operating in groups, the distinctive feature of Dönitz's tactical system, was revealed in British exercises.[85] Remarkably, a Naval Staff post-action report on a Mediterranean fleet exercise in 1935 praised the exploits of one submarine commander who evaded an ASDIC-equipped destroyer screen as well as daylight air cover by attacking a column of heavy ships at night and on the surface.[86] It was precisely this ingenious ploy, which German U-boat officers had used effectively in 1917–18, and which Dönitz would use again with stunning effect with packs in 1940–3. The difficulty here was not insufficient imagination, nor solely faulty links between the surface and subsurface navies.[87] More to the point, what was needed at the Naval Staff level was a different overall strategic framework, in-depth analysis about what German strategy might look like after a failed knockout blow, and a sense of urgency to encourage the rapid elaboration of ASW and *matériel* from below.

Instead, the Naval Staff predicted that optimal ASW readiness would not be needed for some time. How great was this gamble? It is disputable whether ASW failings were as grave as they appeared in wartime or in post-1945 naval oriented histories. From the macro-economic angle, Marc Milner has masterfully shown that it was not the tactical or intelligence rivalry between navies or even evolving technology that was decisive, but the efficient management of the import system and the amassing of a crushing level of resources. Whitehall planners in the 1930s overrated the availability of shipping in war, but they did the same for the amount of imports Britain needed to survive and fight. In 1939, the figure was set at 60 million tons, but by 1942 it was evident that 26 million was enough. In 1941, alleviating port congestion saved nearly as much import capacity as was lost to U-boats.[88] The key point, Milner argues, is that 'the German attack developed slowly enough for the British to take effective countermeasures, and for the improving situation generally to have a decisive influence'.[89] In retrospect, Naval Staff confidence in the Navy's ability to cope with anything short of a true knockout blow against the import system and that British defences would adapt steadily to meet a developing German attack was well placed.

THE SPIRIT OF THE OFFENSIVE AND THE DANGER ZONE

Ostensibly, it may appear odd that the Admiralty did not offer ministers in 1938 a bold plan to exploit the Allied advantage in sea power *vis-à-vis* Nazi Germany. After all, British naval officers were inculcated with a belief that they were blessed with the Nelson touch. It was embedded in the Navy's ethos that by engaging the enemy at close range, its unequalled fighting spirit would prevail. The institutional bias for the offensive,[90] at least at the operational level, was reinforced by abiding recriminations that it was Jellicoe's overcautious tactics that permitted Scheer's numerically inferior fleet to escape annihilation at Jutland. It is, moreover, arguable that the moral ascendancy bred by an offensive doctrine permits a maritime power to derive the full potential benefit from its navy.[91]

Yet war plans framed in 1937 assigned the main fleet a decidedly defensive role. The blockade would be imposed at a distance from the Royal Navy's Scottish bases, and not close to enemy ports. The JPC in 1936 ruled out a Baltic offensive intended to cut off Germany's essential supply of iron ore from Sweden. Germany's geographic advantage in defence, torpedoes, mines and bombers made an offensive too risky for British heavy units for anything but an all-out bid to command the Baltic, but the cost would greatly downgrade the navy's world-wide ranking.[92] The

DCNS, Admiral William James, considered Baltic 'guerrilla warfare' with submarines feasible, provided Soviet bases were available.[93] But unless the enemy ventured from his ports, the prime offensive aim of sea power was to strangle the Nazi war machine with a blockade. Chatfield's maritime war with Germany was to be a prolonged siege, not a *coup de main*.

There were, however, advocates of an offensive strategy. The most vocal was Admiral Sir Reginald Plunket E. E. Drax, the C-in-C Plymouth Station. In September 1937, in a stinging critique of the 'Naval Appreciation of War with Germany (1939)', Drax argued that the Royal Navy should not idly absorb a German knockout blow, but launch its own. He dismissed the current plan as offering little to 'help us actively to win the next war unless they are altered to employ a sustained and early offensive on a scale vastly greater than is here contemplated'. Drax feared that a strategic defensive (in clear contrast with the continual 'lip service' paid to the spirit of the offensive) would encourage a tactically defensive mind-set among junior officers. He was also anxious that if word about current plans leaked to press and Parliament, with the fleet's relative docility during the 1914–18 slaughter well remembered, the naval estimates would be repealed to build up the RAF, and 'the great days of the British navy would then be ended'. And foremost in his mind was the desire to switch the uncertainty of a slow economic strangulation of Germany for a sure and swift offensive. To make this vigorous attack practicable by 1939, Drax recommended that the designated C-in-C of the next 'Grand Fleet' should work with a new offensive planning cell, and that they co-operate with their counterparts in the Air Ministry and the War Office. Specifically, since Germany might operate its surface raiders and U-boats from Spanish bases, he supported the formation of a combined Royal Marine/Army amphibious force to assault these allegedly neutral ports.[94]

Drax's attack on Naval Staff war planning was consistent with a career-long campaign to instil in his colleagues the offensive spirit and an appreciation for the intellectual pursuits of strategy, staff work and history. During the First World War, he had been a follower of the naval historian and reformer Captain (later Admiral Sir) Herbert Richmond, and one of the 'Young Turks' of the Grand Fleet, who were junior officers critical of successive First Sea Lords, especially Jellicoe, for not doing enough to win the war with the main fleet. Richmond and his Young Turks wanted the Admiralty to set up an offensive planning cell and, during the 1917 U-boat crisis, they pushed for the early introduction of the convoy and bold measures to strike the U-boats at source.[95]

Drax's career did not suffer from the stigma attached to Richmond and others for their part in Lloyd George's curt dismissal of Jellicoe in late

1917. Two years later, he was appointed the first Director of the Royal Navy Staff College at Greenwich and developed a reputation as an able strategic and tactical theorist, even if he was not earmarked as a front runner for high command.[96] From his articles in *The Naval Review*,[97] and perhaps as a result of his relative solitude from strategic preparations in Whitehall, it is clear that he was troubled by the fluid diplomatic scene and what he probably diagnosed as a boom in defensive-mindedness in the Naval Staff. He was not a normally cantankerous personality. Drax thought about the likely consequences of his critique for several weeks, and sent it to the C-in-C Home Fleet for scrutiny,[98] long before circulating it to the Admiralty.

Still, the letter arrived at the Admiralty like a bombshell. In November 1937, Chatfield penned a personal reprimand. It was evident that Drax, the CNS pointed out, was oblivious to the CID's innovations in inter-service co-operation, such as the COS and JPC. The Naval Staff viewed the insinuation that they were infected with a feeble offensive spirit and that it was disheartening junior officers as impertinent. 'Our main object has always been and will always be', Chatfield continued, 'to attack the enemy whenever and wherever he appears and to defeat him.' But battle was not the 'primary function of a navy in such a war as envisaged in the German War Plan', but the protection of communications. Although there was scope for the fleet staffs to plan local offensives, they had to be conceived within a sturdy strategic framework. Chatfield rejected Drax's claim that an overwhelming naval strength demanded an offensive war plan: 'I am unable to envisage that in any war we should have overwhelming strength.' Italy and Japan might combine with Germany, Chatfield wrote, 'and so old and weak are our forces to deal with them bound to be that it is highly probable that we shall have to win battles with inferior forces.' He instructed Drax to make any future proposals of a 'definite and tangible nature and not in the form of generalisations'.[99]

Despite the barbed comments, very little actually separated the two points of view. It is important to pursue the similarities and the prime difference between the two men at some length, though, for three reasons. One, it will provide further evidence of what underlay Chatfield's decision-making. Second, it will illuminate the process by which the Naval Staff calculated the probable performance of the British fleet against each of its likely foes. And third, Drax's thinking, especially with his promotion to the Admiralty under Admiral Backhouse in late 1938, represented the only alternative to the strategic policies of the Chatfield period articulated from within the Navy.

In their formative years, both Drax and Chatfield looked to Admiral David Beatty as the prime example of the audacity, broad strategic insight and unshakeable confidence required in a great commander. While serving with the Mediterranean Fleet, both had shown themselves to be like-minded tactical innovators, and stressed the value of seeking close-range fleet engagements, or better yet fighting a night action, to accentuate the Royal Navy's characteristic combat traits.[100] Neither regarded himself as a simple 'materialist' – an appellation reserved for naval officers who concerned themselves strictly with the development of weapons instead of their use.[101] Equally, they both understood the links between the size of ships, finance and diplomacy, although Drax probably appeared to Chatfield to be too much under the influence of Richmond's small capital ship heresy.[102]

In terms of predicting the likely outcome of future combat at sea, neither Admirals Chatfield nor Drax credited any other fleet with an equal fighting capacity to that of the Royal Navy. Indeed, the Naval Staff did not exclusively rely on crude quantitative comparisons:

> We must not lose sight of the superiority which the greater efficiency of our fleet conferred upon us [Chatfield reminded the CID in February 1939]. After all, we should have lost the battle of Trafalgar on a Staff Appreciation since our fleet was inferior to the French. The success or failure of naval operations did not depend entirely on the inferiority, equality, or superiority in capital ships of one fleet in relation to another.[103]

This was not just an archaic form of collective vanity; the First Sea Lord and his colleagues did obtain an intangible sense of moral supremacy by crediting themselves with an innate genius for the offensive that proved tactically efficacious in wartime.[104] In hierarchy among the naval powers, the Royal Navy was at the peak and the others were endeavouring with varying degrees of success to emulate Britain.[105] At the bottom were the Russians, who were 'notorious' for mechanical ineptitude and had a predilection for periodically purging their leading men.[106] As Marder has shown, the Admiralty underestimated the efficiency of the Japanese navy and deplored the lack of initiative they perceived among its senior admirals.[107] The Italians were regarded as 'fair weather sailors' – liable to suffer a severe breakdown in fighting spirit at the first serious reverse.[108]

The German navy, like the Nazi state, was credited with a formidable technical and industrial aptitude. National Socialism was assumed to have corrected many of the defects in morale and discipline that had caused its sailors to mutiny in 1918.[109] Yet, although they were respected as worthy foes, the Admiralty regarded the Germans as soldiers on water, not true sailors. Captain Troubridge had 'the impression that, although their training is admirably designed to work a ship in battle and to operate tactically to the best advantage with other units, there is a lack of that indefinable quality derived from centuries of familiarity with the sea that we call seamanlike'. Despite the new emphasis in German naval thought on the offensive, Chatfield believed that 'Germanic' thoroughness in planning for land war did not work at sea. Raeder's officers were not taught 'to think in oceans', as Troubridge put it.[110] Chatfield later explained:

> Jutland gave the German navy, despite its technical successes, a blow from which it never recovered. The Germans have never been a sea nation; efficient as they are they have not the real seaman's spirit of character. Great as was the navy Kaiser Wilhelm and von Tirpitz created, skilful as had been their preparations, the design of their ships, the experimental work they must have carried out and the skill of the German industrialist, there was something lacking. Was it tradition, character, or something deeper, that caused their first action on contact invariably to be to turn for home? [111]

The above correlation of the presumed national characters and varying yet still inferior levels of efficiency of its potential rivals with the self-image of the Royal Navy as possessing a talent for sea war and the attack should have skewed Admiralty thinking to a bias for offensive fleet operations. Strangely, some historians have censured the Naval Staff for entertaining an exaggerated estimate of Italian power and Japan's eagerness for war in 1938.[112] But the real problem with seizing a chance to knock out any enemy, or boldly to confront all three with numerically inferior forces and trusting in the intangibles, was the knowledge that temporary *matériel* defects in the battle fleet had corrupted the true hierarchy of efficiency.

The danger had been created by the lag behind the Americans and Japanese in capital ship modernisation in the late 1920s and the early 1930s, as well as the extension of the battleship building 'holiday' to 1937. Consequently, a very high proportion of the battleships were relatively obsolete in 1936, including many cruisers and destroyers.[113] The rotation schedule of battleships through extensive rebuilding, including deck armour against long-range plunging fire, meant that three of the total of 15 battleships were quite literally gutted throughout 1938 (see Table 5.1).[114] As C-in-C Mediterranean fleet in the early 1930s, Chatfield had stressed night fighting as a tactical method of seeking close action and hence compensating for the Royal Navy's *matériel* shortcoming in a long-range gun duel or while closing with a foe.[115] Tactical solutions, however, were stopgaps.

The supreme objective was to reach a healthy standing in the quality and quantity of ships. Until then, although the Naval Staff affirmed that it was 'not the gun or torpedo which really counts but the man behind it',[116] it also knew that the Navy was passing through a danger zone – to borrow a term from Tirpitz – in which the battle fleet was perilously flawed. Chatfield wrote in 1936:

> I wish to record my opinion, that the great fighting reserve of power we have in our Navy is our long service system which enables us to have a more highly trained personnel and also our fighting tenacity. Given a good ship, that will not be destroyed by a lucky blow, we will always win. Our efficiency will enable us to fire quicker and more accurately than our foe even if we have slightly fewer guns; but *NO* efficiency or courage will save the ship if she is insufficiently protected and is put out of action. Under such circumstances our fighting qualities will not be able to decide the issue.[117]

Before 1942, when the properly protected capital ships of the 1937–9 building programmes would be ready and the modernisation of the old ships were complete, any battle was one in which potentially a 'lucky blow' from even a third-rate adversary might be lethal for the dominant sea power. In this context, again to borrow from Tirpitz, the navies of all three potential foes represented 'risk fleets' until qualitative renewal was complete; war against any one would probably leave the Royal Navy (and the Empire) fatally exposed to the other two.[118] Thus, the strategic question framed by the Naval Staff was not how to use existing forces in well-timed offensive operations to reduce the disparity in armaments, but how to manage national policy to progress beyond the danger zone to conditions under which the Navy's traditional superiority in fighting skill would count decisively. In the meantime, 'a false step in foreign policy may bring against us a combination of Powers,' Admiral James reminded the CNS in 1938, 'who can marshal an armament far superior to our own and then no superiority in tactical skill or in weapon technique will avail. It is just as true today as it was at the time of Trafalgar that numbers alone can annihilate.'[119]

Of course Drax knew numbers alone could annihilate. Like the CNS he realised that a long and exhausting European struggle commencing in 1939 would herald the decline in Britain's global position. 'I fear there is grave danger of our losing the next war (or winning it too slowly, which is almost the same thing),' he wrote in August 1937, as he pondered his critique, 'if the balance between defensive and offensive requirements is not carefully adjusted.'[120] Unlike Chatfield and his staff, the C-in-C Plymouth accepted the prospect of war with Nazi Germany in 1939. Consequently, the difference between Drax and his superiors was in the handling of time as a strategic commodity.

In Drax's alternative, the offensive was a means to structure the course of the expected 1939 war to Britain's advantage.[121] There was to be no repeat of Jutland. British offensive strikes from the air and sea against Raeder's bases would compel his fleet to contest the North Sea, where it would be annihilated by British numbers and efficiency.[122] If that did not end the German war, at least it would extricate Britain from the dread of Italian and Japanese intervention. Offensive war plans provided the navy with a means to swap the uncertainty and inescapable decline equated with a prolonged macro-economic siege for decisive victories in the Nelsonian tradition.

In a long memo endorsed by his superior intended to refute Drax and entitled 'Speed and Strength', the DCNS reasserted the Naval Staff's policies. Britain needed a 'ubiquitous' navy to defend its global position, not a regional fleet suited to achieve local offensive objectives. In a ubiquitous navy, which had to be properly protected and capable of transfer from one ocean to another, speed (and hence aggressive qualities) suffered. Admiral James continued:

> The attraction of speed is of course that it seems to open the way to various types of adventurous offensive operations, and we are always searching for objectives for offensive operations and means of attacking those objectives. Our plans were criticised recently on the score that the offensive was lacking in them, and those who hold this view probably think that they are echoing the principles which actuated the great war leaders of the past ... 'Offence is the best defence.' But that is not a true interpretation of history. When the great fighting men of the past made their plans they made them carefully and kept constantly before them the main object, which was to win the war...[123]

Winning the war required a sound national policy and an accurate reading of the strategic realities. The CNS judged that a 1939 war entailed the politically unpalatable solutions of conscription (to reduce costs), admitting that 'we cannot afford to have the security that great strength gives', and holding the Empire with inferior forces without certainty of victory.[124]

Chatfield's Jutland was not a lost opportunity. But, in his mind, the only sure way to defeat Germany was by a macro-economic siege. Before that could be faced, however, it was imperative to procure enough time to advance beyond the danger zone towards a restoration of Britain's naval supremacy; only after that would it be practicable to devise aggressive schemes to demoralise an inferior opponent.

Indeed, it is the programmatic dimension of Naval Staff thinking that runs through this chapter. Admiralty policy was formulated to win the battle for global maritime dominance by the mid-1940s, and not on the expectation of waging war against Nazi Germany from September 1939 onwards. Whatever detrimental consequences scholars may link to this policy choice, it is essential to temper hindsight with the knowledge that Chatfield's project was shaped by the attainment of a bold and legitimate grand strategic objective. As we shall see, making time work for British sea power compelled the Admiralty to influence the formation of foreign and defence policy.

6 The Naval Staff and Defence and Foreign Policy, 1937–38

As 1937 drew to a close, it became apparent in London and Berlin that the Anglo-German Naval Agreement had failed to fulfil the variety of divergent expectations that had originally made it possible. In the interval between the first exchange of notes in June 1935 and the second accord of July 1937, naval armaments diplomacy remained at the periphery of Anglo-German relations; the protracted bargaining neither facilitated a comprehensive resolution to the European crisis, nor did it bring about an Anglo-German alliance. Briefly, however, in September 1938, the 1935 Naval Agreement would again move into the foreground of Anglo-German relations.

This chapter reconstructs the Admiralty's efforts to remodel the maritime order and to install naval supremacy as the canon of national policy from the third report of the DRC to Munich. It examines how differences with the FO about how to deal with Germany impelled the Admiralty to back Chamberlain in his effort to bring foreign policy under Downing Street control. While historians have recognised that the COS were steadfast supporters of appeasement, the exposition below reinforces the argument that Admiral Chatfield was driven by the imperatives of his bold programme designed to thwart naval decline, and not by strategic paralysis brought about by imperial decay nor an idiosyncratic propensity for worst-case thinking.

AN OPTIMUM CORRELATION OF NATIONAL POLICIES?

Although the 1935 Naval Agreement augured well for the Navy's programme, the outcome of the DRC had put Chatfield and his planners in a precarious position. The Naval Staff knew that the strategy of a limited European deterrent based on air forces, backed by the Treasury and the FO, provided an economical alternative to its global one based on naval power: air armaments were economical and promised to generate clout for British diplomacy in Europe.[1] While the CID remained tied to a one-power standard with Germany in the air, the Admiralty had no choice but to bide its time, and, as a prerequisite to the fulfilment of its programme, to position itself carefully on the best possible industrial and bureaucratic start-line.

During the second round of the DRC's deliberations in late 1935, Chatfield had profitably played on the resurgence of German sea power to gain approval for a new standard of naval strength to be included among its final recommendations.[2] The DRC report of November 1935, which was approved by the Cabinet in February 1936, marked the shift from the deficiency to the rearmament phase of British defence policy. It set 1939 as the target date to complete defence preparations. Yet for fiscal reasons, warship building would be spread over five years. The Navy would lay down seven battleships in total and five cruisers annually from 1936 to 1939, and four aircraft carriers and five flotillas of destroyers from 1936 to 1942; the army was authorised to prepare a Field Force of five divisions, with reserve formations to follow up to support European allies; and, to fulfil Baldwin's March 1934 pledge to match Germany in air strength, the RAF's scheme of 1512 first-line aircraft (1022 bombers) by April 1937, with scope for further increases, was also sanctioned.[3]

In May 1936, as the DRC had stipulated, the Cabinet asked the Admiralty to study a two-power standard, while reserving its decision about whether it ought to be adopted. Since 1939 was the DRC deadline for rearmament and it was impossible to build much more by that year than a revitalised one-power standard (the DRC fleet – Table 6.1) with existing output capacity, Sir Samuel Hoare, the First Lord, proposed tele-scoping the DRC building timetable over the next three years to include a number of the cruisers, destroyers and submarines planned for 1940–2. His submission was approved.[4] The February 1937 Defence White Paper announced the laying down of the next three *King George V* class ships six months early, an extra aircraft carrier and seven cruisers. A new stand-ard had not been authorised, yet construction planned for 1936–7 corre-sponded with precisely what had to be done to reach it. Although the Third Sea Lord (Controller), Admiral Reginald Henderson, denied Treasury suspicions that this 'acceleration' was nothing more than a clever ruse to locate the Navy on the best possible industrial footing to fight for and sustain maximum output later (Table 6.2), it was evident that this was precisely what the Naval Staff was up to.[5]

In late April 1937, Hoare circulated the Naval Staff's 'New Standard Fleet' proposal to the Cabinet's Defence Plans (Policy) Sub-Committee (DPP).[6] Having learned from Chatfield's error in 1934, the planners no longer claimed that peace in Europe would alone keep Tokyo at bay: 'At present the outside observer sees the German Navy rising, he knows that on

Table 6.1   The DRC and new standard fleets compared

	DRC fleet	New standard fleet
Capital ships	15	20
Aircraft carriers	10	15
Cruisers (all types)	70	100
Destroyers	16 flotillas	22 flotillas
Submarines	55	82

Sources: Gibbs, *Strategy*, 340; 'New Standard Fleet', ADM1/9081.

Table 6.2   A comparison of the Naval Staff's projected DRC and new standard fleet building rates, May 1938

	DRC standard					New standard				
	1937	1938	1939	1940	1941	1937	1938	1939	1940	1941
Capital ships	3	2	2	1	1	3	2	3	2	2
Aircraft carriers	2	1	1	—	—	2	1	3	1	1
Cruisers 8000 tons	5	4	2	—	—	5	4	4	4	4
Cruisers 5300 tons	2	3	—	—	—	2	2	2	2	1
Destroyer flotillas	2	—	—	—	—	2	—	2	1	1
Submarines	7	3	6	—	—	7	7	11	7	5

Source: 'Naval Requirements, 1937–41', ADM116/3631.

our existing declared One-Power Standard we might be able to send a Fleet to the Far East before Germany's programme is complete, but after that date he cannot see how we can do so unless our strength is increased.' To render the colossal building and future upkeep costs more palatable, the planners suggested that economies could be made in smaller classes if a lasting détente with Germany was concluded. Yet, as Chatfield had foreseen nearly a decade before, and despite a sustained diplomatic effort to make warships economical, the soaring price of sea power caused ministers to hesitate. The Admiralty trod cautiously. On 11 May, the First Lord stressed to the DPP that instant approval of the new standard was not being sought; instead, the committee discussed the issue of what the Dominion delegations should be told that month, at the Imperial Conference in London, about the pledge to dispatch the main fleet to Singapore in case of a

Japanese attack. Again the Admiralty scored a tactical victory: the promise was upheld, even though the decision to procure the *matériel* means it presupposed remained in abeyance.[7]

The Admiralty hoped to get the decision it wanted by turning the threat of a Treasury-sponsored defence review into an opportunity. The Treasury of course had its own motives. Although a Minister for the Co-ordination of Defence, Sir Thomas Inskip, had been appointed in March 1936 to bring coherence to military spending, Chamberlain and Warren Fisher had become alarmed at ever inflating service programmes. Before he left the Treasury in May 1937, Chamberlain renewed his efforts to set defence priorities by launching a review of projected service estimates against anticipated revenue.[8] The Treasury proposed a figure of £1500 million (including a £400 million defence loan) as the total available for expenditure on the armed services from 1937 to 1942. In the autumn and winter of 1937, therefore, both Sir John Simon, Chamberlain's successor as Chancellor, and Inskip obtained authority for a system of rationing within this global figure. Although Treasury officials knew that spare expenditure capacity might become available later, and although they may have been unduly anxious about the recurrence of another 1931 slump, their strategic thinking was sound: the forces projected by the ideal service schemes and the income needed to maintain them afterwards would imperil the commercial integrity and the level of economic activity indispensable to waging a protracted war. As Inskip told the Cabinet in December 1937, economic stability should be 'regarded as a fourth arm in defence ... without which purely military effort would fail'.[9]

These developments matched the expectations of Admiral James, the DCNS, and Captain Phillips that the CID would soon face a choice between relinquishing sea power or adopting a less ambitious air strategy. In their minds, the air parity policy violated the key strategic precept of the nineteenth century: the price of British naval supremacy was inferiority on land because simultaneously 'maintaining an army on a Continental scale would spell ruin'. Since they appreciated that the 'overbearing' defence burden endangered Britain's place in the global economy, Chatfield and his colleagues predicted that the Cabinet would come to its strategic senses because the timeless logic of British finance and strategy was on the Royal Navy's side.[10] And this calculation was by no means unrealistic: Inskip's report had after all reaffirmed an essentially maritime-based grand strategy predicated on the steady accumulation of a preponderance of overseas resources for victory over the long haul.

The Cabinet endorsed Inskip's review just before Christmas, and the services were ordered to bring their estimates within a figure of £1500 million (raised to £1650 million in February 1938) for the years 1937–41. The Admiralty naturally rebelled. Tactical victories over this expenditure cap and increases to the 1938–9 building schedule were important, but British ship-yards and related ordnance industries, as the Sea Lords knew, were already at peak capacity. What is crucial to recognise here is that the Admiralty's true objectives in 1937–8 were fundamentally bureaucratic and political:[11] Chatfield wished to liberate the navy after 1938 from annual budgetary battles with the Treasury by installing a Cabinet-endorsed yardstick of naval strength, to advance the industrial strategy of maximising the approved DRC schedule as the springboard for the new standard, and to re-establish the precedence of sea power over other forms of warfare in national strategy.

Besides the pledge to defend the Pacific Dominions and the progress of the Navy's industrial strategy, there were other signs that the trajectory of CID policy matched Naval Staff expectations. The new PM, who acted from his own strategic conceptions rather than any inclination towards the Navy's viewpoint, brought about defence initiatives welcomed by the Naval Staff. First, both as chancellor and premier, Chamberlain championed cutting the armaments required for the army's reserve divisions earmarked for Europe, and then finally, in December 1937, in harmony with Inskip's defence review, those required for the regular Field Force.[12] Chatfield equally advocated a 'limited liability' on the continent.

Second, from the summer of 1937 onwards, as a result of Inskip's enquiry, the Cabinet moved to abandon air parity and the counter-bombing force deterrent. A positive sign came in July with Inskip's decision to restore sole control of naval aviation to the Navy. More importantly, bomber output and plant potential lagged behind the numbers projected by successive expansion schemes, while financial and recruitment targets spiralled upwards; there seemed little chance of perpetually equalling the *Luftwaffe*. Inskip argued, with the backing of Chamberlain, Simon and Fisher, that ultimately it had never been the mission of the bomber force to deliver a knockout blow but to prevent one. He reasoned that a switch to close fighter defences, now more conceivable with the advance of radar, would achieve that end more effectively. Inskip now proposed that the RAF supply strong air defences to parry a knockout blow and only enough bombers initially to augment naval power in economic warfare.[13] The import of this policy U-turn was not lost on the Naval Staff, which had staunchly held that the technological ascendancy of the bomber was fleeting. The Navy in 1938 became a strong supporter of the fighter initiative.[14] Likewise, it pushed ahead with its scheme for an 'objective' JIC enquiry into the air war in Spain to vitiate the RAF's case for a counter-bombing force.[15]

Once again, it is important to appreciate the conditional relationship between the navy's internal and external policy aims: victories in Whitehall would be futile if the Naval Staff's programme collapsed abroad; conversely, a European settlement would dampen support for air parity. How the Naval Staff attempted to ensure that external conditions squared with internal ones is the question to which we must now turn. Here, the principal impetus was the lesson taken from the 1936-7 naval talks, which had convinced senior officers that if a détente with Berlin could not be reached, the Naval Agreements were doomed. At the end of 1937, only fragmentary information about Hitler's growing antipathy to Britain and the Naval Agreements reached the Admiralty, but Admiral Chatfield and his staff knew enough to be worried.

Even with the benefit of hindsight, the course of Hitler's disillusionment with Britain is difficult to chart precisely. But there can be no doubt that the lack of political rewards accrued from his maritime appeasement contributed significantly to the Führer's growing hostility towards Britain between the summer of 1936 and November 1937. During this time, he remained content to watch the election of a Popular Front government in Paris in June 1936 and the outbreak of civil war in Spain a month later divide Europe and draw Italy into his orbit, just as the Ethiopian crisis had done before. German intervention in Spain was confined to extending the conflict with an eye to exploiting the situation to annex Austria. Hitler's immediate aim – with the launch of the Four-Year Plan in September 1936 and its premise of autarky – was to match German war-making capacity with the object of his foreign policy programme, *Lebensraum*.[16]

During 1935-6, Admiral Raeder remained restless: the 35 per cent ratio troubled his blue-water fantasies. In January 1937, though, with the tonnage granted to him by the laying down of three more of the *King George V* class, he ordered his constructors to look beyond the eight capital ships fixed by his 1935 programme and to draft plans for a ninth and perhaps even a tenth battleship. Craigie's hint a few weeks later about Britain perhaps increasing its battlefleet above 15 units encouraged Raeder's belief that the British might launch seven 35 000-ton vessels without scrapping any overage tonnage before 1942.[17] In the following months, Hitler's angry response to intelligence that Moscow was seeking 16-inch gun technology from the Americans, and the Führer's escalating irritation at British mediation in European affairs, permitted Raeder and his planners to add happily to their timetable first four and then in December 1937 six new H-class 56 000-ton ships with 16-inch guns.

Fortunately paper plans were easier to draft than to execute. Even the 35 per cent fleet was well behind schedule due to labour and raw material shortages. Moreover, with Göring, the navy's main rival, commanding the *Luftwaffe* and controlling the Four-Year Plan, and the Reich Chancellor's indolent aloofness from service rivalries, the prospects seemed bleak. At the end of October, in a desperate effort to keep construction on track and forestall imminent cuts in the navy's steel allotment, Raeder appealed to General Blomberg, the Defence Minister, to obtain a prompt decision from the Chancellor on priorities. Evidently out of step with Hitler's thinking, he emphasised that a fleet with only two 35 000-ton ships was inadequate for defence and lacked sufficient alliance value.[18]

On 5 November 1937, Raeder received his answer. At a meeting of top military and foreign policy officials, called to consider the navy's need for steel, Hitler set out his 'unalterable resolve' to acquire *Lebensraum*. Neither autarky nor joining the global economy would solve the need for living space in the long run because of Germany's reliance on seaborne food supplies. The first step was dealing with Austria and Czechoslovakia. This entailed reckoning with 'two hate-inspired antagonists, Britain and France, to whom a German colossus in the center of Europe was a thorn in the flesh'. Hitler attacked the British resolve to join France in blocking German expansion and added that British power was not 'unshakeable', as his generals supposed. Since rearmament would peak in 1942, that was the year for action, but he would move earlier if civil war broke out in France or if a Mediterranean war erupted. While his army colleagues questioned the Führer's calculations, Raeder – true to Tirpitz's dictum 'mouth shut and build ships' – sat silent. Although his war plans called for British neutrality, Hitler's words signalled fresh dividends in Raeder's mind, even if his policy was for now mainly continental. Indeed, during the second half of the meeting, the navy's steel quota was raised from 45 000 to 74 000 tons per month.[19]

Intelligence about the German navy's new steel allotment did not reach the Admiralty; nevertheless, on the same day that the order was issued, Chatfield minuted that positive diplomacy was needed to prevent Germany moving against Britain.[20] To reinvigorate the search for a détente, the CNS turned to Chamberlain. To recount how they arrived at this position, it is necessary to return once again to the final DRC report. The chief message of that document was that no obtainable level of rearmament could secure British interests in three global regions at once, and that the 'cardinal requirement' of security was that diplomacy should prevent the situation in which Britain 'might be confronted simultaneously with the hostility, open or veiled, of Japan in the Far East, Germany in the West and any Power on the main line of communication between the two'.[21] This axiom proved difficult to act upon in practice. The Mediterranean crisis, from

Italy's Ethiopian venture to the Spanish war, vexed the CNS and his staff: they dreaded a costly campaign for the League of Nations and its defunct principle of collective security, and war with a power whose hostility could not be accommodated into their global strategy.[22] Moreover, the threat that foreign intervention in Spain might drive the aggressive powers to combine under the pretence of an ideological affinity appeared to materialise in November 1936 with the Rome–Berlin axis and the Anti-Comintern Pact between Tokyo and Berlin.

The gloomy international situation aggravated tensions between the COS under Chatfield's leadership and Hankey on the one hand, and the FO and the Foreign Secretary on the other. Notwithstanding a broad consensus on appeasement – that war ought to be avoided by promoting peaceful change in Europe until British armaments presented a potent deterrent – divisions developed over how foreign affairs should be conducted in the interim. While the COS called for caution and conciliation abroad, foreign-policy makers became increasingly prepared to take risks with coercive diplomacy.[23] Hence, in a spirit of unveiled reproach to the diplomats, the service chiefs regularly chanted the DRC's reduction-of-potential-enemies formula to the Cabinet.[24]

Differences between the FO and COS over Germany became pronounced after the Rhineland episode. Hitler's refusal to respond to the British questionnaire of May 1936, and his indifference to a joint British, French and Belgian invitation to Germany and Italy to attend a five-power conference, had disillusioned Eden, Vansittart and Central Department officials about the possibility of a worthwhile détente with the Nazis before British bombers posed a credible deterrent. The COS, however, criticised the FO for refusing to frame proposals on a substitute Locarno to exclude Central and Eastern European security issues, as Germany openly wished.[25]

The Admiralty berated the FO (Craigie exempted) for ignoring naval diplomacy as a tool with which to fashion a détente.[26] In May 1936, as we saw in Chapter 2, the apparent success in reversing Hitler's decision to upset the heavy cruiser holiday and the positive test result of 'Craigie's theory' had satisfied the Navy that Berlin was assailable on this flank. This astonished FO officials. Historians have similarly found the Navy's attitude incomprehensible. Roskill saw it as misplaced 'confidence in German good faith'. Wark concludes that the navy's 'egocentric' policy resulted from cosy preconceptions about Berlin's aims, and an unhealthy fixation with parochial service interests.[27] Undoubtedly the Navy's goal to refurbish the naval balance was paramount in its strategic calculus, yet it is useful to contrast in detail FO and Naval Staff outlooks on Nazi Germany and the 1935 Naval Agreement to discover whether the Admiralty did suffer from complacency or warped thinking.

Vansittart and Central Department officials had accepted the June 1935 Naval Agreement as a first step to a general European settlement, but only a year later they had become indifferent to it. Ralph Wigram, the department head and Vansittart's closest associate who had formally objected to the second round of naval talks,[28] in October 1936 derided the notion that the 1935 Naval Agreement was of some 'specially sacrosanct and durable nature'. He believed that Hitler intended to have the largest fleet in Europe as soon as it was feasible.[29] Vansittart agreed:

> The Germans mean to have 'the biggest ever.' One cannot believe a word they say in this respect. (I am not sure that at present one can believe it in *any* respect.) The Naval agreement will not be broken until (a) the Germans are displeased with us, and (b) they are in a position to do so effectively.[30]

In late November, Wigram circulated intelligence from an unnamed diplomatist in London. The source reported a discussion with a friendly German Embassy official about a circular from the Naval Command dated June 1935. It emphasised that the 35 per cent ratio was fixed by German building capacity and that the Agreement would be 'thrown over' once shipyards were available for aggressive expansion.[31]

Craigie, who was at this time negotiating with German and Russian delegations towards qualitative agreements, concluded that Wigram's informant was probably 'mischief-making' and that the existence of such a circular was improbable, but nonetheless reported it to the Admiralty.[32] In reaction, on 22 December 1936, Chatfield candidly set out his perception of German motives and the 1935 Agreement's future:

> It must be remembered that there were two parties to this treaty with Berlin. a. The Führer. b. The Navy. The plan is known to have been the Führer's and no doubt strongly opposed by the latter. It was a political move to secure our friendship and they have got *nothing* for it so far. Once the decision was made Admiral Raeder as a German could accept it ... The memo referred to by Wigram may have been issued by the Naval Staff, annoyed by 'The Führer's' action – I cannot expect however that the Treaty will be kept unless Anglo-German friendship is our policy as well as German policy [otherwise] – they can *easily* find a reason to break it.[33]

He later added:

> I think that the Anglo-German treaty is of the greatest importance not only from a military standpoint but from a Political and international one. Its loss could be serious therefore for both reasons. It was undoubtedly a *most* friendly gesture to us, although it must be admitted that Germany took no great risks since her ship building facilities would have in any case limited the size of the Navy for some years. Göring has also stated that 'no treaty can unceasingly be kept under all circumstances.'[34]

Comparison of the above remarks with those of the FO reveals harmony on core issues. First, the CNS and leading diplomatists agreed that the offer of a 35 per cent ratio was related to German industrial capacity; second, they all admitted that there was nothing 'sacrosanct' or 'durable' about the accord; and third, they all understood that its future depended on the course of Anglo-German relations and the vagaries of the Nazi leadership. The divergent attitudes of the Naval Staff and the FO about the value of the 1935 accord thus did not pivot on incompatible evaluations of Hitler's trustworthiness or the rectitude of his admirals, but on conflicting judgements about the methods for managing German ambitions. In short, they agreed on the prognosis, but differed substantially about an effective remedy.

What Chatfield feared was that the FO might dash Britain's prospects as the leading global maritime power long before his programme of shrewd armaments diplomacy and incremental fleet expansion had paid off. Thus he repeatedly advocated 'taking a long view in foreign policy', in which decisions were governed by the 'final aim', not 'immediate expediency'.[35] As chair and the dominant personality of the COS, he advised ministers that foreign policy had to be brought into line with current war-making capabilities. That translated into a policy of dropping the support of the League of Nations with military sanctions and of avoiding French entanglements in Central and Eastern Europe, especially with a Popular Front government installed in Paris, and building tolerable relations with Japan, Italy and Germany.[36]

In December 1936, Vansittart spelled out his differences with the COS to ministers in an essay entitled 'The World Situation and British Rearmament'. He warned that Germany was assembling an 'international anti-Bolshevik front under her own leadership, with a view to serving as a specific vehicle for ultimate expansion'. The role of the FO was to hold the situation until 1939 by negotiating with the Nazis to encourage 'moderate' elements, and by drawing Italy away from Hitler's grip. Talks should continue about a five-power pact and perhaps a financial or colonial concession should be contemplated (he did not mention the naval talks), but not without 'a full, tested and reliable return'. Yet, since Germany's predatory tendencies on the continent might unexpectedly recoil against Britain, Vansittart gloomily cast doubt on the FO's ability to prevent war even in 1937. Consequently, as some scholars have argued, Vansittart, whose formative years had grounded him in balance-of-power politics, looked to a global equilibrium to solve Britain's dilemma. After Abyssinia, this meant forming links, preferably under the guise of the League, with France and Russia. The aim of this diplomacy was to balance Japanese with Russian power in the Far East (thereby keeping Washington friendly) and creating a web of alignments capable of containing Germany and moderating its policy. Vansittart also advised employing the veiled threat of force, the only 'argument' he thought Berlin recognised, before British armaments were ready, to hearten small European powers into resistance, assure potential allies and to keep Germany 'guessing'.[37]

Significantly, Chatfield's commentary on Vansittart's essay was entitled 'Anglo-German Naval Treaty', but the accord was not mentioned in the text.[38] To appreciate the association, the tactical programme implied by his proposals must be viewed within the Navy's programme. The CNS reiterated his thesis that policy had to be directed at a long-term goal, by which he meant that British statecraft should promote naval supremacy as the mainstay of the Empire. Although he estimated that Germany was unlikely to risk a 'knockout' blow unless Britain became tied to the 'French conception of Europe', he advocated concluding a temporary 'surface' arrangement with Japan to secure sufficient power in Europe to deter a German westward plunge against Britain's 'vital interests'. To rebuild British security, the framework of the qualitative treaties and an extended period of peaceful naval and economic consolidation were needed. Germany's readiness to underwrite this project, regardless of Hitler's true motive, was helpful in 1935 and could be for some time. Chatfield reckoned that the Führer's desire for friendship and German economic and financial weakness under the pressure of the Four-Year Plan (which Vansittart considered 'notorious') could be enlisted to serve British interests.

Accordingly, the CNS wished foreign-policy makers to persuade Paris to abandon the Little Entente and to signal to Berlin that Britain would fight in the West, but not in the East. Germany would expand in that direction and 'run more risks of disaster than dominance by such action, as she will always have behind her armies the growing military strength of England and France'. Similarly, the CNS wished to grant Germany colonies because they would be hostages to British sea power – the very reason why Hitler rejected them. Vansittart and others feared that a German *Drang nach Osten* would upset the European balance of power without acquiring the indispensable moderation in German policy that they sought, but Chatfield predicted that it would restore the balance by encumbering Germany with exhausting liabilities. So he objected to the policy of keeping Germany 'guessing' about British intentions in Eastern Europe because Hitler might miscalculate and strike westward.

In Chatfield's ideal strategic scenario, the inexact Anglo-German *rapprochement* inaugurated by the Naval Agreement was a diplomatic opportunity to find an enfeebling outlet for resurgent German military power in Central and Eastern Europe, while Britain restored its global maritime power; similarly, Hitler and Raeder considered the bilateral accord as a brief renunciation of sea power, intended to secure British acquiescence in continental conquest, until an effective challenge to the Anglo-American sea powers could be launched. The objection to granting Germany liberty in Central and Eastern Europe, raised by the FO during the debate about a five-power pact, was that it would dissolve French power and only postpone the inevitable contest. Chatfield confidently predicted that by the time Berlin could stage such a quarrel with Britain and France, it would be too financially feeble and immobilised by newly acquired vulnerabilities, including a proximate and countervailing Soviet peril, to do so effectively.[39] What the CNS overlooked, however, was that without Anglo-French leadership, the small states were unlikely to hobble the Nazi war machine by armed resistance. And if Hitler moved impromptu in the short run to consolidate his strategic resource base with Czech industries and arms, Austrian steel and iron, and later Romanian oil, he would extensively enlarge Germany's war potential.[40]

The Cabinet, however, had never quite grasped that the 1935 Naval Agreement was founded upon clashing beliefs about what it had signified politically. Chamberlain later admitted that he did not discover that Hitler had composed the deal in exchange for a free hand in Europe until 30 September 1938, when the Führer told him personally.[41] In any case, ministers did not wish to leave Central and Eastern Europe to Nazi mastery, nor could Britain enforce the status quo. The Cabinet had no answer but to leave its public policy 'sufficiently vague' to keep Britain's hands free.[42] Baldwin, in poor health and near retirement, provided little leadership in late 1936. The squabble between Whitehall's military and diplomatic experts intensified.

At CID meetings in December 1936 and February 1937, Chatfield, on behalf of the COS, argued that Eden and his advisors were not interested in a substitute Locarno, but a Franco-British alliance, and, for the same reason, he disowned parts of the COS's annual 'Review of Imperial Defence' drafted by the FO as 'too political in nature'.[43] Likewise, just as reconciliation with Rome appeared closer because of the 'gentleman's agreement' of 2 January 1937, which recognised the Mediterranean status quo, Eden, acting on news that Mussolini was reinforcing his 'volunteers', proposed an effective blockade of Spain. Hoare objected and the Cabinet backed him. The Admiralty were very anxious to coax Italy to join the 1936 London Naval Treaty. The CNS and First Lord resisted any departure from non-intervention and argued that both Franco and the Republicans should be conferred 'belligerent rights' – the right to intercept contraband *matériel* at sea – to free the Navy from guarding British vessels carrying war supplies.[44]

In these circumstances, as Hitler's fabian diplomacy confounded the pursuit of a five-power pact and the Spanish war plagued Anglo-Italian relations, dissatisfaction with FO advice increased, and ministers turned for direction to the leading Cabinet personality and Baldwin's heir presumptive, Neville Chamberlain.[45] For the Navy, despite Chamberlain's awkward proclivities for economy and air power, his policies from 1937 on promised to generate the conditions necessary to realise its strategic vision. In mid-March, the First Lord, Hoare (whose tenure as Foreign Secretary had been cut short in December 1935 when a secret Anglo-French agreement to concede Abyssinia to Italy was leaked to the press), appealed to Chamberlain to prevent anything 'irrevocable' occurring in foreign affairs before he was in control.[46]

Chamberlain, who required no encouragement to distrust professional diplomats, was already convinced that he should take an active role in foreign affairs. Motivated by a loathing of war and by the danger it represented to his own image of a united and mighty Empire, he exploited his powerful executive capacity to bring direction to policy. He revived the Treasury plan to settle with Japan. In June 1936, before the Cabinet had approved, he openly supported the lifting of sanctions against Italy and later *de jure* recognition of the Abyssinia conquest in exchange for Italian co-operation.[47] Chamberlain had an aversion to reviving the 1914 pattern of ententes to deter Hitler because he feared that it would precipitate the calamity he hoped to avert; instead, he advocated regional pacts on the Locarno model, particularly in Eastern Europe,[48] and so rejected projecting an image of uncertainty about the British posture towards change in that region. He therefore sought an unequivocal statement of German grievances from Hitler as a preliminary to talks. And he advanced efforts to induce Berlin to enter into negotiations by offering colonial and economic concessions, which were also intended to strengthen German 'moderates'.[49]

The German Chancellor, however, had no interest in colonies or liberal economics. Chamberlain's efforts stalled. In June, an alleged torpedo attack on the cruiser *Leipzig* in Spanish waters led to the German cancellation of a visit to London by Neurath for talks with Eden. Admiral Chatfield reported to the Cabinet's Foreign Policy Committee (FPC) that the attack was probably not genuine, but it was difficult to prove in either case.[50] For the CNS, the *Leipzig* episode was simply more evidence that the decline in relations was threatening the naval accords.

The Naval Staff's worry about the longevity of the Naval Agreements, however, should not be equated with a fear that Germany might embark on fresh construction. After all, IIC-NID analysis had found that the tempo of German building was declining for technical and industrial reasons that precluded any sudden acceleration in output. Yet promises to Berlin of greater scope for expansion within the 35 per cent framework by large increases in British tonnage – what Craigie had dubbed 'elbow room' – had not reduced tension. In December 1936, Ribbentrop had told Craigie that Hitler was annoyed by the paucity of political return for his naval magnanimity. In response, the CNS took steps to transmit a positive signal to Berlin about the value of the Naval Agreement in the First Lord's speech on the 1937 estimates. In early July, however, in a telegram Vansittart labelled 'ominous', the British ambassador in Berlin wrote that 'Hitler often feels like denouncing the [1935] agreement'.[51]

Reassuring industrial intelligence aside, Chatfield confessed, in agreement with the new First Lord, Duff Cooper,[52] that Hitler could easily find a pretext to discard the Naval Agreements and would certainly do so if the diplomatic deadlock continued. This intensified his calls for a *démarche* in Europe. Encouragement came from the British naval attaché, Captain Troubridge, directly to the CNS and in unofficial 'newsletters' sent to NID. Although he was convinced that the 1935 Naval Agreement would eventually be abrogated, Troubridge also believed until November 1938 that war in the medium term, particularly over Czechoslovakia, was avoidable.[53]

So, as the new PM persisted with his European overtures, the influence of the FO waned and the Naval Staff's expectations waxed. In a confidential memo to the CNS in October, Captain Phillips admitted that the Admiralty had no authority in foreign affairs, but given 'the present turning point in history', he considered forays into the political realm justified: 'If we can settle with Germany, Mussolini would be like a pricked bubble, and Japan would no longer have troubled waters to fish in.'[54] Although the exclusively maritime logic of his pro-appeasement argumentation was truncated by the overriding need to maintain COS credibility by inter-service harmony, Chatfield's broad support was more than sufficient.

After Eden's triumph in September at the Nyon Conference – temporarily ending Italy's Mediterranean submarine piracy – the premier reserved praise for the CNS, and counted him among his allies after Eden resigned in February 1938.[55] Certainly Chatfield did not attempt to openly convert the PM to his way of thinking. Given the latter's views on finance and air forces, that invited certain defeat. But historians have not appreciated that the Naval Staff calculated that if Chamberlain prevailed, he would inescapably promote its master plan to restore British sea power. Undoubtedly the Navy erred, but it is notable that the full contents of Chamberlain's often cited letter of 26 November endorsed one of its fundamental tenets. Remarking on the recent visit to Germany by his future Foreign Secretary, Lord Halifax, the PM buoyantly predicted a settlement in 1938, founded on peaceful treaty revision and limited colonial concessions. Coupled with this prospect, he concluded that disarmament was now only workable by the 'qualitative restriction on matériel ... on the lines of the Washington naval agreement'.[56]

WHEN ASSETS BECOME LIABILITIES

In 1938, the Admiralty's programme to defend British sea power miscarried. As the Naval Staff had recognised, the existing system of naval limitation and the ideas it embodied benefited Britain disproportionately, so long as rivals operated within it; when the revisionist powers departed from naval limitation, what the Naval Staff valued as assets – the two Naval Agreements with Germany and the second London Naval Treaty – became liabilities. Although the following will focus on Nazi Germany's wrecking action, the Japanese of course led the way.

Indeed, Tokyo not only refused in March and June 1937 to join the second London Naval Treaty, but also frustrated efforts to keep the peace in Asia. In July, the outbreak of fighting between Japanese and Chinese forces dashed any residual optimism in Whitehall. For the rest of 1937, Eden pursued joint Anglo-American action against Japan as a means to bolster British diplomacy in Europe; but Chamberlain regarded Washington as an unreliable associate and believed that Eden's plan would push Japan into the Axis. Although Japanese attacks on British and American gunboats in December prompted naval talks in early 1938, Washington later disappointed FO hopes for a truly combined naval demonstration.[57]

To Chatfield, cultivating a rapport with the Americans was important, but, in the event of trouble, he too had little confidence in their aid materialising.[58] Moreover, sanctions might provoke Japan, just when it was 'getting into a mess in Asia and would not trouble us for years'.[59] His chief concern was Japanese naval construction. On this subject, NID was in what the DNC described as a 'colossal' state of ignorance. Although rumours of battleships with 18-inch guns and three 12-inch gun battle-cruisers circulated, the Admiralty wrongly believed that Japan was probably building two 16-inch gun ships of about 40 000 tons.[60]

After brief talks, the London Treaty powers issued warnings on 5 February 1938: unless Japan issued a 'positive assurance' about its plans, they would invoke the 'escalator' clause. Duff Cooper had told the CID that the Navy expected that Tokyo would yield under the threat of Britain's far greater financial and industrial capacity. But the Japanese snubbed the threat on 12 February and turned to qualitative dominance to compensate for the larger productive strength of the Anglo-Saxon powers. Unlike the German H-class battleships, which were paper plans at this stage, the *Yamato* – the first of four 64 000-ton/18-inch gun leviathans with which the Imperial Japanese Navy planned to topple the prevailing naval order – had begun assembly in 1937 under absolute secrecy. At the end of March 1938, France, the United States and Britain raised the upper battleship limit to only 45 000 tons and 16-inch guns.[61] This escalation, plus uncertainty about the naval standard, had grave ramifications for Anglo-German naval relations.

Captain Phillips outlined the predicament in January. The German navy was working out its plans to 1942 on the basis of 35 per cent of the DRC standard of 15 capital ships. In 1937, the British had pledged to inform Berlin of alterations to this five-year tonnage forecast well before the publication of the annual German building programme to provide a firm basis for planning. The Admiralty hoped to increase the battle fleet by assembling 15 modern ships to the new standard of 20. Inskip had proposed in December 1937 a marginal increase by retaining some overage ships. Without a Cabinet decision, though, the number of *Royal Sovereign* class ships (1914–16) to be scrapped as the five new *King George V* class vessels entered service remained open. But Craigie had already told Ribbentrop's deputy in early 1937 that 'there was every probability' Britain would increase its battle fleet. Fearing that any hint of bad faith might furnish Hitler with a pretext to abrogate the Naval Agreements, Phillips pleaded for a prompt decision or some means to brief Raeder before a final ministerial verdict. Perhaps calculating that the CID would find it impossible to cut the fleet later because the 1935 ratio acted as a sort of diplomatic ratchet,[62] Phillips advised announcing that the Navy intended to operate all five overage ships until 1942.[63]

The problem was left hanging until 3 March, when Admiral James confessed that keeping faith with Berlin was incompatible with dragging out the struggle for the new standard. The two issues were securely coupled. Acting before a government decision was ruled out, the DCNS believed that even if the Cabinet did not permit the Admiralty to build new battleships to reach the new standard, ministers would have little choice but to retain all the old tonnage.[64] Chatfield agreed. Yet an early decision to keep 149 700 tons of obsolete ships would award Berlin forthwith enough tonnage for a ninth modern battleship. He decided to play for time. Berlin would be told that 15 capital ships was the planned strength in 1940–1, but Britain reserved the right, governed by the behaviour of the other powers, to keep the *Royal Sovereigns*. Although he expected Raeder to balk at this, at least the situation would remain fluid and a German protest might help his case in Cabinet.[65] The fallout from the *Anschluß* four days later rendered this tactic too risky; however, much to the CNS's relief, Berlin sent its 1938 building plan before receiving the Royal Navy's or the revised forecast for 1942. It was 'unexpectedly small' and confirmed reports that Raeder's slipways were congested. It did not include as expected an eighth capital ship or a third aircraft carrier. 'On the basis of this programme,' Phillips noted, Germany 'will not have built up to her tonnage quota in battleships or aircraft carriers by the end of 1942.'[66] In April, with little immediate prospect of a ninth German battleship on the horizon, the FO briefed the German Embassy about the possible retention of the five *Royal Sovereigns*.[67]

Admiral Chatfield's wish to keep the situation fluid shows that he still reckoned that the Cabinet would underwrite his plan. In early January, he had rejected a compromise for an increase on the DRC fleet within the financial ration because it would tarnish his thesis that the new standard was an immutable axiom of British strategy; furthermore, he anticipated that the Cabinet would accept an increase on the DRC fleet anyway.[68] Accordingly, on 3 February, in the revised financial forecasts for both the DRC and the new standard, Duff Cooper emphasised that the former was not a sound substitute for the latter.[69]

Over the next four months, the Admiralty pressed home the edge it had gained in telescoping the DRC's schedule; concurrently, Simon and his officials applied the financial brake to bring the Navy in line with Cabinet policy. Duff Cooper's proposed 1938 construction plan, which included an extra battleship, aircraft carrier and other vessels, took the Navy within £20 million of the total £225 million projected by the DRC for the years 1936–42. Inskip and Simon accused the Navy of transgressing Cabinet authority by building beyond the approved DRC fleet. The First

Lord revised the plan to two capital ships, one aircraft carrier, seven cruisers and three submarines.[70] As tension over Austria mounted, he appealed to the PM, but in Cabinet Chamberlain voiced his preference for air defence to deter Hitler. The next day, Duff Cooper tried again, claiming tenuously that the Navy was ready to expand 'at the stroke of a pen' and would as a result 'tax [Germany's] limited resources' as Hitler struggled to keep pace.[71]

Yet the First Lord's optimism that the Navy was ready to expand rapidly and the Naval Staff's claim that Japan would be deterred by the marshalling of superior financial and industrial resources belied the reality of the situation. Though the Navy wanted three, it could only lay down two battleships in the 1938 programme, employing emergency reserve slipway space at that. Nevertheless, Chatfield and his planners wished to announce the order of three more capital ships. A steadily increasing element of bluff and bluster was entering into their machinations: 'An unmistakable show of determination on our part to maintain our lead in rearmament at this stage', the Naval Staff maintained, 'may have a most beneficial effect on certain other nations who may well be persuaded to drop out of the race.'[72]

Yet neither financial nor productive capacity was large enough to cope with the intensifying challenge to British sea power by orthodox naval methods. On the contrary, the elegance of Chatfield's programme was that it was composed to forestall the need to employ qualitative escalation by calibrating the naval order to suit the structural realities of British power. As one planner explained in May 1937:

> The truth is that in time of peace it is an obvious British interest to prevent a competition in the size and power of any type of vessel, since an advantage gained in this manner is only temporary and the other power concerned soon goes one better – in war, or if war were known to be coming at a given date, the situation is, however, different and we should be fully justified in starting to build more powerful types so as to be superior on 'the day.'[73]

But unlike Japanese strategists, who could turn to the 'principle of going one better' to be superior on 'the day', the Royal Navy could not pursue this ideal reply to imminent danger. And with the collective analytical powers of the Navy consumed with the realisation of a distant strategic goal, and with the survival of the existing naval order so closely bound to British ascendancy, such a radical reappraisal of means to ends was unlikely to be timely; it would be incremental and belated.

In October 1936, for example, when it still appeared possible that Japan might adhere to qualitative limits, on the recommendation of Admiral Henderson, the Naval Staff confidently resolved to 'gamble' by arming the three ships of the 1937 programme with 14-inch guns, since upgrading to 15 or 16 inches would cause 18 months of delay and result in greater displacement and cost.[74] A year later, rather than pause for Tokyo to play its hand, Phillips called on the Sea Lords to make a prompt decision about the 1938 capital ships to maintain the Royal Navy's production lead. He proposed to press ahead with 14-inch turrets because the 16-inch mounting could not be assembled quickly enough to sustain the building tempo. Unless the 1938 ships were completed by 1942, the Director of Plans foresaw a battleship output gap in 1941–3, during which time the Royal Navy would only be able to array 12 modern and eight unmodernised vessels to combat 20 modern or modernised Japanese and German opponents. On this occasion, the risk of an inferior broadside was deemed too great. The Sea Lords decided to mount 16-inch turrets on the 1938 class battleships.[75]

After escalation in battleship size in March 1938, however, the Naval Staff were bound by the very constraints that British naval armaments diplomacy had been contrived to counterbalance. Rather than dispose of limits altogether, as Washington had proposed, the Admiralty endeavoured to inhibit free escalation.[76] An inquest into the attributes of the new 16-inch gun ships (the future *Lion* class) exposed the problem. The largest – 45 000 tons, with twelve 16-inch guns – was too wide for Home Fleet shipyards. The costs of improving berthing and docking facilities, crew numbers, plus convincing a cost-sensitive Cabinet to order five or more of these £10.5 million weapons, ruled it out. Instead, the Sea Lords settled on a less expensive 40 000-ton ship, with nine 16-inch guns. Again, the Admiralty affirmed that it could produce a ship capable of defeating marginally larger opponents. 'We should aim', the Admiralty resolved, 'at obtaining an upper limit of 40 000 tons and should fight ton by ton against any increase above that, up to a maximum of 43 000 tons.'[77]

As the Admiralty explained to the Cabinet in late May, the only feasible diplomatic strategy for achieving the Navy's goal permitted the Americans to build to the limit. Since war with the US was excluded by Cabinet stricture, the real difficulty was Moscow rejecting qualitative inferiority against Tokyo, which would prompt Berlin to follow suit and so shatter the European equilibrium. To check this, the CNS proposed that Britain should observe a voluntary limit of 40 000 tons and seek to enact it through bilateral deals with Germany, France, Russia, the Baltic states and (after the Anglo-Italian agreement of 16 April) Italy. 'Our hope is that by means of our self-denying ordinance,' the Naval Staff confessed, 'we may produce a European tonnage limit which will prevent [the] disintegrating process.'[78]

But the British effort to induce the powers to follow their lead with 'self-denial' was a diplomatic defensive in the guise of an offensive. Japan led the way, but Germany soon followed with plans to procure ships that exploited the principle of 'going one better', in weight if not gun calibre. Hence the 'self-denying ordinance' gambit flopped as Britain's competitors equivocated about their intentions. And just as the hope of favourable circumstances abroad began to evaporate, the Navy's bid to install naval supremacy as the canon of national policy stalled.

In April, Phillips admitted that the 'psychological moment' to convince the Cabinet to back the Navy was beyond reach. Yet Chatfield and the Sea Lords persevered.[79] The CNS, whose mind was firmly fixed upon the strategic balance of the mid-1940s and who was set to retire shortly, undoubtedly perceived the fight for the new standard as the climax of his career. Acrimonious talks between Duff Cooper and Simon, mediated by Inskip, obtained more money, but not the new standard. By late June, the Chancellor told Chamberlain that 'until the Admiralty is definitely told that it cannot have what it wants, it is impossible to make any progress at all'.[80]

As ministers prepared to rule on naval strength, Chatfield urged Vansittart (now the Cabinet's chief diplomatic advisor) to convert Halifax to his cause.[81] In Cabinet, though, only Hoare spoke up: he invoked the Imperial Conference pledge to send a fleet east in the event of war with Japan, but with little effect. Duff Cooper asked his colleagues to accept the new standard as an ideal target, without fixing a completion date. Hoare considered this reasonable since German ship production had slackened. The Chancellor, however, backed by Chamberlain, refused to commit the government in any way to the new standard. A week later, the Cabinet approved a deal: the Navy's ration of £355 million for 1939–42 was increased to £410 million, only £33 million short of its original demand. In a closing gamble to avert a near total bureaucratic defeat, Duff Cooper requested a revision of the previous Cabinet minutes to reflect that the guidance of the Sea Lords on Britain's proper battle fleet strength had not been rejected, just at present deemed 'not practicable' before 1942, but Chamberlain and Simon could not be outmanoeuvred.[82]

The CNS consoled himself with the knowledge that he had 'shaken' the Cabinet with the ferocity of the Navy's onslaught.[83] Warship output and the funding for future output had benefited from the emphasis on rearmament and measures to mobilise the economy that followed the *Anschluß*. But the building rate was determined by industrial limitations, not financial ones.[84] However, the decision not to build destroyers in 1938, was as much a result of Chatfield's priorities as it was the result of rationing. In July 1935, he told the DRC that if Berlin truly desired war in 1939–40 he would advise jettisoning the 1930 London Naval Treaty, rapidly expanding cruiser and destroyer numbers and advancing battleship building.[85] Instead, he was convinced that war before 1942 was improbable and that his elaborate scheme would have ample time to evolve. Hitler's annexation of Austria on 7 March, however, compressed the strategic horizon. With Czechoslovakia next, Whitehall's policy in Europe switched from war avoidance to crisis management. The fear of war arising from German brinkmanship ensnared the Naval Staff in a conceptual trap of its own making between its long-term goals and the immediate European realities.

Chamberlain was in a similar position. After his close ally Halifax replaced Eden, Chamberlain advanced his plans to divide Mussolini from Hitler. But the Anglo-Italian agreement in April, which settled the thorny issues between London and Rome including Italy's accession to the 1936 London Naval Treaty, remained unratified until Italy withdrew from Spain in late 1938. The PM's hopes, elevated by Halifax's visit, to restrain Berlin by African concessions foundered when Hitler snubbed them in talks with Sir Nevile Henderson, the British Ambassador, in early March. The union of Austria and Germany nine days later underscored the true extent of his ambitions and the hazards of Britain's Locarno obligations. London had already rejected close collaboration with the French in November 1937 and February 1938 because it might block a détente with Berlin and embolden Paris and Prague. In late March, the Cabinet's FPC re-examined policy and arrived at the same verdict. Convinced that Hitler's aims were not boundless, Halifax and Chamberlain planned to deter war by the threat of British intervention, without a formal Anglo-French entente, until the causes of war could be tackled by diplomacy. Accordingly, in April, they persuaded the French to press the Czechs into making concessions to the German minorities within their borders.[86]

Chamberlain had benefited in Cabinet from the prop of COS counsel against war over Czechoslovakia. They had recited the familiar refrain that war with Germany would encourage Japanese and Italian aggression. Little could be done to prevent Germany from defeating the Czechs.[87] The COS resisted staff talks with the French. Indeed, the Navy was foremost in the opposition to such talks. One reason for its reluctance was that there was little to discuss aside from technical matters. But the main objection was the political implications of high-level talks. Admiral James ensured that the FPC was aware of the Navy's fear that Hitler might exploit the news of such talks as an excuse to denounce the Naval Agreements.[88] As it became clear in April that the exchange was needed to fortify the French, Captain Danckwerts of Plans Division proposed 'a very meagre exchange of information'. The concurrence of Chatfield and his colleagues baffled Duff Cooper,[89] and caused one FO official to remark in exasperation that 'what [the Admiralty] would really like to do would be to conduct conversations with the Germans'.[90]

In any case, the Naval Staff's hope that the PM could pilot the impending European storms with the Naval Agreements intact was misplaced. Ribbentrop, at the end of his failed Embassy, labelled Britain Germany's 'most dangerous opponent' and advocated a close co-ordination with Italy and Japan to inflict strategic paralysis on London.[91] Although the Führer judged that he might succeed without British resistance as London's reply to the *Anschluß* seemed to prove, Ribbentrop's appointment as Foreign Minister and Hitler's abolition of General Blomberg's position as War Minister in February helped to tilt the balance to an anti-British policy. The advance of plans to attack Czechoslovakia exposed the incompatibility of Anglo-German images of Europe. The war scare of 20–21 May, initiated by false reports of menacing German military manoeuvres and which resulted in Prague ordering mobilisation and London and Paris issuing warnings, fixed Hitler's previously tentative timetable. Infuriated by the press reports that he had retreated in the face of Anglo-French resolve, Hitler announced to his generals on 30 May his 'unalterable' decision to 'smash' Czechoslovakia 'in the near future'. While Chamberlain hoped his mediator might resolve the dispute, Hitler ordered the German minorities in Czechoslovakia to intensify steadily the agitation campaign.[92]

Likewise, the 'weekend' crisis proved to be the turning point in Anglo-German relations. Hitler vented his resentment at London in demands for more sea armaments. On 24 May, the Chancellor had his naval adjutant, Lieutenant-Commander Karl von Puttkamer, direct Raeder to amend the naval programme: 'The Führer must reckon Britain permanently among his enemies.' His demands were not immediately attainable, but they signalled a departure from his policy of naval abstinence. The C-in-C Navy, who had examined the question of raising U-boat numbers to 100 per cent of the British tonnage in November 1937, placed contracts for eight 750-ton boats and notably gave design priority to U-cruisers, but expansion could not begin before January 1939. While measures for speeding up work on *Bismarck* and *Tirpitz* were feasible, arming the battlecruisers with larger 15-inch gun turrets entailed a year's delay. Construction of extra slipway space for greater output was accepted as a long-term measure.[93] Like the Admiralty, the German Naval Command found itself caught between the imperatives of a long-term project (his December 1937 target provided for 365 ships by 1944) and immediate political realities. After the 5 November 1937 conference, Admiral Raeder procrastinated until 12 April 1938 before briefing his colleagues about the risk of war with Britain entailed in the Führer's vision.[94]

The first clues about the change in German policy did not reach the Admiralty until after Munich. Although Captain Siemens, the new naval attaché, complained in June about the open decision on the *Royal Sovereigns*,[95] the Naval Staff, well acquainted with industrial bottlenecks, were reassured by accurate intelligence and Berlin's official building schedule, which disclosed that Germany was unable to reply with fresh warship contracts. To prevent any inquest about the 1935 Agreement's value, however, Plans Division vigorously challenged any hint that the Nazi defence economy was incapable of accelerating its output of surface warships. In a FO paper prepared to supply Sir Nevile Henderson with ammunition against attacks on the Naval Agreements (Göring had threatened to build to parity in U-boats if London resisted the *Anschluß*), Adrian Holman argued that industrial obstacles precluded German expansion beyond 35 per cent 'for a number of years, possibly indefinitely'. In retort, Danckwerts revived the CID-endorsed report 'German Naval Construction', completed by IIC-NID in July 1936, to convince the FO to tone down Holman's memorandum.[96]

In July, it was decided to transfer the battlecruisers from the Mediterranean to the Home Fleet in late 1938 to check a break-out of German raiders,[97] yet the Naval Staff still hoped that Chamberlain's bilateral diplomacy might restore its strategic timeline. Chatfield told the COS in July that he 'shared the view that Germany aimed eventually at the domination of Europe', in the first stage by subjugating Central Europe, but that the short-term danger was Hitler acting militarily in the Sudetenland to uphold prestige.[98] From the rejection of the new standard in July to Munich in September, the CNS steadfastly opposed any British guarantee of Czechoslovakia.

Relentlessly, however, Berlin and London were steaming towards the conflict of expectations submerged below the 1935 Anglo-German Naval Agreement. These political and strategic waters, though familiar, were shallow and hazardous. In late 1937, Hitler had told Halifax that the naval ratio was the only thing that had not been 'wrecked' in his effort to settle with Britain, and Göring had outlined to Henderson a détente based on two premises: German recognition of British maritime supremacy, and British recognition of German continental hegemony.[99] But as one FO memo put it, in proposing his 35 per cent ratio, Hitler had

> overlooked, as all German politicians have overlooked for many years past, that this country is bound to react, not only against danger from any purely naval rival, but also against the dominance of Europe by any aggressive military Power ... British complaisance can never be purchased by trading one of these factors against the other...[100]

The Munich Agreement appeared to establish peaceful coexistence, but British and German conceptions of Europe remained incompatible. Hitler had told Chamberlain at Berchtesgaden that if Britain continued 'to make it clear that in certain circumstances' it would intervene in Europe, then the preconditions of the naval ratio were void and Germany should be 'honest' and end it.[101] The import of this did not escape the PM. The Anglo-German Declaration of 30 September, which Chamberlain success-fully sprang on the Führer to his subsequent rage, redefined the 35 per cent agreement as symbolic of the desire of the two peoples to renounce armed conflict between them, and stated that the method for resolving existing difference should be 'consultation'. The Naval Staff were euphoric. Still baling furiously to keep qualitative limitation afloat, Admiral James considered that Moscow's rejection of the 40 000-ton self-denying ordinance two weeks before

> might, I think, have been more serious before the events of the last few days. In a document signed a few hours ago by the German Chancellor and our Prime Minister, a special reference was made to the Anglo-German Naval Agreement and I feel that, by good diplo-macy, this question of the German upper limit might be resolved to our satisfaction.[102]

Despite the failure to secure a new standard, at least the vital component of the Navy's external programme was salvageable.

The Admiralty's relief was to be ephemeral. At first reluctant to break the taboo, the German navy quickly adjusted to the new political envi-ronment. The undercurrent of anti-British sentiment in German naval thinking of the Tirpitz era resurfaced.[103] The German Naval Command was anticipating that the entire naval treaty framework would soon col-lapse. In September, Admiral Günther Guse, the Head of the Naval

Command Office, composed a pithy repudiation of the Admiralty's grand design:

> [The German navy has] no interest in supporting the present system of naval agreements which has at the best no other purpose than to stabilise for all times, on all seas, and with the employment of the least resources possible the British superiority at sea.

Admiral Raeder's staff also hammered out plans to wage war against Britain. In tandem they studied the timing and pretext for openly breaking the heavy cruiser holiday and of raising the U-boat ratio to parity.[104] With some justification, the Naval Command grew impatient about the *Royal Sovereigns*. After the CID had decided in late October to operate a battle fleet of 19 ships by the end of 1942, Siemens interrogated Danckwerts about past promises of 'elbow room'. 'The German Admiralty had gained the impression from the late Admiral Wassner's reports', he said, 'that Great Britain was aiming at a total of 21 [battle]ships.'[105] It was a dead issue. In January 1939, with its colossal Z-Plan ready, the Naval Command informed the Foreign Ministry that they should no longer seek the British tonnage forecasts that had been the basis since June 1935 for calculating the 35 per cent ratio.[106]

CONCLUSION

Admiral Chatfield had recognised how close British global power was bound to the existing international naval order. If things changed radically, so too would Britain's ranking among the powers. The Naval Staff's programme anticipated and aimed to regulate that process. The elaborate symmetry of relationships between technology, finance, armaments diplomacy and defence policy that the Navy attempted to spin compelled the Naval Staff to influence policy-making at the highest level. In doing so, Chatfield backed Chamberlain, an unlikely champion with his proclivities for air power and fiscal restraint. But Chamberlainite appeasement was interventionist and hence promised to forge the international context – the longevity of the qualitative treaties, medium-term tranquillity, and a limited liability in Europe – that the navy's programme presupposed. Deprived of this potential international context, in which the prevailing framework of naval limitation and sea power was a British asset, the Naval Treaties became a liability, and the structural impediments to Britain remaining the world's leading maritime power were exposed.

In retrospect, the scale of Chatfield's ambition, the intricate balance of risks and the elaborate and so fragile web of relationships it posited made success improbable. Yet it must be emphasised that Britain was the foremost sea power. Its ascendancy was firmly anchored to the existing naval order. If that order was to survive, British leadership was required to entrench and maintain the political, conceptual and strategic context – the rules of the game – to promote its interests and enhance its status. The trouble was that no matter how adroit the bid, without an alternative course, it was an enormous gamble. To triumph, it needed time to evolve. Chatfield calculated that Hitler's wish for British friendship, with careful handling, could manufacture the time required, well before a fatal German threat to the European balance could develop. Time was not on the Navy's side.

7 The End of Appeasement and the Bid to Transform Admiralty Strategy, 1938–39

The Anglo-German Declaration of September 1938 did not bring about the change in relations with Germany that both Chamberlain and the Naval Staff desired. The collective sense of relief in Whitehall brought about by Chamberlain's novel shuttle diplomacy was short lived. Hitler proved unresponsive to friendly overtures. Profound indignation at having suffered an unseemly humiliation swelled inside and outside the British policy elite. Intelligence from the Nazi camp was often terrifying. In succeeding months, the balance in policy tilted to containment, which was inaugurated in March 1939 with the guarantee to Poland. Concurrently, Admiral Chatfield's successor struggled to adapt Admiralty strategy to match the post-Munich landscape.

Naturally, the closing phase in British interwar diplomacy has received considerable attention. The objective here is not to retraverse this well trodden ground. Rather, this chapter will highlight the significance of naval diplomacy in Anglo-German relations in 1938–9 and will elucidate the policies expounded by the new First Sea Lord, Admiral Roger Backhouse. In different and yet not unrelated ways, both are important to the continuing debate about British policy in the late 1930s. As regards naval diplomacy, no historian has thoroughly examined how Hitler's growing antagonism towards Britain, which expressed itself pointedly in the dismantling of the Naval Agreements in December 1938 and April 1939, influenced British policy-makers. After all, Baldwin had endorsed the Admiralty's suggestion to conclude the 35 per cent agreement on the grounds that it would be a yardstick for Hitler's future intentions.[1] Viewed from this standpoint, naval diplomacy provides some fascinating insights into the minds of Chamberlain, Halifax and subordinate officials as appeasement gave way to containment.

In the case of naval policy, historians have misunderstood the attempt by Backhouse, the CNS from September 1938 to mid-April 1939, with the assistance of his special advisor, Admiral Drax, to forge alternative policies to those of his immediate predecessor.[2] The outcome of this effort shows that the Navy's view on foreign and defence policy in 1937–8 was the product of concrete temporal, material and grand strategic imperatives that could not be transcended simply by the application of an offensive spirit or broad-minded management techniques.

NEW PERSONALITIES

The Cabinet's refusal to endorse the new standard and Munich coincided with a substantial and routine reshuffle of top Admiralty officials. Captain Danckwerts succeeded Phillips as Director of Plans in April 1938. Admiral Andrew B. Cunningham replaced Admiral James as DCNS. Godfrey took over from Troup as DNI in February 1939. Duff Cooper resigned over Munich and Lord Stanhope assumed his Cabinet post. And during the Czech crisis, Admiral Backhouse was appointed CNS.

Historians have been critical of Backhouse's leadership. Although he had held senior positions, namely Third Sea Lord (Controller, 1928–32) and C-in-C Atlantic fleet (1935–8), Roskill implies that his rise to the top was only possible because of a scarcity of good candidates.[3] Due to a lack of records, why he was promoted is likely to remain a mystery.[4] Echoing contemporary naval opinion, both Roskill and Marder portrayed Admiral Backhouse as the 'arch centraliser', who became obsessed with minutiae and stubbornly refused to delegate routine work to subordinates.[5] There may be some truth in these indictments, yet it is not very rewarding to dismiss Backhouse's tenure simply as an unfortunate mistake.[6]

In attempting to describe what Backhouse wanted to achieve, however, the historian meets three obstacles. First, his private correspondence, the main evidence for his inner convictions, is scanty. Second, a great deal of Naval Staff decision-making in 1938–9 was reactive: policies were improvised under the pressure of the fluid international situation and war scares.[7] Third, Backhouse's tenure at the Admiralty was cut short in late March 1939 by a fatal illness. Still, it is possible to identify the central theme of his thinking: that the best way to add clout to British diplomacy and to win the next war was to cultivate the offensive. This tenet was as much a product of his own mind as it was the result of his career-long association with Richmond and Drax.

As early as 1929, Admiral Backhouse was convinced that the Admiralty was suffering from an excess of 'materialism' or, more precisely, a preoccupation with the production of armaments.[8] In late 1937, he complained to Drax that the Naval Staff was doing too little to win a future conflict because it was encumbered by 'dealing with problems concerning Disarmament, League of Nations and Naval Treaties'.[9] To bypass this bureaucratic congestion early in his tenure, Backhouse invited Drax to head for three months, starting in January 1939, a new Offensive Planning Cell, to develop his ideas 'quite independently of any Admiralty Department or Division', and to advise him on strategy.[10] To seek a long-term solution, he convened a special committee in October 1938 to draft proposals for an overhaul of the Naval Staff system.[11]

Of course the promotion of an officer whom Admiral Chatfield had rebuked in November 1937 for proffering generalisations in the guise of practical strategic advice to the position of personnel advisor to the CNS signalled a sharp reversal in Admiralty thinking. As noted, the essential difference between the strategic ideas of Chatfield and Drax was about the use of time as a strategic commodity. If war came, Drax wanted to exploit it with a series of rapid offensives designed to reduce Britain's global disadvantage in naval strength; Chatfield believed that the only way to restore Britain's sea power was through a long cycle of quiet industrial and naval renewal.

Events from October 1938 onwards showed that the timetables of the revisionist states would not permit such an ambitious project to run its course. Drax and Backhouse made this assessment before Munich; the diplomatic crisis vindicated this outlook on world affairs. Two papers composed by Drax in October 1938, for instance, were peppered with what he called the 'unpublished creed of the Prussian Nazi' – 'England is the final enemy' and 'one bold stroke and the British Empire is ours' – and various plots setting out how Hitler might act on these dictums with high-stakes brinkmanship.[12] Likewise, Backhouse confided to the C-in-C Mediterranean 'that 1939 will be a critical year, as it is most unlikely that Hitler will not have some great scheme he wants to put through'.[13]

Previously, Chatfield had believed that the small size of the German navy in 1939–40 would hamstring German policy[14] and that Hitler's desire for British 'friendship' could be managed to the benefit of Britain's interests. NID analysis of the German navy during the Czech confrontation torpedoed these assumptions. In August, a preliminary study concluded that Raeder's forces were 'practically' mobilised.[15] The FO saw this, within the context of the developing crisis, as a rational precaution to ready the German fleet 'for all eventualities', as well as a clumsy attempt at deterrence.[16] The NID post-mortem, however, pointed in an extraordinarily different direction. NID concluded:

A study of the movements of German warships during the end of September 1938, can only indicate the plan which the German Naval

Staff were forced to adopt when rapid and unexpected international reaction to Germany's policy robbed Germany of the initiative. There is no evidence to indicate that the movements of German warships, during this period, were part of their general war plan. The German Navy on the 28th September, 1938, was not 100 per cent ready to cross swords with the sea power of Great Britain and France.[17]

In short, Backhouse was confronted with the disagreeable news that Hitler had impetuously embarked on the break up of a small European state and risked a general war without any concern about the readiness of his fleet or the advice of his admirals.

Consequently, terrifying scenarios, in which Hitler demanded back former German colonies perhaps under the naked threat to bomb London coupled with a 24-hour ultimatum, plagued the imaginations of Backhouse and Drax.[18] Repairing the feebleness they had diagnosed in naval policy, so that British diplomacy had room to manoeuvre before Hitler's next move, became their priority. To put Europe 'into better shape', Drax urged the CNS to ensure the Navy was ready to strike.[19] Precisely how Backhouse expected a new offensive capability at sea would buttress Britain's European policy or, better yet, compensate for the fear of German airpower, remains unclear. Yet a paper later drafted by his private strategic oracle provides some indication of the link. 'People constantly complain that when crisis occurs in Europe the Government never seems to be quite ready to deal with it,' Drax wrote in late March 1939, 'but are not our war plans in the same state ? ... What we need is to have our plans so complete that if war occurs on Monday morning the CNS can signal to any Commander-in-Chief say "execute plan B (or C, or D) tomorrow, Tuesday."'[20] Moving up to Cabinet level, it is reasonable to infer that Drax and Backhouse were likewise convinced that a readiness on the part of the Navy to execute a series of rapid and spectacular blows against the German or Italian fleet, especially in port, would offer ministers an off-the-shelf plan of attack in the event of another crisis, that would also improve the global naval balance.

Given the striking dissimilarity in strategic timetables, the new CNS found much of his predecessor's project unintelligible. On the relative neglect of destroyers and escorts under Chatfield, Backhouse wrote that he 'could not think how [the Navy] got into such a state'. Equally important, the new CNS believed that the Navy was placing too much faith in ASDIC as a solution to the submarine threat.[21] As his correspondence indicates, during and after the Munich crisis, reports about U-boats operating off South America and West Africa caused him great anxiety.[22] Backhouse thus grasped the need to obtain the building potential required for the best currently available model ASDIC equipped vessel, and a sizeable standing force of such units. Early in October 1938, the CNS instructed Goodall to prepare for the mass production of a cheap ASW escort.[23] In November, the Cabinet authorised the inclusion of ten escorts in the 1938 programme and granted provisional authority for more before May 1940.[24] The resulting improvisation (the *Flower* corvettes) served as a mainstay of the Royal Navy's ASW fleet during the war.[25] Probably as a response to the faulty IIC reports about the colossal scale of Germany's mine stocks, the CNS also sought Cabinet approval to convert 12 trawlers to minesweepers.[26]

The new emphasis on light craft did not signify that the Admiralty was content with its battleship strength. But much of the elaborate scheme previously pursued under Chatfield – to induce naval rivals to follow shipbuilding policies compatible with the regeneration of British supremacy at sea – was in shambles. Admiralty decision-makers had few options. Without a Cabinet-authorised standard at which to aim, and without the industrial base to compete globally in battleship numbers and types, the Navy could only 'press forward with the [Cabinet endorsed] new construction of both light and heavy types at the quickest rate that money and building capacity [would] allow'. More sublime and distant goals were in abeyance. By 1944, under the current plan, Japan and Germany would have a capital ship edge of three or four, and together with Italy the margin would be 11 or 12.[27] Worse still, the cycle of refits and modernisation left only ten capital ships operational until September 1939. In early December, the CNS lamented that 1939 would be a bad year: 'Things have been allowed to go too far ...'[28]

This realisation, however, and Britain's industrial and financial plight compelled the CNS, led by Drax, to conceive of fresh ways to escape the limits imposed by time and *matériel*. At the diplomatic level, one consequence was the conviction that American aid was Britain's only salvation from Japan. Drax and Cunningham both looked to an Anglo-American alliance as the substitute for the League of Nations and the guarantor of world peace, without admitting the underlying conflict of interests inherent in such a partnership.[29] At the operational level, the outcome of this process was a proclivity for unorthodox war plans.

SCRAPPING THE NAVAL AGREEMENTS: PART ONE

Munich had cheated Hitler out of the violent end of the Czech state that he had craved. While the rest of Europe saw it as a triumph for Nazi statecraft, he saw it as a defeat. The Führer thereafter aimed his wrath at its British architects. Hitler had hoped to use naval diplomacy to prevent London from interfering with his European conquests. Gratitude for the 35 per cent ratio, in his mind, had not been forthcoming, only more British meddling. From November 1937 onwards, his growing anger at this situation required regular venting with orders for more warships. It was indeed significant that Hitler admitted to Chamberlain at Berchtesgaden in 1938 that he would denounce the 1935 Naval Agreement before going to war with Britain.[30]

Spurred on by Ribbentrop, who was poisoned against his former hosts by what seemed to him to be an incomprehensible reluctance to conclude an alliance, Hitler plotted to rid Europe of British power. The prelude was to finish off the Czech state. By means of a territorial settlement, Poland would be drawn into the German orbit to secure the East. Italy and Japan would be enlisted into a tripartite alliance to paralyse Britain globally and to keep America and Russia in check. An isolated France could then be defeated and Britain blockaded into submission. Weaving this diplomatic web over the next six months, however, proved too much for Ribbentrop. Apart from the Japanese army, key policy-makers in Tokyo would not risk war with Russia and America to serve German ends. The Italians launched a press attack against Paris, in a vain bid to extract concessions on the Sudetenland model. Once frustrated, Rome consented to join Ribbentrop's pact in late December and signed the Pact of Steel in May 1939. In January 1939, the Polish Foreign Minister, hoping to maintain Poland's independence by playing off its two powerful neighbours, refused to settle with Germany and to join the Anti-Comintern Pact, as Ribbentrop had intended.[31]

Once more, the German navy's raw material quota and its dream of a blue-water armada were beneficiaries of Hitler's hostility to Britain. From late 1938 to the summer of 1939, the Führer's naval directives indicate how much Britain counted in his strategic calculus, and conversely, as Donald Cameron Watt has argued, how little Russia figured in it. Hitler's naval policy shows how this anger drove him recklessly to force the pace of events in 1939: a consequence of which was an inability to correlate the scale of his war with German arms output.[32] These issues only stirred Admiral Raeder briefly. Despite his pleas (and a frustrated resignation attempt) in November 1938 in favour of a rapid build-up for *Kreuzerkrieg*, the strategy most promising against the Royal Navy, the C-in-C Navy yielded to Hitler's demand for six 56 000-ton ships by 1944; he later relied on Hitler's belief that an early war with Britain was improbable. The outcome, approved on 17 January 1939, was the mammoth Z-Plan (Table 3.1). Two weeks later, to translate it promptly from paper to steel, Hitler gave the navy top priority over the other arms schemes, and even exports, in raw materials and workers.[33]

Concurrently, Raeder's staff pondered several pressing short- and medium-term issues. January 1939, the point after which it would be possible to lay down more U-boats than permitted under the 45 per cent ratio agreed in June 1935, and after which it would be impossible to conceal the installation of 8-inch guns on cruisers K and L (and so openly break the pledge to observe the A-class cruiser holiday), was rapidly approaching. Both were provided for by the Naval Agreements, but only under mutually agreed circumstances. If unavoidable, the bilateral talks would have to take place in December 1938 at the latest. The bogus pretext – namely excessive Soviet expansion in these classes – had been in cold storage for three years now, but the exact timing still had to be worked out with the Foreign Ministry. The medium term issues – such as would Germany pretend to adhere to the 40 000-ton 'self-denying ordinance' for capital ships, and how much of the Z-Plan expansion could be laid down before it would become necessary to violate openly the 35 per cent ratio – set the technical timetable for the inevitable treaty abrogation. On both counts, Raeder and his advisors were inclined to early denunciation, since they saw the official British forecast of 19 battleships by 1942 as a deliberate ruse intended to restrict German fleet development; yet there was also the incentive of keeping up the pretence of adherence for as long as possible to cloak the new anti-British warship designs.[34]

The objective here is to discover how Hitler's hatred of Britain, expressed in a hunger for more warships and his navy's machinations, influenced British policy-making. Historians have shown that political intelligence, some of it generated by Vansittart's private sources, plus the brief absence (November 1938 – February 1939) of Nevile Henderson, the Ambassador in Berlin, who had a penchant for misrepresentation, promoted the breakdown of the Cabinet's 'best case' analysis of German intentions, and shifted first Halifax and then Chamberlain to a firmer policy.[35] Yet the extent to which German observation of the 1935 Naval Agreement was seen as an indication of Hitler's 'friendship' for Britain and so contributed to this complex process of policy adjustment has been overlooked.

After Munich, Chamberlain hoped to exploit the Anglo-German declaration as the basis for a general settlement. As before, his policy combined rearmament and negotiations. Since it was widely held in Whitehall that extremists and moderates in Berlin struggled for Hitler's ear, efforts to break down Germany's economic isolation to encourage the latter continued.[36] Although there was a consensus (even in the FO), that Germany would dominate Central and Eastern Europe, Chamberlain and Halifax resolved that Romania, Yugoslavia, Greece and Turkey should be shored up economically. Open trade and free currency exchange were one thing, economic hegemony another. But British efforts foundered: German bullying on the international committee overseeing the transfer of the Sudetenland, violent German press attacks, Hitler's anti-British outbursts, and secret reports about Ribbentrop's tripartite diplomacy all inspired apprehension.[37]

To decide on tactics, one crucial problem that confronted the Cabinet was determining the future course of Hitler's policy with reasonable certainty. Depending on Hitler's state of mind, the danger was that too much firmness might stampede him into war, but too much conciliation might tempt him into further belligerence. As students of political intelligence in this period have stressed, the ambiguity generated by the myriad of accurate, inaccurate yet plausible and spurious chaff, plus questions of source credibility, mired appraisal. It was therefore natural that some of the assessors might fix onto certain indicators as alarm signals. One such indicator employed by Halifax was Hitler's attitude to the Naval Agreements. In November 1937, during his visit to Germany, Halifax experienced firsthand Hitler's disappointment with the results of his naval ratio.[38] He grasped that Hitler had intended a tacit deal on spheres of influence.[39] The Führer's remarks along these lines to Chamberlain in September 1938 had also stuck in his mind.

Accordingly, when the CID discussed the forecast of British fleet strength for Berlin on 25 October 1938, the Foreign Secretary raised the Naval Agreement. The main issue was the number of British capital ships in 1942. Backhouse proposed 19 units.[40] Chamberlain, who still had high hopes for the Anglo-German Declaration, enquired whether this might be seen by Hitler 'as an indication of an aggressive attitude on our part'. Halifax did not think so.

> At the same time [he explained], it must be remembered that Herr Hitler had given clear indications that he would denounce the treaty if he thought we visualised the possibility of war with Germany. Continuing, [Halifax] thought that the main point was whether we could trust Germany to adhere to the agreements.

The CNS said that Germany was sticking to the 35 per cent ratio; moreover, he pointed out, although Raeder was impatient for the final tonnage forecast, the German navy was still below the total to which it was entitled under the 1935 Agreement.[41]

The Foreign Secretary's officials were also looking to the Naval Agreement as an augury. During October, in a wide-ranging review of Anglo-German relations and Britain's future European diplomacy initiated by Cadogan, the permanent head of the FO since January 1938, it became evident that they feared that German warship strength might become a lever for Hitler to exact more concessions.[42] For William Strang, the head of the Central Department, German naval diplomacy was the benchmark.[43] Hitler might demand British neutrality under the threat to end the naval ratio; alternatively, the colonial appeasement of Germany could only be contemplated in return for a guarantee of the naval ratio, the scrapping of all its ocean-going U-boats and an undertaking of German neutrality if Britain confronted Italy or Japan.[44]

Signals about which way the pendulum might swing were not long in coming. On 28 October, the petulant reaction of the German naval attaché to the British tonnage forecast was not a hopeful sign.[45] That day, Halifax wrote to Sir Eric Phipps, now the Ambassador in Paris, about other 'disquieting' news. Halifax had been told by Joseph Kennedy, the US Ambassador, that during the final meeting between Hitler and the outgoing French envoy, the former had said 'that he had so far adhered to the Anglo-German Naval Agreement because he genuinely desired Anglo-German understanding and moreover because he had not yet built up to the limit which under the Agreement was permissible'. These clearly conflicting and hypocritical motives for observing the ratio thus far (which Hitler had repeatedly bellowed was permanent) did not encourage Halifax. Again recounting Hitler's remarks in September 1938, the Foreign Secretary instructed Phipps to discover whether the American version was reliable.[46]

Of course the Kennedy report (confirmed by Phipps on 1 November [47]) was not alone sufficient to inspire the resolution in German policy that marked Halifax's contributions in Cabinet from this point onwards.[48] A large volume of alarming SIS briefs, the foreboding tone of the Embassy in Berlin, moral outrage at the anti-Jewish pogrom of 10 November plus annoyance with the lack of results after Munich were also essential.[49] Yet conspicuous was the regular coincidence of intelligence on the Anglo-German Naval Agreement from late October to early November, its connection in Halifax's mind with Hitler's attitude and the firming up of his German policy. In mid-November, hearsay of a possible denunciation or a demand for submarine parity was dispatched to the FO from sources in Berlin.[50] On 3 November, intelligence, probably supplied to Downing Street by T. P. Conwell-Evans, who had often acted before as an informant on Ribbentrop,[51] authenticated the substance of Kennedy's story.

Ribbentrop had said that Germany would delay reconsidering the Anglo-German Naval Agreements overall until the July 1937 Agreement expired in 1942 because there was no immediate reason for raising it and anyway Germany was behind in its programme.[52]

Industrial intelligence upheld the unhappy implication of these assertions: namely, that a principal reason for withholding demands to increase naval armaments and treaty revision was a lack of sufficient productive capacity to exceed the 35 per cent ratio sooner than originally planned. On 2 November, an IIC report, circulated to the Cabinet, correctly described how German shipyards were often protesting to higher authorities about raw materials and skilled workers shortages that were preventing them from completing the current warship programme on schedule.[53] The DNC concluded from an analysis of German armour output that the only means by which Berlin could rapidly expand its surface fleet at this stage was to convert mercantile ships to auxiliary cruisers.[54]

One must be cautious, however, in assigning primacy to any single index in complex and not entirely rational cognitive processes. On 14 November, the Foreign Secretary treated the FPC to a catalogue of clandestine material about 'the crazy persons who had managed to secure control' of Germany, plus Ribbentrop's remarks.[55] But the emerging split between Halifax and Chamberlain pivoted on the degree to which each had faith in Munich. Halifax accepted the gist of the SIS reports – that Hitler was twisted against conciliation – because he was certain that the Führer was chafing at the naval accords. The PM had inserted into the draft Anglo-German Declaration a reference to the 1935 Naval Agreement; but he was not ready to see that an attack on the latter was an assault on the former. His continuing desire to build on the Naval Agreements with air warfare rules backs this interpretation.[56] Chamberlain was thus sceptical about 'alleged conversations with various prominent Germans to the effect that Hitler and his entourage were becoming more and more hostile to this country'. The Foreign Secretary's proposals for a national service register and higher aircraft output were put on hold. Instead, the Cabinet accepted an approach to Hitler via Mussolini by seeking a visit to Rome which took place in January 1939.[57] Italy at least had recently joined the 1936 London Naval Treaty and the 40 000-ton battleship limitation.[58]

After Chamberlain and Halifax had cleared the way for a visit to Rome by mending their fences with the French in late November, clear proof of German antagonism was again delivered to Downing Street. On 9 December, the German Foreign Ministry received orders from Hitler to inform the British about the decision to escalate to parity in U-boats and to break the heavy cruiser holiday.[59] That day, perhaps motivated by erroneous reports from the Ambassador in London, Dr Herbert von Dirksen, which suggested that Chamberlain's grip on office was tenuous without a positive sign from Hitler, one of Ribbentrop's agents in London made a feckless attempt to mitigate the impact of the escalation. Dr Hesse, head of the German News Agency in London, informed George Steward, Chief Press Officer at Downing Street, with whom he had been in unofficial contact, about what was in the pipeline. Hesse said that he wanted the PM briefed before the FO so that he could take account of it in his forthcoming speech to the Foreign Press Association.[60]

It has been argued that Chamberlain used Steward to send signals to Hesse in an effort to short-circuit the FO News Department and its pugnacious head, Sir Reginald Leeper, in pursuit of appeasement.[61] On 28 November, an MI5 source in the German Embassy exposed Steward to Cadogan, reporting that the Press Chief had told Hesse that any demands Hitler made in 1939 would be granted. Halifax challenged Chamberlain about the liaison; the PM was 'aghast at the news' and professed that Steward was acting independently. Steward's activities were curtailed. Richard Cockett suggests that Chamberlain, fully aware of the approach, feigned his dismay.[62] This view, however, does not match up with Chamberlain's behaviour after Hesse's 9 December message about the cruisers and U-boats. Chamberlain's thoughts on the German breach of the spirit of the naval accords have not survived in the records, but since Hesse's object was to influence his upcoming speech, it may be taken as a guide to his thinking.

The speech on 13 December did not refer to the naval build-up, which had not been made public,[63] and its negotiations and peace padding rendered it overall 'very feeble and bad' in Cadogan's mind. Still, the PM had emphasised 'expanded' and 'accelerated' rearmament 'while we see others accumulating force and making no response to any suggestion for disarmament'. He spoke of the Anglo-French relationship transcending legal bonds and of the need to rearm to fulfil such obligations. He warned of the 'futility of ambition, if ambition leads to the desire for domination'.[64] Dirksen and the German press corps balked at the text (circulated in advance), especially its attack on the German propaganda vilifying Britain, and boycotted the dinner.[65] Cadogan thought the address flopped, but Dirksen's account of it depicted Chamberlain as 'playing the strong man *vis-à-vis* Germany' to bolster his standing.[66] This was nonsense. More plausibly, the firm messages that Dirksen dismissed as political posturing were a riposte to the naval measures and an expression of the PM's chagrin at Hitler's silence. Anyway, the idea that Steward's messages divulged the true content of Chamberlain's mind is untenable. In fact, probably unhappy with his performance, the PM sought the advice of Cadogan and Leeper with his next foreign-affairs statement to the House of Commons. Ironically, on 19 December, this 'stiffer' script delivered by Chamberlain was portrayed by Dirksen as 'positive and friendly'.[67]

Formal notice of the German move reached the FO on 12 December. The note explained that the naval build up was triggered by Russian naval expansion. Dirksen told Cadogan that he hoped that publication could be avoided altogether.[68] This was impossible. London had just issued proposals to increase the official trade in warship information. Yet the FO and Cabinet were anxious to give it a low profile. The First Lord briefed the Cabinet the next day and added that he was afraid that public opinion might take the view that 'Germany was now definitely rearming against us and that there was no hope of any real appeasement between the two countries'. Though nothing could be done to stop the German naval measures, the Cabinet agreed to use the joint talks required by the 1935 Naval Agreement to mitigate the public impact of the escalation.[69] Industrial intelligence made clear that submarine parity and installing 8-inch guns in its fourth and fifth heavy cruisers was the most that Germany could accomplish at the moment, but the First Lord was anxious not to provoke Hitler into trying to do more.[70] Nevertheless, NID was aware that the German excuse was spurious. On 8 December, the Director of Plans was satisfied that Russia had not exceeded its heavy cruiser quota.[71]

Halifax secured German assent to talks, and challenged Dirksen with the lack of progress on détente,[72] but naval diplomacy was set aside in view of the first of a series of war scares that plagued Whitehall in 1938–9. On 15 December, the First Secretary of the Embassy in Berlin delivered news that Hitler intended to bomb London in March without warning. The next day, an emergency CID meeting was convened to accelerate defence preparations for completion in three months.[73]

Against this background, the FO and the Naval Staff acquiesced in the 'bad precedent and loss of prestige' of accepting the German invitation to hold the naval talks in Berlin.[74] The British team, led by Admiral Cunningham, consisted mostly of naval officers. The FO brief emphasised that the talks were 'exclusively exploratory'. The Admiralty intended to dispute the German Naval Command's claims about excessive Soviet naval construction, to obtain a mutual 40 000-ton capital ship limit, and to induce the Germans to fix dates for each stage of U-boat expansion.[75]

The talks, which took place on 30 December, were friendly but futile.[76] Admiral Schniewind, Raeder's new chief of staff, was reluctant to lock U-boat building to a firm schedule and dodged the capital ship issue with a promise that new vessels would conform to the 40 000-ton limit even if they did not formally adhere to it. Schniewind blocked protests about the threadbare Soviet pretext with the retort that 'it was natural for every country to trust its own intelligence Services more than that of other countries'.[77] The implication was clear to Strang and his colleagues. The new U-boats would promptly augment German capacity to launch a knockout blow. And 'we shall not have very long to wait, I fear before the naval Agreement itself is threatened with termination.'[78] As Schniewind himself put it, the German navy was calculating that the whole treaty relationship would soon 'sink into oblivion'.[79]

WAS THE DESIRABLE FEASIBLE ?

In the first months of 1939, in his effort to transform naval policy to match post-Munich realities, Backhouse found himself confounded at every turn by the irreparable and intensifying grand strategic calamity that his predecessor had worked to bypass. Naval intelligence on Japan made distressing reading. In November 1938, the DNI minuted (incorrectly) that the Japanese had laid down two or three battleships, plus two pocket battleships with 12-inch guns.[80] Worse still, relations with Japan steadily deteriorated after October 1938 as the war in China expanded, which pressured the Navy to reconsider the 1937 Imperial Conference pledge to send the main fleet to Singapore in the event of war. Craigie, now the Ambassador in Tokyo, and other FO officials, urged the CNS to base capital ships at Singapore to impress Japan. These proposals, however, which amounted to dividing the battle fleet into penny packets, were rejected.[81]

For Backhouse, though, the bad news from Asia did not compare with his Hitlerian nightmares. In January 1939, SIS and other sources disclosed that the Führer, consumed with a hatred of Britain, was bent on another confrontation. The CNS warned his commanders that 'Germany is preparing for war as hard as she can, so as to be ready for any eventuality'.[82] Naval intelligence on Germany was also unpleasant. The Embassy in Oslo discovered from a Norwegian printing firm that its order for machinery from a German manufacturer could not be met because it was too busy building U-boat motors.[83] And, perhaps in a deliberate move to unnerve the Royal Navy, the Germans released to the press covertly obtained design details of the new *King George V* class.[84]

Meanwhile, the CNS's initiative to inject an offensive spirit into the naval policy was gaining pace. Drax, aided by Admiral Dickens, the former DNI, and a small staff, drafted a variety of offensive sea-based operations. Both the CNS and his personal strategist saw air attack against naval bases as a way to rapid victory: 'If we had been able to do it in 1914–18,' Backhouse speculated, 'the war would never have lasted so long.' Drax's plans employed, in co-operation with aircraft carriers, RAF bombers to cripple Raeder's fleet in port, along with torpedo attacks against warships in the Kiel Canal. He also formulated a knockout-blow strategy against Italy, combining coastal bombardment by the Royal Navy, and air and ground attacks by the RAF and the French armed forces.[85] The common features of these plans were an emphasis on obtaining prompt and final results and obviating the need for large-scale trade defence by pre-emptive strikes to destroy potential attackers.[86]

The parallels here with the 'Young Turks' of the Grand Fleet are obvious. But the Backhouse-Drax initiative should not be seen only as an effort to surpass past glories. These were bold and progressive ideas; the difficulty was translating them into real capabilities. It was one thing to draft a memo about RAF fighters flying from carriers or to imagine torpedoes and magnetic mines ready for RAF crews to drop into German harbours, another to manufacture them rapidly. The Chatfield system of priorities, combined with the general neglect of the Fleet Air Arm and air warfare at sea by the Air Ministry, meant that the *matériel*/technical means as well as the practical expertise were wanting.[87]

Two examples will suffice. The first concerns Drax's plan for offensive mining close to German bases. The goal was to compel Raeder's heavy units to expose themselves to attack while covering light minesweeping units. The Naval Staff's divisional heads concluded that the scheme could not be executed with the 'means available at present'. This was not obstinacy. The proper mines would not be available before 1940. The danger of air attack, and progress since 1918 in radio location, favoured the defence. Moreover, it was correctly argued that Drax presupposed the doubtful premise of British air-sea supremacy in the Heligoland Bight.[88] The second example concerns the hope in September 1939 of achieving a two-power standard by destroying Hitler's navy while his army conquered Poland. But the Director of Naval Air Division excluded the Fleet Air Arm (the only torpedo aircraft suitable for the precision task) from the project. The lack of speed, low ceiling and poor defensive armament made the navy's Swordfish and Skua aircraft 'easy meat' for high-performance land-based fighters. Probable losses would disable the embryonic naval air arm. Subsequent raids to knock out the German fleet by airforce medium bombers produced no results.[89]

The important conceptual consequence of *matériel* obstacles (and the burst of escort building) was to force the new CNS to project the Navy's optimal state of readiness into the future. Even if Backhouse was not looking to 1946, his eyes were nevertheless fixed on 1940–1.[90] The logic generated by standing policy and the regular tempo of CID decision-making stymied his effort to effect radical change; this tended to magnify his already inflated images of totalitarian efficiency.[91] Characteristically, Drax was sure that he could devise a solution. 'Our Admiralty should be just as efficient as the German Admiralty,' he claimed, 'and the dictator-ship has the serious disadvantage that every major decision must go through one bottleneck, viz., the neck of the dictator.' He proposed to accelerate the decision-making process and to create 'speed merchants' to hustle work along.[92] The impetus behind this proposal was similar to the one for assuming the offensive: Drax hoped to structure bureaucratic processes by taking the initiative in the same way he desired to structure battle by taking the offensive.[93] It was this effort to circumvent the organ-isation (like Drax's OPC) that amplified the CNS's tendency for centrali-sation that his critics condemned. But, as Backhouse readily discovered, no amount of jerry-rigging, improvisation or intervention could break the fetters imposed by time, scarce *matériel* and past policy.

As to the future battle fleet, the Cabinet had approved four 40 000-ton/16-inch gun *Lion*s for the 1938–9 programmes. Owing to the inability to produce guns and gun mountings for the second ship, though, in March, Danckwerts suggested using the four triple 15-inch turrets held in reserve to build one 40 000-ton battlecruiser. Thus, the CNS and his staff began to reverse another of Chatfield's key precepts by resurrecting the battle-cruiser concept. Inspired by false intelligence about new Japanese pocket battleships and plans to send a flying squadron east, Cunningham minuted that he 'would sooner build two battlecruisers mounting six 15-inch guns each with good protection and a speed of 33–35 knots'. Backhouse, who as Controller in 1929–32 had witnessed the contraction of Britain's ship industries at its worst, confessed that he was perplexed by the situation, but he was inclined to agree that two 20 000-ton battlecruisers were the best cost-effective alternative to one 40 000-ton ship.[94]

Oddly, one reason why the CNS found the issue so vexing was his ten-dency to exaggerate grossly the tempo of German output. In January, the British naval attaché confirmed that even the 35 per cent fleet was unreal-isable by 1942.[95] Yet when the CID discussed retention of all five *Royal Sovereign*s on 24 February, raising the fleet to 21 ships by 1942, the CNS feared that Hitler would build an extra battleship in reply. But Chatfield, who had just replaced Inskip as Minister for the Co-ordination of Defence, 'was inclined to doubt whether the Germans would actually lay down an extra ship'. The new CNS retorted that 'Herr Hitler had stated categorically, when launching the battleship *Bismarck*, that he intended to build up to the full 35 per cent of our strength.'[96] This was the first skirmish in a bitter clash between the two admirals.

The main battle was over an Admiralty proposal to concentrate on the Mediterranean at the expense of the Far East. In January, the CNS saw an occasion to advance Drax's war plan for a knockout blow against Italy during Cabinet deliberations over a rumoured German move on Holland and upcoming Anglo-French staff talks. Chamberlain stated that he thought it would be more important to emphasise to the French the security of the Eastern Mediterranean than the Far East, where he predicted that Japan would play it safe *vis-à-vis* Russia and America.[97] Concurrently, the COS circulated the 'European Appreciation, 1939–40', which studied Britain's chances, with France, against Germany and Italy, with Japan eager to pounce. The COS survey found that to retain a capable fleet in the Mediterranean would mean reneging on the pledge to the Dominions to send a large force to Singapore; conversely, executing the Singapore strategy would leave the Mediterranean devoid of capital units and so tempt Italy to move against South-Eastern Europe and even the Middle East.[98] Chamberlain raised the conundrum and wondered whether the Dominions should be informed when the CID met to examine the 'European Appreciation' on 24 February. The First Lord, Stanhope, pressed the Mediterranean first scheme, but Chatfield successfully had the matter referred to a special Strategic Appreciation Committee (SAC).[99]

The task of the SAC, which met from March to April, was to prioritise the proposals in the COS survey, to relate them to expenditure outside the approved plan, and to set policy for the upcoming talks with the French. The main point of dispute, however, was naval strategy. The CNS called for the authority to strike 'Italy a series of hard blows at the start of hostilities [so] she might be counted out and the whole course of the war [would] turn in our favour'. Chatfield, who had manoeuvred to make it government policy, invoked the promise to come to the rescue of the Dominions if Japan moved South: 'We must do this, or risk the Empire.' A Mediterranean attack might climax in disaster, he continued, leaving Britain helpless in Asia. European exigencies, though, had eroded the basis of Chatfield's former policies. As Strang said, the French would balk at an allied war plan that envisaged the fleet sailing East as fighting raged in Europe. Co-operation with the United States, Stanhope argued, was Britain's only hope in Asia. Chatfield was fighting a losing battle. Backhouse realised that what was needed was some policy statement that would permit the Cabinet to bow out of the guarantee to Australia and New Zealand gracefully.[100]

He sent his staff to work on a formula. Drax revised his overall plan to include a scenario in which Italy remained neutral and an offensive in the Far East remained an option. But his criterion for the principal target was still the enemy that could be vanquished the quickest – Italy, in six months, with careful planning. The idea of a flying squadron based at Singapore to keep the Japanese at bay was also considered. Yet the search for a convincing and coherent formula was futile. 'There is no getting away from the fact,' Backhouse confessed, 'that we started to rebuild our Battlefleet too late and that we are now several years behind.' In early April, when the CNS was steadily incapacitated by illness, the task was left to his deputy. Admiral Cunningham thus proposed that there were 'so many variable factors which cannot at present be assessed' that it was impossible to state definitely how soon after Japan played its hand the main fleet would sail east.[101]

By this stage, after Hitler had entered Prague and Mussolini had grabbed Albania, the Cabinet required little convincing to drop Far Eastern commitments. As the Admiralty wished, feelers were sent out to Washington, which made encouraging signals in reply, and a path was cleared for secret naval talks.[102] On 20 March, Chamberlain warned the Dominions about a likely delay in the relief of Singapore. On 17 April, the SAC endorsed Admiral Cunningham's 'variable factors' formula, which was approved by the CID, along with the Mediterranean offensive, on 2 May. Guarantees issued to Greece, Romania and Turkey underscored the change in strategic focus.[103]

Nonetheless, shortly after the CID endorsed the Mediterranean-first strategy, the JPC issued a stinging refutation of the entire scheme. As the joint planners asserted, within the wider strategic context, the initiative rested with the Axis powers, who had the early lead in offensive weapons.[104] During staff talks, the French made it clear that they did not have the spare land or air forces to back up a sea-based offensive which Drax had called for in his plan.[105] British naval power alone was insufficient to implement the Backhouse-Drax scheme. The Mediterranean offensive, moreover, was not a solution to the German problem, only a method to brace 'our prestige throughout the world' while the Nazis attacked 'where and when they pleased'.[106] It delighted ministers, but proved difficult to convert into workable plans. Admiral Dudley Pound, who replaced Backhouse in May, wrote:

I do not know who gave the politicians the idea that it could be done but it seems they expect it and they are now undergoing the rather painful process of being undeceived. Italy can only be 'knocked out' either by her armies being defeated, or by Italy being laid waste by air. We cannot do either of these things at the beginning of the war and it is left to the Navy to do the 'knocking out'. I can only imagine that they thought the Fleet would steam slowly along the Italian coast and blow it to bits, which, even were it possible, would not 'knock Italy out.'[107]

The trouble was that technological advance had made the small naval powers invulnerable in their home waters except at great cost to an attacker. As Drax and Backhouse saw, sea-based air power was the key to engaging foes that refused the one-big-battle. Although the attack on the poorly defended Italian fleet at Taranto in late 1940 was impressive, the Fleet Air Arm was too backward for knockout results. Even plans for a Baltic *coup de main* turned on the wishful hope that a halt to Germany's access to Swedish iron ore would bring victory, not on sinking Hitler's battleships. In the event, as argued in Chapter 5, the COS's long-versus-short war framework of expectations was sound: ultimately, Nazi continental power had to be defeated on land. A pronounced fixation with the offensive can compel strategists to see 'the necessary as possible'.[108] This was true of Backhouse and Drax. Not only did their ideas outpace current *matériel* resources, but they also overrated the potential payoff from the realisation of their plans.

SCRAPPING THE NAVAL AGREEMENTS: PART TWO

On 23 January, Halifax presented the FPC with an intelligence dossier that painted a terrifying picture of the Nazi camp. Hitler, a fanatic, was on the verge of a pre-emptive strike against London, to be heralded by the occupation of Belgium and the Netherlands to extend the radius of his bombers. Chamberlain, Halifax and Cadogan were sceptical, but the cycle of misunderstanding, alarm often verging on panic and improvisation, which typified the transformation of British strategic policy in 1939, was thus set into motion. An attack on Holland was acknowledged as a *casus belli*. It was decided to forewarn Washington. Rearmament was accelerated. Approaches were made to the Low Countries and staff talks were opened with the French. The first steps to building a continental army in peace were taken. On 6 February, the British government openly committed itself to the defence of France.[109]

Yet the failure of the nightmarish Nazi attack to materialise fostered a sense of relief in succeeding weeks. Chamberlain wrote that at last Britain was 'getting on top of the dictators'.[110] Satisfaction with the Rome visit plus encouraging signals from Washington added up to misplaced elation. New-found COS confidence in Anglo-French ability to withstand an initial German onslaught and to prevail in a protracted conflict (inspired by Backhouse's call for the offensive in JPC studies) certainly helped. Chamberlain also perceived signs that economic troubles and anti-war opinion in Germany were putting the brake on further Nazi adventurism, just as British rearmament was gaining steam.[111] Where a few months before he had been concerned that setting a total of 19 capital ships by 1942 would be regarded by Hitler as offensive, the PM readily endorsed in late February a new target of 21 battleships.[112]

In naval diplomacy, although attempts were made to persuade Berlin to adopt formally the 40 000-ton limitation and to join the global trade in warship details, no progress was made because Admiral Raeder obfuscated to the end. That end came with the invasion of the rump Czech state on 15 March. It was a brutal abrogation of the Anglo-German Declaration and with it the 1935 Naval Agreement. In the aftermath, which saw a new British deterrence policy based on an Eastern front and a long war, the continuation of the naval ratio was less of an issue than the potential, if unlikely, survival of qualitative limitation and its benefits. Nonetheless, it is worthwhile to proceed with Anglo-German naval diplomacy to its termination in April–June 1939 to recount the significant post-mortem on the naval relationship conducted by the Cabinet and for the light it sheds on the expectations harboured by policy-makers of relations with Berlin.

In this respect, the ill-timed euphoria of February caught Chamberlain in the unpleasant fix of uttering optimism on the eve of the Prague coup. The Cabinet, though, prepared by the January war scares, quickly recovered its bearings. Halifax delivered to Dirksen a stinging rebuke of Germany's lunge for European domination and, on 17 March, Chamberlain modified his speech in Birmingham to do the same in public. This was followed by a frenzy of diplomatic activity to construct a set of East European and Balkan links to contain Germany. The first was the British guarantee to Poland on 31 March. It was hoped that Warsaw would reply with a promise to Romania and that Russia could be persuaded to proclaim unilaterally its intent to assist Hitler's victims, and thereby undercut the repugnance of Moscow by the small powers. This ambitious design, however, was promptly trampled on by French pressure, rumours of German plans to seize Romanian oil fields and to attack Poland, and Italy's invasion of Albania on 7 April. Consequently, the Anglo-French guarantee of Poland was followed by pledges to Romania, Turkey and Greece, conscription was ordered on 26 April and hesitant talks with the Soviets proceeded.[113]

Hitler exploded at the British guarantee to Poland: 'I shall brew them a devil's drink.' Typically, on 1 April, in his speech at the launch of the *Tirpitz* at Wilhelmshaven, he called into question the continuance of the 1935 Naval Agreement when Britain continued to pry into German affairs, and hereafter inflamed press attacks against British 'encirclement'. That day, in case Warsaw continued to oppose his designs, military plans to destroy Poland were initiated. Apart from the Pact of Steel, the failure of Ribbentrop's tripartite diplomacy led instead to a search for a deal with Moscow.[114]

In London, the threat to the Naval Agreement came as no surprise. The British naval attaché and the Berlin Embassy had reported that Hitler had wished to denounce the Naval Agreement straight away after Duff Cooper had called him a liar in the House of Commons.[115] For the Admiralty, however, it heralded two naval scares that damaged its credibility. On 3 April, Admiral Canaris, the head of the *Abwehr* (military intelligence), had told a British Embassy contact that the Führer intended to knock Britain out with a surprise bomb strike on the fleet during its Easter leave. Halifax told the First Lord to make it known that the Navy was at the ready. On 4 April, Stanhope announced on the *Ark Royal* that the Navy had information that required the manning of its anti-aircraft defences. Downing Street and the FO were flabbergasted by the blunder: Berlin was handed a propaganda coup.[116]

A week later, the German naval attaché informed the DNI that Raeder hoped to conduct four weeks of fleet exercises around Spain, including the *Panzerschiffe*, from 18 April onwards. NID's newly founded Operational Intelligence Centre and Vansittart's private sources had already reported suspicious U-boat activity close to home and abroad.[117] Cunningham, now *de facto* CNS, told his colleagues that Raeder – 'a good friend' – had said that no threat was intended. Despite French anxiety that the Axis was hatching a fresh plot, therefore, the Admiralty reassured ministers that the German exercises were not camouflage for a seaborne coup.[118] Later, however, confusing Naval Staff advice about precautionary naval movements, and its proclamation after Hitler denounced the Naval Agreement on 28 April that the formerly benign German cruise now posed a real threat, affirmed FO misgivings about Admiralty competence.[119]

Hitler's abrogation of the Anglo-German Naval Agreement and the 1934 Non-Aggression Pact with Warsaw was a rejoinder to the British bloc building and intended to pressure the Poles. The question for the Nazi leadership was whether it could destroy Poland without igniting a general conflict. As his timetable unfolded, mesmerised by a lust for bloodshed, Hitler overrode fears that the West meant business. As he told his generals in late May, Poland could not be spared even if it meant war with France and England.[120] His remark that 'nothing will be changed in the shipbuilding programme' delighted Raeder (now promoted to Grand Admiral) that the war would be localised and the naval build-up would be completed. Orders for the first of six 56 000-ton Type H class in April had required a denunciation of the Naval Agreements. Significantly, Admiral Raeder and his staff feared that the British might concoct a fresh ploy in naval armaments diplomacy to dash their fantasies of global sea power status. In April, with perverse logic, Schniewind argued that any future talks would have to be avoided because 'the English might have the opportunity to show themselves generous and reaffirm the treaty as such'. More ominously, he hoped to dodge the obligation to notify London of the details of the first three of 12 *Kreuzerkrieg* type *Panzerschiffe* – 26 000 tons, 34 knots and 11-inch guns – to steal a march of 15 months on the Royal Navy.[121]

To set this trap, however, it was necessary in the memo abrogating the 1935–7 accords to cancel the information-exchange clauses, to leave qualitative limits in force, and to bait it with the prospect of more negotiations.[122] The note confronted Whitehall with a dilemma: reject it outright and hasten the collapse of the naval treaty framework entirely or keep the door open to future talks. 'Whatever Herr Hitler may say,' FO officials agreed, 'there seems no doubt that his denunciation of the Naval Agreement opens up the vista of a naval race and we must face this unpalatable fact.' Even Craigie telegraphed from Tokyo to censure Hitler and Ribbentrop for outright treachery.[123]

The Cabinet discussed the problem on 3 May. Stanhope assured his colleagues that 'at [the] present time Germany was building ships as fast as she could but that she would not be able to exceed the 35 per cent ratio before 1942 or 1943'. Halifax and Chamberlain argued that it was important to counteract the propaganda point Hitler scored in denouncing the Naval Agreement on the grounds of encirclement by setting out the true history of the naval relationship in a reply. Chatfield emphasised that Hitler had cancelled the Naval Agreement because he had 'persuaded himself' that Britain had given him a free hand in Eastern Europe in exchange for the 35 per cent ratio. This sparked a controversy: the minutes underscored that no such understanding had ever been made, tacitly or otherwise. Significantly, Chamberlain said that the first time he had become aware of this notion was during his talks with Hitler in Berchtesgaden. Anyway, he did not believe that any purpose would be served by making another agreement because Hitler could not be trusted and any new German proposals would likely be unacceptable. On the other hand, Chamberlain conceded that it might promote British interests globally if they tried to salvage qualitative limitation.[124]

Approval of the British reply was delegated to the FPC. While the FO drafted the document, the German navy invited the Royal Navy to the Kiel Regatta in July to wave the false promise of a new deal,[125] and sinister yet inexact intelligence about German naval building began to arrive in London. It was assumed that the end of the 35 per cent ratio would have little effect on the output of German yards for two or three years, and precedence would go to air and land forces anyway.[126] Short of espionage, it was difficult to discover the details of the Z Plan or Hitler's directive that it should get top priority. Allowing for the interval between command and execution, the British detected the large transfer of resources to naval purposes quite readily. On 6 June, Troubridge arrived in Whitehall with rumours that a large volume of steel production had been redirected to the navy. Rumours that the Führer in April had ordered Raeder to triple ship output regardless of the cost were also circulating.[127]

On 13 June, when the FPC convened to discuss the draft reply,[128] it became evident that Chamberlain had not been briefed about these reports (a failure for which the Berlin Embassy was 'called to task'[129]). The PM enquired whether there was any news to confirm a recent press report of a public speech by Raeder in which he spoke of greater sea expansion. Stanhope recounted his meeting with Captain Troubridge: 'It was understood that the German authorities had recently diverted a considerable volume of their steel production to Naval purposes.' On whether this was an acceleration of the 35 per cent programme or marked a departure from it was uncertain. It could not have been otherwise. Despite impressive results with the extra resources, German constructors could lay down nothing more than U-boats for over a month, and then only the first two heavy ships.[130]

The intelligence predicament was significant because it reflected badly on the Navy's desire to press Berlin for firm proposals on the scope and purpose of new talks. Halifax, arguing from his FO brief,[131] which was drafted by officials for whom the Navy's April blunders were a fresh memory, questioned whether Germany could be relied on to adhere to treaty limits without promising to publish ship characteristics. To undermine the First Lord, he pointed to the apparent discrepancy between the Navy's desire to uphold qualitative limits and its confessed inability to detect German cheating in time to counter it. 'The real objection was', the Foreign Secretary rightly cautioned, 'that in the present temper of

Germany we might find ourselves caught in a trap, e.g. the Germans might build without our knowledge a number of vessels of a new type highly dangerous to us.' Chamberlain agreed that it was 'useless to contemplate another agreement' without the confidence that 'Germany would play straight'. Chatfield, who in mid-April was still hoping that Hitler would not denounce the 1935–7 accords,[132] rescued Stanhope. Probably citing the *Gorizia* episode, he explained that qualitative limitation benefited Britain even if the other powers cheated.[133]

The FPC accepted that it was in Britain's interests to salvage qualitative limits if possible on a firmer basis. Chatfield also convinced his colleagues that they could not skirt the political imperative behind the 1935 Anglo-German Naval Agreement by characterising it in the British note as a 'purely technical' agreement. He suggested

> that we might say that we now understood that Herr Hitler had in 1935 thought that we had given him a free hand in Eastern and Central Europe in return for his acceptance of the 100 : 35 ratio, but that as we could not accept the correctness of this view it might be better that the 1935 arrangements should be abrogated.

The PM and the others admitted the veracity of this statement, yet the final draft of the British reply did not make this point. Instead, the diplomatic reply exclusively disputed the accusation that Britain was pursuing a policy of encirclement.[134]

Although there was no chance of saving the treaty framework, the Cabinet post-mortem on the naval relationship with Germany reveals significant findings. It underscores that the Naval Agreement was only possible because each party hoped to satisfy irreconcilable policy aspirations with it. Chatfield's remarks reinforce the view that he had planned to exploit Hitler's 35 per cent ploy to advance the interests of British sea power globally. Admiral Schniewind's plot to trump the Royal Navy confirms that Britain benefited from the web of conceptual and contractual boundaries defined by the treaty framework because it discouraged such developments earlier and would have continued to do so had the qualitative treaties remained in force. Likewise, in 1939, the lack of alternatives but to trust to armaments diplomacy exposed how little flexibility British naval policy possessed to cope with an intensifying strategic disaster. The Royal Navy's blunders in April made the FO resistant to this insight thereafter. Finally, although this is not the place to review every argument about whether Chamberlain obstructed effective deterrence after March 1939 by keeping the prospect of a détente alive, it should be acknowledged that in the sphere of naval armaments diplomacy, Chamberlain was entirely realistic about the likelihood of concluding a reliable deal with Hitler, and neither he nor the Cabinet recklessly encouraged further naval negotiations that summer to the detriment of deterrence.

Chatfield's desire to make explicit publicly the conflict of aims that underlay the 1935 Agreement requires explanation. He had hoped in mid-April that Hitler would not end the accords (not from fear of German ship output in the short term, but to sustain Britain's prospects at sea), but he had seen that Munich had failed. In November 1937, Chatfield had minuted that the alternative to appeasement was fighting with weak forces and conscription.[135] In February 1939, as noted, he argued that Britain should defend its Far Eastern Empire with an inferior battle fleet at the expense of the Mediterranean. Conscription was ordered on 26 April. He supported the Eastern Front strategy because, like Chamberlain, Admiral Chatfield premised deterrence on the belief that Hitler would pause at the thought of a protracted struggle.[136] From this, and his hope that Germany would discover its equipoise in the East, the Minister for the Co-ordination of Defence's vigorous backing for the guarantee to Poland (even if it did not make military sense)[137] and the pursuit of an alliance with Moscow followed.[138] It was Chatfield who proposed that the offensive-minded Admiral Drax, sent to Leningrad with the rest of the allied staff mission to Moscow on a heavy *Southampton* class cruiser, should speak for Britain.[139] Unfortunately, the final choice of a slow civil liner aside, sea power turned out to be as little empowering to British alliance diplomacy with Soviet Russia as it had been in deterrence diplomacy against Nazi Germany.

Briefly, in June, the Admiralty made one last bid at a crash project to install the plant capacity to keep the Royal Navy competitive against the fleets of Germany, Japan and Italy. The Naval Staff's timing was propitious. That month, largely due to FO complacency, London's clash of interests with Tokyo in China culminated in a potentially explosive local dispute over the British concession at Tientsin. Chatfield made it clear that a force of seven capital ships could be dispatched in August but that it was inadvisable at the moment. Fortunately, by 19 July, Craigie had staged a graceful climb down from the affair.[140] Accordingly, with ministers focused once again on imperial defence, the navy made its move. The two *Lion* class ships planned for 1941 had already been cut in February, but the Admiralty now sought CID authority to study a crash programme to acquire the industrial plant to lay down three (instead of the available maximum of two) 16-inch gun battleships annually.[141]

In its brief, the Admiralty projected the demise of British sea power unless output potential was now calibrated to match a full-blown armaments competition against the revisionist naval powers. It cited Admiral Raeder's speech calling for a powerful fleet, intelligence that since March the German navy had received top priority in raw materials, and Japanese and Italian shipbuilding to illustrate that if the strategic future unfolded according to maximum capital ship assembly, then 'the British Empire is almost certainly doomed' by the mid-1940s (see Figure 7.1). The Naval Staff underlined that acquiring the specialised plant to produce guns, armour, fire control instruments, etc., did not commit the CID to a new standard of strength; yet there was 'no time to lose' since the Edwardian heyday of 1908 when the Navy could promptly lay down eight dreadnoughts to plug the capital ship gap against Tirpitz was long since past.[142]

On 6 July, the CID studied the Navy's gloomy prophecy. As before, Chamberlain and Simon, the Chancellor, questioned the project for its potentially damaging long-term financial and industrial implications. With his ambitious programme largely defunct, Chatfield dryly 'observed that it was a

Figure 7.1   Admiralty, forecast of comparative capital ship strengths, June 1939 (assuming: (a) no scrapping; (b) German *Panzerschiffe* and Japanese pocket battleships alleged to be being built counted as 1/2 capital ship).

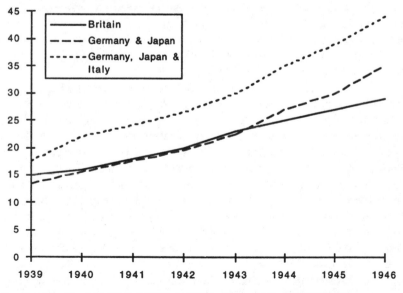

Source: 'Needs of the Navy', 15 June 1939, Appendix I, ADM167/104.

national failing not to look far enough ahead'. Stanhope's request that a third capital ship should be included in the 1940 building schedule using the spare 15-inch turrets to bypass production bottlenecks was approved; but a decision on the larger issue of a crash plan to lay down the foundations for expanded capital ship output in future was postponed for three months. The declaration of war on 3 September permanently shelved the project.[143] As to the naval treaty system, the Admiralty concluded that 'even with the greatest exercise of ingenuity so little could be saved that the only practical course would be to denounce the Treaties in toto.'[144] And in 1940, the compressed strategic time-line imposed by the struggle dictated that the four *Lion* class ships were abandoned to concentrate industrial capacity on war needs.

CONCLUSION

On 24 August, Ribbentrop returned to Berlin from Moscow with the Nazi–Soviet Pact signed. From July onwards, in contrast with the desultory approaches of his rivals, Ribbentrop's insistent tactics, offering what his interlocutors could not easily resist, had paid off. Hitler and his Foreign Minister were convinced that France and Britain had been bluffing all along. Now they would surely step aside to permit the end of Poland. This of course did not happen. After only a brief pause, heedless of its ultimate scale and scope, Hitler willed his war. Raeder was deflated. The first two H-class battleships were barely on the stocks and none of the improved *Panzerschiffe* had even been laid down. As the admiral admitted on 3 September in his war diary, there was now little chance of 'settling the British question conclusively'.[145]

The way in which this antagonism, so concisely phrased by Raeder and practised by Hitler in regular orders for more naval armaments in 1939 and in the Führer's outbursts against the Naval Agreements, contributed to the formation of British policy after Munich illustrates that the 1935 Agreement did operate at times as Baldwin had foreseen. It was indeed a vital yardstick of Hitler's intentions for Halifax and the FO at the end of 1938. Chamberlain held out hope longer, yet not much longer. In the light of reliable intelligence about German building capacity, Berlin's unfounded demand to exercise its right to parity in submarine tonnage and to break the heavy cruiser holiday was probably seen by Chamberlain and others as the effective end of the Naval Agreements. Regardless, the war scares of January 1939 rendered the issue irrelevant. The occupation of the rump Czech state in March killed the naval accord. Chamberlain was not even moved to note its demise.[146] After that, there was no enthusiasm in

Cabinet for more Anglo-German naval diplomacy, and only a cautious operation to salvage the beneficial structure of qualitative limitation globally was attempted.

With notable exceptions, Admiral Backhouse's bid to transform naval policy remained disconnected from the mainstream of Whitehall decision-making. After his departure, Admiralty policy continued to adjust from peace to war. Churchill's posting as First Lord in the War Cabinet brought to the Navy a strategist whose offensive-mindedness equalled that of Backhouse and Drax. The latter joined the cadre of freelance admirals (such as Lord Cork, who led the ill-fated expedition to Norway) who fed Churchill's appetite for adventure. In fairness, bizarre operations like 'Catherine', a reckless battleship sortie into the Baltic, were only at the extreme end of a coherent strategic design,[147] but the First Lord also suffered from a capacity to see 'the necessary as possible'. More to the point, as the impracticalities of 'Catherine' show, no dosage of offensive spirit, intestinal fortitude or even the application of modern staff methods could have bypassed the concrete imperatives of the standing strategic framework, time, and *matériel* which stymied Backhouse in 1939.

Conclusion

Admiral Chatfield arrived at the Admiralty in January 1933 with a clearly defined policy aim. The First Sea Lord believed that the preservation of the Empire and the security of Britain's rank as the leading global power and maritime trading nation depended upon its fleet. He desired to make the fleet equal to this task. Chatfield and his staff, however, were acutely aware that British sea power had entered a period of vulnerability. This was the legacy of the 1930 London Naval Treaty and the economic depression. The former had delayed until 1936 the capital ship replacement plan that the Admiralty had expected to begin in 1930, and the latter had wrecked a sizeable portion of Britain's contract-starved shipbuilding industries. Despite the damage, Britain still possessed the world's greatest building capacity. Yet that capacity would not be large enough until the early 1940s to replace the old battle fleet and, concurrently, to check determined challenges from its principal rivals.[1]

This risky situation would not have been serious if a stable global order had developed. Unfortunately, while Britain's naval armaments capacity shrank rapidly in 1930–5, the world scene became much more volatile. Consequently, the question facing the Naval Staff was how to ensure that the naval contest did not outstrip Britain's ability to win it. The solution was naval armaments diplomacy. If the expiring 1922 Washington and 1930 London Naval Treaties could be replaced by one better suited to British interests, then the period of vulnerability that had opened up in the early part of the decade could be safely passed through.

Broadly, the Naval Staff recognised that the framework created by the Naval Treaties had worked and would continue to work in its favour. Qualitative limitation served two functions. First, it helped to keep the cost of sea power down to an affordable level. Second, it discouraged radical escalations in warship power and design. Even if rivals cheated on the agreed standards, the Royal Navy was certain that it could design and build better fighting vessels. Likewise, by abolishing the contentious ratio system, the Admiralty hoped to temper the ambitions of the other major powers. During the resulting decade-long cycle of calm industrial and naval renewal, Chatfield and his planners aimed to expand the fleet to an unchallengeable two-power standard over Japan and the largest European navy.

Co-opting the other naval powers into this venture was a formidable task. Germany could easily throw a huge spanner into the works by freeing itself from the Versailles Treaty and provoking a European naval competition. In 1935, however, Hitler made explicit his willingness to settle for a fleet of only 35 per cent the size of the Royal Navy. The Naval Staff were aware that this was probably the most that Admiral Raeder could build up to during the lifespan of the proposed multilateral naval treaty. Nonetheless, since the maximum size for any European fleet compatible with British sea security was 35 per cent, and since the German offer would boost British naval armaments diplomacy globally, the Admiralty and the American Department of the FO pressed the Cabinet to accept it.

The other obstacle to the Naval Staff executing its programme was opposition within Whitehall. The Treasury and the FO advanced the idea of a limited European deterrent, based on air forces, that promised to draw Berlin into a general settlement. The Naval Staff regarded this departure from the historic British policy of supremacy at sea as a temporary aberration. It bided its time, confident that in due course strategic, diplomatic and fiscal imperatives would vindicate its programme.

From 1935 onwards, however, the diplomatic scene became steadily worse. The Italian adventure in Abyssinia, the Rhineland crisis, the Spanish Civil War and the renewal of Japan's advance in China fuelled a quarrel between British military and diplomatic experts. All agreed that even the level of strength projected for 1939 by the rearmament plan of 1936 could not possibly protect the Empire simultaneously in three separate regions of the globe. The COS wanted the FO to reduce the number of Britain's likely foes. The FO, disillusioned with the chances of a détente with Nazi Germany, sought alternative ways to stabilise the global balance before defence preparations were complete. Vansittart warned that the FO might not be able to forestall a general European conflict before 1939.

Sufficient time was indispensable for the realisation of the Admiralty's programme. The Naval Staff had never accepted the DRC's five-year timetable as a serious strategic forecast. The naval negotiations from July 1935 and July 1937, however, had taught Admiral Chatfield and his staff a distressing lesson: despite the slow rate of German shipbuilding, and despite Craigie's promises of future 'elbow room', it was clear that if the search for an Anglo-German détente failed Hitler would easily find a pretext to cancel both the 1935 and 1937 Anglo-German Naval Agreements. Although the Admiralty knew that the Third Reich could not at once expand its output of warships, it feared that an early end to the naval accords would wreck its long-term programme for maritime security.

Admiral Chatfield believed that with a resolute effort this outcome could be avoided. He shared his critics' misgivings about the Nazi leaders, but he was convinced that the Führer's desire for good relations could be exploited once again to Britain's advantage. He predicted that Germany's predatory policies could be diverted eastward into strategic overstretch; before a German threat to the West could develop, the Naval Staff's project would have restored Britain's global sea power. Vansittart and others feared that a German *Drang nach Osten* would upset the balance of power; but Chatfield predicted that it would restore the balance by encumbering Germany with substantial liabilities, including a proximate Soviet threat. Accordingly, the Admiralty wished policy-makers to induce the French government to abandon the Little Entente and to make it explicit that Britain would fight for the West, but not for the East.

The Cabinet could not accept such a policy. Yet there was much support for a fresh effort at a European settlement. This was Chamberlain's priority upon assuming the premiership in May 1937. Ironically, given the new PM's proclivities for air forces and financial probity, the Naval Staff regarded his policy as its best prospect to promote the Navy's master plan for sea power. In fact the trend in foreign and defence policy under Chamberlain appeared to bear this out. Inskip's report to the Cabinet at the end of 1937 underscored a limited liability on the continent and the long-war strategy. The switch to air defence in 1938 was interpreted as a positive sign by the Naval Staff that the 'ascendancy' of the bomber and the goal of bomber parity were on the wane. The Pacific Dominions had been promised that the main fleet would be sent to their rescue if Japan moved against them. And the DRC's naval construction programme had been maximised, so that although the Admiralty's two-power standard had not been endorsed by the Cabinet, the warship building tempo for 1936–7 corresponded precisely with what had to be done to reach it.

In 1938, however, the progress of both the internal and external dimensions of the Naval Staff's programme stalled. Although British naval building was proceeding at top speed, and the Navy's estimates had benefited from the sense of urgency that followed the *Anschluß* on 12 March, the Cabinet rejected the new naval standard. Concurrently, in the face of threats from the signatories, Japan refused to join the 1936 London Naval Treaty. On the continent, in late 1937 to 1938, Hitler grew steadily more impatient with the pace of events and irritated at London for interfering with his plans for wars of racial conquest. Indeed, the public climb-down he was compelled to endure during the weekend of 20–21 May made Hitler determined to destroy Czechoslovakia at the first available opportunity.

From the standpoint of coming out on top in the global order of sea power by the mid-1940s, the timing of the Czechoslovakian crisis signalled the imminent demolition of the Admiralty's master programme: a general war beginning in September 1938 would mean the end of the Naval Treaties and incite warship innovation and expansion globally, and it would *prematurely* divert Britain's national effort from a systematic one on the oceans to an impromptu one on the continent. In the COS, Admiral Chatfield argued against a guarantee to Czechoslovakia, and informed the Cabinet that there was little that could be done immediately to save the Czechs. In any case, Chamberlain was bent on a diplomatic solution, and flew three times to Nazi Germany to induce Hitler into one. The Führer was forced into a corner. Britain and France would not stand aside. Despite his determination to 'smash' Czechoslovakia, he could not do so without revealing to the world the extent of his true ambitions. He accepted Mussolini's offer of mediation.

The Munich Agreement and the Anglo-German Declaration were shortlived. The agreements did not bring about the change in relations with Nazi Germany that both Chamberlain and the Naval Staff desired. Hitler was infuriated. He regarded Munich as a defeat. As he had done in November 1937, the Führer vented his anger at London for blocking him in September by ordering more sea armaments, in the shape of the Z Plan, as part of a design to rid Europe of the meddling British. Admiral Raeder and his senior planners set the timetable for the dismantling of the 1935–7 Anglo-German Naval Agreements. In December 1938, they would break the heavy cruiser holiday and claim parity in U-boats. By the summer of 1939, when the keels of the first H-class battleships could no longer be concealed from observers, the 35 per cent tonnage ratio would have to be jettisoned. Although not alone decisive, information reaching the FO and the Cabinet after Munich about Hitler's attacks upon the Anglo-German Naval Agreement did contribute in a complex fashion to the unravelling of Chamberlain's policy of appeasement.

At the same time, the new leadership at the Admiralty struggled to adjust naval policy to post-Munich realities. Admiral Backhouse was caught in an impossible predicament. The Chatfield programme was unworkable. The future prospects of British sea power were now perilously exposed. As a consequence of his predecessor's priorities, the Royal Navy was not at maximum readiness for a European war. Nor was there enough time to realise Admiral Drax's quick-fix schemes to bring an offensive spirit to naval planning and policy. The *matériel* means to execute them were not available. Furthermore, Drax and Backhouse overrated the potential pay-off from these offensive plans. Above all, their most novel stratagem, a knockout blow against Italy, would not have solved the problem of Nazi aggression. As the COS and JPC had long recognised, the only way to defeat Nazi Germany was through a prolonged macro-economic slugging match.

Ultimately, Hitler propelled Europe to war. By marching into Prague on 15 March 1939, he ended the Anglo-German Declaration and with it the Anglo-German Naval Agreement. The British response of bloc building in Eastern Europe, especially the Anglo-French guarantees to Poland, provoked Hitler's formal denunciation of the 35 per cent ratio in April. Heedless of signs that this time London and Paris would stand firm, the Führer was now resolved to conquer the Poles. Meanwhile, the Admiralty, once again under new leadership, in one final bid to restore Britain's capacity to remain competitive on the world's oceans, asked the CID to consider a crash project to expand the industrial base for capital ship production to bear the strains of an all-out race against the three revisionist naval powers. The outbreak of war in September 1939 rendered a formal decision on the Admiralty's crash-recovery proposal superfluous.

The story of Anglo-German naval relations in the 1930s exemplifies the degree to which the two governments (as well as their naval experts) were working at cross purposes. Hitler interpreted the 35 per cent deal as a precursor to a wider political arrangement on maritime and continental spheres of influence. Such a compact had long been a precondition in his programme of racial tyranny and conquest in Central and Eastern Europe. The British accepted the 35 per cent deal for a number of reasons. The Admiralty wished to advance the cause of naval armaments diplomacy. Baldwin held that it would serve as a yardstick of Hitler's intentions. In the main, the Cabinet and the FO accepted the 35 per cent offer as a measure to pave the way for later arms limitation agreements within the framework of a stable European settlement. The 1935 Anglo-German Naval Agreement failed to satisfy the principal foreign-policy aspirations of either government because they were irreconcilable. Despite Hitler's growing anger, and the Cabinet's frequent disappointment, regular naval talks continued until July 1937, and on occasions thereafter, because the negative consequences of ending them entirely were deemed greater than those of proceeding.

Still, there was something tangible at stake: opposing ideas about force structure. It was no coincidence that top planners in both navies (Captain King in 1934, Commander Heye in 1938) envisaged for Nazi Germany essentially identical anti-British sea armaments strategies. A *Kreuzerkrieg* fleet would have generated for the resources expended a greater wartime return than the surface fleet that Admiral Raeder actually built. Yet the Anglo-German Naval Agreements committed Berlin to a pattern of naval development which was *the least* threatening to British security. Diplomacy was important in bringing this about, but so was the German navy's craving to obtain the Washington Treaty or battle fleet standard. As Heye had grasped (and indeed lamented), Britain profited from the abstract influence exerted by the prevailing norms and historically conditioned responses about what constituted true sea power.[2] The value-laden terms the planners employed – 'freak', 'balanced', 'special' and 'normal' fleets – points to the effect. The interwar Naval Treaties, by codifying this historical legacy into the international system, reinforced its power. In this connection, it is significant that the British government had no success at all in obtaining European-wide treaties to regulate the instrument of state power with the briefest history, and the one closely associated with Hitler's revisionist diplomacy, the bomber.[3]

On a larger scale, it is clear that a profound cause of the Second World War was this clash between Britain's desire to uphold the essentials of the international status quo and the Nazi regime's nationalistic impulses towards its violent overthrow.[4] At one level, appeasement was designed to enmesh the Third Reich into the rules and conventions governing the European system with offers to facilitate peaceful revision and the build-up of an air deterrent. As the primary commercial and imperial beneficiary of the status quo, British intervention was needed to entrench and modify the political and strategic environment – the rules of the game – to promote its interests and enhance its power. In retrospect, it is tempting to conclude that the normative aspect of appeasement was flawed, without substance and misguided. But the evidence from naval armaments diplomacy shows that there were genuine strategic pay-offs at hand. Its political counterpart was the way in which Chamberlain put Hitler on the spot in September 1938. To grasp how this rule-building diplomacy impinged on even the Führer's twisted solipsism, one only has to look at Hitler's later rage at having been cheated out of his Czech war, his resolve to never be trapped into talks again and his determination to rid Europe of Britain.[5]

As we have seen, in assessing the Admiralty's input into foreign policy, it is important to probe beyond the arguments made by Chatfield at the COS and the CID to grasp the exclusively maritime logic to his stance. Although they shared much common ground about the need to defend Britain's prospects as a global power, the CNS and the Prime Minister had substantial differences. By the beginning of 1937, Chatfield was certain that Hitler would not be satisfied for much longer with having received nothing in return for the 35 per cent ratio: the solution was to feed Germany the poison pill of Central and South Eastern Europe. The outcome would be, Chatfield calculated, an optimal correlation of national policies, whereby German land power would be hobbled and British sea power enhanced. 'Peoples, not rulers, now have to be conquered,' he reasoned: 'Can they be? I do not think so.'[6] Here lies his principal error. The First Sea Lord did not see that the small powers would only resist the German advance with Franco-British leadership. Nor did he see that Berlin would acquire, as Vansittart had warned, the resource base and overland supply routes it needed to become immune to blockade and to develop into a lethal threat.

Although Admiral Chatfield was not alone in speculating about the merits of an unopposed German *Drang nach Osten,* the idea was unacceptable to the Cabinet. To promote its goal, the Naval Staff pinned its hopes on Chamberlain's positive effort at appeasement. Ironically, it had precisely the opposite effect from what Chatfield had anticipated. From Hitler's statements on economic preparations, it is clear he did not intend a general European conflict until about the mid-1940s.[7] But British attempts in 1938 to mediate and conciliate incited him to act sooner. After Munich, Hitler's belief in a lack of British will was confirmed, and the scale of his enmity to London was expressed in orders for warships. As he tried in 1939 to manipulate events to turn westwards, and confounded by Poland's refusal to succumb, his miscalculations multiplied. The scale of the war that broke out in September 1939 was out of step with his plans to ready the German economy for total war. The victories of 1938–40 supplied the Third Reich with the resource base it required to prolong the conflict. Among other *strategic* consequences, Hitler's war disrupted the Royal Navy's timetable for Britain's renaissance as the world's leading sea power.

In exercising their strategic imaginations, did the Naval Staff officers suffer from an inability to exploit intelligence? A proclivity for confusing German capabilities with intentions? Or a wrongheaded aversion to the gloomy predictions of the FO? The evidence indicates that the Admiralty was better at grasping the German navy's offensive posture, the details of German naval building, assessing the quality of Admiral Raeder's warships and U-boats and monitoring the output capacity of his shipyards than has previously been supposed. But getting the details right is only the first step. In using this knowledge to assist policy-making and war planning, on the whole, within reasonable limits, the Admiralty's performance was quite good when compared with the realities with which it was presumed to correspond.

On the issue of prediction, it must be underscored that Admiral Chatfield and his top planners believed that war with Nazi Germany before the 1940s was *improbable*, not *impossible*. They understood what Hitler was up to with his 35 per cent offer. In 1936–7, the Naval Staff realised how quickly things could change unless statecraft cultivated a stable international environment for sea power renewal. In short, the Naval Staff hoped that the future could be made to unfold roughly according to its programme. In the event, it proved impossible for Britain in tandem to secure its empire at sea and to forestall a serious challenge to the balance of power on the continent.

The programmatic structure to Chatfield's naval policy had a cumulative effect. As time progressed, the stakes increased, and the Royal Navy's options narrowed. The link between Chatfield's maritime objectives and his advice to the Cabinet is clear. As chairman of the COS, the First Sea Lord consistently advised against war over Czechoslovakia in 1938. The long-term war-winning combination of sea power, economic staying power and blockade proved to be little consolation. In striking contrast to the debilitating effect that the dread of a knockout blow delivered by the *Luftwaffe* had on British diplomacy in 1938, the COS repeatedly warned ministers that economic warfare was a very blunt and unwieldy coercive instrument when it came to attempts to deal with Hitler.

All of this leads one to speculate about what might have happened had the Admiralty accepted war in 1939 as a certainty and adjusted its goals accordingly. Similarly, what would naval strategy have looked like if Admirals Backhouse and Drax had control in early 1933 instead of late 1938? As we saw from Drax's memo of September 1937 he was prepared to take the DRC's 1939 forecast seriously. Although no doubt battleship building would still have been a major feature of naval policy, it is conceivable that financial imperatives would have propelled Backhouse and Drax to a fundamental shift in strategic thinking. There was a precedent for this in 1913–14. Under Churchill, due to fiscal restraints, the Admiralty was prepared to abandon the two-power fleet and to exploit the offensive capacity of submersibles to attack Tirpitz's fleet.[8] Certainly, Backhouse would not have taken Chatfield's calculated risk over U-boat defences, and perhaps Drax's offensive spirit might have encouraged the early development of the technical means to strike at Raeder's fleet in port. We know that Chamberlain was heartened on 27 September 1938 when the Chief of the French General Staff told him that his forces would conduct an offensive into Nazi Germany if war broke out over Czechoslovakia.[9] If

Admiral Backhouse had been in a position to announce in Cabinet during the crisis that the Home Fleet was ready to launch 'offensive plan B, tomorrow', perhaps this injection of Nelsonian confidence might have inspired different decisions.

Yet this was not the strategic future that the Admiralty selected in 1933. The Royal Navy would have had to scale down its historic aspirations, against the grain of its self-image as the world's foremost navy, just at a time when a revival of its fortunes seemed workable. Admiral Chatfield and his staff knew that their policy was a calculated risk, but the potential prize was worth it. Once the decision was made to remodel the naval order over a decade to suit Britain's rank as the global power, there was no shortcut back to a fresh start – except, as the CNS wrote in late 1937, to fight with inferior forces. In other words, the Naval Staff embarked in 1933–5 on a complex programme to rebuild British sea power that left it with no option but to back Chamberlain's policy of appeasement in 1937–8.

Notes

INTRODUCTION

1. D. C. Watt, 'The Historiography of Appeasement', A. Sked and C. Cook, eds, *Essays in Honour of A. J. P. Taylor* (London, 1976); P. Kennedy, 'Appeasement', G. Martel, ed., *The Origins of the Second World War Reconsidered* (London, 1986).
2. The classic statement is Cato [M. Foot, F. Owen, and P. Howard], *Guilty Men* (London, 1940), 38–41; C. Bloch, 'Great Britain, German Rearmament and the Naval Agreement of 1935', in H. Gatzke, ed., *European Diplomacy between the Two Wars, 1919–39* (Chicago, 1972); R. Best, 'The Anglo-German Naval Agreement of 1935: An Aspect of Appeasement', *Naval War College Review* 34 (1981). Despite access to the British archives, E. H. Haraszti, *Treaty-Breakers or "Realpolitiker"? The Anglo-German Naval Agreement of June 1935* (Boppard am Rhein, 1974), advances a 'Guilty Men' style hypothesis. But, as A. J. P. Taylor pointed out, her evidence is in conflict with her conclusion: see his 'The Anglo-German Naval Agreements', *New Hungarian Quarterly* 16 (1975), 161.
3. H. Hall, 'The Foreign Policy Decision-Making Process in Britain, 1934–1935, and the Origins of the Anglo-German Naval Agreement', *Historical Journal* 19 (1976); N. H. Gibbs, *Grand Strategy* Vol. I, (London, 1976), 155–70. In 'The Anglo-German Naval Agreement of 1935: An Interim Judgement', *Journal of Modern History* 28 (1956), D. C. Watt anticipated the revisionist case before British documents became available.
4. S. Roskill, *Naval Policy Between the Wars* 2 vols (London, 1968–76), II, 321.
5. P. Kennedy, *The Rise and Fall of British Naval Mastery* (London, 1983), 289.
6. W. Wark, *The Ultimate Enemy: British Intelligence and Nazi Germany, 1933–1939* (Oxford, 1986), 124–54.
7. G. Post Jr, *Dilemmas of Appeasement: British Deterrence and Defence, 1934–1937* (Ithaca, 1993), explores the temporal dimension to British defence and diplomacy more thoroughly than most accounts, and recognises that the Admiralty entertained a different timescale from other Whitehall departments. Yet Post wrongly assumes that this was a result of a Naval Staff preoccupation with the Japanese threat.
8. J. R. Ferris, '"It is our business in the Navy to command the Seas": The Last Decade of British Maritime Supremacy, 1919–1929', in K. Neilson and G. Kennedy, eds, *Far Flung Lines: Studies in Imperial Defence in Honour of Donald Mackenzie Schurman* (London, 1996). Also see G. Martel, K. Neilson, J. Ferris and B. McKercher in *International History Review* 13 (1991).

9. S. Aster, '"Guilty Men": The Case of Neville Chamberlain', in R. Boyce and E. M. Robertson, eds, *Paths to War* (London, 1989); R. A. C. Parker, *Chamberlain and Appeasement* (London, 1993). W. Murray argues that the appeasers failed as strategists in *The Change in the European Balance of Power, 1938–1939* (Princeton, 1984).
10. Gibbs, *Strategy*, 767–92.
11. General W. Jackson and Lord Bramall, *The Chiefs* (London, 1992).
12. J. R. Ferris, *Men, Money, and Diplomacy* (Ithaca, 1989), 1–14; B. McKercher, 'Old Diplomacy and New: The Foreign Office and Foreign Policy, 1919–1939', in M. Dockrill and B. McKercher, eds, *Diplomacy and World Power* (Cambridge, 1996); G. Peden, *British Rearmament and the Treasury, 1932–1939* (Edinburgh, 1979).
13. A. Duff Cooper, *Old Men Forget* (London, 1955), 195; S. Hoare, *Nine Troubled Years* (London, 1954), 204–5.
14. Ferris, *Diplomacy*, 6.
15. M. Murfett et al., *The First Sea Lords* (London, 1995), 157–71.
16. Sir Oswyn Murray, 'The Admiralty', *The Mariner's Mirror* 33 (1937).
17. J. Gooch, 'The Chiefs of Staff and the Higher Organisation for Defence in Britain, 1904–1984', in J. Hattendorf and R. Jordan, eds, *Maritime Strategy and the Balance of Power* (London, 1989); A. J. Marder, *From Dreadnought to Scapa Flow* Vol. IV (London, 1969); Murfett, *First Sea Lords*, 48; Command 1343 (1921), 'The Distribution of the Duties of the Naval Staff'.
18. Murfett, *First Sea Lords*, 128.
19. D. C. Watt, *Personalities and Appeasement* (Austin, 1991), 9.
20. *Instructions for Naval Staff* June 1934, CE674/34, ADM1/8778/183.
21. 'The Work of Plans', 16 April 1935, PD04884/35, ADM116/3366.
22. C. M. Andrew, *Secret Service* (London, 1985), 139–94.
23. F. H. Hinsley et al., *British Intelligence in the Second World War* Vol. I (London, 1979), 3–43; E. Thomas, 'The Evolution of the JIC System Up to and During World War II', in C. Andrew and J. Noakes, eds, *Intelligence and International Relations 1900–1945* (Exeter, 1987). Before 1939, the JIC acted more as a joint study group on specific issues (such as air warfare in Spain) than as a central cell for the appraisal of intelligence.
24. 'Organisation of Intelligence Division', February 1924, ADM 116/1842.
25. R. Young, 'Spokesmen for Economic Warfare: The Industrial Intelligence Centre in the 1930s', *European Studies Review* 6 (1976).
26. In the 1930s, the Admiralty employed about fifty men at its wireless interception stations at Scarborough and Flowerdown, which sent by teleprinter intercepted messages for decryption to the Naval Section at the Government Code and Cypher School. The Home, Mediterranean and the Reserve fleets at Portsmouth and Devonport made interceptions to decrypt foreign naval codes. On naval signals intelligence between the two world wars, see 'Before September 1939: NID Revives', n.d. [1947?], ADM223/469 and ADM116/6320, 6322–4.
27. Hinsley, *Intelligence*, 3–43; D. C. Watt, 'British Intelligence and the Coming of the Second World War in Europe', in E. May, ed., *Knowing One's Enemies* (Princeton, 1984).

CHAPTER 1   THE NAVAL STAFF AND THE ANGLO-GERMAN
NAVAL AGREEMENT OF JUNE 1935

1. C. Hall, *Britain, America, and Arms Control, 1921–1937* (London, 1987);
    S. Pelz, *Race to Pearl Harbour* (Boston, 1984); E. Goldstein and J. Maurer,
    eds, 'The Washington Conference, 1921–1922', *Diplomacy and Statecraft* 6
    (1993); J. R. Ferris, 'The Symbol and the Substance of Seapower: Great
    Britain, the United States and the One-Power Standard', in B. McKercher
    ed., *Anglo-American Relations in the 1920s* (London, 1990).
2. B. McKercher, *The Second Baldwin Government and the United States,
    1924–1929* (Cambridge, 1984).
3. J. Ferris, 'Last Decade', 124–70; G. Gordon, *British Seapower and
    Procurement between the Wars* (London, 1988), passim.
4. Ferris, 'Last Decade', 159–61.
5. Gibbs, *Strategy*, Chp II; Roskill, *Policy*, II, Chs. III–VI.
6. Plans, 14 November 1932, Case 11431, ADM 116/3434.
7. Roskill, II, 70, 125–6, 150–1, 153–4.
8. Monsell to Chatfield, 26 June 1932, CH[a]T[field Papers NMM]2/1/55.
9. Roskill, II, 154–5; A. J. Marder, *Old Friends, New Enemies* (Oxford, 1981),
    30–1; Gordon, *Procurement*, 109–11.
10. His remarks to Sir Warren Fisher, Permanent Under-Secretary of the
    Treasury, 16 July 1934, CAB21/434 and 4 June 1934, CHT3/1.
11. Gordon, *Procurement*, 109–12.
12. Ferris, 'Last Decade', 124–70.
13. DCNS, Controller (Chatfield), and ACNS, joint minute, 21 December 1926,
    M03056/26, ADM1/8699/118.
14. J. Sumida, *In Defence of Naval Supremacy* (London, 1989); Kennedy,
    Mastery, 267–98; Ferris 'Last Decade', 124–70.
15. Roskill, I, 499, II, 50; 'Proposed Classification and Limitations of Warships',
    Table W, M03056/26, December 1926, ADM1/8699/118; Plans, 'Capital
    Ships', December 1932, Templewood Papers, Vol. IX, folios 5–6, Cambridge
    University Library.
16. Ferris, 'Symbol and Substance', 55–80.
17. See 'Maritime Power' in DRC37, 21 November 1935, CAB16/112.
18. DCNS, Controller (Chatfield), ACNS, 21 December 1926, M03056/26,
    ADM1/8699/118; FO/Admiralty mtg., 20 March 1934, A2416/1938/45,
    FO371/17596.
19. This account of the Naval Staff's proposals unless otherwise stated is based
    on the following: Sir Robert Craigie, Head of the American Department,
    FO, 9 January 1934, A1977/22/45, FO371/17596; 'Strategic Requirements',
    14 March 1934, M0687/34, ADM116/2999; NCM(35)23, 30 October 1934,
    CAB29/148; FO/Admiralty, '1935 Naval Conference', 23 March 1934,
    NCM(35)1, CAB29/148.
20. Admiral R. Bellairs, 7 September 1933, W10329/117/38, FO371/17382.
21. The opposite practice, 'global limitation' – whereby each power expended
    its assigned tonnage as it liked – was advanced by the French and later
    adopted by the Japanese.

22. The non-construction zone became paras three and four of Article IV of the Treaty for the Limitation of Naval Armament, London, 25 March 1936, Command Paper 5136.
23. Sumida, *Supremacy*, 39; NCM(35)23, 30 October 1934, CAB29/148.
24. The committee papers and the records of talks are in CAB29/147–9.
25. 'Admiralty Paper No.1', para. 6, April 1934, PD04493/34, ADM 116/3373.
26. Hall, *Arms Control*, 144.
27. Craigie, 9 January 1934, A1977/22/45, FO371/17596.
28. For instance para. 18, Annex III, NCM(35)50, 5 June 1935, CAB29/150.
29. Chatfield to Admiral W. Fisher, 2 August 1934, CHT4/5; 'New Standard', 25 September 1936, PD05892/36, ADM1/9729; Ferris, 'Last Decade', 124–70.
30. Chatfield to Admiral Charles Madden, former First Sea Lord, 1927–30, 4 October 1934, CHT/3/2.
31. The DRC papers are in CAB16/109; Gibbs, *Strategy*, 93–131; Peden, *Treasury*, passim.
32. U. Bialer, *The Shadow of the Bomber* (London, 1980).
33. DRC14, 28 February 1934, CAB16/109.
34. NCM(35)3, 19 April 1934, CAB29/148; D. C. Watt, *Personalities and Policies* (London, 1965), 83–99; Hall, *Arms Control*, 149–60.
35. The DCM's records are in CAB16/110. It included the three service ministers, the Chancellor, the FO Under-Secretary, the Lord Privy Seal, the President of the Board of Trade, the Colonial Secretary and Hankey. In July 1935, it became the Defence Policy and Requirements Committee, which vetted later DRC reports for the CID.
36. DCM(32), 55th mtg, 24 July 1934, CAB16/110; DCM(32)120, 20 June 1934, CAB16/111; Chamberlain, diary, 6 and 31 July 1934, 9 and 25 October 1934, NC2/23A, Birmingham University Library.
37. Director of Plans, 20 June 1934, DCNS to CNS and First Lord, CNS to First Lord, 21 June 1934, and 'General Basis of Proposals', 23 June 1934, Case 11431, ADM 116/3436; Chamberlain to Hilda Chamberlain, 28 July 1934, NC18/1/881; G. Till, 'The Strategic Interface: The Navy and Air Force in the Defence of Britain', *Journal of Strategic Studies* 1 (1978).
38. DCM, 55th mtg, 24 July 1934, CAB16/110.
39. Kennedy, *Mastery*, 288–9 and Wark, *Intelligence*, 129–30. Hankey to Chatfield, 9 August 1934, H[an]KY [Papers, CCC]1/7. Hankey assured Chatfield that most ministers would back substantial naval building if they could be persuaded to voice their opinions; Captain T. Phillips to CNS, 4 April 1938, ADM205/80.
40. Sir H. Rumbold, British Ambassador Berlin, to FO, 7 November 1930, C8290/657/18, FO371/14370; Admiralty to FO, 27 May 1931, and FO to Admiralty, 22 January 1932, C3683/C9515/116/18, FO371/15219.
41. Admiralty to FO, 13 April 1931, C2526/116/18, ibid.; Craigie, 3 September 1931, A5309/21/45, FO371/15122; Admiralty to FO, 18 February 1932, M0197/32, FO371/15951. For British draft disarmament proposals, see Command Papers 4122 (1931–2), 4279 (1932–3) and 4498 (1933–4).
42. Director of Plans, 27 February 1932, M0197/32, ADM116/2945; Record of a conversation between Captain Bellairs and Baron von Rheinbaben and Admiral von Freyberg, 27 July 1932, W8566/1466/98, FO371/16464. For

German policy, see J. Dülffer, *Weimar, Hitler, und die Marine: Reichspolitik und Flottenbau, 1920–1939* (Düsseldorf, 1973), 254–66; G. L. Weinberg, *The Foreign Policy of Hitler's Germany* Vol. I, (Chicago, 1970), 42–7, 159–68.

43. Captain H. R. Moore, 10 March 1932, M889/32, and draft memo, July 1932, M01517/32, ADM116/2945.
44. Dülffer, *Marine*, 256–7.
45. Conversation on 29 April 1933 between Bellairs and Rheinbaben and Freyberg, 5 May 1933, W4844/117/98, FO371/17381.
46. Sir E. Phipps, British Ambassador Berlin to FO, 21 November 1933, PH[i]PP[S Papers CCC]1/11; and Captain Muirhead-Gould, British naval attaché Berlin, 11 December 1933, C10627/404/18, FO371/16730.
47. Record of a private conversation, 1 April 1933, CHT/3/1.
48. Muirhead-Gould to DNI, 30 November 1933, C10777/404/18, FO371/16730; Captain King, 21 December 1933, PD04407/33, ADM116/2890; Dülffer, *Marine*, 267.
49. Principal Under-Secretary, Admiralty, 22 December 1933, PD04407/33, ADM116/2890; Bellairs to FO, 8 January 1934, Craigie, 16 January 1934, W465/82/98, FO371/18535.
50. C. Thomas, *The German Navy in the Nazi Era* (London, 1990), 78–9.
51. Weinberg, *Foreign Policy*, I, 1–24, 42–7.
52. A. Hitler, *Mein Kampf* (London, 1992), 129–31. The history of the German navy is important to the debate about whether Hitler had a master plan of world domination or improvised his foreign policy. M. Salewski, in *Die deutsche Seekriegsleitung 1935–1945* 3 vols (Frankfurt, 1970–5), asserts that Hitler had a flexible foreign/naval policy; Dülffer, in *Marine*, persuasively argues that Hitler's naval policy reveals his long-term plans. Dülffer sees the June 1935 accord as a temporary measure on the road to a final showdown with the Anglo-American sea powers; Salewski views it and the planned Anglo-German alliance as Hitler's desired but not indispensable preconditions for the conquest of Central and Eastern Europe.
53. Thomas, *German Navy*, 65–6, 71; Dülffer, *Marine*, 204–24.
54. G. Schreiber, 'Zur Kontinuität des Groß- und Weltmachtstrebens der deutschen Marineführung', *Militärgeschichtliche Mitteilungen* 26 (1979).
55. Dülffer, *Marine*, 274–7; *DGFP* C, II, No. 45; German Naval Command, 'Thoughts on the Naval Conference', 12 December 1933, D. C. Watt, ed., *Anglo-German Naval Relations: Documents*, British Library of Political and Economic Science, London.
56. W. Deist et al., *Germany and the Second World War* Vol. I (Oxford, 1990), 458–9, Dülffer, *Marine*, 244–9, 268–9, 566; Thomas, 78–84; Salewski, 'Marineleitung und politische Führung, 1931–1935', *Militärgeschichtliche Mitteilungen* 10 (1971).
57. Dülffer, *Marine*, 249–51.
58. Sir H. Rumbold to FO, 11 March 1932, W2910/1466/9, FO371/16460.
59. Dülffer, *Marine*, 274–5, 279–99; Deist, *Germany*, 460–1; Salewski, I, 9–13 and his 'Marineleitung', 132–44.
60. On 26 March 1935, during his conversation with Simon and Eden, Hitler simultaneously demanded equality with the French and a 35 per cent ratio with the Royal Navy. The British emissaries pointed out that these were not

the same thing, a fact confirmed by Neurath, who was also present at the conference: *DGFP* C, III, No. 595.

61. *DGFP* C, III, Nos 25 and 32; Dülffer, 'Determinants of German Naval Policy, 1929–1939', in W. Deist, ed., *The German Military in the Age of Total War* (London, 1985).

62. *DGFP* C, III, No. 298.

63. Muirhead-Gould to DNI, 27 November 1934, C8066/2134/18, FO371/17765; Phipps to FO, 28 November 1934, C8045/20/18, F0408/64; *DGFP* C, III, No. 360; Dülffer, *Marine*, 299–302.

64. Muirhead-Gould to DNI, 30 November 1933, C10777/404/18, and various Central Department officials, 11 December 1933, C10627/404/18, FO371/16730. Dülffer, *Marine*, 268–9; Salewski, I, 10 and his 'Marine-leitung', 131.

65. Phipps to FO, 5 February 1934, W1237/82/98, FO371/18535. He wrote that the naval attaché had learned that diesel engines for ship D had not been ordered.

66. Phipps to FO, 11 April 1934, C2352/2134/18, FO371/17765; Conversation between Muirhead-Gould and Admiral Groos, 18 October 1934, C7129/20/18, FO371/17696.

67. The Committee on German Rearmament issued its report on 18 December 1934, CP300, CAB24/251. J. Perowne, Central Department, 20 December 1934, C8799/2134/18, FO371/17765; NCM(35)46, 17 January 1935, ADM116/3433.

68. DCNS, 26 February 1935, PD04831/35, ADM116/3373.

69. Cabinet, 27 February 1935, 12(35), CAB23/81.

70. Roskill, II, 303–5; Wark, *Intelligence*, 130–8.

71. NCM(35)1, 23 March 1934, CAB29/148; NCM, 1st mtg., 16 April 1934, CAB29/147; Admiral Charles Little, DCNS, 9 March 1934, M0687/34, ADM116/2999.

72. Captain King, 29 June 1934, PD04586/34, ADM116/3373.

73. King, December 1934, PD04754/34, ibid.

74. DNI, 5 December 1934, ibid.

75. King, 21 December 1934 and DCNS, 31 December 1934, ibid.

76. Plans, 15 January 1935, PD04786/35, ibid.

77. DRC, 2nd mtg, 27 November 1933, CAB16/109; Dülffer, *Marine*, app. B, 570.

78. Phipps to FO, 31 January 1934, W1237/82/98, FO371/18535; Muirhead-Gould to Phipps, 9 April 1934, C2353/2134/18, FO371/17765.

79. Hinsley, *Intelligence*, 50; Dülffer, *Marine*, app. B, 570. Hinsley records that MI6 discovered shipbuilding in violation of Versailles taking place at Kiel, but offers no specifics. At that time, E was still being built to displace 18 000 tons. Alternatively, the information might have been about the stock-piling of U-boat parts. NID was advised on 15 May 1934 that Krupp was building engines for ocean-going U-boats. This report is cited in 'Germany – New Submarine Construction', 16 October 1935, NID0673/35, in Ship's Covers (Foreign Submarines), No. 439, folio 46, NMM.

80. Dülffer, *Marine*, 293–4; M. Whitley, *German Capital Ships of World War II* (London, 1989), 31–6.

81. Naval attaché, 1934 annual report, 3 January 1935, C233/233/18, FO371/18863; naval attaché Berlin to DNI, 7 January 1935, NID36/35, FO371/18860.
82. Naval attaché to DNI, 14 January and 11 February 1935, NID36/35, FO371/18860; FO, minute, 5 March 1935, C1767/55/18, FO371/18828.
83. E. Rössler, *The U-Boat* (London, 1981), 88–98; L. Farago, *The Game of the Foxes* (London, 1972), 117–120.
84. Rössler, *U-Boat*, 98–100; *International Military Tribunal* No. C–189, Vol. 34, 775.
85. Department of Naval Construction, Ship's Covers (Foreign Submarines), No. 439. This volume contains technical intelligence about various German U-boat types from 1925 onwards. See, for example, folios 21 and 21A, 'German built Spanish Submarine', 1932, NID841/32, which contains rough sketches and design details of the boat, and folio 26, 'Specifications for a 250 ton submarine', 9 January 1933, NID0476/32, which describes the details of the Spanish and Finnish U-boats.
86. Naval attaché Berlin to FO, annual report, 27 January 1930, C685/657/18, FO371/14370; British Legation Helsingfors to FO, 12 April 1932, C3167/1450/18, FO371/15951.
87. DNI, 9 June 1933, M01653/33 and 22 July 1933, M02138/33, ADM116/2945; British Legation, Helsingfors to FO, 21 June 1933, C6165/6165/18, FO371/16755. In Section 2 of 'Naval Intelligence Report: Germany', 28 August 1936, NID1517/36, ADM178/137, NID enumerates accurately the dates, types and locations of boats built by Inkavos before 1933.
88. DRC, 2nd mtg, 27 November 1933, CAB16/109.
89. British Embassy Paris to FO, 8 November 1934; Phipps to FO, 22 November 1934; Muirhead-Gould's report to FO, 28 November 1934, C7485/2134/18, FO371/17765. The NID report of 15 May 1934 is cited in 'Germany – New Submarine Construction', 16 October 1935, NID 0673/35, in Ship's Covers, No. 439, folio 46. Orders for parts for two 700-ton U-boats had been issued: Rössler, *U-Boat*, 99.
90. Rössler, *U-Boat*, 102; Dülffer, *Marine*, 575
91. 21 March 1935, NID0176/35 in C2418/206/18, FO371/18860. Wark argues that the report was 'a confession of the Admiralty's state of ignorance' about German construction: see his *Intelligence*, 134. The work on D and E as 31 800-ton battlecruisers began 6 June and 15 May 1935: Dülffer, *Marine*, 575.
92. Wark, *Intelligence*, 37–51.
93. FO official, 1 May 1935, C3544/206/18, FO371/18860. The first was launched on 15 June 1935: Dülffer, *Marine*, 575.
94. *DGFP* C, III, No. 595.
95. Craigie, 7–29 March and 4 April 1935, A2843/A2878/A3139/A3323/22/45, FO371/18732. Monsell told Eden that he also did not believe Germany had the capacity to build to 35 per cent by 1942. Eden, 1 March 1935, A2877/22/45, FO371/18732. Central Department officials disagreed with the talks taking place before Stresa, but not with a naval exchange of views as such: Hall, 'Foreign Policy', 495–8.

96. Captain Danckwerts to Gore-Booth, FO, 18 April 1935, A3748/22/45, FO371/18733; *DGFP* C, IV, No. 51. Earlier, on 5 March, Muirhead-Gould presented a memo to the German navy, which he had prepared for Phipps, that set out what a 33 per cent ratio would look like in each ship category. FO instructions that he should not hand it over to Raeder because it differed slightly from Admiralty figures did not reach him in time. As well, Captain Wassner, the German naval attaché in London, reported to Raeder on 19 March 1935 that he had been told by an NID officer (Commander Schwerdt) that the Admiralty was not opposed to a 35 per cent ratio: Dülffer, *Marine*, 319; FO to Phipps, 27 February 1935, C1536/206/18, FO371/18860.
97. *DGFP* C, III, No. 560; Dülffer, *Marine*, 320.
98. Phipps to FO, 12 April 1935, C3119/206/18, FO371/18860; *DGFP* C, IV, No. 25.
99. *The Defeat of the Enemy Attack on Shipping, 1939–1945* (London, 1954), 14, ADM234/578.
100. Phipps to FO, 25 March 1935, C2632/206/18, FO371/18860.
101. Dülffer, *Marine*, 306; *DGFP* C, IV, Nos 51, 52, 54.
102. NID report 0236/35 of 26 April 1935 about the submarines is cited but not reproduced in full in ADM/3433. It was circulated to the FO, as the DNI note in this file indicates, but no copy is enclosed. Commander Schwerdt to FO, 30 May 1935, C4372/206/19, FO371/18860. It is also cited in 'Germany – New Submarine Construction', 16 October 1935, NID0673/35, in Ship's Covers, No. 439, folio 46. The information about the large boats was probably an exaggerated report about the two 700-ton boats (U25–26) planned for Bremen yards. The engines for these two boats were being built by the MAN plant. Dülffer, *Marine*, 575; Rössler, *U-Boat*, 334.
103. Phipps to Simon, enclosure No. 1, 2 May 1935, C3557/206/18, FO371/18860; *DGFP* C, IV, Nos 58, 59, 60.
104. Orme Sargent, Central Department, 27 April 1935, C3446/206/18, FO371/18860.
105. Craigie described his negotiating strategy for the PM, and added that the French naval minister had told him that he thought they would be 'lucky' to set a limit on German fleet expansion: Craigie to MacDonald, 17 May 1935, PRO30/69/546.
106. Sir R. Clive, Tokyo, to FO, 3 May 1935, A4086/22/45, FO371/18733.
107. Little to Craigie, 4 May 1935, and Craigie, 9 May 1935, A4086/A4333/22/45, ibid. The order but not the meaning of his words have been altered. Little, 26 February 1935, PD04831/35, ADM116/3373; Craigie to PM, 17 May 1935, PRO30/69/546.
108. FO to Phipps, 10 May 1935, Telegram No. 102, cited in ADM116/3433; Phipps to FO, 13 May 1935, A4439/A4733/22/45, FO371/18733.
109. Conwell-Evans to Leo A. Kennedy, 14 May 1935, and diary entry, 11 May 1935, L[eo A.]KEN[nedy Papers CCC]1/8.
110. Muirhead-Gould to DNI, 28 May 1935, NID818/35, in ADM116/3433; DNI to Muirhead-Gould, 3 June 1935, C4405/206/18, FO371/18860.
111. J. Wheeler-Bennett and S. Heald, eds, *Documents on International Affairs 1935* Vol. I (London, 1936), 173.
112. Cabinet, 22 May 1935, 30(35), CAB 23/81.
113. Phipps to FO, 23 May 1935, A4661/22/45, FO371/18733.

114. Craigie, 25 May 1935, ibid.
115. Chatfield to Admiral F. Dreyer, C-in-C China, 31 May 1935, CHT/4/4.
116. Plans, 27 May 1935, PD04928/35, ADM116/3373.
117. The records are in CAB29/150; *DGFP* C, IV, passim.
118. M. Bloch, *Ribbentrop* (London, 1992), 68–73; Dülffer, *Marine*, 325–8; *DGFP* C, IV, No. 100.
119. Cabinet, 32(35), 5 June 1935, CAB23/81.
120. *DGFP* C, IV, Nos 135, 136, 137.
121. Craigie, 4 June 1935, A5214/22/45, FO371/18733.
122. NCM(35)50, 5 June 1935, CAB29/150.
123. NCM(35), 6 June 1935, 11th mtg, CAB29/147; K. Middlemas and J. Barnes, *Baldwin* (London, 1969), 826–8. MacDonald had approved the insertion of a 'more rapid replacement' in the text: N. M. Butler to PM, 1 June 1935, PRO30/69/546.
124. Ibid.; letter to Vansittart, 13 June 1935, A5414/22/45, FO371/18734 and 22 December 1936, PD06012/36, ADM116/3378.
125. Bloch, *Ribbentrop*, 69–75.
126. Salewski, 'Marineleitung', 148–9.
127. Chamberlain wrote to Hilda on 22 June 1935 that 'I am not surprised that the French were annoyed [by the Naval Agreement], but there was not time to be lost and I believe Eden will have been able to show them that the treaty is good not for us but for them,' NC18/1/923.
128. *DGFP* C, IV, No. 154; Hall, 'Foreign Policy', 495–8.

CHAPTER 2   ANGLO-GERMAN NAVAL RELATIONS, JUNE 1935 TO JULY 1937

1. Two exceptions are D. C. Watt, 'Anglo-German Naval Negotiations on the Eve of the Second World War', *Journal of the Royal United Services Institute* 610–611 (1958); Dülffer, *Marine*, 391–419.
2. For more details, see Pelz, *Pearl Harbour*.
3. Craigie to Soviet Ambassador, 5 February 1937, A1221/180/45, FO371/20657.
4. NC(G)12, Annex I, 23 June 1935 and NCM(35)55, 29 June 1935, CAB29/150.
5. Craigie to FO, 4 May 1939, A3236/1/45, FO371/22785.
6. What follows is based on NCM(35)56, and Annex II, 4 July 1935, CAB29/150.
7. Dülffer, *Marine*, 392–4, 397, nn. 2, 4.
8. *DGFP* C, IV, No. 275.
9. Dülffer, *Marine*, 392–4; Bloch, *Ribbentrop*, Chs III–V.
10. Dülffer, ibid.
11. *DGFP* C, IV, No. 273.
12. Craigie, 4 December 1935, A10060/22/45, FO371/18742.
13. Conversation between Vansittart and French Ambassador, June 19, 1935, A5485/22/45, FO371/18734.
14. Craigie to Captain Phillips, 18 November 1935, A9565/5/45, FO371/18726.

15. Craigie, 16 September 1935, A7787/22/45, FO371/18739.
16. Captain Danckwerts, 23 September 1935, PD05075/35, ADM 116/3377.
17. 'Memorandum Communicated', 16 October 1935, A8992/22/45, ibid.; Craigie, 17 October 1935, A8992/22/45, FO371/18740.
18. Dülffer, *Marine*, 393–4.
19. 'German Answer', 27 November 1935, A10060/22/45, ADM116/3377.
20. Craigie, 4 December 1935, A10060/22/45, FO371/18742.
21. Craigie, 3 June 1935, A5810/22/45, FO371/18735.
22. Conversation between Danckwerts and Wassner, 12 August 1935, A7574/22/45, FO371/18739.
23. Craigie, 16 August 1935 and FO to Plans, 26 August 1935, ibid.
24. *DGFP* C, IV, No. 59, n.7.
25. Ibid., No. 273; DNI to Craigie, 7 December 1935, Muirhead-Gould to Sir E. Phipps, 7 October 1935, A9440/A10605/5/45, FO371/18726; Berlin Embassy to FO, 19 February 1936, A1628/12/45, ADM116/3368.
26. Muirhead-Gould to Phipps, 1 November 1935, A9440/5/45, FO371/18726.
27. Conversation between Craigie and Wassner, 9 November 1935, Craigie to Wassner, 19 November 1935, Craigie to DNI, 13 November 1935, A9316/A9565/5/45, ibid.
28. L. Kennedy, Diaries, 30 April 1936, LKEN1/20.
29. Naval attaché Berlin to FO, 17 September 1935, A8087/22/45, FO371/18739.
30. Craigie, 11 November – 14 December 1935, A9440/A10605/5/45, FO371/18726.
31. DNI to Craigie, 1 November 1935, A9316/5/45, ibid.
32. Vansittart to DNI, 20 December 1935 and DNI to Vansittart, 2 January 1936, A67/4/45, FO371/19803.
33. Berlin Embassy to FO, 19 February 1936, A1628/12/45, ADM116/3368; DNI, 28 February 1936, PD05471/36, ADM116/3377; DNI to Craigie, 6 March 1936, A2044/12/45, FO371/19822.
34. FO to Wassner, 25 January 1936, A383/4/45 and 'Reply', 19 February 1936, A1731/4/45, ADM116/3377.
35. One dispute over capital ship lifespans was quickly settled: Danckwerts, 28 February 1936, PD05471/36, ibid.
36. W. N. Medlicott, 'Britain and Germany: The Search for Agreement, 1930–1937', in D. Dilks, ed., *Retreat From Power* Vol. I (London, 1981).
37. Eden replaced Sir S. Hoare in December 1935, who resigned over the fiasco of the Hoare-Laval plan.
38. *DGFP* C, IV, No. 555.
39. Ibid., No. 595.
40. J. T. Emmerson, *The Rhineland Crisis* (London, 1977), 72–103.
41. Ibid., 39–70.
42. Commander R. K. Dickson to his father, 8 March 1936, Box No. 13526, folios 42–9, National Library of Scotland, Edinburgh; Backhouse to Chatfield, 29 March 1936, CHT4/1; Commander J. Hughes-Hallett (Plans Division), 'The Outlook in Europe', *The Naval Review* 24 (1936), 287–94.
43. A. J. Marder, 'The Royal Navy and the Ethiopian Crisis of 1935–36', *American Historical Journal* 75 (1970); COS441(JP), 16 March 1936, CAB53/27.

44. Captain T. Phillips, 'The European Situation', July 1934, in the possession of Mr T. R. V. Phillips.
45. Chatfield to Backhouse, 27 March 1936, CHT/4/1. First Lord's indiscreet remarks of January1936 in *DGFP* C, IV, No. 531.
46. Craigie, 12 March 1936, A2571/4/45, FO371/19812.
47. Vansittart, 13 March 1936, ibid.
48. Cabinet, 16 March 1936, 20(36), CAB23/83; Craigie, 18 March 1936, A2571/4/45, FO371/19812.
49. Emmerson, *Rhineland*, 104–230.
50. Cabinet, 18 March 1936, 21(36), CAB23/83.
51. *DGFP* C, V, No. 303; F. Gannon, *The British Press and Germany, 1933–39* (London, 1971), 43–50.
52. Craigie's record in A4708/4671/45, FO371/19838; *DGFP* C, V, Nos. 309.
53. *DGFP* C, IV, No. 585; Cabinet, 27 May 1936, 39(36), CAB23/84.
54. Dülffer, *Marine*, 402–5.
55. Ibid., 382; M. Whitely, *German Cruisers of World War II* (London, 1985), 51–2.
56. Weinberg, *Foreign Policy*, I, 271–82; A. Hillgruber, 'England's Place in Hitler's Plans for World Dominion', *Journal of Contemporary History* 9 (1974).
57. *DGFP* C, V, No. 336; Craigie, 19 May 1936, A4708/4671/45, FO371/19838.
58. Craigie, Vansittart and Eden, 20–5 May 1936, A4708/4671/45, FO371/19838; Phillips and Little, 25–6 May 1936, PD05723/36, ADM116/3377.
59. Conversation between Eden and Bismarck, 29 May 1936, A4708/4671/45, FO371/19838; Bloch, *Ribbentrop*, 94–5.
60. Conversation between Monsell and Ribbentrop, 29 May 1936, A4891/A4772/4671/45, FO371/19838; *DGFP* C, V, No. 303.
61. Craigie, 3 June 1936, A4773/4671/45, ADM116/3377.
62. Dülffer, *Marine*, 404–5; Bloch, *Ribbentrop*, 95–6; *DGFP* C, V, No. 361.
63. Phillips, 15 June 1936, PD057747/36, ADM116/3377.
64. Vansittart and Eden, 10–12 June 1936, A5054/4671/45, FO371/19839; Cabinet, 17 June 1936, 42(36), CAB23/84.
65. Craigie to Phipps, 3–11 June 1936, A4773/A5038/4671/45, FO371/19838.
66. Vansittart and Wigram, 3–11 June 1936, ibid.
67. Phipps to Craigie, 19 June 1936, A5540/4671/45, ibid.
68. See editor's n. 1, *DGFP* C, V, No. 309.
69. *DGFP* C, IV, No. 585; Bloch, *Ribbentrop*, 78.
70. *DGFP* C, V, No. 361, n. 6.
71. Watt, 'Negotiations', 203–4; Dülffer, *Marine*, 404–5, 413–14; *DGFP* C, VI, No. 35.
72. Phillips, 7 December 1936, PD06012/36, ADM116/3378; DNI, 28 February 1936, PD05471/36, ADM116/3377.
73. *DGFP* C, IV, No. 602; Dülffer, *Marine*, 399.
74. Eden to FO, 26 March 1935, A2936/22/45, FO371/18732; Craigie, 4 March 1936, A2230/4/45, FO371/19811.
75. D. C. Watt, 'Stalin's First Bid for Seapower 1935–1941', *Proceedings of the US Naval Institute* 90 (1964); J. Rohwer and M. Monakov, 'The Soviet Union's Ocean-Going Fleet, 1935–1956', *International History Review* 28 (1996).

206   *Notes*

76. 'Summary of Results', 29 July 1936, A6338/4811/45, FO371/19840.
77. Craigie, 10 June 1936 A5054/4671/45, FO371/19839; conversation between Craigie and the Soviet Ambassador, 22 July 1936 and Craigie, 30 October 1936, A6266/A8790/4811/45, FO371/19840.
78. Moscow Embassy to FO, 8 August 1936 and 17 August 1936, Naval attaché Moscow to FO, 1 December 1936, N4119/N6018/58/38, FO371/20344; Admiralty to FO, 15 October 1936, A8286/A8214/4811/45, FO371/19840; M. Muir, 'American Warship Construction for Stalin's Navy Prior to World War II: A Study in Paralysis of Policy', *Diplomatic History* 5 (1981).
79. Craigie, 10 June 1936, A5054/4671/45, FO371/19839; Captain H. Clanchy to FO, 22 February 1937, A1557/180/45, FO371/20657; V. Gribovski, 'The "Sovetskii Soiuz" Class Battleship', *Warship International* 30 (1993).
80. *DGFP* C, V, Nos. 431, 453, 459; Dülffer, *Marine*, 406–7.
81. *DGFP* C, V, Nos. 431, 633.
82. Phipps to FO, 1 July 1936, A5551/4671/45, FO371/19838; *DGFP* C, V, No. 445; Dülffer, *Marine*, 407; L. Pratt, *East of Malta, West of Suez* (London, 1975), 141–4.
83. Craigie to Phipps, 12 September 1936, A7954/4671/45, FO371/19838; *DGFP* C, V, No. 571.
84. *DGFP* C, VI, No. 40; 'Soviet Russian Warships', 19 November 1936, A9852/4/45, FO371/19821; British Embassy Moscow to FO, 14 December 1936, A9967/4811/45, FO371/19840; British Embassy Rome to FO, 22 January 1937, A624/180/45, FO371/20657. Intelligence about a Soviet approach to Washington to purchase the design for a 16-inch naval gun also came to the attention of Raeder and Hitler in early 1937: Whitley, *Capital Ships*, 56.
85. *DGFP* C, V, No. 421; Dülffer, *Marine*, 268, 409.
86. Dülffer, *Marine*, 407–9; Watt, 'Negotiations', 386.
87. *DGFP* C, V, Nos 496, 563.
88. *DGFP* C, VI, Nos 40, 68.
89. Craigie to Phipps, 2 July 1936; First Lord's Private Secretary to Craigie, 3 July 1936; Craigie, Wigram, and Vansittart, 24–30 July 1936, A5635/A5567/A6340/4671/45, FO371/19838; Cabinet, 29 July 1936, 55(36), CAB23/85.
90. Phillips, 17 November 1936, PD05996/36, ADM116/3378.
91. Craigie, 18 December 1936, A54/54/45, FO371/20652.
92. Phillips, 23 December 1936, PD06030/36, ADM116/3929.
93. Conversation between Craigie and Woermann, 25 February 1937, A1654/6/45, FO371/20646 and A1723/A1690/54/45, FO371/20652. Official and unofficial British signals about a *possible* increase in the British battle fleet, however, were received by the Naval Command as a definite intention to expand by new construction and the retention of overage tonnage: Watt, 'Negotiations', 205; Dülffer, *Marine,* 417–18.
94. Craigie, 5 March 1937, A1984/54/45, FO371/20652; conversation between Craigie and Maisky, and Craigie, A. Cadogan and Vansittart, 8–9 March 1937, A2080/180/45, FO371/20658.
95. Hoare to Eden, and Eden to Hoare, 12–13 March 1937, A[nthony Eden] P[apers Birmingham University Library], 13/1/56.

96. Conversations between Eden and Maisky, 15 and 23 March 1937, A2062/180/45, FO371/20657 and A2284/A2228/180/45, FO371/20658; Cabinet, 24 March 1937, 13(37), CAB23/88.
97. A. Holman, American Department, 30 March 1937, A1385/6/45, FO371/20656.
98. DNC, 8 December 1936, M05260/36, ADM116/3368.
99. See Chapter 4.
100. Anglo-German mtg, 15 December 1936, A10124/A10085/4671/45, FO371/19839; *DGFP* C, VI, No. 160; Craigie, 2 July 1937, A5236/54/45, FO371/20653.
101. Captain T. Troubridge, annual report, 27 January 1938, C1360/1360/18, FO371/23055
102. Nevile Henderson to FO, 1 July 1937, C4958/270/18, FO371/20753.
103. 19–20 June 1935, NC(G), CAB29/150; *DGFP* C, IV, No. 161.
104. Cf. Wark, *Intelligence,* 139–40.
105. Dülffer, *Marine,* 303–15, 378–80; Deist, *Germany,* 464–6.
106. DNI to Vansittart, 2 January 1936, A67/4/45, FO371/19803; naval attaché, annual report 1935, 6 January 1936, C143/143/18, FO371/19938.
107. CID No. 1252-B, 22 July 1936, CAB4/24.
108. CID, 281st mtg, 30 July 1936, CAB2/6.
109. Cf. Wark, *Intelligence,* 139–40. Wark appreciates that the Naval Staff's object in circulating the report was to back up its case for further naval talks, but he wrongly concludes that the navy actually embraced its message.
110. Dülffer, *Marine,* 378–82, 419–34, 446, 505–12, 568–9; Deist, *Germany,* 465–71; Watt, 'Negotiations', 202–3.
111. The naval attaché's report is cited by Phipps, 21 May 1936, A4708/4671/45, FO371/19838; naval attaché, 1936 annual report, 12 January 1937, C357/357/18, FO371/20743; IFC/286, 1 May 1937, T160/846/F14141/3.
112. ICF/505, 'Germany: Rate of Output of Armament in 1937', 20 November 1937, C8223/136/18, FO371/20732; naval attaché Berlin, 1937 annual report, 10 January 1938, C250/250/18, FO371/21692.
113. Chatfield to Phillips, 10 November 1937, ADM205/80.

CHAPTER 3   NAVAL STAFF PERCEPTIONS OF GERMAN NAVAL STRATEGY, 1934–39

1. J. Gooch, *The Prospect of War* (London, 1981), 1–35; I. F. Clarke, *Voices Prophesying War* (Oxford, 1992), 27–93. The COS discounted the possibility of a successful invasion throughout the 1930s: COS545(JP), 7 January 1937, CAB53/30.
2. Ferris, 'Symbol and Substance', 57–9.
3. DRC, 3rd mtg, 4 December 1933, CAB16/109.
4. J. Neidpath, *The Singapore Naval Base and the Defence of Britain's Far Eastern Empire, 1919–1942* (Oxford, 1981); C. Bell, '"Our Most Exposed Outpost": Hong Kong and British Far Eastern Strategy, 1921–1941', *Journal of Military History* 60 (1996).

5. CNS, 'British Naval Strategy', 14 January 1930, LNC(E)10, ADM116/2746; 'Capital Ships', December 1932, Templewood Papers, Vol. IX, folios 5–6; 'Appreciation of Requirements', April 1934, ADM116/3373.
6. Pratt, *Malta*, 108–17.
7. W. Wegener, *The Naval Strategy of the World War* (Annapolis, 1989), 77.
8. D. Morton, 'Economics in Modern War', lecture précis for Royal Naval Staff College, 1938, G[o]D[frey]FR[ench Papers CCC]5/17; D. C. Watt, *Too Serious A Business* (London, 1975), 110–16.
9. W. N. Medlicott, *The Economic Blockade* (London, 1952).
10. JP155, 'War against Germany', 26 October 1936, CAB55/8.
11. A. Marder, 'The Influence of History on Sea Power', *From Dardanelles to Oran* (London, 1974); Roskill, I, 534–7, II, 227–8, 332, 430–31; P. Kennedy, 'British "Net Assessment" and the Coming of the Second World War', in A. Millett and W. Murray, eds, *Calculations* (New York, 1992). In contrast, see J. Sumida, '"The Best Laid Plans": The Development of British Battle-Fleet Tactics, 1919–1942', *International History Review* 14 (1992).
12. Wark, *Intelligence*, 124–54.
13. Ibid., 188–224.
14. By tracing file numbers, it was possible to identify that Case 00244 contained the draft war plans against Germany. It probably comprised several volumes: Deputy Records Officer, Ministry of Defence, to the author, 22 February 1993.
15. 'Capital Ships', December 1932, Templewood Papers.
16. T. Ropp, 'Continental Doctrines of Sea Power', in E. M. Earle, ed., *Makers of Modern Strategy* (Princeton, 1943); C. Gray, *The Leverage of Sea Power* (New York, 1992), 80–5; J. Creswell, *Naval Warfare* (London, 1936), 162–3.
17. D. Henry, 'British Submarine Policy, 1918–1939', in B. Ranft, ed., *Technical Change and British Naval Policy, 1860–1939* (London, 1977).
18. R. M. A. Hankey, 23 September 1932, C7995/211/18, FO371/15940.
19. 'Home Fleet Exercises DA', November 1933, CB1769/33, ADM186/153.
20. Creswell, *Warfare*, 139–72.
21. 'Mediterranean Fleet Exercise', April 1934, CB176933(2), ADM186/154.
22. DRC, 2nd mtg., 27 November and DRC5, November 1933, CAB16/109.
23. COS351, 23 October 1934, CAB53/24.
24. JPC, 63rd mtg, 12 November 1934, CAB55/1.
25. COS, 114th mtg, 12 October 1933, CAB53/4.
26. COS, 153rd mtg, 29 October 1934, CAB53/5; DRC, 14th mtg., 19 Jul. 1935, CAB16/112.
27. This phrase is borrowed from Gray, *Leverage*, 218.
28. DRC37, 21 November 1935, CAB16/112; Chatfield, *It Might Happen Again* (London, 1947), 10.
29. King, 21 December 1934, PD04754/34, ADM116/3373.
30. DNI, 27 August 1934, NID0583/34, ibid.
31. DNI, 5 December 1934, PD04754/34, ibid.
32. Gray, *Leverage*, 56–91. The Royal Navy understood this point: see 'Disparity between Capital Ships and Cruisers' in 'Capital Ships', December 1932, Templewood Papers; war game debriefing notes, Captain Tennant, instructor 1936–8, Naval Staff College, 1937 session, TEN[nant Papers NMM]42/4.

33. 'War against Germany', 6 December 1934, PD04756/34, ADM1/27413.
34. Schreiber, 'Kontinuität', 101–31, and his 'Reichsmarine, Revisionismus und Weltmachtstreben', in J. Müller and E. Opitz, eds, *Militär und Militarismus in der Weimarer Republik* (Düsseldorf, 1978).
35. Dülffer, *Marine*, 297–8, 342–53, 534–55.
36. Salewski, *Seekriegsleitung*, I, 29–35.
37. Salewski, I, 29–35; Dülffer, *Marine*, 440–3.
38. Salewski, I, 44–5.
39. The final draft dated 25 October 1938 is reproduced in Salewski, III, 28–63.
40. Salewski, I, 45–50.
41. Salewski, I, 44–5; Dülffer, *Marine*, 475–6.
42. Salewski, I, 51–7; Dülffer, *Marine*, 481–6, 492; Carl-Axel Gemzell, *Raeder, Hitler, und Skandinavien* (Lund, 1965), 84–104.
43. Salewski, I, 57–9; Dülffer, *Marine*, 470, 486–98, 501–2; Deist, *Germany*, 474–80.
44. Gray, *Leverage*, 64–85; D. Steury, 'The Character of the German Naval Offensive', in T. Runyan and J. Copes, eds, *To Die Gallantly* (Boulder, 1994).
45. J. Showell, ed., *Fuehrer Conferences on Naval Affairs, 1939–1945* (London, 1990), 36–7
46. G. Till, 'The Battle of the Atlantic as History', in S. Howarth and D. Law, eds, *The Battle of the Atlantic, 1939–45* (London, 1995).
47. Steury, 'Naval Offensive', 75; P. K. Lundeberg, 'The German Critique of the U-boat Campaign, 1915–18', *Military Affairs* 27 (1963).
48. Salewski, I, 22–5, 46–7.
49. Watt, 'Negotiations', 384.
50. Till, 'History', 584–95.
51. Deist, *Germany*, 478–80; Dülffer, *Marine*, 503–12; Salewski, I, 61–3; H. H. Herwig, 'The Failure of German Sea Power, 1914–1945: Mahan, Tirpitz, and Raeder Reconsidered', *International History Review* 10 (1988).
52. The limited success of the German fleet in the Second World War shows what might have been possible: in November 1940, *Admiral Scheer* succeeded in suspending North Atlantic convoy traffic for 12 days following its attack on convoy HX84, causing considerable disruption to the entire system: Steury, 'German Offensive', 84.
53. Gemzell, *Innovation*, 275, n. 71.
54. Dülffer, 'Determinants', in Deist, *Total War*, 165.
55. Herwig, 'German Sea Power', 68–105; Gray, *Leverage*, 64–85.
56. The import system encompassed more than just ships on the trade routes. It included the focal points at the approaches to home ports, terminal ports and specialised unloading equipment, and the inland rail and road networks serving those ports. The object of attacking these targets was not simply to destroy the immediate targets, but to disrupt the efficient management of shipping and inland distribution: M. Doughty, *Merchant Shipping and War* (London, 1982).
57. 'War with Germany' and 'Courses of Action', 20 March 1935, PD04853, ADM1/27413.
58. 'Naval Intelligence Report: Germany', CB1818, summer 1936, ADM178/137.

59. In March 1935, the Admiralty and the Air Ministry began to study with the Distribution of Imports Committee the air menace to east coast shipping and to prepare measures to divert it to west coast ports without serious congestion in unloading and inland distribution: Doughty, *Shipping*, 132–76.

60. DNI, Director Plans, and DCNS, 26–7 March 1935, PD04853/35, ADM1/27413; CID No. 1167-B, 21 February 1935, in C1767/55/18, FO371/18828.

61. JP105, 31 October 1935, CAB55/7.

62. 'Aircraft for Attack on Trade', 5 March 1936, PD9167/37, ADM116/3596; DRC, 26th mtg, 14 November 1935, CAB16/112.

63. JP157, 2 July 1936, CAB55/8; G. Till, *Air Power and the Royal Navy* (London, 1979), 142, 148–9. CID planning overestimated the amount of diversion that could take place without overloading the distribution network: Doughty, *Shipping*, 154–76.

64. COS, 186th mtg, 16 October 1936, CAB53/6.

65. JP183, 15 December 1936, and JP241, 11 October 1937, CAB55/8 and 10.

66. COS539(JP), 22 December 1936, CAB53/29.

67. Phillips, 23 July 1936, NID1242/35, ADM178/137. Phillips was rightly sceptical about the capacity of the west coast ports and the rail network to handle as much as 75 per cent of east coast imports: Doughty, *Shipping*, 144–5, 154–5.

68. Wark, *Intelligence*, 195–201; Post, *Dilemmas*, 255–6.

69. JP155, 26 October 1936, CAB55/8.

70. Cf. Wark, *Intelligence*, 201–2; Post, *Dilemmas*, 255–6

71. COS, 192nd and 194th mtgs, 12 and 22 January 1937, CAB53/6.

72. 'Naval Appreciation (1937) of War with Germany', spring 1937, M00599/37, ADM199/2365; JP290, July 1938, CAB55/12.

73. 'Operation Instructions', 24 September 1938, M01862/39, and 'Africa Station', 19 June 1939, M05898/39, ADM116/3874.

74. Captain Hermon-Hodge, 20 July 1937, NID1521/37, ADM178/137. Wark writes in *Intelligence* 142 that the version completed in August 1936 represented the 'orthodox' view and remained so until the outbreak of war. Minutes in the file, however, show that the manual was extensively *rewritten* in 1937.

75. 'Naval Intelligence Report: Germany', summer 1936, ADM178/137.

76. Ibid., 12.

77. Naval attaché Berlin to FO, 10 January 1938, C250/250/18, FO371/21692.

78. 'Before September 1939: NID Revives', n.d. [1947?], ADM223/469.

79. Sumida, '"Best Laid Plans"', 692.

80. DCNS, 18 October 1937, PD06476/37, ADM1/9729.

81. Tactical Division, 14 September and 18 November 1938, TD482/38, ADM1/10076. The fleet exercises of March 1938 were conceived to test related tasks: 'the protection of a large convoy when attacked by Surface, Submarine, and Airforces', and 'the location and bringing to action of a fast enemy raiding force': 'Exercises and Operations 1938', February 1939, CB1769/38, ADM186/159.

82. Ibid. The NID report is cited as No. M03392 of 1938. NID believed that German merchant ships were designed and equipped to act as raiders in war: 'Enemy Merchant Ships', 7 February 1939, DRAX2/10, CCC.

83. 'War against Germany', 6 December 1934, PD04756/34, ADM1/27413. In early 1936, Captain Phillips correctly expressed concern that the new capital ships would have insufficient endurance to intercept German battleships in the Atlantic: Director of Plans, 15 January 1936, PD05489/36, ADM1/9411.
84. 'Convoy at the Outset of a War', 3 March 1938, PD06700/38, ADM1/9501; 'Setting for Atlantic Trade Defence War Game', 28 January 1938, PD016250/38, ADM1/9466; COS, 310th mtg., 2 August 1939, CAB53/11.
85. 'Combined Fleet Exercise [March 1935]', September 1937, CB1769, ADM186/157 and 'Home Fleet Exercises and Operations [June–July 1937]', July 1938, CB1769/37, ADM186/158.
86. 'War with Germany', 3 March 1938, PD06700/38, ADM1/9501. In 1937, the Admiralty reserved the right to substitute two small trade defence aircraft carriers for part of the cruiser programme: Board Minute, 9 December 1937, ADM167/96.
87. 'Possible Staff Conversations', 23 December 1937, PD06569/37, ADM116/3379.
88. Salewski, I, 50–1.
89. Salewski, I, 35–6, 69–71, 75; Dülffer, *Marine*, 442–3; Gemzell, *Skandinavien* and *Innovation*, 278–85.
90. Admiralty to FO, 23 December 1938, N6367/4973/30, FO371/22283. Raeder at one point agreed: Salewski, I, 71.
91. COS, 250th mtg, 13 September 1938, CAB53/9; 'Africa Station', 19 June 1939, M05898/39, ADM116/3874.
92. Deputy DNI and Director of Plans, October 1936–June 1937, NID00827/36, ADM116/4391. Rumours that Germany was building U-boat bases on the island were discounted in 1939: NID, 17 January 1939, NID105/39, ibid.
93. C-in-C American to Admiralty, 3 September 1937, A1031/1031/51, FO371/21457.
94. Watt, 'British Intelligence', in May, *Enemies*, 237–70; Wark, *Intelligence*, 141–3.
95. Wegener, *Naval Strategy*, passim.
96. Vansittart to Backhouse, 14 April 1939, and naval attaché Berlin to DNI, 15 May 1939, NID1428/39, ADM1/9956.
97. B. Hunt, *Sailor-Scholar* (Waterloo, 1982), passim; J. Goldrick, 'The Irresistible Force and the Immovable Object: The Naval Review, the Young Turks, and the Royal Navy, 1911–1931', in J. Goldrick and J. B. Hattendorf, eds, *Mahan Is Not Enough* (New Port, RI, 1993).
98. Commander Kleikamp, 'Intelligence in Cruiser Warfare' [from *Marine Rundschau*], *The Naval Review* 14 (1926), 844–51; Capitaine De Frègate P. Chack, 'The German Strategy in the Distant Seas' [serialised from *Revue Maritime*], *The Naval Review* 14–15 (1926–7), 80–103, 500–522, 697–718.
99. Ibid., 17 (1929), 825–8, and again in 27 (1939), 721–4.
100. Ibid., 26 (1938), 36–7.
101. Ibid., 'List of Members', 14 (1927).
102. K. Bird, 'The Origins and Role of the German Naval History in the Interwar Period, 1918–1939', *Naval War College Review* 29 (1976); Herwig, 'Introduction', in Wegener, *Strategy*, xv–lv.
103. Gemzell, *Skandinavien*, 49–57 and *Innovation*, 278–9; D. Steury, *Germany's Naval Renaissance: Ideology and Sea Power in the Nazi Era* Phd, University

of California, Irvine, 1990, 167–87, 207–12. Steury shows that, despite Raeder's attack on Wegener, the key features of his 'revisionist' critique of Tirpitz were adopted by Admiral Kurt Aßmann, who was the navy's archivist, historian and an influential lecturer at the naval academy.

104. See MIR Nos 222–3, 15 November and 15 December 1937, 41–3, 39, Admiralty Library: it is an indication of the importance of these reports that Captain G. A. French cited both in his 'German Naval Strategy', May 1938, lecture notes for the Royal Navy Staff College, GDFR5/15.

105. Naval attaché Berlin to FO, 10 January 1938, C250/250/18, FO371/21692.

106. 'Organisation Plan', April–June 1938, H10/38, ADM203/91.

107. Naval attaché Berlin to FO, 10 January 1938, C250/250/18, FO371/21692.

108. 'Germany', summer 1936, ADM178/137.

109. British Embassy Berlin to FO, app. X, 30 June 1937, C4958/270/18, FO371/20735; Naval attaché Berlin to FO, 10 January 1938, C250/250/18, FO371/21692.

110. Dülffer, *Marine*, 495–504.

111. DNI, 9 June 1933, M01653/33, citing NID0499/30, ADM116/2945; CID No. 1167-B, 21 February 1934, CAB4/23; IIC reports, 'Naval Mines', 14 September 1934–10 January 1935, T161/894/S.29222/01/1.

112. ICF/286, 1 May 1937, T160/846/F14141/3.

113. DNI, 22 July 1937, NID0687, ADM1/9074; Rössler, *U-Boat*, 110.

114. Consul-General Hamburg to FO, 11 September 1938, C9536/3096/18, FO371/21759; *Progress in Torpedo, Mining, A/S Measures and Chemical Warfare* June 1939, p.33, CB3002(39), ADM189/116.

115. This para. is based on ICF/128, 11 April 1939, C5327/1061/18, FO371/23054.

116. JIC(40)11, 13 March 1940, p. 16, CAB81/96.

117. CB3002(39), June 1939, p. 33, ADM189/116.

118. The mine establishment, HMS *Vernon*, did conduct prewar experimental work with magnetic sweeps and magnetic mines: 'Half Yearly Progress Report', December 1938, p. 32, TO384/39, ADM253/756.

119. Salewski, I, 141–7; H. Bauermeister, 'Die Entwicklung der Magnetminen bis zum Beginn des Zweiten Weltkrieges', *Marine Rundschau* 55 (1958); C. Barnett, *Engage the Enemy More Closely* (London, 1991), 90–2.

120. The lack of co-operation between the Royal Navy and the RAF in the development of maritime aviation and its negative consequences are thoroughly covered in the literature: see especially Till, *Air Power*, Roskill, I–II, passim, and J. Buckley, *The RAF and Trade Defence, 1919–1945* (Keele, 1995).

121. Bialer, *Bomber*, 56–8; COS, 130th mtg., 27 June 1934, CAB53/4; DRC, 26th mtg, 14 November 1935, CAB16/112; CID, 349th mtg., 3 March 1939, CAB2/8.

122. JIC, 8–10th mtgs, 26 April – 28 September 1937, CAB 56/1.

123. JIC89, 10 June 1939, CAB56/4. In January 1939, though, the Committee on Bombing and Anti-Aircraft Gunfire Experiments questioned the usefulness of gun fire to protect convoys from bombers: Doughty, *Shipping*, 58–9.

124. H. Boog, 'Luftwaffe Support of the German Navy', in Howarth and Law, *Atlantic*.

125. 'Foreign Development of the Torpedo as an air weapon', 17 May 1938, NID0520/38, ADM1/9649. The *Luftwaffe*, as a result of a war game in

May 1939, concluded that units assigned to the fleet and the air force as a whole were ill-prepared to attack the British fleet, shipping or ports. Boog, 'Luftwaffe', 306. But, as the Royal Navy was to learn to its cost off Greece and Crete in the Second World war, the *Luftwaffe* deployed its divebombers against warships to great effect.

126. DNI to Troubridge, 30 January 1939, NID01026/37, AIR2/9376.
127. Vachell to Air Ministry, 20 February 1939, AA155/39, ibid.
128. Troubridge to DNI [draft], February 1939, ibid.
129. Bialer, *Bomber*, 151–60; Wark, *Intelligence*, 66–9, 76–9.
130. 'Summer Leave', 5 June 1939, PD07754/39, ADM116/4293.
131. 'Protection of Merchant Shipping', 10 May 1939, M05200/39, ADM1/10041, issued in June 1939 as CID No. 1557-B, CAB4/30.
132. Doughty, *Shipping*, 154.
133. JIC(39)18, 9 October 1939, CAB81/95.

CHAPTER 4   ADMIRALTY TECHNICAL INTELLIGENCE AND THE GERMANY NAVY, 1936–39

1. Wark, *Intelligence,* 124–54; G. Till, 'Perceptions of Naval Power Between the Wars: The British Case', in P. Towle, ed., *Estimating Foreign Military Power* (London, 1972); Hinsley, *Intelligence*, 505–7.
2. J. H. Godfrey, 'The Navy and Naval Intelligence, 1939–1942', ADM223/619; *The Naval Memoirs of Admiral J. H. Godfrey* (London, privately printed, 1964–6), Vol. V, Part II, 248–58, NMM.
3. 'Control of AA guns by Infra-red cell', 22 December 1937, NID031/38, ADM1/9713; 'US Aircraft Bombing', 31 December 1938, NID02169/37, ADM1/9072.
4. Admiral G. Ross, assistant naval attaché, Tokyo, 1933–6, *Memoirs*, 249–50, MS 86/60/1, Imperial War Museum, London.
5. Sir Stanley V. Goodall Diaries, MS 52790, 19 May 1937, British Library, London.
6. 'Collection of Intelligence', 1 December 1934, ADM116/3871.
7. Home Fleet, 19 February 1937, and Director of Naval Ordnance, 18 June 1937, NID0213/37, ADM1/9073.
8. DNI, 30 June 1937, NID0600/37, ibid.
9. *Foreign Major War Vessels,* CB1815, April 1939, ADM239/46.
10. CID No. 1326-B, 24 May 1937, CAB4/26.
11. Goodall Diaries, MS 52789, 1–2 November and 14–17 December 1936.
12. The weight of a warship is equal to that of the amount of water it displaces. The Washington Treaty defined standard displacement as the weight of a ship complete, fully manned, engined and equipped ready for sea, but without fuel or reserve feed-water on board.
13. Plans to FO, 23 November 1937, A8503/771/45, FO371/20669.
14. Salewski, 'Marineleitung', 147.
15. Godfrey, *Memoirs*, 248–58.
16. Captain Wassner to FO, 21 November 1935, A9864/5/45, FO371/18726.
17. 'German Naval Construction', 21 March 1935, NID0176/35, in C2418/206/18, FO371/18860.

18. DNC, 'Germany: Large Naval Guns', 23 February 1939, NID0177/39, ADM229/20. The original December 1936 report is cited in this minute as NID0992/36.
19. DNC, '"Gneisenau" and "Scharnhorst"', 19 December 1938, ADM229/19.
20. Ibid.
21. Whitley, *Capital Ships,* 35–6; Dülffer, *Marine*, 314.
22. Goodall, 28 February 1936, M01230/36, ADM116/3368.
23. *Foreign Major War Vessels,* CB1815, April 1939, p. 57, ADM239/46.
24. Whitley, *Capital Ships*, 20–30.
25. *Foreign Major War Vessels*, p. 57, ADM239/46.
26. COS, 192nd mtg, 12 January 1937, CAB53/6.
27. '"Gneisenau" and "Scharnhorst"', 19 December 1938, ADM229/19.
28. 'Progress of Foreign Naval Construction and Engineering', 18 September 1935, NID0568/35, Ship's Cover (Foreign Capital Ships) No. 426b; 'Notes on Foreign Office letter', 1 October 1937, paras E–F, in R8381/1932/22, FO371/21181; 'Strategical and Tactical Problems', 14 September 1938, TD482/38, ADM1/10076; JP290, July 1938, CAB55/12.
29. Wassner to FO, 1 July 1936, M03699/36, ADM116/3368.
30. DNC, 5 September 1936, ibid.
31. Sir Eustance T. D'Eyncourt, 'German Warship Construction', and Goodall, 'Ex-German battleship Baden', *TINA* 63 (1921), 1–7, 13–48.
32. Director of Plans, 8 September 1936, M03699/36, ADM116/3368.
33. *TINA* 91 (1949), 438.
34. DNC, 5 September 1936, M03699/36, ADM116/3368; 'Bismarck', 7 March 1942, Goodall Papers, MSS 52793.
35. Whitley, *Capital Ships*, 43–7; Dülffer, *Marine*, 313, 379.
36. Goodall Diaries, MS 52789, 1–2 November, 14–17 December 1936.
37. CID, 294th mtg, 17 June 1937, CAB2/6.
38. Eden, 15 March 1937, A2062/180/45, FO371/20657.
39. Director of Plans to FO, 6 April 1937, A2062/A2549/180/45, ibid.
40. Craigie to Maisky, 11 June 1937, A2062/180/45, FO371/20657. Craigie's letter asking for details is in the file, but not Maisky's reply.
41. Godfrey, *Memoirs*, 248–58.
42. Ibid.
43. Ibid. and para. 2 of CID No. 1326-B, 24 May 1937, CAB4/26. Ironically, the DNC anticipated in January 1936 that the *King George V* might exceed treaty limits without strict weight savings. By May 1939, its standard displacement was 36 230 tons. Ship's Cover (King George V) No. 547/1, folios 41 and 57.
44. Battlecruisers were battleships with the high speed but limited protection of cruisers. The interwar generation of battleships represented a further merging of the cruiser and battleship concepts into fast battleships: battleships with both the speed of cruisers and the protection of battleships. For a discussion of Fisher's battlecruiser policy: C. Fairbanks Jr, 'The Origins of the Dreadnought Revolution', *International History Review* 13 (May 1991); Sumida, *Supremacy*.
45. Minutes by FO officials on a naval attaché report (Rome), 10 September 1937, R6125/R8381/1932/22, FO371/21181.

46. Admiralty, 'Notes on Foreign Office letter', 1 October 1937, R8381/1932/22, FO371/21181, and DNI to naval attaché, Tokyo, telegram, 19 January 1937, PD06129/37, ADM116/3379. The notes were probably drafted in Plans because they dealt with FO queries. The telegram explains the rationale for 14-inch guns. A. Raven and J. Roberts, *British Battleships of World War Two* (London, 1976), 273–82. Once committed to 14-inch guns in 1936, it proved difficult to mount 15-inch guns on the three ships of the 1937 programme: Roskill, II, 328–9.

47. 'Notes', 1 October 1937, R8381/1932/22, FO371/21181. Similar views were entertained about the Imperial Japanese Navy. Admiral Reginald Henderson, the Third Sea Lord and Controller, who was responsible for ship construction and design, with Chatfield's assent, assumed that Japan would probably construct 35 000-ton ships and 16-inch guns, but with inferior armour, against which 'our new 14-inch ships should be able to engage ... with every chance of success'. See his M04798/36, 25 September 1936, ADM116/3382.

48. D'Eyncourt, 'German Warship Construction', Goodall, 'Baden', and the audience discussion, *TINA* 63 (1921), 1–48; D'Eyncourt's October 1913 remarks cited in Sumida, *Supremacy*, 262–3.

49. D. Brown, *A Century of Naval Construction* (London, 1983), 157–8.

50. Goodall Papers, 'Bismarck', 7 March 1942, MSS 52793; *TINA* 91 (1949), 439.

51. Chatfield, *The Navy*, 138–52; Gordon, *Procurement*, 110–16, 172–3.

52. G. Till, 'Airpower and the Battleship in the 1920s' in Ranft, *Technical Change*.

53. Chatfield, 12th NCM mtg, 21 October 1935, CAB29/147; note his confidence in the superiority of British gunnery, even if the foe had more or larger guns, Board minute 3357, 3 April 1936, ADM167/94.

54. *TINA* 62 (1920), 14; Chatfield's 'Note by Minister for Co-ordination of Defence', 16 March 1940, CHT6/4; Gordon, *Procurement*, 110–11, 172–5.

55. Goodall Diaries, MS 52789, 6 February and 18 March 1936; CNS, 20 March 1936, MFO102/36, in Ship's Cover No. 547/1, folio 41.

56. H. Hutchinson, 'Intelligence: Escape from Prisoner's Dilemma', *Intelligence and National Security* 7 (1992).

57. CNS, 20 March 1936, MFO102/36, in Ship's Cover No. 547/1, folio 41; 'Battleships Policy', June 1937, Templewood Papers, Vol. IX, folios 1–4.

58. NCM(35)23, 30 October 1934, CAB29/148.

59. Goodall Diaries, MS 52790, 2 November 1937.

60. DNI, 'German Naval Construction', 18 January 1938, M06532/37, ADM116/3368. It cites the differences between the DNC's projected speed and horsepower figures in the pre-January 1938 NID reference book, and the German ones. The German figures were published in the April 1939 edition, which contained only 'known' discrepancies, suggesting that the question was still open. See *Foreign Major War Vessels*, CB1815, April 1939, p. 85, ADM239/46.

61. CID, 299th mtg, 14 October 1937, CAB2/6.

62. Craigie, 11 June 1937, A4075/6/45, FO371/20647.

63. CID, 319th mtg, 11 April 1939, CAB2/7.

64. Captain Siemens, German naval attaché, to FO, 4 December 1937, A8765/771/45, FO371/20669.
65. Fitzmaurice, 8 December 1937, ibid.
66. FO to Plans, 10 December 1937, ibid.
67. DNI, 'German Naval Construction', 18 January 1938, M06532/37, ADM116/3368.
68. FO minute, 11 March 1938, A8765/771/38, FO371/20669.
69. See the analysis under 'German Action at Sea' in JP290, July 1938, CAB55/12.
70. 'Capital Ship Construction', 17 July 1939, CHT/6/4.
71. DNC, 'Speed of Battlecruiser "Gneisenau"', 14 September 1938, NID0943/38, ADM229/18.
72. DNC, '"Gneisenau" and "Scharnhorst"', 19 December 1938, ADM229/19.
73. Godfrey, *Memoirs*, 248.
74. 'Germany: 35,000 ton Battleship', 11 November 1938, ADM229/19. *Bismarck*'s first armoured deck was 2.5 to 4 inches and the second was 3.2 to 4 inches. The main and middle decks of *King George V* were 6 and 5 inches; Whitley, *Capital Ships*, 48; Raven and Roberts, *British Battleships*, 409.
75. DNC, 'Bismarck', 19 January 1940, ADM229/22.
76. German naval attaché to FO, 14 March 1939, A2095/87/45, FO371/22806; Showell, *Fuehrer Conferences*, 37; Whitley, *Capital Ships*, 55–60.
77. Goodall Diaries, MS 52790, 23 May 1939.
78. 'Naval Intelligence Report: Germany', 1935 edition, CB1818, ADM 178/137.
79. DNI, 18 May 1936, M02798/36, ADM 116/3368; Captain Troubridge to FO, 1936 annual report, 12 January 1937, C357/357/18, FO 371/20743.
80. M. J. Whitley, *German Destroyers of World War Two* (London, 1991), 22–4.
81. DNC, 'LEBERECHT MAAS Class Destroyers', 14 July 1938, NID0707/38, ADM 229/18; Whitley, *Destroyers*, 16.
82. DNC, 19 February 1936, M05295/35, ADM 116/3368.
83. Whitley, *Destroyers*, 16–17
84. Admiral J. Somerville, Commander, Mediterranean Fleet Destroyer Flotillas Proceedings, 27 June 1937, S[o]M[er]V[i]L[le Papers CCC]5/5; Whitley, *Cruisers*, 22–32.
85. DNC, 'Germany: Cruisers "K" and "L"', 15 July 1938, NID0701/38, and 'Particulars of Cruisers "M" "N" "O"', 8 February 1939, M076898/38, ADM 229/20.
86. Farago, *Foxes*, 117–20.
87. Godfrey, *Memoirs*, Vol. IV, Part I, 77.
88. Plans to FO, 18 July 1935, A6479/22/45, FO371/18737.
89. ICF/118, 'Submarine Construction: Germany', 8 April 1936, CAB104/29.
90. Rössler, *U-Boat* 101, 118–19; Wark, *Intelligence*, 155–87.
91. IIC/NID, July 1936, No. 1252-B, app. D, CAB48/4.
92. 'Naval Intelligence Report: Germany', 1935, CB1818, ADM178/137.
93. Ship's Cover (Foreign Submarines), No. 439, contains intelligence about various U-boats from 1925 onwards. For example, folios 21 and 21A, 'German built Spanish Submarine', 1932, NID841/32, include rough sketches and design details, and folio 26, 'Specifications for a 250 ton

submarine', 9 January 1933, NID0476/32, describes the particulars of the Spanish and Finnish U-boats. Also DNI, 9 June 1933, M01653/33, and 22 July 1933, M02138/33, ADM116/2945; British Legation Helsingfors to FO, 21 June 1933, C6165/6165/18, FO371/16755; also G. Simpson, *Periscope View* (London, 1972), 55–67.

94. Wassner to Craigie, 1 July 1935, A5828/G, ADM116/3377; again, 4 November 1935, NID0785/35, ADM116/3368.

95. Goodall Diaries, MS 52788, 6 to 19 December 1935; NID, 'Advantage of Double Hull', 1935, NID841/35, Ship's Cover No. 439, folio 45. *Progress in Torpedo, Mining, and A/S Measures* 1935, CB3002/35, ADM186/522, p. 58, notes the general increase in submarine hull strength and diving depth. Yet the DNC greatly underrated the capacity of U-boats to resist attack by deep diving because no premium was placed on deep diving in British submarines. D. Brown, 'Submarine Pressure Hull Design and Diving Depths Between the Wars', *Warship International* 3 (1987).

96. Rössler, *U-Boat*, 105–7.

97. DNI, 18 May 1936, M02798/36, ADM116/3368.

98. Goodall, analysis of IIC report, 14 May 1936, NID0336/36, Ship's Cover No. 439, folio 67.

99. DNC, 'Germany – New Submarine Construction', 8 November 1935, NID0751/35, Ship's Cover No. 439, folio 46.

100. Goodall Diaries, MS 52789, 11 May 1936.

101. Rössler, *U-Boat*, 67–75, 102–19; Dönitz, *Memoirs*, (London, 1959), Ch. IV; Dülffer, *Marine*, 386–9, 419–20; Salewski, I, 22–9.

102. 'German Submarine Aircraft Carriers', 1925, NID0239/25, 'Mine-Laying Submarine', 1926, NID0267/26, and 'German – Caustic Soda Boiler Design', 7 May 1927, NID0107/27, Ship's Cover No. 439, folios 2, 6 and 8.

103. Extracts from secret reports in 'Germany – New Submarine Construction', 16 October 1936, NID0673/35, Ship's Cover No. 439, folio 46.

104. 'German Built Spanish Submarine', 1932, NID841/32; DNC, 'New Submarine Construction', 8 November 1935, NID0751/35, Ship's Cover No. 439, folios 21–21A, 46; F. Bryant for DNC, 10 June 1936, NID0785, ADM115/3368; DNC, report on captured U39, December 1939, NID01920/39, ADM1/9964.

105. Goodall, 26 October 1936, M05271/36, ADM116/3368.

106. DNI, 4 December 1936, M05353/36, ibid.; DNI, 22 July 1937, NID0687/37, ADM1/9074.

107. *Foreign Major War Vessels,* April 1939, CB1815, ADM239/46, records it as 2000 miles. Rössler and Dönitz, depending on the variation, cite for the Type VII a surface endurance from 4000 to 6000 miles at 12 knots.

108. Captain Troubridge to FO, 10 January 1938, C250/250/18, FO371/21692.

109. Rössler, *U-Boat*, 104–5; Dönitz, *Memoirs*, 31.

110. NID, 'German Naval Construction', 18 January 1938, M06532/37, ADM116/3368.

111. Captain Troubridge to FO, 10 January 1938, C250/250/18, FO371/21692.

112. J. Keegan, *The Price of Admiralty* (London, 1988), 252–5.

113. Rössler, *U-Boat*, 168–77; Dönitz, *Memoirs*, 235–6, 265–6, 352–4.

114. 'Propellant for German Submarines', 17 July 1935, and 'Hydrogen as Fuel for Aircraft and Marine Engines', 29 September 1936, NID0278/35,

ADM116/6325. Godfrey cites Captain Tower's remarks that 'reports of the Walter boat had been received [in NID] for many years', in 'The Navy', ADM223/619.

115. Rössler, *U-Boat*, 31–2.
116. 'The Erren Motor System of Propulsion, 1930–43', Case 6857, ADM116/6325.
117. Director of Scientific Research, 7 January 1931, NID2033/30, ibid.
118. Muirhead-Gould to DNI, 28 August 1933, DSR715/32, ibid.
119. Director of Scientific Research and Engineer-in-Chief, 11 May 1935 – 4 May 1937, NID0278/35, ibid.
120. DNI, 7 July 1937, NID0278, and Director of Scientific Research, 17 March 1938, DSR225/38, ibid.
121. W. Honan, *Bywater* (London, 1990).
122. *Daily Telegraph* 15, 16, 21 September 1936 and MIR No. 209 15 October 1936, 51–2. A report had also appeared in *The Morning Post,* April 1935.
123. Goodall Diaries, MS 52789, 17, 21 September 1936.
124. Goodall Papers, 'Bismarck', 7 March 1942, MSS 52793 and Raven and Roberts, *British Battleships*, 408–16.
125. W. Garzke, R. Dulin, and D. Brown, 'The Sinking of the Bismarck: An Analysis of the Damage', *Warship* (1994); Salewski, I, 381–2; 'Germany', 1935, CB1818, ADM178/137.
126. Dönitz pinned his hopes on the Type XXI 'Electro' submarines. F. Kökl and E. Rössler, *The Type XXI U-Boat* (London. 1991).

CHAPTER 5   THE NAVAL STAFF, BRITISH STRATEGY AND THE GERMAN MENACE, 1934–38

1. Admiral E. Chatfield, *The Navy and Defence* (London, 1942), 168, 212–13.
2. Bialer, *Bomber*, 56–8; DRC, 26th mtg, 14 November 1935, CAB16/112; CID, 349th mtg, 3 March 1939, CAB2/8.
3. JP253, 23 December 1937, CAB55/11. The original study, 'Naval Air Targets' in CAB48/9, pointed out that bombers could be employed to attack German facilities for the mass production of U-boats.
4. DCNS to CNS, 17 February 1938, Chatfield Papers MS78/189; COS, 190th mtg., 21 December 1936, CAB53/6. The Admiralty was not certain that it would be able to break German codes once more: 'Wireless Intercepts' para. in draft 'Naval War Manual', October 1938, Captain J. CRES[well Papers CCC]1/1.
5. Creswell, *Warfare*, 173–84; Medlicott, *Blockade*, 3–12.
6. The only CID study, A. C. Bell, *A History of the Blockade of Germany* (London, 1937), was judged to be inadequate by the Admiralty: S. H. Phillips, 13 July 1936, M2461/36, ADM116/3303.
7. A. S. Milward, 'Economic Warfare', *War, Economy and Society, 1939–45* (London, 1977); Watt, *Too Serious a Business*, 110–16.
8. In 1936, 'economic warfare' and 'economic pressure' began to be substituted for the obsolete term 'blockade' in Admiralty documents: Director of Plans, 8 September 1936, NID1517/36, ADM178/137.

9. Major D. Morton, Director IIC, 1931–9, 'Economics in Modern War', lecture précis for the Royal Naval Staff College, 1938, G[o]D[frey]FR[ench Papers]5/17; Watt, *Business*, 111–12.
10. Medlicott, *Blockade*, 12–14.
11. CID No. 1139-B, May 1934, CAB48/4.
12. JP155, 26 October 1936, para. 109 and app. I, CAB55/8; CP73(37), 25 February 1937, CAB24/268; JP290, July 1938, CAB55/12; COS843, 20 February 1939, CAB53/45.
13. Wark, *Intelligence*, 166–87; ATB191, 22 July 1938, CAB47/6; C. E. Fayle, 'Economic Problems in War Plans', lecture précis, GDFR5/17.
14. M. Howard, *The Continental Commitment* (London, 1972), 96–120.
15. CP24(38), February 1938, CAB24/274; Cabinet, 16 February 1938, 5(38), CAB23/92; Watt, *Business*, 111–16; for a thorough study of the often amorphous concepts of deterrence elaborated in Whitehall in the early 1930s, see Post, *Dilemmas*.
16. Medlicott, *Blockade*, xi.
17. M. Smith, 'Rearmament and Deterrence in Britain in the 1930s', *Journal of Strategic Studies* 1 (1978).
18. Plans, 16–23 May 1933, PD04298/33, and 'Economic Pressure on Germany' and 'Blockade of Germany', 19 May 1933, PD04853/33, ADM1/27413.
19. ATB101, 30 October 1933, ATB106, 25 January 1934, and ATB116, 3 June 1935, CAB47/5.
20. Captain Moore, 23 May 1933, PD04298/33, and 'Economic Pressure on Germany', 26 June 1933, PD04316/33, ADM1/27413; ATB(EP)4–5, 27 June 1933, CAB47/6.
21. 'Naval Construction Programme', 17–25 November 1937, ADM167/98–9; 'Naval Construction Programme', 13 December 1938, ADM167/101; 'Additional Needs of the Navy', 15 June 1939, ADM167/104. Ferris, 'Last Decade' and Gordon, *Procurement*. One of the most vexing bottlenecks in all classes of warships was the lack of gun-forging and gun-mounting capacity.
22. Nonetheless, in the 1930s, British building capacity still remained the single largest in the world: Ferris, 'Last Decade', 159, and I. Buxton, 'British Warship Building and Repair', in Howarth and Law, *Atlantic*.
23. DRC, 14th mtg, 19 July 1935, CAB16/112; General Sir Henry Pownell, *Chief of Staff* Vol. I, ed. B. Bond (London, 1973), 87.
24. ATB137, 12 March 1936, CAB47/5.
25. COS549, 15 February 1937, CAB53/30. In April 1937, the ATB's Economic Pressure Sub-Committee was reconstituted as the Economic Pressure on Germany Sub-committee.
26. Wark, *Intelligence*, 174–87; D. Morton, 'JPC War Planning', 9 June 1936, CAB104/34.
27. ATB176/181, 18 July 1938, CAB47/6. In 1939, as confidence in the long-war strategy waned, British strategists searched for a key commodity of which the creation of a sudden shortage would cause the German war effort to collapse: IFC66, 25 June 1937, CAB47/13; P. Salmon, 'British Plans for Economic Warfare against Germany, 1937–1939: The Problem of Swedish Iron Ore', *Journal of Contemporary History* 16 (1981), 53–71.

28. COS697(JP), 'German Aggression against Czechoslovakia', 21 March 1938, CAB53/37. The final version, COS698, 28 March 1938, CAB53/37, was circulated to the Foreign Policy and Defence Plans Policy subcommittees. Also COS769, 23 September 1938, and COS770, 24 September 1938, CAB53/41; COS765, 14 September 1938, CAB53/41 [circulated to Cabinet as CO199(38), CAB24/278].

29. W. Strang, 10 September 1938, C9741/9726/18, FO371/21782; entries of 10–11 September 1938, *Diaries of Sir Alexander Cadogan, 1938–1945*, ed. D. Dilks, (New York, 1972), 96–7; Roskill, II, 439–42.

30. Chamberlain to Ida, 11 September 1938, NC18/1/1068. On 12 September 1938, Halifax informed the Cabinet about the DNI's interview with Siemens: Cabinet, 12 September 1938, 37(38), CAB23/95. Consequently, additional measures were taken to bring into service overage destroyers and minesweepers from reserve. Unfortunately, Siemens's report of the conversation did not reflect the British version of events: *DGFP* D, II, No. 451.

31. 11 September 1938 entry, Sir Thomas INSK[i]P[diaries CCC]1/1.

32. Telephone conversation between US Ambassador and A. Cadogan, 12 September 1938, C9727/9726/18, FO371/21782; cf. Roskill, II, 441.

33. Cadogan, *Diaries*, 96–7.

34. Cabinet, 14 September 1938, 38(38), CAB23/95; cf. W. Wark, 'Naval Intelligence in Peacetime: Britain's Problems in Assessing the German Threat, 1933–39', in D. Masterson, ed., *The Sixth Symposium of the U.S. Naval Academy* (Delaware, 1987).

35. Narrative of events leading to mobilisation, October 1938, ADM1/9910; Cabinet, 27 September 1938, CS(38)15, CAB27/646.

36. Hitler's letter (*DGFP* D, 2, No. 635) reached London at 10:30 p.m.; according to Vansittart's private intelligence network, news of the British mobilisation reached Berlin at about midnight: Cadogan, *Diaries*, 108–9; Wark, 'Naval Intelligence', 200–1.

37. Cf. Weinberg, *Foreign Policy*, II, 451 with the accounts by W. N. Medlicott, *The Coming of War in 1939* (London, 1963), 16, and Deist, *Germany*, 670. Göring said that Hitler had subsequently told him that the British mobilisation had greatly influenced his decision: D. Irving, *The War Path* (London, 1978), 148.

38. Weinberg, *Foreign Policy*, II, 384–6, 451–63; D. C. Watt, *How War Came* (London, 1989), 28–31.

39. Cf. Wark, 'Naval Intelligence', 191–205; 'German Naval Activities During the Czecho-Slovakian Crisis', February 1939, NID00151/39, ADM223/483.

40. Murray, *Change in the European Balance of Power*; Wark, *Intelligence*, 202–11; Kennedy, 'British "Net Assessment"', in *Calculations*, 19–59.

41. Murray, *Change*, passim.

42. R. A. C. Parker, 'The Pound Sterling, the American Treasury and British Preparations for War, 1938–1939', *English Historical Review* 98 (1983); G. Peden, 'A Matter of Timing: The Economic Background to British Foreign Policy, 1937–1939', 69 *History* (1984).

43. Kennedy, '"Net Assessment"', 54–6, and his *Mastery*, 295–8, 312.

44. Cf. Murray, *Change*, 363; Wark, *Intelligence*, 210–11.

45. COS, 153rd mtg., 29 October 1934, CAB53/5.

46. CNS, 10 November 1937, ADM205/80.

47. Chatfield, *Navy*, 174–5.
48. CNS, 10 November 1937, ADM205/80; CNS to PM, 25 January 1938, CHT3/1.
49. B. McKercher, '"Our Most Dangerous Enemy": Great Britain Pre-eminent in the 1930s', *International History Review* 13 (1991).
50. R. J. Overy, 'Hitler's War and the German Economy: A Reinterpretation', *Economic History Review* 35 (1982).
51. Gray, *Leverage*, 218–19, 236–7.
52. Primarily Marder and Roskill; also see P. Gretton, 'Why Don't We Learn From History', *The Naval Review* 46 (1958).
53. H. Willmott, 'The Organisation: The Admiralty and the Western Approaches', in Howarth and Law, *Atlantic*.
54. W. Murray, 'Neither Navy Was Ready', *United States Naval Institute Proceedings* 107 (1981).
55. Till, *Air Power*; Sumida, '"The Best Laid Plans"'.
56. 'Convoy at the Outset of a War', 19 February 1938, PD06700/38, ADM1/9501; Doughty, *Shipping*, 43, 48–9, 65. On the importance of aircraft, compare para. 25 of JP183, 15 December 1936, CAB55/8, with J. Buckley, 'Air Power and the Battle of the Atlantic, 1939–45', *Journal of Contemporary History* 28 (1993).
57. 'Naval Appreciation', sec. VII, 1937, M00599/37, ADM199/2365.
58. A. Lambert, 'Seapower 1939–1940: Churchill and the Strategic Origins of the Battle of the Atlantic', *Journal of Strategic Studies* 17 (1994).
59. D. Brown, 'Naval Rearmament, 1930–1941: The Royal Navy', *Revue Internationale D'Histoire Militaire* 73 (1991).
60. Follow, for instance, the review of destroyer policy, 18 October 1937 – 28 June 1938, PD0647/37, ADM1/9729.
61. DRC14, 28 February 1934, CAB16/109, envisaged a five-year programme of £250 000 for 200 ASDIC and depth charge sets for reserve ASW ships. Another 200 would be required to be put into production in war. New vessels were built equipped.
62. 'Construction of A/S Vessels', 13 March 1936, PD05617/36, ADM116/3375.
63. CID No. 1318-B, 24 March 1937, CAB4/26; D. O'Connell, *The Influence of Law on Sea Power* (Manchester, 1975), 44–52.
64. Gordon, *Procurement*, 271–2.
65. 'Sloops, Minesweepers, and A/S Craft', 2 July 1936, PD05782/36, ADM1/11596. Phillips advocated developing one design that could function as an ASW/anti-aircraft vessel or minesweeper.
66. 'Naval Construction', 25 November 1937, ADM167/99; Gordon, 175, 271–4; Lambert, 'Seapower', 93.
67. D. Brown, 'Atlantic Escorts 1939–45', in Howarth and Law, *Atlantic*; A. Watson, 'Corvettes and Frigates', *TINA* 89 (1947), 85–111.
68. The Admiralty recognised in war plans the limited overseas range of the German U-boat fleet. In November 1935, however, technical intelligence reached NID about possible refuelling at sea for U-boats via submersible oil tankers and specially installed pipes to enhance their offensive reach: 'Pipe work for German Submarines', 11 November 1935, NID0747/35, Ship's Cover No. 439, folio 37.

69. Lambert, 'Seapower', 93–4.
70. W. Hackmann, *Seek and Strike* (London, 1984).
71. ACNS, 27 July and 15 September 1921, A1555/21, ADM1/8609/138.
72. D. MacGregor concludes that the Royal Navy's emphasis on integrating ASDIC into a coherent tactical doctrine in the 1930s laid the foundations for wartime successes: *Innovation in Naval Warfare* (PhD, Rochester, 1990), 159–185, and Hackmann, *Seek and Strike*, 125–35.
73. For instance 'Home Fleet Submarine Exercise AF', CB1769/33, November 1933, ADM186/153.
74. CID No. 1318-B, 24 March 1937, CAB/4/26; cf. Roskill, II, 226–8, 306, 429.
75. Roskill, II, 383; F. Willard, Jr, 'Politico-Military Deception at Sea in the Spanish Civil War, 1936–39', *Intelligence and National Security* 5 (1990).
76. Director of Tactical Division, 25 January 1938, M01126/38, ADM116/3534.
77. Deputy DNI, 27 January 1938, ibid.; Willard, 'Deception', 103.
78. Director of Tactical Division, 5. February 1938, M01126/38, ADM116/3534.
79. Hackmann, *Seek and Strike*, 132–4.
80. CB3002/38, June 1938, p. 35, ADM186/551.
81. Salewski, I, 22–9, 73–4.
82. Muirhead-Gould to DNI, 26 November 1934, C8064/2134/18, FO371/17765. The German literature was not revealing, including Dönitz's *Die U-Bootwaffe* (Berlin, 1939). See Lundeberg, 'German Critique of the U-boat Campaign', 111, n. 39.
83. Admiral Sir Thomas Troubridge, Diaries, 1936–9.
84. MacGregor, *Warfare*, 182; *Submarine Operations* 1935, CB01913(4), ADM186/499.
85. 'Exercise RT', April 1934, CB1769/33(2), ADM186/154.
86. 'Combined Fleet Exercise ZL', September 1937, CB1769(1-2), ADM186/157: see under 'Submarine Operations' and 'Night Surface Attack'.
87. Cf. Roskill, I, 536–7.
88. M. Milner, 'The Battle of the Atlantic', *Journal of Strategic Studies* 13 (1990); cf. G. Till, 'History', in Howarth and Law, *Atlantic*, 584–7.
89. Milner, 'Atlantic', 49.
90. J. Snyder, *The Ideology of the Offensive* (New York, 1984).
91. Gray, *Leverage*, 23.
92. JP155, 26 October 1936, paras 48–50, CAB55/8.
93. Deputy Chiefs of Staff, 11th mtg, 24 November 1936, CAB54/1.
94. C-in-C Plymouth to Admiralty, 3 September 1937, No. 1509, DRAX [Papers CCC]2/8.
95. Hunt, *Sailor-Scholar*, Ch. IV; Marder, *Dreadnought*, IV, 170–1, 179, 193–4, 254–5.
96. 'Senior Admirals', n.d., n.s., in DUFF[Cooper Papers CCC]2/12.
97. Drax [RX], 'Prophecy', and 'Five Foreign Policies', *The Naval Review* 23/25 (1935/37), 705–8, 47–50.
98. Backhouse to Drax, 27 August 1937, DRAX2/8.
99. First Sea Lord to C-in-C Plymouth, 5 November 1937, CHT3/1: Pratt, *Malta*, 98, 114–15.

100. Sumida, '"Best Laid Plans"', 681–700. According to Drax, Chatfield had expressed agreement with a lecture he delivered on 'Battle Tactics' at Malta in 1929: 21 November 1929, DRAX2/2.
101. Chatfield, *Navy*, 190, 213. For the long-running tension between the imprecisely definable 'materiel' and 'historical' schools: B. Semmel, *Liberalism and Naval Strategy* (London, 1986), 134–51.
102. In a commentary on a draft 'Naval War Manual' (n.d. 1934?), Drax argued that from the standpoint of Imperial defence, infrastructure and cost, it was better to build a superior number of 30 000-ton ships with 15-inch guns even if some powers build 50 000-ton ships with 16-inch guns or larger: DRAX2/1 and Hunt, *Sailor-Scholar*, 189–205.
103. 348th mtg, 24 February 1939, CAB2/8; Chatfield, *Navy*, 175.
104. Historians have generally agreed upon the improved tactical performance of the Royal Navy in the Second World War as compared with the First: see for instance Barnett, *Engage the Enemy*.
105. For studies of 'efficiency', 'national character' and 'ethnocentrism' in British intelligence: W. K. Wark, 'British Intelligence and Small Wars in the 1930s', *Intelligence and National Security* 2 (1987); J. Ferris, '"Worthy of Some Better Enemy?"': The British Estimate of Imperial Japanese Army 1919–41', *Canadian Journal of History* 28 (1993). For an insight into the naval aspect of this process: DNI to FO, 17 October 1935, W9084/91/50, FO371/19619. The DNI sets out standard questions for 'Naval Intelligence Reports', under the heading of 'national characteristics'. 'Nelson's advice to close with a Frenchman and out manoeuvre a Russian,' he wrote, 'based as it was on an appreciation of Latin quickness and Slav passivity, is an illustration of the application of this sub-section.'
106. Admiral James, 30 September 1938, ADM116/4053.
107. COS, 207th mtg, 18 May 1937, CAB53/7; Marder, *Old Friends*.
108. Naval attaché Rome to DNI, 28 April 1938, R3639/70/22, FO371/23810; Pratt, *Malta*, 108–17.
109. CB1818, summer 1936, Sec. 2, Part 5, ADM178/137.
110. Naval attaché Berlin, annual report 1938, 27 January 1939, C1360/1360/18, FO371/23055; on the 'Germanic' frame of mind, see Chatfield, *Navy*, 226, 230–1.
111. Chatfield, *Navy*, 150.
112. Kennedy, '"Net Assessment"', 56–7; Murray, *Change*, 362.
113. Ferris, 'Last Decade', 159.
114. Of the 15 British battleships, five had to be rotated through the shipyards to modernise their guns, armour and engines: Gordon, *Procurement*, 116–17.
115. Sumida, '"The Best Laid Plans"', 687–9.
116. Phillips, 25 March 1938, PD016250/38, ADM1/9466.
117. 'Capital Ship Design 14.0', 20 March 1936, MFO0102/36, ADM167/94.
118. Cf. Chatfield, *Happen Again*, 115.
119. DCNS to CNS, 17 February 1938, Chatfield Papers MS78/189; Chatfield, *Navy*, 175; W. Hughs, *Fleet Tactics* (Annapolis, 1986), 34–9. The extent to which the development of radar for air-warning and gunner ranging provided an incentive to wait for operational sets to be installed in the fleet is difficult to determine. In May 1938, the Admiralty Board informed the

C-in-C Home Fleet about radar's great potential. Two ships were to be fitted with experimental sets that summer. It is possible that the Admiralty thought that radar might give the fleet a combat edge. NID, however, did not know about German progress on naval radar: H. Howse, *Radar at Sea* (Annapolis, 1993), 24, 45–9.
120. Drax to Hore-Belisha, 9 August 1937, DRAX2/12.
121. Snyder, *Ideology*, 29–30.
122. C-in-C Plymouth to Admiralty, 3 September 1937, No. 1509, p. 1, and 'Battle Tactics,' 1 November 1929, 11, DRAX2/8.
123. DCNS, 23 November 1937, PD06808/38, ADM1/9730.
124. Chatfield and Phillips, 10 November 1937, ADM205/80.

CHAPTER 6   THE NAVAL STAFF AND DEFENCE AND FOREIGN POLICY, 1937–38

1. M. Smith, *British Air Strategy Between the Wars* (Oxford, 1984), 140–72.
2. DRC, 13th–14th mtgs, 11 and 19 July 1935, CAB16/112.
3. DRC37, 21 November 1935, ibid. This report was reviewed for the Cabinet by the Defence Policy and Requirements Sub-Committee and the Defence Requirements Inquiry Committee. The former was chaired by the PM and included the Foreign Secretary, the Chancellor, the service ministers and the COS. The latter was modified slightly and included the permanent under-secretaries of the FO and Treasury. See CAB16/123, and 136–40 and Gibbs, *Strategy*, 254–68.
4. DPR88, 22 June 1936, CAB16/140; DPR, 22nd and 24th mtgs, 11 June and 2 July 1936, CAB16/137; 'Construction Programme 1937', and secret note, 20 October 1936, ADM167/95.
5. Peden, *Treasury*, 162–4.
6. Set up in February 1937, the DPP reviewed war plans and acted as a nucleus for the war cabinet. It was chaired by the PM and included the Chancellor, the Home and Foreign Secretaries, the Minister for the Co-ordination of Defence, the service ministers and the COS. Its records are in CAB16/181–3.
7. 'New Standard', 29 April 1937, ADM1/9081; DPP, 2nd mtg, 11 May 1937, and First Lord's DP(P)3, CAB16/181. Gibbs, *Strategy*, 332–9; S. Roskill, *Hankey* Vol. III (London, 1974), 280–8.
8. Peden, *Treasury*, 60–149; Gibbs, *Strategy*, 275–371.
9. CP316(37), 15 December 1937, CAB24/273; Cabinet, 22 December 1937, 49(37), CAB23/90A; Gibbs, *Strategy*, 282–5; Peden, 'A Matter of Timing', 15–28.
10. James and Phillips, 1 July 1937, ADM205/80; Peden, *Treasury*, 117.
11. Gordon, *Procurement*, 258–65; senior policy-makers mtg, 5 April 1938, ADM205/80; Peden, *Treasury*, 165.
12. 'Defence Expenditure', 10 November 1937, Cabinet 276, ADM116/3631; Peden, *Treasury*, 121–8, 134–9.
13. Peden, *Treasury*, 128–34; Smith, *Strategy*, 173–226.
14. DCNS, secret staff memo, 6 July 1938, ADM205/80.

15. Phillips, 1 July and 10 November 1937, ibid.; Chatfield to Admiral D. Pound, C-in-C Mediterranean, 16 February 1937, CHT/4/1; JIC, 8th–10th mtgs, 26 April – 28 September 1937, CAB56/1; JIC32, 22 April 1937, CAB56/2.
16. Weinberg, *Foreign Policy*, I, 264–364; Deist, *Germany*, 620–5.
17. Craigie, 25 February 1937, A1654/6/45, FO371/20646; Dülffer, *Marine*, 417–18, 434, 463; Salewski, *Seekriegsleitung*, I, 43.
18. Whitley, *Capital Ships*, 55–9; Deist, *Germany*, 468–70; Dülffer, *Marine*, 434–8.
19. *DGFP* D, I, No. 19; Dülffer, *Marine*, 299, 446 – 51; Weinberg, *Foreign Policy*, II, 35–41; J. Wright and P. Stafford, 'Hitler, Britain, and the Hoßbach Memorandum', *Militärgeschichtliche Mitteilungen* 42 (1987).
20. CNS, 10 November 1937, ADM205/80; COS, 228th mtg, 29 January 1938, CAB53/8.
21. DRC37, 21 November 1935, CAB16/112.
22. Marder, 'Ethiopian Crisis'; Pratt, *Malta*, 29–106.
23. Post, *Dilemmas*, 247–67.
24. COS491(JP), 3 July 1936, CAB53/28; Cabinet, 8 December 1937, 46(37)10, CAB23/90A.
25. Compare FO, 19 August 1936, CP220(36), with COS, 1 September 1936, CP218(36), CAB24/263; Cabinet, 2 September 1936, CAB 56(36)3, CAB23/85; Post, *Dilemmas*, 249–53; Medlicott, 'Britain and Germany', in Dilks, *Retreat*; Parker, *Chamberlain and Appeasement*, 59–69.
26. Chatfield, 8 January 1937, PD06030/36, ADM116/3929.
27. Roskill, *Policy*, II, 309, 323, 355; Wark, *Intelligence*, 137–8, 144–5, 151–3.
28. Wigram, 21 October 1936, A8350/4/45, FO371/19819.
29. Wigram, 21 October 1936, C7271/3790/18, FO371/19946.
30. Vansittart, 21 October 1936, ibid.
31. Wigram, 20 and 26 November 1936, A9482/46771/45, FO371/19839. The circular probably existed: its alleged content is similar to Naval Command memo, 25 August 1935, *DGFP* C, IV, No. 275.
32. Craigie to Phillips, 3 December, and Phillips, 7 December 1936, PD06012/36, ADM116/3378.
33. Chatfield, 22 December 1936, ibid.
34. Chatfield, 8 January 1937, PD06030/36, ADM116/3929 and 3596.
35. COS, 174th, 179th and 187th mtgs, 13 May, 25 June and 20 October 1936, CAB53/6.
36. Hankey, 21 December 1936, MO(36)10, CAB63/51; D. Dilks, '"The Unnecessary War"? Military Advice and Foreign Policy', in A. Preston, ed., *General Staffs and Diplomacy* (London, 1978).
37. Vansittart, 16 and 31 December 1936, W18355/18355/50, FO371/20467, and 31 December 1936, C8998/8998/18, FO371/19787; Vansittart to Chatfield, 1 January 1937, FO800/395. For a reassessment of Vansittart see the essays [especially M. Roi] in B. J. C. McKercher, ed., Special Section, 'Robert Vansittart and the Unbrave World, 1930–1937', *Diplomacy and Statecraft* 6 (1995).
38. This and the next para. are based on CNS to Vansittart, 25 December 1936, FO800/394 and CNS, 5 January 1937, CHT/3/1 and CAB21/541; DRC, 14th mtg, 19 July 1935, CAB16/112; COS, 187th and 195th mtgs,

20 October 1936 and 5 February 1937, CAB53/6; CID, 285th and 288th mtgs, 10 December 1936 and 11 February 1937, CAB2/6; Chatfield to Backhouse, 26 March 1936, CHT/4/1. The War Office harboured similar ideas on a German move eastward: Wark, *Intelligence*, 88–9 and cf. 143–4.

39. COS, 195th mtg, 5 February 1937, CAB53/6. It is significant that Chatfield as Minister for the Co-ordination of Defence, and Hoare, as Home Secretary, supported an Anglo-Soviet alliance in May 1939: FPC, 47th mtg., 16 May 1939, FP(36), CAB27/625.

40. See Murray, *Change in the European Balance of Power*; D. Kaiser, *Economic Diplomacy and the Origins of the Second World War* (Princeton, 1980).

41. Cabinet, 3 May 1939, 26(39), CAB23/99.

42. Cabinet, 6 July 1936, 51(36), CAB23/85.

43. CID, 285th and 288th mtgs, 10 December 1936 and 11 February 1937, CAB2/6.

44. Pratt, *Malta*, 40–8, 63–5; Roskill, *Policy*, II, 374–7.

45. Cf. Post, *Dilemmas*, 267–330.

46. Hoare to Chamberlain, 17 March 1937, Templewood Papers, Vol. IX.

47. K. Middlemas, *Diplomacy of Illusion* (London, 1972), Chs II–IV; Watt, *How War Came*, 76–87, and his *Personalities and Appeasement*; D. Dilks, '"We Must Hope for the Best and Prepare for the Worst": The Prime Minister, The Cabinet and Hitler's Germany, 1937–1939', *Proceedings of the British Academy* 73 (1987); Parker, *Chamberlain*, passim.

48. Chamberlain to Ida, 30 March 1934, NC18/1/911; Post, *Dilemmas*, 257.

49. C. MacDonald, 'Economic Appeasement and the German "Moderates" 1937–1939', *Past and Present* 56 (1972); A. Crozier, *Appeasement and Germany's Last Bid for Colonies* (London, 1988).

50. Cabinet, 21 June 1937, 25(37), CAB23/88; FPC, 14th mtg, 21 June 1937, FP(36), CAB27/622. The FPC was set up in April 1936 in response to the Abyssinian and Rhineland crises to advise the Cabinet on foreign policy. Chaired by the PM, it consisted of top ministers, including the Foreign Secretary, the Chancellor of the Exchequer and the Minister for the Co-ordination of Defence, but not the Service ministers.

51. See chapter 2; Sir N. Henderson to FO, and Vansittart, 1 July 1937, C4958/270/18, FO371/20735; CNS, marginal note on draft Commons Resolution, 9 January 1937, PD9167/37, ADM116/3596; Phillips, 22 July 1937, and his letter to FO, 12 August 1937, PD06331/37, ADM116/3378.

52. First Lord, 7 August 1937, PD06331/37, ADM116/3378.

53. Admiral Sir Thomas Troubridge, Diaries, 1936–39. For his views and the reference to 'newsletters', see 31 May 1937, 16 July, 13–29 September, 15 November 1938, 18 March and 14 April 1939. He convinced Duff Cooper that a deal with Göring was possible: First Lord to FO, 12 August 1938, FO800/309. Also see Troubridge to FO, 15 February 1939, C2135/2198/18, FO371/23059.

54. 'Defence Expenditure', 10 November 1937, ADM205/80.

55. Chamberlain to Ida and Hilda, 30 October 1937 and 27 February 1938, NC18/1/1026/1040.

56. Chamberlain to Ida, 26 November 1937, NC18/1/1030.

57. A. Best, *Britain, Japan and Pearl Harbor* (London, 1995), 1–60; M. Murfett, *Fool-Proof Relations* (Singapore, 1984).
58. Murfett, *Relations*, 54–138; CNS to Backhouse, 8 October 1937, CHT4/1.
59. Goodall Diaries, 1 October 1937, MS 52790.
60. Ibid., 23 September 1938; DNI and CNS, 22 December 1937, PD06563/37, ADM116/3735.
61. S. Toyama, 'The Outline of the Armament Expansion of the Imperial Japanese Navy During the years 1930–41', *Revue Internationale D'Histoire Militaire* 73 (1991); Phillips, 21 and 31 January 1938, PD06563/37, ADM116/3735; CID, 306th mtg, 13 January 1938, CAB2/7. Protocols establishing the new limits between the 1936 London Treaty powers, Germany, Russia and eventually Italy, were signed in June and July 1938.
62. Fitzmaurice, 4 November 1938, A8124/4/35, FO371/21513; CID, 348th mtg, 24 February 1939, CAB2/8.
63. Phillips, 11 January 1938, PD06592/38, ADM116/3929.
64. DCNS, 3 March 1938, ibid.
65. CNS, 7 March 1938, ibid.
66. Phillips, 17 March 1938, M399/38, ADM116/3369.
67. Admiralty to FO, 22 April 1938, FO to German Embassy, 26 April 1938, PD06592/38, ADM116/3932. Raeder and his staff were disappointed by this forecast and began to calculate when the programme of six H class would clash with the 35 per cent ratio: Dülffer, *Marine*, 463–4.
68. CNS, 12 January 1938, ADM205/80; Phillips, 10 November 1937, Cabinet 276, ADM116/3631.
69. Duff Cooper to Inskip, 3 February 1938, CAB21/534.
70. Cabinet, 16/23 February 1938, 5/9(38), CAB23/92; Gibbs, *Strategy*, 345–51; Peden, *Treasury*, 164–5.
71. Cabinet, 12 March 1938, 12(38), CAB23/92; Duff Cooper to PM, 12–13 March 1938, PREM1/346.
72. 'Construction Programme 1938', 25 November 1937, ADM167/99; Gordon, *Procurement*, 279, n. 23.
73. 'Cruiser Building Policy', 6 May 1937, Templewood Papers, Vol. IX.
74. Director of Plans, Controller, CNS, and First Lord, 3 July – 16 October 1936, PD05795–05932/36, ADM116/3382; Roskill, *Policy*, II, 328–9. The CNS noted that the five *King George V* class would match the European ships under construction, while more powerful ships were built for Far East operations. He was confident that Britain could build faster than Japan: CNS, 11 November 1936, PD05932/36, ADM116/3382.
75. Director of Plans, DCNS, Controller, and CNS, 15 October – 18 November 1937, PD06489/37, ADM1/9729.
76. Phillips, 8 April 1938, PD06687/38, ADM116/3735.
77. Sea Lords mtg, the DNC and the Director of Plans, 4 May 1938, PD06786/38, and '1938 Programme Capital Ships', 10 May 1938, PD06823/38, ibid.; Board Minute 3581, 17 November 1938, ADM167/100.
78. CP129(38), 27 May 1938, CAB24/277; Cabinet, 1 June 1938, 27(38), CAB23/93. The Germans and Russians were informed on 2–3 June 1938: A4435/55/45, FO371/21521.
79. Phillips, 4 April 1938 and First Lord's mtg, 5 April 1938, ADM205/80.

80. First Lord to CNS, 6 and 9 May 1938, ibid.; Chancellor to PM, 24 June 1938, PREM1/346.
81. Chatfield to Vansittart, 26 July 1938, ADM205/80.
82. Cabinet, 20 and 27 July 1938, 33 and 35(38), CAB23/94.
83. Chatfield to Pound, 3 August 1938, CHT/4/10.
84. Gordon, *Procurement*, Part VI; Peden, *Treasury*, 165–7; 'Acceleration of Naval Defence Programmes', 1 April 1938, ADM205/80.
85. Roskill, *Policy*, II, 422–3; DRC, 14th mtg, 19 July 1935, CAB16/112.
86. Compare Dilks, 'Hope for the Best', 309–27, with Parker, *Chamberlain*, 124–46; FPC, 11–21 March 1938, FP(36)24–7, CAB27/623; Cabinet, 22 March 1938, 15(38), CAB23/93.
87. COS697(JP), 21 March 1938, CAB53/37 and CAB27/267.
88. COS701, 24 March 1938, CAB53/37; JP286, 8 April 1938, CAB55/12.
89. Danckwerts and other officials, 6–9 May 1938, PD06792/38, ADM116/3379.
90 W. Strang, 9 April 1938, C3129/37/18, FO371/21653.
91. *DGFP* D, I, No. 93.
92. Weinberg, II, 313–77; D. C. Watt, 'Hitler's Visit to Rome and the May Weekend Crisis: A Study in Hitler's Response to External Stimuli', *Journal of Contemporary History* 9 (1974); Deist *Germany*, 641–55.
93. Dülffer, *Marine*, 451–70; Salewski, I, 41–2; Watt, 'Naval Negotiations'; Rössler, *U-Boat*, 115. Weinberg disputes the Watt-Dülffer interpretation of Hitler's May 1938 naval directives as evidence of a 'turn' in the Führer's policy. He sees them as a refinement of Hitler's long-standing plans as well as a disclosure of his true intentions to the navy: *Foreign Policy*, II, 372, n. 229.
94. Dülffer, *Marine*, 461–75; Salewski, I, 40–4; Deist, *Germany*, 462–80.
95. Danckwerts, 30 June 1938, PD06912/38, ADM116/3929.
96. Henderson to Halifax, 20 April 1938, A4384/55/45, FO371/21521; Danckwerts to FO, 13 May 1938, ADM116/3378; Holman to Commander Bell, 22 June 1938, Director of Plans to Holman, 27 June 1938, and various FO officials, 29–30 June 1938, A5032/55/45, FO371/21522; cf. Wark, *Intelligence*, 144–5.
97. CNS, 7 July 1938, M03903/38, ADM1/9919.
98. COS, 245th mtg, 25 July 1938, CAB53/9.
99. Halifax, 19 November 1937, PREM1/330; CP218(37), 12 September 1937, CAB24/271.
100. Halifax to N. Henderson, Berlin, 17 August 1938, A5032/55/45, FO371/21522.
101. Compare the record of the 15 September 1938 talks by Schmidt, Hitler's interpreter, in C11970/11169/18, FO371/21785, with Chamberlain's account in C10084/1941/18, FO371/21738; Cabinet, 17 September 1938, 39(38), CAB23/95; W. Strang, *Home and Abroad* (London, 1956), 146–7.
102. DCNS, 30 September 1938, ADM116/4053.
103. Schreiber, 'Kontinuität', 101–31.
104. Watt, 'Naval Negotiations', 204; Salewski, I, 42.
105. Plans, 7 and 28 October 1938, PD07146/38, ADM116/3929; CID, 335th mtg, 25 October 1938, CAB2/8; Cabinet, 26 October 1938, 50(38), CAB23/96; Salewski, I, 43.
106. *DGFP* D, IV, No. 297; cf. Salewski, I, 59–60.

CHAPTER 7   THE END OF APPEASEMENT AND THE BID TO
TRANSFORM ADMIRALTY STRATEGY, 1938–39

1. Middlemas and Barnes, *Baldwin*, 826–8.
2. Pratt, *Malta*, examines Backhouse's Italy-first offensive in the context
   of Britain's Mediterranean policy. J. Pritchard, *Far Eastern Influences Upon
   British Strategy Towards the Great Powers, 1937–39* (New York, 1987),
   looks at the Mediterranean-first policy in terms of the Singapore strategy.
3. Roskill, *Policy*, II, 356–7, 462–3.
4. Admiral William Fisher was Chatfield's choice. The official correspondence
   on this topic in PREM1/281 is not very illuminating.
5. Marder, *Old Friends*, 32; Admiral James to Roskill, 21 May 1969, Roskill
   [Papers CCC]7/196; 'Senior Admirals', n.d., n.s., in DUFF2/12; Admiral A.
   Cunningham, *A Sailor's Odyssey* (London, 1951), 195.
6. Murfett, *First Sea Lords*, 173–84.
7. Improvements to Scapa Flow's defences, for example, were overlooked, and
   resulted in the loss of the *Royal Oak* to a U-boat: Roskill, II, 446.
8. Hunt, *Sailor-Scholar*, 196.
9. Backhouse to Drax, 27 August 1937, DRAX2/8.
10. Backhouse to Drax, 15 October and 24 November 1938, DRAX2/10.
11. CNS, 6 October 1938, M07778/38, and 'Organisation', CE3693/39,
    ADM116/4194.
12. 'Future German Policy', 12 October 1938, DRAX2/8; '[German] Programme
    for the Second World War (1939?)' 19 October 1938, DRAX2/16.
13. Backhouse to Pound, 11 October 1938, ADM205/3.
14. DRC, 14th mtg, 19 July 1935, CAB16/112.
15. Admiralty to C-in-C Mediterranean, 31 August 1938, ADM1/9542.
16. I. Kirkpatrick, R. L. Speaght, and O. Sargent, 29 August 1938,
    C8862/C8863/3096/18, FO371/21759.
17. 'German Naval Activities', February 1939, NID00151/39, ADM223/483.
18. Backhouse to Pound, 11 October 1938, ADM205/3; '[German]
    Programme', par. 9, 19 October 1938, DRAX2/16.
19. Drax to Backhouse, 12 October 1938, DRAX2/12.
20. 'European Naval War Plan', 21 March 1939, DRAX2/8.
21. Goodall Diaries, 8 May 1933, MS52786.
22. Backhouse to Pound, 11 October 1938 and Backhouse to Inskip, 13 October
    1938, ADM205/3.
23. *TINA* 89 (1947), 85–111, 112–13.
24. Cabinet, 7 November 1938, 53(38), CAB23/96.
25. Gordon, *Procurement*, 271–3; Lambert, 'Seapower', 86–108.
26. Roskill, II, 450–1; Board Minute 3581, 17 November 1938, ADM167/100;
    CID No. 1521-B, 3 February 1939, CAB4/29.
27. 'Construction Programme 1939', 13 December 1938, ADM167/102.
28. Backhouse to Somerville, 5 December 1938, MOO690/38, ADM1/9767;
    SAC4, 28 February 1939, CAB16/209.
29. Cunningham to Admiral Baillie-Grohman, 9 March 1936, XGRO/1, NMM;
    Drax [RX], 'Five Foreign Policies', *The Naval Review* 25 (1937), 47–50;
    'War Plans', 21 October 1938, DRAX2/8.

30. Watt, *How War Came*, 30–45; G. Weinberg, *Germany, Hitler, and World War II* (Cambridge, 1995), 109–120; Cabinet, 17 September 1938, 39(38), CAB23/95.

31. Watt, *How War Came*, 41–75; Weinberg, *Foreign Policy*, II, 465–513.

32. Watt, *How War Came*, passim, 40–5.

33. Salewski, I, 57–63; Dülffer, *Marine*, 471–504. Dülffer interprets the Z-Plan, and Hitler's refusal to adjust the timetable according to the requirements of cruiser warfare, as evidence that Hitler already had the 'world-power phase of his programme', including an inter-continental struggle against the United States, in mind. Salewski sees in the Z Plan elements of Tirpitz's 'risk' and 'alliance' fleet strategies. On the United States in Hitler's foreign-policy programme and the Z Plan: Weinberg, *Germany, Hitler, and World War II*, 182–204 and J. Thies, *Architekt der Weltherrschaft* (Düsseldorf, 1976), 128–48.

34. Watt, 'Naval Negotiations'; Salewski, I, 63–4; Dülffer, *Marine*, 513–16.

35. Watt, *How War Came*, 90–108; W. Wark, 'Something Very Stern: British Political Intelligence: Moralism and Grand Strategy in 1939', *Intelligence and National Security* 5 (1990); J. Ferris, '"Indulged In All Too Little"?: Vansittart, Intelligence, and Appeasement', *Diplomacy and Statecraft* 6 (1995); B. Strang, 'Sir George Ogilvie-Forbes, Sir Nevile Henderson and British Foreign Policy, 1938–39', *Diplomacy and Statecraft* 5 (1994).

36. MacDonald, 'Economic Appeasement', 55–135.

37. D. C. Watt, 'Misinformation, Misconception, Mistrust: Episodes in British Policy and the Approach of War, 1938–1939', in M. Bentley and J. Stevenson, eds, *High and Low Politics in Modern Britain* (Oxford, 1983); cf. Kaiser, *Economic Diplomacy*, 245–59, 290–5.

38. Halifax, November 1937, PREM1/330.

39. Halifax to N. Henderson, Berlin, 17 August 1938, A5032/55/45, FO371/21522.

40. First Sea Lord's mtg, 14 October 1938, PD0697/38, ADM116/3929.

41. CID, 335th mtg, 25 October 1938, CAB2/8.

42. D. Lammers, 'From Whitehall After Munich: The Foreign Office and The Future Course of British Policy', *Historical Journal* 16 (1973).

43. Strang recalls telling the PM in September 1938 that the 1935 Agreement was 'not a thing to be proud of': see his *Home and Abroad*, 146–7

44. Strang, 10 October 1938, C14471/42/18, FO371/21659.

45. A report of the Siemens-Danckwerts mtg was sent to the FO: A8343/55/45, FO371/21523.

46. Halifax to Phipps, 28 October 1938, FO800/311: a copy was sent to the PM.

47. Phipps to Halifax/Halifax to J. Kennedy, US Ambassador, 1/7 November 1938, FO800/311

48. Historians agree that there was a shift in influence in Cabinet after Munich from Chamberlain to Halifax: see A. Roberts, '*The Holy Fox': A Biography of Lord Halifax* (London, 1991), and J. Charmley, *Chamberlain and the Lost Peace* (London, 1989), for differing emphasis.

49. As Ferris cautions, one could underline a variety of factors, but what was most important was the outcome: 'Vansittart', 163–8.

50. A. Ogilvie-Forbes to FO, 14–18 November 1938, A8837/A8842/55/45, FO371/21523.

51. Leo A. Kennedy, diary entry 3 November 1938, LKEN1/22.
52. FPC, 32nd mtg, 14 November 1938, FP(36), CAB27/624.
53. IFC/185, 2 November 1938, C13557/65/18, FO371/21670.
54. 'Germany: Recent Activity in the Armour Industry', 16 November 1938, NID01215/38, ADM229/19.
55. 32nd mtg, FP(36), CAB27/624; 'Germany: The Crisis and the Aftermath', 14 November 1938, CAB104/43; Wark, 'Very Stern', 154–6.
56. Strang, *Home and Abroad*, 146–7. Strang, who accompanied Chamberlain to Munich, recalls that one reason why Chamberlain cited the 1935 Naval Agreement in the Munich accord was to clear the way for a similar arrangement. For the futile attempts from October 1938 – February 1939 to progress with air warfare rules: Bialer, *Bomber*, 124–5.
57. 32nd mtg, FP(36), CAB27/624; P. Stafford, 'The Chamberlain-Halifax visit to Rome: A Reappraisal', *English Historical Review* 98 (1983).
58. On Italy's accession to the 1936 London Naval Treaty: A8837/A8842/55/45, FO371/21523. The Italians were cheating on their latest battleship designs.
59. Watt, 'Negotiations', 388.
60. Steward to Sir Horace Wilson, Chief Industrial Advisor, 9 December 1938, A9348/55/45, FO371/21523; *DGFP* D, IV, No. 251.
61. R. Cockett, *Twilight of Truth* (London, 1989), 85–6.
62. Andrew, *Secret Service*, 387; Cadogan, *Diaries*, 127, and cf. manuscript entries for 28–30 November and 1–6 December 1938, Sir A[lexander]CAD[ogan diaries CCC]; Cockett, *Twilight*, 85–6.
63. Announcements were made on the eve of the talks, but rumours had been circulating in press circles: Assistant Director of Plans, 24 December 1938, ADM116/3765.
64. N. Chamberlain, *The Struggle For Peace* (London, 1939), 369–78; Cadogan, *Diaries*, 129–31
65. Editor's note, *DBFP*, Third Series, III, p. 434.
66. *DGFP* D, IV, No. 281. Cadogan recorded that the speech 'got applause in the wrong places' [references to improved relations with the US and France, but not to Munich] and that the PM had lost an opportunity [presumably to demand a German reply to Munich]: Cadogan, *Diaries*, 129–31; J. Harvey, ed., *The Diplomatic Diaries of Oliver Harvey, 1937–40* (London, 1970), 227–8. Harvey was the Private Secretary to the Foreign Secretary, 1936–9.
67. Cadogan, *Diaries*, 129–31; Harvey, *Diaries*, 227–9; *Hansard*, Fifth Series, Vol. 342 (1938), Cols 2523–4; *DGFP* D, III, No. 286.
68. German Embassy to FO, 10 December 1938; Sir A. Ogilvie-Forbes, Berlin, to FO, 12 December 1938; Cadogan, conversation with the German Ambassador, 12 December 1938, Halifax to Ogilvie-Forbes, 16 December 1938, A9339/A9348/55/45, FO371/21523.
69. Cabinet, 14 and 21 December 1938, 59 and 60(38), CAB23/96.
70. CID, 340th mtg, 1 December 1938, CAB2/8. Backhouse and Stanhope probably inflated the danger of German expansion at sea to win over the CID to expanded naval building.
71. Danckwerts, 8 December 1938, and DNI, 13 December 1938, PD07276/38, ADM116/4053.

72. Halifax to Ogilvie-Forbes, 15 December 1938, C15529/42/18, FO371/21523; Dirksen to Cadogan, 20 December 1938, A9519/55/45, FO371/21524.
73. Cadogan, *Diaries*, 130–1; Wark, 'Very Stern', 157–60; CID, 342–3th mtgs, 16–22 December 1938, CAB2/8.
74. Director of Plans, 20 December 1938, PD07325/38, ADM116/3765; Strang, 21 December 1938, A9646/55/45, FO371/21524.
75. 'Guidance' and 'Discussions', n.d., A9648/55/45, FO371/21524.
76. Cunningham, *Odyssey*, 197–8.
77. The record is in A130/1/45, FO371/22785 and *DGFP* D, IV, No. 288; conversation between German naval attaché and DCNS, 19 January 1939, ADM116/3765.
78. Strang, 10 January 1939, A297/1/45, FO371/22785.
79. *DGFP* D, IV, No. 297.
80. DNI, 22 November 1938, NID001278/38, ADM116/5757.
81. Best, *Pearl Harbor*, 60–71; Marder, *Old Friends*, 42–6, 48–9, 76; Commander T. C. Hampton, Plans Division, 'A Far Eastern War', 7 October 1938, F10819/10819/61, FO371/22176.
82. CNS to C-in-C America and West Indies, 9 January 1939, C-in-Cs Atlantic and Mediterranean Fleets, 13 January 1939, and C-in-C Africa, 23 January 1939, ADM205/3.
83. Sir C. Dormer, Oslo, to FO, 3 and 25 January 1939, C1061/C1297/C1539/C1629/1061/18, FO371/23054.
84. Goodall Diaries, 13 February 1939, MS52790: 'D[aily] Express today has copy from German paper of d[ra]w[in]g of KGV,' the DNC wrote, 'looks like leakage, saw DNI.'
85. 'Major Strategy', 1 February 1939, DRAX2/11.
86. Backhouse to Drax, 27 August 1937, DRAX2/8; Drax and Dickens, 'WP Papers' and 'Summary of OPC Proposals', 19 September 1939, DRAX2/10.
87. Plans for the RAF to attack the German navy in its bases had been proposed long before 1939 but were not very advanced: Danckwerts to Group Captain J. Slessor, Air Staff Director of Plans, 16 September 1938, S50218 and the draft plans in AIR9/83.
88. Directors of Plans, Tactical and Operations Divisions, 26 March to 4 April 1939, TD127/39, ADM116/5452.
89. Director of Naval Air Division, 7 September 1939; Director of Plans, 20 September 1939, PD07981/39, ADM1/9899. Attacks by submarines and torpedo boats were also proposed but rejected on similar grounds. On Bomber Command and the plans to bomb Kiel and Wilhelmshaven: Smith, *Strategy*, 301–2. On the Fleet Air Arm's weaknesses: Till, *Air Power*, 99–105.
90. CNS to C-in-C America and West Indies, 9 January 1939, ADM205/3
91. CNS to C-in-C Africa, 23 January 1939, ibid.
92. OPC7, 17 February 1939, DRAX2/3.
93. Snyder, *Ideology*, 29–30.
94. Danckwerts, Cunningham and Backhouse, 3–5 March 1939, PD07537/39, ADM229/20; Roskill, II, 450–4.
95. Troubridge to FO, 27 January 1939, C1360/1360/18, FO371/23055.
96. CID, 24 February 1939, 348th mtg, CAB2/8.
97. FPC, 36th mtg, 26 January 1939, FP(36), CAB27/624; Gibbs, *Strategy*, 654–7.

98. COS843, 20 February 1939, CAB53/45; Gibbs, *Strategy*, 657–67; Wark, *Intelligence*, 211–21.
99. The CNS later complained that he had not had the opportunity to express his views: CID, 24 February 1939, 348th mtg, CAB2/8. The SAC proceedings are in CAB16/209. It consisted of the Minister for the Co-ordination of Defence (chair), a FO delegate, the service ministers and chiefs.
100. SAC, 1st–2nd mtgs, 1 and 3 March 1939, CAB16/209; Backhouse, 14 March 1939, M02268/39, ADM1/9897.
101. Stanhope, Backhouse, Cunningham and Drax, 16 March – 3 April 1939, M02268/39, ADM1/9897; cf. Pritchard, *Influences*, 138–43.
102. Murfett, *Relations*, 199–248.
103. SAC, 6th mtg, and SAC16, April 1939, CAB16/209; CID, 355th mtg, 2 May 1939, CAB2/8.
104. JP382, 27 March 1939, CAB55/15. The navy's JPC representative, Captain Danckwerts, a Chatfield appointee, was not an enthusiast of Backhouse or Drax. In March 1940, Churchill sacked Danckwerts and others for a lack of offensive mindedness.
105. 'Major Strategy', 1 February 1939, DRAX2/11; Pratt, *Malta*, 181–3; Pritchard, *Influences*, 146–9.
106. 'European Appreciation: Notes', n. d. [February 1939?], para. 5, DRAX2/11.
107. CNS to Cunningham [now C-in-C Mediterranean], 24 July 1939, Cunningham Papers, MS 52560, British Library, London. Admiral Pound was not opposed an offensive in principle, he was just realistic about its potential results: Pratt, *Malta*, 167–8, 186.
108. Snyder, *Ideology*, 18, 211–14.
109. FPC, 35–6th mtgs, 23 and 26 January 1939, FP(35–6), CAB27/624; FP(36)74, January 1939, CAB27/627; Watt, *How War Came*, 99–123.
110. Chamberlain to Hilda, 5 February 1939, NC18/1/1084.
111. Watt, *How War Came*, 164–7; Wark, *Intelligence*, 212–18. Wark traces the new COS optimism, but does not credit Backhouse with initiating it. Cf. COS, 266/276th mtgs, 5 January/15 February 1939, CAB53/10; the JPC letter of 23 December 1938 (CAB104/76), deflecting accusations of defensive mindedness, was probably a reply to the CNS.
112. CID, 24 February 1939, 348th mtg, CAB2/8.
113. C. A. MacDonald, 'Britain, France, and the April Crisis of 1939', *European Studies Review* 22 (1972); Watt, *How War Came*, 162–87.
114. Watt, *How War Came*, 188–94.
115. Kirkpatrick, Cadogan and other officials, 1–4 April 1939, C4727/C4567/C4566/15/18, FO371/22968; Troubridge Diaries, 21 March 1939; Ogilvie-Forbes to FO, 22 March 1939, C3746/19/18, FO371/22995.
116. Goodall, diaries, 25 April 1939, MS 52790; FO to Washington, 5 April 1939, C4567/15/18, FO371/22968; Ogilvie-Forbes to FO, 6 April 1939, C4855/3778/18, FO371/23076; Harvey, *Diaries*, 273–4; Cadogan, *Diaries*, 169.
117. DNI, 12 April 1939, CAB21/943; OIC reports, 27 March – 16 May 1939, IC008–0064/30, ADM223/79; Wark, *Intelligence*, 147–8; draft JIC history by C. Morgan, ADM223/465.
118. Notes by Admiral Forbes, C-in-C Atlantic, 14 April 1939, Cunningham MS 52565; Chamberlain to Hilda, 15 April 1939, NC18/1/1094; Cabinet,

19 April 1939, 21(39), CAB23/96; 'Significance of the German Cruise', 18 April 1939, C5684/1061/18, FO371/23054; Chatfield to Halifax, 19 April 1939, FO800/323.

119. Cadogan, *Diaries*, 176; Harvey, *Diaries*, 287.
120. German Embassy London to FO, 28 April 1939, A3092/1/45, FO371/22785; Watt, *How War Came*, passim; *DGFP* D, VI, No. 433.
121. Dülffer, *Marine*, 503–4, 517; Schniewind, 'Notes for a Conference', 21 March 1939, and 'Notes for a Conference', 4 April 1939, in Watt, *Documents*. On the design of the 12 improved *Panzerschiffe* as well as the three new 32 000-ton/15-inch gun battlecruisers ordered in August 1939: Whitley, *Capital Ships*, 60–2.
122. *DGFP* D, VI, No. 277.
123. Perowne, Fitzmaurice, Kirkpatrick, Craigie, 4–5 May 1939, A3092/A3236/1/45, FO371/22785.
124. Cabinet, 3 May 1939, 26(39), CAB23/99.
125. The source of this promise was Dirksen: Chamberlain, Diaries, 15 May 1939, NC2/23A.
126. Cadogan, 24 March 1939, C3746/19/18, FO371/22995.
127. Troubridge, Diaries, 6–20 June 1939; Harisson, Berlin Embassy, to FO, 19 June 1939, C8893/1061/18, FO371/23054.
128. This account is based on FPC, 51st mtg, 13 June 1939, FP(36), CAB27/625; 'Draft Reply to the German Government', and Plans, June 1939, FP(36)86, CAB27/627.
129. CID Paper No. 1559-B, June 1939, CAB55/17; Cadogan, Sargent, 13–17 June 1939, C8829/C8824/ 1061/18, FO371/23054. Cf. Wark, *Intelligence*, 150–1.
130. Salewski, I, 57–63; Dülffer, *Marine*, 505–12, 571.
131. Kirkpatrick, 'Naval Disarmament', 30 May 1939; Kirkpatrick and Vansittart, 16 June, A3857/1/45, FO371/22786.
132. CID, 319th mtg, 11 April 1939, CAB2/7.
133. Though this point was not made explicit in the FPC minutes, it is reasonable to infer from internal evidence that Chatfield deployed the argument since the decision was taken to try to salvage qualitative limitation despite the possibility that the German navy would cheat: 51st mtg, 13 June 1939, FP(36), CAB27/625. Cf. Wark, *Intelligence*, 150–1.
134. Halifax, draft note, 22 June 1939 and N. Henderson to FO, 29 June 1939, A4372/A4477/A4558/1/45, FO371/22786. The British note was handed to the German Foreign Ministry on 28 June 1939. The German press ridiculed it.
135. CNS, 10 November 1937, ADM205/80.
136. Chamberlain to Ida, 23 July 1939, NC18/1/1108.
137. See Wark, *Intelligence*, 219–21.
138. Chamberlain had appointed Chatfield as Inskip's replacement to reinforce his grip on the Cabinet. Their differences over the approach to Moscow later caused him consternation: FPC, 47th mtg, 16 May 1939, FP(36), CAB27/625.
139. Kirkpatrick, 25 July 1939, C10525/3356/18, FO371/23071; FPC, 60th mtg, 1 August 1939, FP(36), CAB27/625.
140. COS927(JP), 16 June 1939, CAB55/17; CID, 362nd mtg, 26 June, 1939, CAB2/9; Best, *Pearl Harbor*, 71–81.

141. Board Minute 3646, 15 June 1939, ADM167/103.
142. 'Needs of the Navy', 15 June 1939, ADM167/104; DP(P)63, 27 June 1939, CAB16/183A.
143. CID, 364th mtg, 6 July 1939, CAB2/9; Gibbs, *Strategy*, 355–7.
144. Head of Military Branch, 24 August 1939, M08132/39, ADM1/10524.
145. Watt, *How War Came*, 430–98; Showell, *Fuehrer Conferences*, 37.
146. Chamberlain to Hilda, 29 April 1939, NC18/1/1096.
147. Churchill devised his own offensive plans before becoming First Lord: 'Memorandum of Sea-Power' PREM1/345. On 'Catherine' and interdicting Swedish iron ore: P. Salmon, 'Churchill, the Admiralty and the Narvik Traffic, September–November 1939', *Scandinavian Journal of History* 4 (1979); T. Munch-Petersen, *The Strategy of the Phoney War* (Stockholm, 1981); Lambert, 'Seapower', 98–9.

CONCLUSION

1. Ferris, 'Last Decade', 124–70.
2. See the 'composition of a fleet' in 'Essay by Vice-Admiral Heye', 15 October 1945, NID1/gp/13, ADM223/690.
3. In fact, the CID contemplated trading some of Britain's traditional belligerent rights to blockade foodstuffs in exchange for a convention to prevent the bombing of civilians: Bialer, *Bomber*, 121–2.
4. D. C. Watt, 'The European Civil War', in W. Mommsen and L. Kettenacker, eds, *The Fascist Challenge and the Policy of Appeasement* (London, 1983).
5. Watt, *How War Came*; Weinberg, *Hitler, Germany, and World War II*, 109–20.
6. Chatfield to Vansittart, 25 December 1936, FO800/394
7. Overy, 'Hitler's War', 272–91.
8. N. A. Lambert, 'British Naval Policy, 1913–14: Financial Limitation and Strategic Revolution', *Journal of Modern History* 67 (1995).
9. Cadogan, *Diaries*, 106–7.

Select Bibliography

For reasons of space, the following list of printed sources is confined to those most useful in the preparation of this study. The relevant bibliographies are Aster, S., *British Foreign Policy 1918–1945* (Wilmington, Delaware, 1991); Bird, K. W., *German Naval History* (1985); Kimmich, C. M., *German Foreign Policy 1918–1945* (Wilmington, Delaware, 1991); and Rasor, E. L., *British Naval History Since 1815* (New York, 1990). Unless otherwise stated, London is the place of publication.

PRIMARY SOURCES

Unpublished Documents

Admiralty Library, London: Monthly Intelligence Reports, 1928–39

National Maritime Museum, Greenwich: Department of the Controller, Ship's Covers

Public Records Office, London:
Admiralty:

ADM 1	Admiralty and Secretariat Papers
ADM 116	Admiralty and Secretariat Case Books
ADM 167	Admiralty Board Minutes and Memoranda
ADM 178	Admiralty Papers and Cases, Supplementary Series
ADM 186	Publications for Official Use
ADM 189	Torpedo and Anti-Submarine School Reports
ADM 199	War of 1939–45, War History Cases
ADM 203	Royal Naval College, Correspondence and Papers
ADM 204	Admiralty Research Laboratory Reports
ADM 205	First Sea Lord Papers
ADM 219	Directorate of Naval Operations Studies
ADM 223	Admiralty Intelligence Papers
ADM 229	Director of Naval Construction Reports
ADM 234	Navy Reference Books
ADM 239	Confidential Books

Air Ministry:

AIR 2	Registered Correspondence Files
AIR 9	Director of Plans Papers

Cabinet Office:

CAB 2	Minutes of the Committee of Imperial Defence
CAB 4	Committee of Imperial Defence Memoranda
CAB 16	Committee of Imperial Defence, Ad Hoc Sub-Committees
CAB 21	Cabinet Office Registered Files
CAB 23	Minutes of Cabinet Meetings
CAB 24	Cabinet Memoranda

CAB 27	Cabinet Committees, General Series
CAB 29	International Conferences
CAB 47	Advisory Committee on Trade Questions in Time of War
CAB 48	Industrial Intelligence in Foreign Countries
CAB 53	Chiefs of Staff Committee
CAB 54	Deputy Chiefs of Staff Committee
CAB 55	Joint Planning Sub-Committee
CAB 56	Joint Intelligence Sub-Committee
CAB 64	Minister for the Co-ordination of Defence
CAB 81	Joint Intelligence Sub-Committee (Wartime)
CAB 104	Cabinet Registered Files, Supplementary Series

Foreign Office:

FO 371	General Correspondence, Political
FO 408	Berlin Embassy Correspondence
FO 800	Private Papers

Prime Minister's Office:

PREM 1	Prime Minister's Office

Treasury

T 160	Finance Files
T 161	Supply Files

British Library of Political and Economic Science, London School of Economics:
D. C. Watt, ed., *Anglo-German Naval Relation: Documents* (unpublished MSS).

Private Papers, Diaries, Memoirs and Correspondence

Birmingham University Library:
Neville Chamberlain
Lord Avon (Anthony Eden)

British Library, London:
1st Viscount Cunningham of Hyndhope
Sir Stanley Vernon Goodall

Cambridge University Library:
1st Earl Stanley Baldwin
Viscount Templewood (Sir Samuel Hoare)

Churchill College Archives, Cambridge:
Sir Alexander Cadogan
1st Viscount Caldecote
Captain John Creswell
Admiral Sir Reginald Plunket-Ernle-Erle Drax
Captain Godfrey A. French
1st Baron Maurice P. A. Hankey
Aubrey Leo Kennedy
1st Viscount Norwich of Aldwich (Duff Cooper)
Captain Stephen W. Roskill
Sir Eric Phipps
Admiral Sir James F. Somerville

Imperial War Museum, London:
  Admiral Sir G. C. Dickens
  Admiral J. H. Godfrey
  Rear Admiral G. C. Ross

Public Records Office, London:
  CAB 63   Lord Hankey
  FO 800   Private Papers, Various Officials
  PRO/30/69   Ramsay MacDonald

National Library of Scotland:
  Rear Admiral Robert K. Dickson

National Maritime Museum, Greenwich:
  Vice Admiral H. T. Baillie-Grohman
  Admiral of the Fleet A. Ernle M. Chatfield
  Sir E. Tennyson D'Eyncourt
  Admiral Sir Barry Domville
  Admiral J. H. Godfrey
  Admiral Sir William Tennant

Published Sources

Diplomatic Correspondence

Documents on British Foreign Policy, 1929–1939, Second Series: 21 vols; Third Series: 9 vols. HMSO, 1946–85.
Documents on German Foreign Policy, Series C (1933–6), 7 vols; Series D (1936–9), 7 vols. HMSO, 1949–83.
Wheeler-Bennett, J. W. and Heald, S., eds, *Documents on International Affairs 1935* (1936).

Government Publications

The Duties of the Naval Staff, Command 1343 (1921).
Exchange of Notes, the United Kingdom and Germany, Regarding the Limitation of Naval Armaments, Command 4930, 4953, 5519, 5637, 5795 and 5834 (1935).
Draft Disarmament Conventions, Command 4122 (1931–2), 4279 (1932–3), and 4498 (1933–4).
Parliamentary Debates: House of Commons, 5th Series.

International Military Tribunal

Trial of the Major War Criminals Before the International Military Tribunal, Nuremberg, 1945–6, 42 vols. Nuremberg, 1947–9.

Naval Documents

Fuehrer Conferences on Naval Affairs 1939–1945, Foreword by Mallmann Showell, J. P. (Trowbridge, 1990).

Professional Journals

The Naval Review
Transactions of the Institution of Naval Architects

Diaries, Speeches, Memoirs

Cadogan, A., *The Diaries of Sir Alexander Cadogan, 1938–1945*, ed. Dilks, D. (1971).
Chamberlain, N., *The Struggle For Peace* (1939).
Chatfield, Admiral E., *The Navy and Defence* (1942).
——, *It Might Happen Again* (1947).
Cunningham, Admiral A. B., *A Sailor's Odyssey* (1951).
Dönitz, Admiral K., *Memoirs: Ten Years and Twenty Days*, trans. Stevens, R. H. (Cleveland, 1959).
Duff Cooper, A., *Old Men Forget* (1953).
Eden, A., (Lord Avon) *The Eden Memoirs: Facing the Dictators* (1962).
Halifax, Earl of, *Fullness of Days* (1957).
Harvey, J., ed., *The Diplomatic Diaries of Oliver Harvey, 1937–1940* (1970).
Hitler, A., *Mein Kampf*, trans. Manheim, R. (1992).
Hoare, S. (1st Viscount Templewood), *Nine Troubled Years* (1954).
Pownell, Lieutenant-General H., *Chief of Staff: The Diaries of Lieutenant-General Sir Henry Pownell* ed. Bond, B., 2 vols (1973–4).
Raeder, Admiral E., *Mein Leben*, 2 vols (Tübingen, 1956–7).
Ribbentrop, J., *The Ribbentrop Memoirs*, ed. Ribbentrop, A. (1954).
Schmidt, P., *Hitler's Interpreter* (Köln, 1950).
Strang, W., *Home and Abroad* (1956).

SECONDARY SOURCES

Biographies

Bloch, M., *Ribbentrop* (1992).
Feiling, K., *The Life of Neville Chamberlain* (1946).
Honan, W. H., *Bywater: The Man Who Invented the War in the Pacific* (1990).
Hunt, B., *Sailor-Scholar: Admiral Sir Herbert Richmond* (Waterloo, Ontario, 1982).
Middlemas, K. and Barnes, J., *Baldwin: A Biography* (1969).
O'Halpin, E., *Head of the Civil Service: A Biography of Sir Warren Fisher* (1989).
Roberts, A., *'The Holy Fox': A Biography of Lord Halifax* (1991).
Rose, N., *Vansittart: Study of a Diplomat* (1978).
Roskill, S., *Hankey: Man of Secrets*, 3 vols (1970–7).
Simpson, Admiral G. W. G., *Periscope View* (1972).

Monographs

Andrew, C. M., *Secret Service: The Making of the British Intelligence Community* (1984).

Barnett, C., *Engage the Enemy More Closely: The Royal Navy in the Second World War* (1991).

Bell, A. C., *A History of the Blockade of Germany* (1937).

Best, A., *Britain, Japan and Pearl Harbor: Avoiding War in East Asia, 1936–1941* (1995).

Bialer, U., *The Shadow of The Bomber: The Fear of Air Attack and British Politics, 1932–1939* (1980).

Boyce, R. and Robertson, E. M., *Paths to War: New Essays on the Origins of the Second World War* (1989).

Brown, D. K., *A Century of Naval Construction* (1983).

Buckley, J., *The RAF and Trade Defence, 1919–1945* (Keele, 1995).

Cato [M. Foot, F. Owen and P. Howard], *Guilty Men* (1940).

Charmley, J., *Chamberlain and the Lost Peace* (1989).

Clarke, I. F., *Voices Prophesying War: Future Wars 1763–3749* (Oxford, 1992).

Cockett, R., *Twilight of Truth: Chamberlain, Appeasement and the Manipulation of the Press* (1989).

Creswell, Captain J., *Naval Warfare* (1936).

Crozier, A., *Appeasement and Germany's Last Bid for Colonies* (1988).

Deist, W., Messerschmidt, M., Volkmann, H. and Wette, W., *Germany and the Second World War Vol. I: The Build-up of German Aggression* (Oxford, 1990).

Dingman, R., *Power in the Pacific: The Origins of Naval Arms Limitation, 1914–1922* (Chicago, 1976).

Doughty, M., *Merchant Shipping and War: A Study of Defence Planning in Twentieth Century Britain* (1982).

Dülffer, J., *Weimar, Hitler, und die Marine: Reichspolitik und Flottenbau, 1920–1939* (Düsseldorf, 1973).

Emmerson, J. T., *The Rhineland Crisis of 7 March 1936: A Study in Multilateral Diplomacy* (1977).

Farago, L., *The Game of the Foxes* (1972).

Ferris, J. R. *Men, Money, and Diplomacy: The Evolution of British Strategic Policy* (Ithaca, 1989).

Friedman, N., *Battleship Design and Development, 1904–1945* (New York, 1978).

Gannon, F. R., *The British Press and Germany, 1933–39* (Oxford, 1971).

Garzke, W. H. Jr and Dulin, R. O. Jr, *Battleships: Allied Battleships in World War II* (Annapolis, Maryland, 1980).

Gemzell, C.-A., *Raeder, Hitler, und Skandinavien: Der Kampf für einen maritimen Operationsplan* (Lund, 1965).

——, *Organization, Conflict, and Innovation. A Study of German Naval Strategic Planning, 1880–1940* (Lund, 1973).

Gibbs, N. H., *Grand Strategy Vol. I: Rearmament Policy* (1976).

Goldrick, J. and Hattendorf, J. B., eds, *Mahan Is Not Enough: The Proceedings of a Conference on the Works of Sir Julian Corbett and Admiral Sir Herbert Richmond* (Newport, Rhode Island, 1993).

Gooch, J., *The Prospect of War: Studies in British Defence Policy, 1847–1942* (1981).

Gordon, G. A. H., *British Seapower and Procurement between the Wars: A Reappraisal of Rearmament* (1988).

Gray, C., *The Leverage of Sea Power: The Strategic Advantage of Navies in War* (New York, 1992).

Hackmann, W., *Seek and Strike: Sonar, Antisubmarine Warfare and the Royal Navy 1914–1954* (1984).

Haggie, P., *Britannia at Bay: The Defence of the British Empire against Japan, 1931–1941* (Oxford, 1981).

Hall, C., *Britain, America and Arms Control, 1921–1937* (1987).

Haraszti, E. H. *Treaty-Breakers or 'Realpolitiker'? The Anglo-German Naval Agreement of June 1935* (Boppard am Rhein, 1974).

Hattendorf, J. B., and Jordan, R. S., eds, *Maritime Strategy and the Balance of Power: Britain and America in the Twentieth Century* (1989).

Hinsley, F. H. et al., *British Intelligence in the Second World War: Its Influence on Strategy and Operations*, Vol. I (1979).

Howard, M., *The Continental Commitment: The Dilemma of British Defence Policy in the Era of the Two World Wars* (1972).

Howarth, S. and Law, D., eds, *The Battle of the Atlantic, 1939–45* (1995).

Howse, H., *Radar at Sea* (Annapolis, 1993).

Hughs, W. P., *Fleet Tactics: Theory and Practice* (Annapolis, Maryland, 1986).

Irving, D., *The War Path: Hitler's Germany, 1933–1939* (1978).

Jackson, B., and Bramall, D., *The Chiefs: The Story of the United Kingdom Chiefs of Staff* (1992).

Kaiser, D. E., *Economic Diplomacy and the Origins of the Second World War: Germany, Britain, France, and Eastern Europe, 1930–1939* (Princeton, 1980).

Keegan, J., *The Price of Admiralty: The Evolution of Naval Warfare* (1988).

Kennedy, P., *The Rise and Fall of British Naval Mastery* (1983).

Kökl, F., and Rössler, E., *The Type XXI U-Boat* (Annapolis, Maryland, 1991).

McIntyre, W. D., *The Rise and Fall of the Singapore Naval Base, 1919–1942* (1979).

McKercher, B. J. C., *The Second Baldwin Government and the United States, 1924–1929* (Cambridge, 1984).

Maier, K., Rohde, H., Stegemann, B. and Umbreit, H., *Germany and the Second World War Vol. II: Germany's Initial Conquests in Europe* (Oxford, 1991).

Marder, A. J., *From Dreadnought to Scapa Flow*, 5 vols (Oxford, 1961–70).

——, *From the Dardanelles to Oran: Studies of the Royal Navy in War and Peace, 1915–1940* (1974).

——, *Old Friends, New Enemies Vol. 1: The Royal Navy and the Imperial Japanese Navy: Strategic Illusions, 1936–41* (Oxford, 1981).

May, E. R., ed., *Knowing One's Enemies: Intelligence Assessment Before the Two World Wars* (Princeton, 1986).

Medlicott, W. N., *The Economic Blockade*, Vol. I (1952).

——, *The Coming of War In 1939* (1963).

Michalka, W., *Ribbentrop und die deutsche Weltpolitik, 1933–1940* (München, 1980).

Middlemas, K., *Diplomacy of Illusion: The British Government and Germany, 1937–1939* (1972).

Millett, A. R. and Murray, W., eds, *Calculations: Net Assessment and the Coming of World War II* (New York, 1992).

——, *Military Innovation In The Interwar Period* (Cambridge, 1997).

Müller, J., and Opitz, E., eds, *Militär und Militarismus in der Weimarer Republik* (Düsseldorf, 1978).

Munch-Petersen, T., *The Strategy of the Phoney War: Britain, Sweden and the Iron Ore Question, 1939–1940* (Stockholm, 1981).

Murfett, M., *Fool-Proof Relations: The Search for Anglo-American Naval Cooperation during the Chamberlain Years, 1937–1940* (Singapore, 1984).

—— et al. *The First Sea Lords* (1995).

Murray, W., *The Change in the European Balance of Power, 1938–1939: The Path to Ruin* (Princeton, 1984).

Neidpath, J., *The Singapore Naval Base and the Defence of Britain's Eastern Empire, 1919–1941* (Oxford, 1981).

O'Connell, D. P., *The Influence of Law on Sea Power* (Manchester, 1975).

Overy, R. J. and Wheatcroft, A., *The Road to War* (1989).

Parker, R. A. C., *Chamberlain and Appeasement: British Policy and the Coming of the Second World War* (1993).

Peden, G. C., *British Rearmament and the Treasury, 1932–1939* (Edinburgh, 1979).

Pelz, S. E., *Race to Pearl Harbor: The Failure of the Second London Conference and the Onset of World War II* (Boston, 1984).

Post, G. Jr, *Dilemmas of Appeasement: British Deterrence and Defence, 1934–1937* (Ithaca, 1993).

Pownell, Sir H., *Chief of Staff*, Vol. I, ed. B. Bond (1973).

Pratt, L. R., *East of Malta, West of Suez: Britain's Mediterranean Crisis, 1936–1939* (1975).

Preston, A., ed., *General Staffs and Diplomacy before the Second World War* (1978).

Pritchard, R. J., *Far Eastern Influences upon British Strategy Towards the Great Powers, 1937–1939* (New York, 1987).

Ranft, B., ed., *Technical Change and British Naval Policy, 1860–1939* (1977).

Raven, A. and Roberts, J., *British Battleships and World War Two: The Development and Technical History of the Royal Navy's Battleships and Battle Cruisers from 1911 to 1946* (1976).

Roskill, S. W., *Naval Policy between the Wars Vol. I: The Period of Anglo-American Antagonism*; *Vol. II: The Period of Reluctant Rearmament* (1968–76).

Rössler, E., *The U-Boat. The Evolution and Technical History of German Submarines* (1981).

Salewski, M., *Die deutsche Seekriegsleitung 1935–1945*, 3 vols (Frankfurt, 1970–5).

Semmel, B., *Liberalism and Naval Strategy: Ideology, Interest, and Sea Power During the Pax Britannica* (1986).

Shay, R. P., *British Rearmament in the 1930s: Politics and Profits* (Princeton, 1977).

Smith, M., *British Air Strategy Between the Wars* (Oxford, 1984).

Snyder, J., *The Ideology of the Offensive: Military Decision Making and the Disasters of 1914* (Ithaca, New York, 1984).

Sumida, J. T., *In Defence of Naval Supremacy: Finance, Technology, and British Naval Policy, 1889–1914* (1989).

Thies, J., *Architekt der Weltherrschaft: Die 'Endziele' Hitlers* (Düsseldorf, 1976).

Thomas, C. S., *The German Navy in the Nazi Era* (1990).
Till, G., *Air Power and the Royal Navy, 1914–1945* (1979).
Wark, W. K., *The Ultimate Enemy British Intelligence and Nazi Germany, 1933–1939* (Oxford, 1986).
Watt, D. C., *Personalities and Policies* (1965).
——, *Too Serious a Business: European Armed Forces and the Approach of the Second World War* (1975).
——, *How War Came: The Immediate Origins of the Second World War 1938–1939* (1989).
——, *Personalities and Appeasement* (Austin, Texas, 1991).
Wegener, Admiral W., *The Naval Strategy of the World War*, trans. and intro. Herwig, H. H. (Annapolis, Maryland, 1989).
Weinberg, G. L., *The Foreign Policy of Hitler's Germany Vol. I: Diplomatic Revolution in Europe, 1933–1936; Vol. II: Starting World War Two, 1937–1939* (Chicago, 1970/80).
——, *Germany, Hitler, and World War II* (Cambridge, 1995).
Whitley, M. J., *Destroyer: German Destroyers of World War II* (Annapolis, Maryland, 1983).
——, *German Cruisers of World War II* (Annapolis, Maryland, 1985).
——, *German Capital Ships of World War II* (1989).

Articles

Allard, D. C., 'Naval Rearmament, 1930–1941: An American Perspective', *Revue Internationale D'Histoire Militaire* 73 (1991).
Baldwin, D. A., 'Power Analysis and World Politics: New Trends versus Old Tendencies', *World Politics* 31 (1979).
Bason, A. V., 'Der Bau der Seekriegsflotte der UdSSR vor dem Zweiten Weltkrieg–1921 bis 1941', *Revue Internationale D'Histoire Militaire* 73 (1991).
Bauermeister, H., 'Die Entwicklung der Magnetminen bis zum Beginn des Zweiten Weltkrieges', *Marine Rundschau* 55 (1958).
Bell, C., '"Our Most Exposed Outpost": Hong Kong and British Far Eastern Strategy, 1921–1941', *Journal of Military History* 60 (1996).
Best, R. Jr, 'The Anglo-German Naval Agreement of 1935: An Aspect of Appeasement', *Naval War College Review* 34 (1981).
Bird, K., 'The Origins and Role of the German Naval History in the Interwar Period', *Naval War College Review* 29 (1976).
Bloch, C., 'Great Britain, German Rearmament and the Naval Agreement of 1935', in Gatzke, H., ed., *European Diplomacy between the Two Wars, 1919–1939* (Chicago, 1972).
Brown, D. K., 'Submarine Pressure Hull Design and Diving Depths Between the Wars', *Warship International* 3 (1987).
——, 'Naval Rearmament 1930–1941: The Royal Navy', *Revue Internationale d'Histoire Militaire* 73 (1991).
Buckley, J., 'Air Power and the Battle of the Atlantic', *Journal of Contemporary History* 28 (1993).
Burdick, C. B., '"Moro": The Resupply of German Submarines in Spain, 1939–1942', *Central European History* 3 (1970).

Dilks, D.,'"We Must Hope for the Best and Prepare for the Worst": The Prime Minister, The Cabinet and Hitler's Germany, 1937–1939', *Proceedings of the British Academy* 73 (1987).

Dülffer, J., 'Determinants of German Naval Policy, 1929–1939', in Deist, W., ed., *The German Military in the age of Total War* (1985).

Fairbanks, C. H. Jr, 'The Origins of the Dreadnought Revolution', *International History Review* 13 (1991).

Ferris, J. R. 'The Symbol and the Substance of Seapower: Great Britain, the United States and the One-Power Standard, 1919–1921', in McKercher, B. J. C., ed., *Anglo-American Relations in the 1920s: The Struggle for Supremacy* (1991).

——, '"Worthy of Some Better Enemy?": The British Estimate of the Imperial Japanese Army 1919–1941, and the Fall of Singapore', *Canadian Journal of History* 28 (1993).

——, '"Indulged In All Too Little"?: Vansittart, Intelligence, and Appeasement', *Diplomacy and Statecraft* 6 (1995).

——, '"It is our business to command the Seas": The Last Decade of British Maritime Supremacy, 1919–1929', in Neilson, K. and Kennedy, G., eds, *Far Flung Lines: Studies in Imperial Defence in Honour of Donald Mackenzie Schurman* (1996).

Garzke, W., Dulin, R. and Brown, D., 'The Sinking of the Bismarck: An Analysis of the Damage', *Warship* (1994).

Goldstein, E. and Maurer, J., eds, Special issue on 'The Washington Conference, 1921–1922', *Diplomacy and Statecraft* 6 (1993).

Gribovski, V. Iu., 'The "Sovetskii Soiuz" Class Battleship', *Warship International* 30 (1993).

Hall, H., 'The Foreign Policy Making Process in Britain, 1934–35, and the Origins of the Anglo-German Naval Arms Agreement', *Historical Journal* 19 (1976).

Herwig, H. H., 'The Failure of German Seapower, 1914–1945: Mahan, Tirpitz, and Raeder Reconsidered', *International History Review* 10 (1988).

Hillgruber, A., 'England's Place in Hitler's Plans for World Dominion', *Journal of Contemporary History* 9 (1974).

Hutchinson, H., 'Intelligence: Escape from Prisoner's Dilemma', *Intelligence and National Security* 7 (1992).

Kennedy, P., 'Appeasement', in Martel, G., ed., *The Origins of the Second World War Reconsidered: The A. J. P. Taylor Debate After Twenty-Five Years* (1986).

Lambert, A., 'Seapower 1939–1940: Churchill and the Strategic Origins of the Battle of the Atlantic', *Journal of Strategic Studies* 17 (1994).

Lambert, N. A., 'British Naval Policy, 1913–14: Financial Limitation and Strategic Revolution', *Journal of Modern History* 67 (1995).

Lammers, D., 'From Whitehall After Munich: The Foreign Office and The Future Course of British Policy', *The Historical Journal* 16 (1973).

Lundeberg, L. K., 'The German Critique of the U-boat Campaign, 1915–18', *Military Affairs* 27 (1963).

MacDonald, C. A., 'Economic Appeasement and the German "Moderates" 1937–1939', *Past and Present* 56 (1972).

——, 'Britain, France, and the April Crisis of 1939', *European Studies Review* 22 (1972).

McKercher, B. J. C., '"Our Most Dangerous Enemy"': Great Britain Pre-eminent in the 1930s', *International History Review* 13 (1991).

——, 'No Eternal Friends or Enemies: British Defence Policy and the Problem of the United States, 1919–1939', *Canadian Journal of History* 28 (1993).

——, ed., Special Section, 'Robert Vansittart and the Unbrave World, 1930–1937', *Diplomacy and Statecraft* 6 (1995).

——, 'Old Diplomacy and New: The Foreign Office and Foreign Policy', in Dockrill, M. and McKercher, B. J. C., eds, *Diplomacy and World Power: Studies in British Foreign Policy, 1890–1950* (Cambridge, 1996).

Marder, A., 'The Royal Navy and the Ethiopian Crisis of 1935–36', *American Historical Journal* 75 (1970).

Martel, G., 'The Meaning of Power: Rethinking the Decline and Fall of Great Britain', *International History Review* 13 (1991).

Masson, P., 'Réarmament et Marine Française', *Revue Internationale D'Histoire Militaire* 73 (1991).

Medlicott, W. N., 'Britain and Germany: The Search for Agreement, 1930–1937', in Dilks, D., ed., *Retreat From Power: Studies in Britain's Foreign Policy of the Twentieth Century*, Vol. I (1981).

Milner, M., 'The Battle of the Atlantic', *Journal of Strategic Studies* 13 (1990).

Milward, A. S., 'Economic Warfare', *War, Economy and Society,1939–45* (1977).

Muir, M. Jr, 'American Warship Construction for Stalin's Navy Prior to World War II: A Study in Paralysis of Policy', *Diplomatic History* 5 (1981).

Murray, O., 'The Admiralty', *The Mariner's Mirror* 33–5 (1937–9).

Murray, W., 'Neither Navy Was Ready', *United States Naval Institute Proceedings* 107 (1981).

Newton, S., 'The "Anglo-German Connection" and the Political Economy of Appeasement', *Diplomacy and Statecraft* 2 (1991).

Overy, R. J., 'Hitler's War and the German Economy: A Reinterpretation', *Economic History Review* 35 (1982).

——, 'Air Power and the Origins of Deterrence Theory Before 1939', *Journal of Strategic Studies* 15 (1992).

Parker, R. A. C., 'The Pound Sterling, the American Treasury and British Preparations for War, 1938–1939', *English Historical Review* 98 (1983).

Peden, G. C., 'A Matter of Timing: The Economic Background to British Foreign Policy, 1937–1939', *History* 69 (1984).

Prazmowska, A., 'The Eastern Front and the British Guarantee to Poland of March 1939', *European History Quarterly* 14 (1984).

Rohwer, J. and Monakov, M., 'The Soviet Union's Ocean-Going Fleet, 1935–1956', *International History Review* 28 (1996).

Roi, M. L., 'From the Stresa Front to the Triple Entente: Sir Robert Vansittart, the Abyssinian Crisis and the Containment of Germany', *Diplomacy and Statecraft* 6 (1995).

Ropp, T., 'Continental Doctrines of Sea Power', in Earle, E. M., ed., *Makers of Modern Strategy: Military Thought From Machiavelli to Hitler* (Princeton, 1943).

Salerno, R., 'Multilateral Strategy and Diplomacy: The Anglo-German Naval Agreement and the Mediterranean Crisis, 1935–1936', *Journal of Strategic Studies* 17 (1994).

Salewski, M., 'Marineleitung und politische Führung, 1931–1935', *Militärgeschichtliche Mitteilungen* 10 (1971).

Salmon, P., 'Churchill, the Admiralty and the Narvik Traffic, September–November 1939', *Scandinavian Journal of History* 4 (1979).

——, 'British Plans for Economic Warfare against Germany, 1937–1939: The Problem of Swedish Iron Ore', *Journal of Contemporary History* 16 (1981).

Santoni, A., 'Italian Naval Policy from 1930–1941', *Revue Internationale D'Histoire Militaire* 73 (1991).

Schreiber, G., 'Zur Kontinuität des Groß- und Weltmachtstrebens der deutschen Marineführung', *Militärgeschichtliche Mitteilungen* 26 (1979).

——, 'Die Rolle Frankreichs im strategischen und operativen Denken der deutschen Marine', in Hildebrand, K., and Werner, K. eds, *Deutschland und Frankreich, 1936–39* (Munich, 1981).

Smith, M., 'Rearmament and Deterrence in Britain in the 1930s', *Journal of Strategic Studies* 1 (1978).

Stafford, P., 'The Chamberlain-Halifax Visit to Rome: A Reappraisal', *English Historical Review* 98 (1983).

Steury, D. P., 'The Character of the German Naval Offensive', in Runyan, T. and Copes, J., eds, *To Die Gallantly* (Boulder, 1994).

Strang, B., 'Sir George Ogilvie-Forbes, Sir Nevile Henderson and British Foreign Policy, 1938–39', *Diplomacy and Statecraft* 5 (1994).

Sumida, J. T., '"The Best Laid Plans": The Development of British Battle-Fleet Tactics, 1919–1942', *International History Review* 14 (1992).

Taylor, A. J. P., 'The Anglo-German Naval Agreements', *New Hungarian Quarterly* 16 (1975).

Thomas, E. E. 'The Evolution of the JIC System Up to and During World War II', in Andrew, C. and Noakes, J., eds, *Intelligence and International Relations 1900–1945* (Exeter, 1987).

Till, G., 'Perceptions of Naval Power Between the Wars: The British Case', in Towle P., ed., *Estimating Foreign Military Power* (1972).

——, 'The Strategic Interface: The Navy and Air Force in the Defence of Britain', *Journal of Strategic Studies* 1 (1978).

——, 'Naval Power', in McInnes, C. and Sheffield, G., eds, *Warfare in the Twentieth Century: Theory and Practice* (1988).

Toyama, S., 'The Outline of the Armament Expansion of the Imperial Japanese Navy During the Years 1930–41', *Revue Internationale D'Histoire Militaire* 73 (1991).

Wark, W. K., 'Baltic Myths and Submarine Bogeys: British Naval Intelligence and Nazi Germany, 1933–39', *Journal of Strategic Studies* 6 (1983).

——, 'British Intelligence and Small Wars in the 1930s', *Intelligence and National Security* 2 (1987).

——, 'Naval Intelligence in Peacetime: Britain's Problems in Assessing the German Threat, 1933–39', in Masterson, D. M., ed., *Naval History. The Sixth Symposium of the U.S. Naval Academy* (Wilmington, Delaware, 1987).

——, 'Something Very Stern: British Political Intelligence: Moralism and Grand Strategy in 1939', *Intelligence and National Security* 5 (1990).

Watt, D. C., 'The Anglo-German Naval Agreement of 1935: An Interim Judgement', *Journal of Modern History* 28 (1956).

——, 'Anglo-German Naval Negotiations on the Eve of the Second World War', *Journal of the Royal United Services Institute* 610–611 (1958).

——, 'German Strategic Planning and Spain', *The Army Quarterly* 80 (1960).

——, 'Stalin's First Bid for Seapower 1935–1941', *Proceedings of the US Naval Institute* 90 (1964).

——, 'Hitler's Visit to Rome and the May Weekend Crisis: A Study in Hitler's Response to External Stimuli', *Contemporary History* 9 (1974).

——, 'The Historiography of Appeasement', in Sked, A. and Cook, C., eds, *Essays in Honour of A. J. P. Taylor* (1976).

——, 'The European Civil War', in Mommsen, W. and Kettenacker, L., eds, *The Fascist Challenge and the Policy of Appeasement* (1983).

——, 'Misinformation, Misconception, Mistrust: Episodes in British Policy and the Approach of War, 1938–1939', in Bentley, M. and Stevenson, J., eds, *High and Low Politics in Modern Britain* (Oxford, 1983).

Willard, C. F. Jr, 'Politico-Military Deception at Sea in the Spanish Civil War, 1936–39', *Intelligence and National Security* 5 (1990).

Wright, J. and Stafford, P., 'Hitler, Britain, and the Hoßbach Memorandum', *Militärgeschichtliche Mitteilungen* 42 (1987).

Young, R., 'Spokesmen for Economic Warfare: The Industrial Intelligence Centre in the 1930s', *European Studies Review* 6 (1976).

PhD Dissertations

MacGregor, D., *Innovation in Naval Warfare in Britain and the United States Between the First and Second World Wars*, University of Rochester, 1990.

Steury, D. P., *Germany's Naval Renaissance: Ideology and Seapower in the Nazi Era*, University of California, Irvine, 1990.

Index